THE RISE OF MODERN EUROPE
Edited by WILLIAM L. LANGER

REACTION
AND REVOLUTION

1814 - 1832

BY

FREDERICK B. ARTZ

Oberlin College

ILLUSTRATED

NEW YORK and LONDON
HARPER & BROTHERS PUBLISHERS

REACTION AND REVOLUTION

To
LOVE
JÁSZI AND
STETSON

*

TABLE OF CONTENTS

LIST OF ILLUSTRATIONS

The illustrations, grouped in a separate section, will be found following page 174.

ix

INTRODUCTION

OUR age of specialization produces an almost incredible amount of monographic research in all fields of human knowledge. So great is the mass of this material that even the professional scholar cannot keep abreast of the contributions in anything but a restricted part of his general subject. In all branches of learning the need for intelligent synthesis is now more urgent than ever before, and this need is felt by the layman even more acutely than by the scholar. He cannot hope to read the products of microscopic research or to keep up with the changing interpretations of experts, unless new knowledge and new viewpoints are made accessible to him by those who make it their business to be informed and who are competent to speak with authority.

These volumes, published under the general title of *The Rise of Modern Europe*, are designed primarily to give the general reader and student a reliable survey of European history written by experts in various branches of that vast subject. In consonance with the current broad conceptions of the scope of history, they attempt to go beyond a merely political-military narrative, and to lay stress upon social, economic, religious, scientific and artistic developments. The minutely detailed, chronological approach is to some extent sacrificed in the effort to emphasize the dominant factors and to set forth their interrelationships. At the same time the division of European history into national histories has been abandoned and wherever possible attention has been focussed upon larger forces common to the whole of European civilization. These are the broad lines on which this history as a whole has been laid out. The individual volumes are integral parts of the larger scheme, but they are intended also to stand as independent units, each the work of a scholar well qualified to treat the period covered by his book. Each volume contains about fifty illustrations selected from the mass of contemporary pictorial material. All non-contemporary illustrations have been excluded on principle. The bibliographical note appended to each volume is designed to facilitate further study of special aspects touched upon in the text. In general every effort has been made to give the reader a clear idea of the main movements in European history, to embody the monographic contributions of research workers, and to present the material in a forceful and vivid manner.

*   *   *

The present volume deals with a much neglected part of European history, the aftermath of the Napoleonic period. It is not an age of spectacular personalities or great international conflicts, but Professor Artz, who is the author of a study of *France under the Bourbon Restoration*, shows very clearly the deeper significance of European development from the abdication of Napoleon to the passage of the first Reform Bill in England. Prefacing his narrative with a survey of conditions after twenty-five years of almost uninterrupted war, he analyzes the great conflict of interests and principles between the old privileged orders and the rising middle classes. The study of the reaction in the first five years of the period is succeeded by an account of the abortive revolutionary movements of 1820 and the following years, while the latter part of the book is devoted to the new generation of liberalism, its outlook and organization, and its victory in western Europe in the movements of 1830-1832. Particular emphasis is placed throughout on the general European character of the issues fought out in these years, and to the reflection of conflicting viewpoints in religion, literature and art.

WILLIAM L. LANGER

PREFACE

Back of this book lie certain assumptions. Among these is my Liberal point of view, which I have tried to minimize but which I have not attempted to conceal. Moreover, I am of the conviction that the most significant political, social, and intellectual movements of the nineteenth century took place in the period 1815 to 1870. I am also of the opinion that there was in the nineteenth century, as in earlier ages, a general European civilization and that the time has come when the history of this period should be conceived from a non-national point of view. Finally, the whole structure of the book rests on the assumption that the widening influence of English institutions and inventions, and of the French conceptions of liberty and equality, on the feudal and agricultural states of Europe constitutes the basis of nineteenth-century history. With this in mind, the reader may the more easily understand what I have undertaken to do.

I am deeply indebted for help to a large number of my friends; especially to William L. Langer, Georges Weill, Kent R. Greenfield, Crane Brinton, A. P. Usher, M. M. Karpovich, E. J. Knapton, Oscar Jászi, H. D. Jordan, H. J. Marks, and F. E. Manuel. W. B. Briggs, R. H. Haynes, Julian S. Fowler and the staffs of the Harvard and Oberlin Libraries have greatly facilitated my labors. Genevieve Brandt and Warren Taylor helped to prepare the manuscript for the press; E. J. Knapton read the proofs.

FREDERICK B. ARTZ

April 1, 1934

xiii

REACTION AND REVOLUTION

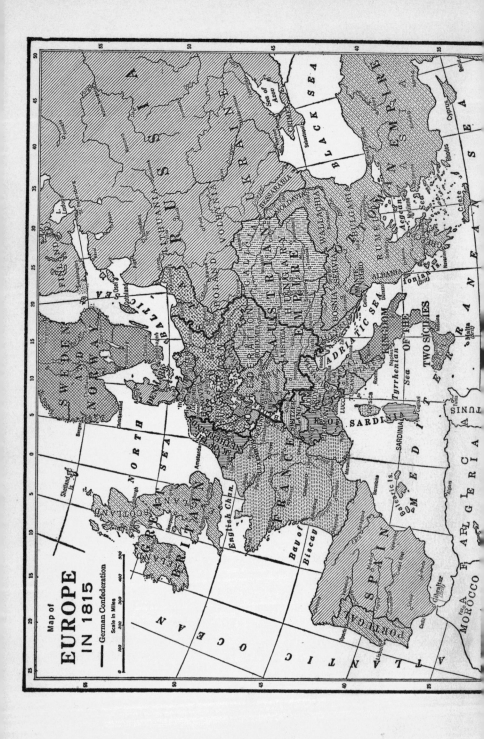

Map of
EUROPE
IN 1815

— German Confederation

Scale in Miles
0 100 200 300 400 500

Chapter One

EUROPEAN SOCIETY AFTER THE NAPOLEONIC WARS: THE THRONE AND THE ALTAR

I. THE MONARCHS, THE STATESMEN, AND THE ARISTOCRACIES

A FRENCH CARTOON of 1815 shows an eagle leaving the Tuileries and five geese waddling in. The flight of Napoleon and the return of the Bourbons to the palace of their ancestors were symbolic of the great changes that were taking place from one end of Europe to the other during the years 1814 and 1815, and to a war-weary generation they were proof enough that the French Revolution had come to an end. During a quarter of a century, amidst revolutionary conquests and political and economic reconstruction, an ancient society had been dissolved into its constituent elements. Old feudal, industrial, political, and ecclesiastical bonds had been loosened or completely severed. A new society was everywhere in process of formation, when suddenly the downfall of the Napoleonic empire threw the political, and to some extent the social and economic, control back into the hands of the governing classes of the Ancien Régime. The Restoration thus represents one of the most striking reversals in modern history.

The return of the monarchs was due to the general exhaustion and the widespread desire for peace. Everywhere from the Neva to the Seine, and from the Tagus to Stockholm the horror of war and the growing economic anarchy had led to the belief that peace and order were worth having at any price. The streets of Paris in 1814 and again in 1815 echoed to the cry of *Vive la paix*! far more frequently than to that of *Vive les Bourbons*! The return of royal authority seems to have been accepted with indifference by everyone, except small groups who either through deep conviction or through interest were ardently hostile or rapturously enthusiastic. The continuance of the new order, however, would inevitably depend on the capacity of the monarchs, the aristocracies, and the higher clergy whom the wheel of fortune was again bringing into power. A study of their ideas and policies shows that exile and suffering had not made many of them the wiser.

Of the monarchs who had witnessed the revolution without losing their thrones, the most influential in general European affairs was Alexander I of Russia. He was aware of the significance of the revolutionary era, and his project of 1804 for a European confederation undoubtedly represented one of the most original and constructive political ideas of his generation. His conceit and emotional unsteadiness, however, played havoc with the fulfillment of his program, and, able though he was, he proved to be a false Messiah. The King of Prussia and the Emperor of Austria were less competent and at the same time far less aware of the real forces in the world about them than had been a number of their more able and more enlightened predecessors in the eighteenth century. In England the regent, who in 1820 became George IV, was a man whose mediocre intelligence and scandalous private life had shorn him of all prestige.

Of the monarchs who had suffered exile, all except Louis XVIII of France returned embittered and resentful. The Spanish king, Ferdinand VII, was a stupid reactionary who had occupied himself in exile with embroidering a robe for the Virgin of a pilgrimage shrine. None of the rulers of the petty states of Italy and Germany except Goethe's patron, the Duke of Saxe-Weimar, seems to have possessed any real capacity for governing in such trying times. Ignorant of the society in which they were living, and with fantastic lack of judgment, they busied themselves with matters of court etiquette, and, like the King of Piedmont, vented their rage on the immediate past by uprooting the French plants in their botanical gardens, and throwing the French furniture out of their palaces.[1] Their governments they turned over to their confessors and their executioners. By contrast, Louis XVIII of France stands

[1] Typical of the ideas of the monarchs of the time is the following statement of Charles Felix of Savoy, "At the beginning of my reign (1820) everything was a mystery to me. I did not know what to write or what to answer. Then I made the sign of the cross, recommended myself to the adorable Trinity, and God willed that my decisions should be worthy of a Christian prince." F. Lemmi, *Carlo Felice* (Turin, 1931), 165 note.

out as the shrewdest royal statesman among the rulers of his generation. His unerring *tact des choses possibles*, expressed in his dictum of "nationalizing the monarchy and of royalizing the nation,"
and his success in achieving at least a part of this program led
Gambetta to say later that he was "the greatest French king since
Henry IV."

In most states the rulers surrounded themselves with very conservative advisers. The pattern of the perfect statesman of the absolutist governments was Prince Metternich, the Austrian minister
for foreign affairs, and later chancellor. Admired by the conservatives of all Europe as an infallible oracle, and hated by the liberals
as the incarnation of the spirit of obscurantism, he hardly merited
either estimate. The key to his policy is found in a remark made
by Castlereagh in 1814: "Austria, both in army and government,
is a timid power; her minister is continually temporizing."[2] Metternich's policy of stability was inspired primarily by the peculiar
nature of the Austrian monarchy. While he dressed out the needs
of his Hapsburg masters in the elaborate phraseology of legitimacy
and in talk about "the support of the moral order," it was quite
evident that he was directing the destinies of an empire that was
merely a governmental machine without any genuine national
basis. The mere introduction of democratic or nationalist ideas anywhere in Europe could easily stir up disruptive movements in this
strange conglomerate of half the races and religions of Europe that
was Austria. Hence, revolutionary ideas in speeches, books, or newspapers frightened Metternich, even if they appeared as far away
as Spain, Sweden, or Sicily. His personal convictions, formed during
the French Revolution, led him to believe that political and social
changes could be effected only by gradual evolution and in accordance with historical tradition. He had little sympathy for, or understanding of, the aspirations of the middle and lower classes, but
he saw that the upper bourgeoisie, posing as "the people," were
often narrow and selfish in their aims and were bent chiefly upon
usurping the position and privileges of the ruling aristocracy. After
1815 Metternich's extraordinary diplomatic skill enabled him to erect
a complete system of European conservatism in harmony with his

[2] C. K. Webster, *The Foreign Policy of Castlereagh 1812-1815* (London, 1931), 218.

own convictions and in consonance with the peculiar needs of the Hapsburg monarchy.[3]

In Spain, and in the small Italian and German states, the leading ministers tried to pattern their policies upon those of Metternich, but none of these statesmen showed anything approaching the ability of their Austrian model. In the *Chartreuse de Parme* Stendhal, characterizing this type, spoke of the perfect courtier as a man without either honor or humor. The hero of the novel, Fabrizio, found himself suspected of liberal leanings. To clear himself he had to be sure "to go to mass every day, to choose as his confessor some man devoted to the monarchy; . . . secondly he was not to consort with any man who had the reputation of being clever, and when occasion offered, he was to speak of rebellion with horror; he was never to be seen in a café; . . . he was to express dislike of reading in general, and he was never to peruse any works printed later than 1720, the only possible exception being Scott's novels; and lastly, he must not fail to pay open court to some pretty woman in the district, which would prove that he had none of the gloomy and discontented spirit of the conspirator. . . . For the rest, he must be simple—no wit, no brilliancy, no swift repartee." After this description of the man, Stendhal proceeds to discuss his policy: "Everything which has been done since the death of Louis XIV in 1715 is at once a folly and a crime. Man's foremost interest must be his own salvation—there cannot be two opinions on that score. The words *liberty, justice,* and *happiness of the greatest number* are criminal; they give men's minds a habit of discussion. Man ends by distrusting the commands of the Church and the authority of the princes set up by God."[4]

The statesmen of the period in England were mostly mediocre men, though Castlereagh and, after 1822, some of the younger

---

[3] The learned biography of Metternich by Heinrich Ritter von Srbik, *Metternich, der Staatsmann und der Mensch* (2 vols., Munich, 1925) has led to a far-reaching revision of historical opinion. The book was bitterly attacked by Viktor Bibl, *Metternich in neuer Beleuchtung* (Vienna, 1928), and questioned by Eduard von Wertheimer, "Gibt es einen neuen Metternich?" *Forschungen zur brandenburgischen und preussischen Geschichte,* XXXVIII, 1926, pp. 339-367, but has been generally supported by scholars like Arnold O. Meyer, "Fürst Metternich" *Archiv für Politik und Geschichte,* II, (1924), 134-166, Erich Kittel, "Metternichs politische Grundanschauungen" *Historische Vierteljahrschrift,* XXIV (1928), 443-483 and H. du Coudray, *Metternich* (New Haven, 1936).   [4] Stendhal, *La Chartreuse de Parme,* chaps. v and vii.

Tories were leaders of great capacity. Lord Liverpool, the Prime Minister, was a characteristically obstinate though good-humored conservative who knew how to turn the displeasure of the public against his colleagues. In the eyes of the Liberals the personification of the Tory statesman was not the able Castlereagh, although he was far more hated than he deserved to be, but Lords Eldon and Sidmouth. In Eldon's opinion—and he was much given to making pronouncements—the man who wanted to do away with any ancient privilege was laying his hands on the sacred constitution; yet, as he showed in his support of the Six Acts (1819), no one was more ready than he to set aside this constitution. Castlereagh and the Duke of Wellington among the older Tory leaders, and among the younger group, Canning, Huskisson, and Peel, who were willing to compromise with the business interests in England, showed that a conservative policy did not need to be a reactionary one.

The ablest statesmen of the restoration in France were the Duc de Richelieu, Decazes, and Villèle. The Duc de Richelieu and Decazes worked with Louis XVIII to steer a middle course between reaction and revolution, but the steady pressure exerted by the king's brother, the Comte d'Artois, drove them from power. Villèle was an able financier, but in other fields of domestic policy he was under the influence of the reactionary party and, after 1824, of Artois, now become Charles X. It was only with the Prince de Polignac, the last head of the ministry before the revolution of 1830, that Charles could fully agree. Polignac was a strange visionary—a Spanish, or Russian type of statesman—who found in apparitions of the Virgin assurance that he was right in issuing the July Ordinances.

In Prussia and Russia the monarchs year by year chose more reactionary ministers. The King of Prussia, instead of listening to Stein and Hardenberg, took advice from men like Wittgenstein and Schmalz. The Russian tsar's earlier liberalism had led him to select as ministers the liberal Speransky and Czartoryski. Later they were set aside, and by the end of his reign (1825) Alexander had placed in power dark reactionaries like the priest Photius, and the brutal Count Arakcheiev. It was useless to complain of such men, whose irresponsible abuse of authority irritated and alarmed even the loyal supporters of the monarchy, for neither Frederick William III nor Alexander I would believe any charges against their favorites. The idea of governing held by the majority of the statesmen of the time was well expressed by Metternich, who once remarked, "it is only necessary to place four energetic men, who know what they want and are agreed on the manner of carrying out their wishes, in the four corners of Europe. Let them raise their voices and their arms at the same moment and the whole agitation vanishes like so much smoke."[5]

During the Napoleonic era, the development of the secret police—often combined with the use of agents provocateurs—and of centralized bureaucracies greatly increased the power of the monarchs. Moreover, after 1815 many of the administrators were ex-officers who brought the severity and the summary methods of army rule into civilian life. Only rarely had the governments of the Ancien Régime known how to keep themselves well informed of what went on within their borders. But in the early nineteenth century the records of the police in every country contained detailed information about all important persons, not only in the capital, but even in the smaller towns. Letters were opened, in Austria even the correspondence of Gentz, who stood highest in Metternich's confidence, was tampered with. Conversations at table were reported, and travelers were shadowed. This extended activity of the secret police forms one of the most characteristic features of the period after Waterloo; the archives of every European capital contain hundreds of dossiers of their reports.

The surviving administrative personnel of the Ancien Régime returned in some numbers from hiding or exile to their old positions. In France, for example, many of the prefects of the period were old *émigrés*. These officials hated many of the new laws and institutions that had come into force since 1789 and they often did everything possible to interfere with their functioning. The revolution had cleared away many old administrative anomalies, and in every state the government now had a better control over law-enforcement and

---

[5] Chateaubriand, in his *Monarchie selon la charte* (1816), 16, set forth the same idea, "A bishop, an army commander, a prefect, a police commandant; if these are for God and the King I will answer for the rest!"

taxation. All governments were furnished with the indispensable apparatus, often lacking in the eighteenth century, for all kinds of repressive measures. The policies devised by Metternich and his contemporaries for the internal control of the various European states represent, then, not only a changed administrative outlook but a greatly increased administrative power. Back of all this spying and despotic control was plain fear, the dread that the horrors of the revolution would suddenly begin again. Employers were afraid of their workmen, the nobles were afraid of the peasants and of the middle class, the governments acted as though they were afraid of everyone. Statesmen opposed all change lest it release unknown and destructive forces. Börne satirized this fear and the behavior of the governments: "When the world catches fire and the fat begins to melt off the upper classes, the police will make the announcement, 'Alarmists have spread the rumor that the world is overheated. This is an insidious fabrication. The weather was never cooler or finer. All people are cautioned against making ill-considered remarks and lounging about the streets. Parents should keep their children, teachers their pupils, and employers their workmen off the streets. *Keep the peace. To keep the peace is the citizen's first duty!* "[6]

The tone of society, as before the revolution, was set by the kings and their courts. The upstarts who had flourished in the entourage of the Napoleonic rulers were now rudely thrust aside and their places given to aristocrats of ancient lineage. In states like England, Russia, and Austria, which Napoleon had never been able to annex, there was less of an upset. But in all countries, whatever was of long and established standing enjoyed after 1815 a social prestige which the eighteenth century would have found difficult to understand. An ancient title was, more than ever before, the surest guarantee of favor at court or of a position in the army, the navy, the administrative personnel, or the established church.

England possessed the most enlightened nobility and the one most experienced in governing. Unlike the continental aristocracies it was not a closed caste, for its members did not refuse to intermarry with the banking and commercial classes. For generations it had found the joint-stock company an admirable device for the associa-

[6] J. Legge, *Rhyme and Revolution in Germany 1813-1850* (London, 1918), 57.

tion of blood with brains. This social mobility, together with the custom of ennobling the wealthiest leaders of the mercantile class, had kept the English aristocracy in close contact with the life of the nation. The highest nobility sat in Parliament or devoted itself to the diplomatic service. The lesser aristocracy policed and ruled the countryside, managed parliamentary elections, and supplied the army, the navy, and the church with its leaders. As a class it was accustomed to traveling and to taking an interest in public affairs. The large libraries collected by some of these lords were apparently not left unread if we may judge by the copious fragments of Virgil, Horace, Shakespeare, and Milton which they deftly hurled at each others' heads in Parliament and with which they adorned their correspondence. The Continental Blockade had raised the price of cereals, and, together with the spread of improved agricultural methods had doubled the rents of landowners in the three decades between 1790 and 1820. Benighted as they seemed to the radicals of the time, in their knowledge of public affairs and in their sense of public responsibility the English aristocracy was the most active and alert in Europe.

On the continent, the nobles had by the eighteenth century lost many of the political powers they had once possessed. This was especially true in France and in the petty despotisms of Italy and Germany, where the aristocracy usually knew little of foreign affairs or of the developing world of trade. During the Revolution many of them had been separated from their homes by years of war and emigration. After 1815 there were not a few in France, Italy, and Germany who foolishly believed they had been called back in a passion of national repentance. They returned hating the revolutionary principle, though rarely understanding it.

In all countries the greatest noble families formed a class apart. They usually maintained residences in the capital and often intermarried with the upper aristocracy of another capital. Since on the continent their language and their culture were largely French, they formed something of an international caste. It was among these families, rather than among the country gentry, that the greatest interest in politics and in literature was to be found. Everywhere the nobles lived much as they had before the revolution. Not even in England was the primacy of the aristocracy in society challenged. James Fenimore Cooper discovered that in London no bourgeois plutocrat would have thought of trying to build a town house on a scale grander than that of the great mansions of the nobility. The priest, the parson or the pastor, and the dancing master still directed the education of the children. The boys looked forward to a career in the army or the church and the daughters waited for their parents to find husbands for them. In parts of Europe a redistribution of property had reduced the income of the aristocracy, but even in France, where the revolution had wrought the greatest changes, the nobles who had survived the upheaval were usually able to return to their old ways of living. In East Prussia, in Russia and in other parts of central and eastern Europe, the aristocracy discharged many of the political duties which the possession of their large estates entailed. They lived like great feudal lords, administering law and preserving a prestige which the monarchy had never dared attack. The Spanish aristocracy was considered the proudest in Europe and the Russian the most prodigal, the most ignorant, and the most brutal.[7]

Although the social status of the noble class had been little affected by the revolution, the temper of the aristocratic salons of Paris, Rome, Vienna, and the other capitals after 1815 showed clearly that the revolutionary era had profoundly modified their attitude and outlook. Piety and a fear of all innovations had largely replaced the frivolity, the wit, and the love of bold ideas which characterized the salons of the Enlightenment. Many nobles joined the religious societies for laymen which sprang up in both Catholic and Protestant countries. An obscurantism that could never have flourished in the days of Voltaire seized many members of the aristocracy and gave a strange tone to the higher circles of society. One eighteenth-century trait remained, however—a literary, artistic, or musical reputation was still as effective an entrée to a salon as a dukedom. The Americans, Washington Irving, Ticknor, Edward Everett, and Cooper, were accepted in the best circles of aristocratic society, often with the most haphazard of introductions.

[7] Pushkin's father was a characteristic Russian noble of the time. Living all his life in a house half-furnished and half-empty, fond of entertaining and of reading French novels, he squandered a large fortune. Cf. descriptions of nobles in Gogol's *Dead Souls*.

A few aristocratic families in every country maintained a liberal point of view. This was strikingly true of England where many nobles were attached to the traditions of Whiggism. In France some representatives of the highest nobility, like the Broglies, took an active part in liberal movements, and generally maintained close relations with the Whig aristocracy of England.[8] But the opposition of many aristocrats in Italy, Poland, and Belgium to the existing régime arose from hatred of foreign rule rather than from dislike of conservative or undemocratic policies. Military campaigns and diplomatic missions had for the first time brought large numbers of Polish, Hungarian, and Russian nobles into contact with the society of western Europe, and some of them, on their return, formed small groups which began to agitate for reform and for the introduction of western institutions.

These striking exceptions, however, do not essentially modify the fact that the monarchs and the aristocracies of Europe were more in agreement than they had been in earlier centuries. Years of disaster had brought them together, and by 1815 both had joined the clergy to combat the ravages of revolutionary change. The old struggles between the monarchy and the aristocracy, like the Fronde in France, and the old differences between the monarchy and the church, like the Gallican and Febronian controversies, were now forgotten in a new alliance of the throne and the altar. For good or for ill, Europe in 1815 was in the control of kings, nobles, and priests as it had not been since the Age of Louis XIV.

II. THE CHURCHES AND THE CLERGY

No institutions had suffered more from the influence of the Enlightenment than the churches in both Protestant and Catholic countries. During the eighteenth century their membership had fallen off, particularly among the upper classes. Indifference had affected even the clergy, and, some decades before the outbreak of the French Revolution, there had been widespread discussion as to whether organized Christianity would not disappear entirely in the new age of reason. Then came the dramatic changes in the position of the church in France. The clergy were suddenly deprived of

[8] Cf. M. E. Elkington, *Les relations de société entre l'Angleterre et la France 1814-1830* (Paris, 1929).

their property and of their independence. During the Terror priests married, the church bells were melted into cannon, and the altars were stripped. From the violence of this extremism, which had never affected the masses, a sharp reaction among the governing classes appeared at the close of the century, and in 1801 Napoleon made his terms with the pope.

Outside France the clergy in every state had, during the revolution, grown increasingly bitter against anything that smacked of French rationalism. By 1815 they were everywhere proclaiming that the fall of the Napoleonic empire was not alone a political event, but also a victory of religion over free-thought. In this view they were supported by the governing classes who during the revolution had seen how easily thrones and estates could follow altars to their ruin, and who now regarded organized religion as the most substantial bulwark against revolutionary change.

In 1815 the church was everywhere a privileged institution. It was either supported by grants from the government, or, if still in possession of its lands as in England and in most Catholic countries, it enjoyed a wide influence in public affairs. The dramatic changes of the time are best seen in the history of the Catholic Church. At the end of the eighteenth century it was widely assumed that Catholicism was tottering on the edge of extinction. When the Roman Republic was proclaimed in 1798, a statue of Liberty with her heel on the triple crown of St. Peter was erected, and in 1799 Novalis wrote: "Catholicism is almost played out. The old Papacy is laid in the tomb, and Rome for the second time has become a ruin."[9] Yet by 1815 a great Catholic reaction was under way, and even in Protestant states there had grown up a sympathy for the Catholic Church as one of the most effective forces in Europe for holding the revolutionary spirit in check. The governments were now convinced that if the papacy, the oldest and most legitimate monarchy in Europe, were not reinstated, no other monarchy could count on saving itself. The spirit of the time is in no way better shown than in the efforts made by the three non-Catholic powers, England, Russia, and Prussia, to restore the papacy to a position of influence in European affairs. The passive dignity of Pius VII be-

[9] H. Lichtenberger, *Germany and Its Evolution in Modern Times* (London, 1913), 218.

fore the bullying of Napoleon had given him a prestige which no pope had possessed for centuries. His return to Rome in 1814 was a triumphal progress. After his arrival he set to work, with the help of his chief minister, Cardinal Consalvi, to repair the ravages made by the revolution.

Henceforth the spirit of ultramontanism reigned at Rome. The dominant note of a new age in the history of the church was struck at once by the reëstablishment of the Jesuit Order. The Jesuits, it is true, had been reëstablished in Russia in 1801, and in Sicily in 1804, but now the Order was given its former international organization and placed in a position of high favor at the papal court. Soon it was reorganizing its forces all over Europe and the United States. Even in France, where there were laws against them, the Jesuits were active in preaching and teaching. In 1820, Alexander expelled the Order from Russia because it interfered with the work of another of his religious experiments, the Bible Societies; and the French Chambers in 1828 passed new laws restricting Jesuit teaching activities. In spite of these minor setbacks, however, the Order was more powerful than it had been since the Age of Louis XIV. The Inquisition was reëstablished at Rome and in Spain, and the Index was reconstituted.[10]

The chief activity of the papacy after the return of the pope to Rome was centered in efforts to recover its influence in the public affairs of Europe, to eradicate Gallicanism in France, Febronianism in Germany, and Josephism in Austria, and thereby to gain for Rome a greater influence in the delimitation of bishoprics and in the appointment of the clergy. Toward the accomplishment of this program, Consalvi negotiated a series of concordats with various European governments. In 1816-17 agreements were drawn up with the governments of Spain, France, Sardinia, and Bavaria. The new French concordat, however, failed to satisfy the king and the Chambers, and after extended negotiations the Napoleonic arrangement of 1801 was renewed. Concordats were made with Naples in 1818, with Prussia in 1824, with Holland in 1827. In Ireland, Canada,

[10] The literature on the Jesuit Order in modern times is very inadequate, but the reader may consult, on this period, M. J. Rouët de Journel, *Un collège de Jésuites à Saint-Pétersbourg, 1800-1816* (Paris, 1922); A. Boudou, *Le Saint-Siège et la Russie* (Paris, 1922), I, especially chap. iii; J. Burnichon, *La Compagnie de Jésus en France; Histoire d'un siècle, 1814-1914* (4 vols., Paris, 1914-1922).

the United States, and the new states of Latin America, the governments allowed the papacy a free hand in fixing the limits of the dioceses and in appointing the clergy. The political activities of the papacy after 1815 somewhat overreached themselves, and even in Catholic countries met with opposition. Metternich and the Austrian emperor refused to make a concordat with Rome, and Louis XVIII was hostile to the new ultramontane policies of the papal curia; in fact the governments of Austria and France gave favors to prelates of Josephist or Gallican views.

Wherever the Catholic Church was powerful, the clergy worked after 1815 for the restoration of the privileges which the church had enjoyed under the Ancien Régime. They strove to recover the church lands which had been seized by the revolutionary governments, to control education, and in general to fight all the forces that favored free-thought and democracy. The struggle was particularly bitter in France, where the Catholic Church had lost most from the revolutionary upheaval. With the backing of the Comte d'Artois (after 1824 Charles X), the clergy saw some chance of recovering its lands, of abolishing the Napoleonic Université with its state control of education, and of removing the obligation of civil marriage established by the Code Napoléon. The influence of the clerical party in the Bourbon government in France was the chief cause of the Revolution of 1830.

Munich became the center of ultramontanism and of clerical reaction in Catholic Germany. Ludwig I tried to make the newly organized University of Munich (1826) a successful rival of the Protestant University of Berlin, and he called Görres, Baader, Möhler, and Döllinger to the faculty there. But the Austrian government looked with some distrust upon the ultramontanism of Friedrich Schlegel, Werner, and Adam Müller. Both the emperor and Metternich still clung to the traditions of Joseph II. Spain, Portugal, the Italian states, Hungary, Ireland, Belgium, and Poland—these countries were all strongholds of clerical power after the Napoleonic period, though the clergy were often unfavorable to the existing political régime.[11]

[11] A good brief account of the situation in France may be found in C. S. Phillips, *The Church in France, 1789-1848* (London, 1929), chaps. ix to xi; on Germany see G. Goyau, *L'Allemagne réligieuse, Le Catholicisme* (Paris, 1910), I, Book I, chap. iv. and Book II *passim*.

The life of the parish priests of the Catholic Church, except in a few of the larger cities where the clergy had become affected with the spirit of Jesuitism, went on very much as it had before the revolution. The country priests were usually very poorly educated, even in France, Belgium, and South Germany, though they were more hard-working and conscientious than their superiors. The higher clergy were largely recruited from the nobility. There were among them a few men of great learning, and some able administrators and controversialists, but the number of clerics with any clear conception of what the church would have to do to regain its old prestige was very small. Although in a few states subject to foreign political control—Ireland, Poland, and Belgium—the clergy, especially after 1820, played an important rôle in stimulating and guiding discontent, the Catholic clergy in general preached obedience to the established order, and were even more given to denouncing the race of atheists and democrats who made revolutions than were the statesmen who directed the governments of the period. Clerical meddling in politics was a marked characteristic of almost every country. In France, for example, the bishops frequently issued orders to the faithful to vote for the royalist candidates, and certain bishops used their priests as electoral agents.

Among the important activities of the Catholic clergy, besides the daily round of diocese and parish, were the propagation of the faith through revivalist methods and the organization of societies of Catholic laymen. The revivalist missionaries were particularly active in France. Bands of priests were sent out from the larger centers to hold services even in the most remote districts, services which frequently took place in the open air and were conducted in an atmosphere of intense emotion. A large mixed chorus was usually organized to sing hymns set to the popular tunes of the day. The missionaries always ended their sojourn in a community with a great "ceremony of reparation." On this occasion, a large wooden cross was borne in solemn procession, and, in the presence of the prefect or the mayor or some other important government official, was planted in some prominent place. Public penance for the outrages of the revolution was then made before it. The ceremony usually closed with a burning of the works of Voltaire and the writers of the Enlightenment, and an oath was taken by all assembled to maintain religion and legitimate government. Sometimes the violent attacks of the missionaries on the great men of the revolution, especially on the "Ogre of Corsica," and on those who had acquired national lands, led to hostile demonstrations in which the police were obliged to intervene. State officials came in such numbers to these services that the liberals always insisted that they were sent by order of the government.[12]

The societies for Catholic laymen had a much wider influence. Most of them were either founded or fostered by the Jesuits. Characteristic of this type of society were the Congrégation de la Vierge in France, the San Fedists and other groups in Italy, and the Society of the Exterminating Angel in Spain. The Congrégation brought together laymen and ecclesiastics who were agreed to use for the general good of the church any useful information or influence which they might be able to command. Subject to the central society were a large number of auxiliary groups organized among students, laboring men, and prisoners. It is estimated that there were fourteen hundred in the central society and forty-eight thousand in the affiliated groups. The Comte d'Artois, the Prince de Polignac, Franchet d'Espérey, the director of police, and many other men eminent in the government and in French society took part in the movement. Members of the society acknowledged that they used their influence to have men favorable to the church appointed to educational and administrative posts. The exact relation of the Congrégation to the Jesuit Order and to the Bourbon government is unknown, though their close association has never been successfully disproved.[13]

The secret societies organized by the Catholic Church in Italy were founded primarily to combat the influence of the liberal Carbonari groups. The San Fedists and Consistoriali of the Papal States, the Calderari of Naples, the Society of Catholic Friendship of Piedmont were all similar in purpose to the Congrégation. They received help from the Jesuits and from the Zelanti, the reactionary party at the papal court. The principles which these societies tried to inculcate

[12] Cf. G. Vauthier, "Les missions religieuses sous la Restauration," *Revue des études historiques,* 1920.
[13] Phillips, *op. cit.* chap. ix; Geoffroy de Grandmaison, *La Congrégation, 1801-1830* (Paris, 1889), chaps. viii, ff.; P. Nourrisson, *Histoire légale des congrégations religieuses en France* (Paris, 1928), I, chap. iv.

are well summed up in a San Fedist publication, *La Voce della Verità*. "God has made hell," it said, "and the most pious prince is he whose prime minister is the executioner."[14] Francis, Duke of Modena, the "Butcher" as he was commonly called and the villain of the revolt of 1831, was especially active in these societies. It was at the instigation of the San Fedists that Pius VII in 1821 promulgated a bull against the Carbonari. During the same period (1820-21) the San Fedists tried to drive Consalvi from office. Proclamations denouncing him appeared on the streets of Rome along with manifestoes of the Carbonari proclaiming death to the priests and calling for a republic. From one end of the peninsula to the other these Italian societies formed a kind of secret police whose denunciations were nominally directed against the members of the Carbonari but were in practice used by the governments against all inconvenient persons. Moreover, they were active in stirring up the lower classes in the towns against the liberal leaders of the bourgeoisie. When disturbances broke out, their propaganda bore fruit. The Italian revolts of the early nineteenth century all failed not only because of the steady indifference of the masses but also because of the hostility stirred up by the clericals.

A similar organization in Spain, the Society of the Exterminating Angel, founded by the Bishop of Osma, had branches all over the country. It brought together, for the defense of conservative principles, the higher clergy, the monarchy, the aristocracy, and the masses. Don Carlos, the king's brother, was one of its leaders. After the Revolution of 1820 it was active in ferreting out revolutionaries, and the only two newspapers that were allowed to exist were published under its influence. Even the reactionary king, Ferdinand VII, was regarded as too liberal by the members of the society.

The Protestant governments, like the Catholic, enjoyed the support of the clergy in their efforts to reimpose an authoritarian régime. The Anglican Church was, in this matter, one of the most conservative. While dissent had long been permitted in England, the established church forced everyone to pay taxes for its maintenance. According to the law, Anglican clergymen alone could perform

[14] B. King, *A History of Italian Unity* (2nd ed., London, 1912), I, 140. Some historians have denied the existence of these Italian societies; cf. D. Spadoni: *Sètte, conspirazioni, e conspiratori nello stato pontificio* (Turin-Rome, 1904), cxl-cxlv.

marriages; no service except that of the Prayer Book could be read over the dead. Most of the charitable and educational endowments were in the control of the Anglican clergy, and both the universities and the great public schools were entirely dominated by the state church. The Presbyterians had a similar monopoly in Scotland. Nearly all the Anglican bishops were nobles or were closely affiliated with the nobility. Of twenty-seven English and Welsh bishops in 1820, eleven were nobles, eleven more had been tutors in aristocratic families, while the other five had received their positions through the patronage of some nobleman. These bishops lived in dignified ease apart from the parish priests, entertained the country gentry, attended the king's levees and occasionally published books on points of classical scholarship. In the House of Lords they fought as an almost solid phalanx against any reform of the penal laws, against Catholic Emancipation, and against the Reform Bill.

The country parsons, recruited largely from the rural gentry, lived like squires. Unlike similar groups in the continental countries, the country clergy in England had the tastes of the aristocracy; they found little to do but shoot and fish. Some went in for a dilettante scholarship, though, unlike the Protestant clergy in Germany, very few could boast a serious theological training. Jane Austen's novels depict a variety of clergymen, some amiable, some ridiculous, but few who seem to have anything to do with religion. The novelist never even notes this deficiency. The temper of the Anglican clergy is shown in the chief theological textbook of the time, Paley's *Evidences of Christianity* (ed. of 1794). Christ, according to Paley, was quite unlike the Methodists; he was not a man of "impassioned devotion," there was "no heat in his piety," for he was a "person of moderation and soundness of judgment." Throughout its life and organization, the ecclesiastical constitution of England harmonized with the political constitution because the same social groups controlled both.[15]

The laity of the Anglican Church were greatly influenced by a group of broad churchmen known as the Evangelicals. While remaining within the official church, these men took over many of the ideas and attitudes of the Methodists. They wished to minimize

[15] See J. H. Overton, *The English Church in the Nineteenth Century, 1800-1833* (London, 1894), chaps. i, ii; and P. H. Ditchfield, *The Old-Time Parson* (London, 1908).

ritual and ceremony, and to arouse the religious interest of the lower classes. They founded a series of reform societies to extend Sunday schools at home and foreign missions abroad, to fight the slave trade, and to distribute religious tracts. The movement affected the Anglican laity far more than the clergy. Politically very influential was a small group of these humanitarians, led by Wilberforce and Zachary Macaulay, called the "Clapham Sect," and, by those who disliked them, "The Saints." Their liberal enemies accused them of ignoring crying abuses at home, particularly those which arose from enclosures and from the factory system, while they were distributing Bibles to the heathen or were working to abolish slavery in the British West Indies. Bentham's friend, Francis Place, called Wilberforce an "ugly epitome of the devil," and Cobbett made bitter fun of Evangelical piety.[16]

Among the dissenting sects in England, the Methodists were the strongest. The evangelizing efforts of the Wesleys and their followers had raised the total number of Nonconformist churchgoers from about a twentieth of the total population to nearly one-half. The successes of the Methodists had stimulated the Presbyterians, the Baptists, the Congregationalists, the Quakers, and the Evangelicals to greater activities which resulted in bringing an emotional type of Christianity to thousands among the lower classes. No movement, in the long run, did more to inoculate the English people against revolutionary ideas. While, under French influence, radicals of all sorts were trying to establish by force a kingdom of heaven on earth, Methodism, as an influence in all the churches, set men's hearts on a kingdom which was not of this world, and one which certainly could never be established by violence. In the chapels of all the Nonconformist sects the virtues of hard work, frugality, and self-respect were being preached by enthusiastic, though usually ignorant, exhorters. The lower classes, the small shopkeepers, farmers, artisans, and agricultural laborers joined the dissenting sects by the thousand. The leaders in these congregations were usually the élite of this group— the skilled workers, the more energetic shopkeepers, and the more

---

[16] Especially of Hannah More, one of their pamphleteers, in his *Hannah More's account of the celestial death of an Evangelical mouse, who though starving, would not touch the master's bread and cheese.* Cf. on the Evangelicals L. E. Binns, *The Evangelical Movement in the English Church* (London, 1928), and W. L. Mathieson, *English Church Reform 1815-1840* (London, 1923).

successful small landowners. When, finally, a dissenting family became wealthy, it usually went over to the Church of England, for if a successful man of business wished to enter the governing class, to entertain at his country seat the clergy or gentry of the neighborhood, to obtain a title or a government appointment, it would not do to be a dissenter. So Nonconformity tended to become a transitional creed, a stage in the history of a rising English family.[17]

The world of German Protestantism had been stirred in the eighteenth century by Pietism, and its intellectual outlook was being broadened in the early nineteenth century by the teaching and writing of Schleiermacher. German universities offered the most thorough training in Europe in theology, Greek and Hebrew history and philology, and general Biblical exegesis. The German Protestant clergy was therefore better supplied with well-educated leaders than any other ecclesiastical group. Still, there was no dearth of ignorant and reactionary pastors, and Germany experienced no great popular movement like Methodism in England. Frederick William III of Prussia made the tercentenary of the Reformation (1817) the occasion for working out a project for reuniting the Lutheran and Calvinist churches in order to strengthen religious resistance to the teachings of liberalism. Schleiermacher lent his assistance and Bunsen drew up for the United Church a sort of German Book of Common Prayer. Official sanction was given the movement by the governments of Baden, Hesse, Württemberg, and some of the smaller states. But the Lutherans refused to compromise on their doctrine of consubstantiation and the Calvinists objected to the Lutheran ideas about the power of the crown in ecclesiastical affairs. The orthodox on both sides were opposed to the attempt to introduce some of the doctrines of Schelling and Schleiermacher into the statement of faith. Although the Prussian government for a time used pressure to enforce the union, the arrangement never worked satisfactorily.[18]

Several international Protestant movements of the time brought

[17] See W. J. Warner, *The Wesleyan Movement in the Industrial Revolution* (London, 1930), Elie Halévy, *A History of the English People in 1815* (New York, 1924), E. R. Taylor, *Methodism and Politics* (Cambridge, 1935) and M. J. Edwards, *After Wesley, Social and Political Influence of Methodism* (London, 1935).

[18] A good account of the movement may be found in J. B. Kissling, *Der deutsche Protestantismus, 1817-1917* (2 vols., Münster, 1917-1918), chaps. i and ii. Cf. G. Goyau, *L'Allemagne religieuse le Protestantisme* (Paris, 1924).

more intellectual coöperation among the different national Protestant churches than had existed since the time of the Reformation. One of these, the *Réveil*—a society to promote religious revivals— was originated by a group of English and Scotch Methodists, some of whom preached on the continent. The chief center of the movement came to be Geneva, whence their conservative theological and political ideas spread into France, largely through the efforts of the Monod brothers. Another international Protestant movement aimed at the founding of Bible Societies to collect funds for the printing and distribution of the Scriptures. The mother society was founded in England in 1804. By 1820 similar organizations existed not only in Germany and the Scandinavian countries, where the royal families of Prussia, Bavaria, Württemberg, Sweden, and Denmark patronized their work, but also in France, Holland, Hungary, Russia, the United States, and even in Iceland. In Russia, where they were introduced by Alexander I, there were, by 1820, almost three hundred branches. Metternich, on the other hand, would never allow the founding of Bible Societies in Austria, apparently because he feared they might bring men into contact with English ideas.

The Orthodox clergy in Russia were completely under the thumb of the state. Seraphim, Metropolitan of Moscow, and Photius were the leaders of the most reactionary forces in the Russian Church. In the earlier part of the reign of Alexander I, they had had to accept the liberal views of the tsar, but after 1822, when he grew more conservative, they took the lead in a clerical war on the press and the universities. The majority of the Russian clergy had small incomes and their lives differed little from those of the peasants about them. But since only the sons of secular priests were admitted to the clerical schools, and as parishes were handed down in the family, the clergy formed a separate group in society. The higher clergy after 1825 exerted an important influence in the growth of Slavophil ideas. In the Balkan states, the Orthodox clergy were under the control of the Greek Patriarch of Constantinople who was, in turn, merely an official of the Ottoman despotism. A small number of priests among the subject nationalities were beginning to revive the national legends and history of their own peoples, but the majority of the higher clergy, who were Greek, frowned on such interests and joined with the Ottoman officials in keeping the population in bondage. Among the Turks themselves, the Mohammedan learned caste, opposed to all new ideas, fought the reforms of Mahmud II and backed the Janissaries in their quarrel with the sultan.

From one end of Europe to the other, the churches and the clergy were, with few exceptions, everywhere regarded as the chief supports of the throne. The close coöperation between church and state to combat change, the growing sympathy of the Catholic and Protestant groups, and the widespread acceptance by the governing classes of the ideals of the Holy Alliance are all indicative of the close connection between throne and altar. Guizot expressed the spirit of the age when he exhorted Catholics and Protestants to work together, "Do not quarrel among yourselves, quarrel only with those who do not believe; that is your field."[19]

Viewing their activities as a whole, it is evident that after 1815 the monarchs, nobles, and clergy were trying to reconstitute the society of the Ancien Régime.[20] Statesmen were endeavoring to carry through much more than a merely political program. In the same way, the policies and activities of the churches—Catholic, Protestant, and Orthodox—were not confined to spiritual fields. How the clerical, aristocratic, and royal interests worked together can be seen only in a detailed study of the period, but their general plan of procedure becomes evident from a consideration of the policies of Villèle, head of the ministry in France from 1822 to 1827, and of the coöperation he got from churchmen, nobles, and king. Under Villèle's direction, they strove together to transform the whole order. The Law of Primogeniture and the Law for the Indemnification of the Nobles were intended to give the French aristocracy their old economic and social status. The Law of Sacrilege and the attempts to abolish the Université de France were directed toward the restoration of the church to the position it had had before the revolution. In the Laws of Press Censorship, and in the elaborate attempt to nullify the purposes of the Charter of 1814 by controlling elections, Villèle and his followers sought to undo the political changes that had come since 1789.

[19] G. Weill, *L'éveil des nationalités et le mouvement libéral* (Paris, 1930), 196.
[20] With the addition in France of the Napoleonic administrative system, and in other states of similar systems which had greatly strengthened the power of the central government.

The survival of old differences, and, in certain cases, the development of new ones, made complete agreement among the conservative forces impossible. Catholics and Protestants continued to distrust each other, particularly in France, England, and the Low Countries, while in Germany Lutherans and Calvinists could not be brought together. Metternich refused to allow Bible Societies in Austria, and they were condemned by the pope in 1817 and again in 1824. Louis XVIII in France and the Hapsburg government in Vienna declined to make certain concessions to a papacy pursuing ultramontane policies. The papacy refused to join the Holy Alliance, as did England; Turkey was not asked to join. A change in the Tory ministry led England in 1822 to withdraw from the European Alliance. At the same time a part of the aristocracy and of the Catholic clergy in Ireland, Belgium, Poland, Hungary, and northern Italy became increasingly hostile to the prevailing political order. In Russia, a group of young nobles, the Decembrists, embraced the liberal ideals of western Europe and conspired against the political and religious tyranny of the imperial government. These important exceptions, and others that might be cited, must not, however, obscure the fact that the throne and the altar joined in sharing the first fruits of Waterloo and in trying to hold them. This collaboration of the conservative forces gives the age its peculiar character.

Chapter Two

EUROPEAN SOCIETY AFTER THE NAPOLEONIC WARS: THE MIDDLE CLASS AND THE PEASANTS

I. THE UPPER BOURGEOISIE AND INDUSTRIAL CHANGE

THE fortunes of war had restored the monarchies and aristocracies to political control, but the economic power, at least within the society of western Europe, was slowly passing into the hands of the bourgeoisie. This process did not escape the notice even of the landed aristocracy. In 1814 the French *émigré*, the Comte de Montlosier, published a tract in which he said: "We are going to see how in the midst of an ancient state will arise a new state. We are going to see a dual state, a dual people, advancing side by side, attacking each other. The movable properties are being balanced against the immovable, money against the land, the cities against the châteaux. The people, rising ever higher, alters the old forms or does away with them. It ends by sitting at the council table of the king and from there imposing its laws and institutions."[1]

The bourgeoisie was a large and ill-defined class which showed within itself wide variations in social and economic status. In fact there was not at that time one economic system, but several, functioning alongside of one another. Moreover, the extent of social change was very unequal from country to country and even from district to district. Some countries and some districts were being rapidly transformed while others were as yet hardly touched. Side by side with cities like Manchester in England and Lille in France, with their masses of factory chimneys, were hundreds of towns where economic life had not greatly changed since the time of St. Louis and Dante.

The range of interest and outlook among the bourgeoisie was much broader and more varied than among the members of the aristocracy. In the larger cities the leaders of the old mercantilist

[1] Montlosier, *De la monarchie française* (Paris, 1814), I, 135-136.

plutocracy formed a compact group which stood socially just below the town-dwelling nobility. In England, France, and the Low Countries, this plutocracy was beginning to share its leadership in the world of business with a small number of factory owners, the new "captains of industry," as Carlyle was soon to name them. Beneath both types of wealthy magnates were a large number of small shop-keepers and professional men whose status had not been greatly changed for several generations. Indeed, the term *bourgeoisie* can hardly be confined to those who dwelt in cities, for there were some artisans, freeholding farmers, and country doctors, lawyers, and school-teachers, especially in England, and in parts of France, Germany, Italy, and the Low Countries, who shared the point of view of the middle class in the towns, read the same newspapers and often discussed politics with as much interest.[2]

At the top of this large and vaguely defined bourgeois world were the old patrician families of the larger cities of western Europe. Their fortunes had been founded on the profits of colonial enterprise, and after 1815 most of them were, as before the revolution, bankers and merchants rather than manufacturers. To this group, as to the middle class in general, the amassing of riches had not yet come to be an end in itself. Wealth was considered only as a means of assuring a man leisure to enjoy his family and his friends. Such a merchant in the early nineteenth century, regarding his customers as a landed proprietor might have regarded a feudal fief, considered it beneath his dignity to advertise, to try to get trade away from another merchant, or to attempt to extend his output indefinitely. His ideal of life was an assured income, the possibility of an early retirement from business, and the acquisition of an estate in the country. As a type these men were usually self-reliant and cautious and, after 1815, anxious to maintain peace. They disliked all extremes, absolutism or republicanism, atheism or the rule of priests, and were for order, security, and authority, provided these were not so oppressive as to throw the world again into revolution. They desired a voice in the government through which they might influence law-making to the advantage of their commercial interests. They were usually careful to go to church—in England it was often to a Non-

[2] Cf. W. Sombart, *Le bourgeois* (Paris, 1926).

conformist chapel—and they were philanthropic toward the inferior classes, so long as these were willing to remain inferior. In England the wealthier members of this plutocracy often intermarried with the old aristocracy and in France with the Napoleonic nobility.

The upper bourgeoisie in France resented the airs of superiority of the old nobility. To a minister who offered Royer-Collard the title of count, he answered indignantly, "Count, yourself!" When Louis XVIII accorded the Sieur Hervier de Charin letters of relief to wipe away the stigma of his ancestors who had engaged in commerce, Ternaux, the greatest factory owner on the continent and a member of the Chamber of Deputies, rose in the assembly and said, "After the last exposition of our arts, where I presented before the public some products of my industrial labors, I received from His Majesty the title of baron. This title, which I did not solicit, has now lost all value in my eyes."[3] The July Ordinances of 1830 disfranchised many of the wealthier merchants of Paris, and they showed their hostility to the government by closing their shops, and arming their employees to fight for the maintenance of the Charter of 1814. Elsewhere on the continent the aristocracy looked down on the wealthier bourgeoisie, though as a class the latter were better educated, more widely traveled, and more interested in new movements in literature, science, and politics. The economic life of nearly all the large cities was in the hands of this mercantile plutocracy, which, like the highest aristocracy, shared across all national frontiers something of a common culture and outlook. Its ideals, which eventually passed down to lower strata of the middle class, are well set forth in the early comedies of Scribe and in the novels of Jane Austen.

The business life of the larger cities included all the older types of local trading, usually centered in a weekly market, together with some wholesale buying and selling of colonial wares and of local manufactures. Except in parts of England, France, and the Low Countries where there were large factories equipped with water or steam power, manufacturing was carried on either by the craft system, or by the newer putting-out or domestic system. In the case of the latter, an entrepreneur bought the raw materials, distributed

[3] *Archives parlementaires*, 2 Série (Paris, 1876), XXXII, 707.

them for manufacture to the home-workers, and then marketed the finished product. But the greater part of the industry of western Europe in 1815 was still conducted by independent craftsmen, who might or might not belong to a guild, producing on a small scale in workshops of their own. It is this parallelism and overlapping of several types of manufacture, very characteristic of the period, which makes all generalization difficult.

Even in the larger towns where some manufacturing was done, the separation of the world of industry from that of agriculture was not clearly marked. The larger manufactures, which were usually still produced on the putting-out system, diffused industry through the countryside. This interpenetration of agriculture and industry gave the town life of the early nineteenth century a character much like that of earlier centuries. The horn of the cowherd called together the cows of the townsmen, and orchards and vegetable gardens often adorned the front yards. There was hardly a town-dwelling family without a garden inside or directly outside the town wall. Every household not only had most of its clothing made at home, but also brewed and baked and slaughtered there. It was taken for granted that the pig was the town scavenger, and that sewers, street-paving, sidewalks, and gas-lighting were wonders that belonged to a few great cities like London and Paris. With the exception of the few factory towns in western Europe, even the larger cities still fitted easily into their old ramparts. The high church spires and the walls of a few public buildings rose above a mass of roofs from which one could see the surrounding plowlands. Economically the world of Metternich was much like the world of Voltaire.

The similarity must not, however, obscure the changes actually in progress. Besides the break-up of the guilds and the growth of the putting-out system, other innovations were taking place. Trading was being facilitated by striking improvements in roads and canals. Indeed, not since Roman times had western Europe possessed so many miles of good roads as it did after 1815, and even in antiquity the same region had not been so well supplied with canals. Travel by stagecoach was improved in comfort and increased in speed before the steamboat and the locomotive were introduced in the 1830's and 1840's to give this transformation a new impulse. In eastern and in much of southern Europe, however, all communication still depended on rivers which might freeze in winter or run shallow in summer, and on dirt roads that were quagmires in spring and autumn. Trade was also blocked by innumerable local customs barriers, though these were less numerous than they had been in the eighteenth century.

If the building of better roads and the opening of canals, together with the abolition of many internal customs barriers, gave an impetus to business, there was after 1815 a temporary decline due to the economic maladjustments of twenty-five years of war. The Continental Blockade had ruined the colonial commerce of France, Spain, and Holland and had, in every country, seriously dislocated most industries. The peace in 1815, from which so much was hoped, proved to be only another sudden disturbance for business. Many industries lacked capital, others found their markets gone, and their old customers ruined or at least impoverished. On the continent nearly all industries were for a time depressed by the dumping on their markets of accumulated English stocks which undersold the home manufactures created or developed by the blockade. This led after 1815 to a great drive on the part of the manufacturing groups to force the governments to introduce high tariffs. The result soon appeared in the establishment of national protective systems for local industries which the blockade had created. This was true in every country from the United States to Russia. The immediate dislocation and confusion which followed the Napoleonic wars convinced many business men that the royal and aristocratic direction of the state was the cause of business depression and instability. Much of the political strife of the time is understandable only when this is kept in mind.[4]

Alongside this older commercial and industrial world, which had not changed fundamentally since the eighteenth century, a new society was forming, rapidly in parts of England, and more slowly in France and the Low Countries, wherever industries were being transformed through the introduction of machinery and the steam engine. The common type of leader in this change was a hard-

[4] An interesting comparison between conditions as they were after 1815 and after 1918 is made by Mrs. H. A. L. Fisher, in her essay *Then and Now, Economic Problems after the War a Hundred Years Ago* (London, 1925).

working, self-made man, usually of little education but of great energy. Spending his days over his machines or his accounts, he allowed neither himself nor his mill-hands leisure or recreation. His one all-absorbing ambition was to increase the output of his machines to the very limit. He hoarded every farthing so as to reinvest it in the business, for capital still was the laborious result of parsimony. For that reason he believed that high wages and most government regulations were disastrous to business. At the same time he found in the strain of competition an excuse for opposing expenditures for human welfare. Such a factory owner kept his own secrets, tried to discover those of his neighbors, strove for personal gain, took personal risks, and made his way by personal initiative and hard work. He was often a member of one of the Nonconformist sects whose exhorters were preaching the evils of extravagance and of worldly pleasures, and the virtues of self-denial and self-discipline, a code that was likewise required for modern business.

Beside this group of enterprising "captains of industry," as representatives of a new social order, were a number of great bankers, Laffitte of Paris, the Hopes of Amsterdam, the Barings of London, and above all the Rothschilds, whose system of banking extended from London to Naples. After 1815 these great financiers played a much larger rôle in European society than they had in the preceding century. Like the few great factory owners of the period, they represented only a small element in the society of the time though they stand out as the forerunners of a new order. The insistence of these new groups on the obligation of everyone to do something useful, and their will to power and to wealth—what Balzac called their *stratégie des intérêts*—had begun by 1830 to affect the whole tone of British and French society. Their ideal of a life of hard work differed sharply from the ideal of the nobility, shared to some extent by the older bourgeoisie, of a life of leisure and of personal cultivation. Great Britain was the leader in these economic changes. As the nineteenth century proceeded England was praised, envied, and imitated, much as the United States has been in the twentieth. English ideas, machines, and men were borrowed, as well as her accumulated wealth; and from England the idea of the possibilities of an industrialized society spread across the continent.

The term *Industrial Revolution*[5] as applied to these changes, many of which were due to the introduction of the steam engine, is no longer so widely used as it was a generation ago. Even in England, where the transition to industrialism came most rapidly, a close examination of the situation has shown that the changes were too gradual to warrant calling them a revolution. Recent studies point to the persistence and the great importance of the putting-out system of manufacture all through the first half of the nineteenth century, as well as to the limited application of machinery and of steam power to industry, and to the small size of most industrial establishments. Indeed, it is now clear that while many industries by 1830 had been affected by mechanization, nevertheless no single British industry had by that time passed through a complete technical transformation.[6]

The history of banking and investment shows the same evidence of steady development, although the total effect of such change could not by 1830 be called a revolution. In England more credit was available than in the eighteenth century, though even bankers like the Rothschilds were still reluctant to lend money freely, and most banks would lend only in small amounts and on short term credits. The joint-stock company was now permitted by law but it was still hedged about with elaborate regulations. Thus wherever the story of English industrial change is picked up it shades from a remote and somewhat similar past on into a similar future.

In France the changes came even more slowly. Although Sheffield, Birmingham, Manchester, Liverpool, and Leeds increased by forty per-cent between 1821 and 1831, it took a half century for cities like Paris, Lyons, and Bordeaux to double their population. Here, as elsewhere on the continent, mechanization had to make way against fixed habits and the routine of old business forms and usages. Credit was almost nonexistent, means of communication were inadequate, markets were restricted. Such industries as were

[5] Cf. T. S. Ashton, "The Industrial Revolution," a bibliographical article, *Economic History Review*, 1934.
[6] Among recent studies the most detailed is J. H. Clapham, *An Economic History of Modern Britain* (2nd. ed., Cambridge, 1930), I; see also L. W. White and E. W. Shanahan, *The Industrial Revolution and the Economic World of To-day* (London, 1932).

organized on any considerable scale lacked qualified workmen and technical improvements.[7]

The sane and shrewd handling of public finance in both England and France was a help to business, although severe financial panics in 1816-17, in 1819, and above all in the great crisis of 1825-26 offset much that the governments were able to do. In spite of all short-comings in the banking and credit situation, however, a new mech-anism of national and international banking and investment was slowly making its way. Western Europe was gradually becoming a single commercial and industrial society with certain common economic interests and common economic diseases. England needed the continental markets and the continent needed some of Eng-land's manufactures and capital as never before. A situation had already developed in which nations were so closely interlocked financially that pressure on the economic nerve-centers in Paris, London, Amsterdam, Hamburg, or New York was felt nearly everywhere.

Thus, in spite of all manner of disorders and changes of political conditions, there was from the days of the Ancien Régime, through the revolutionary era into the period of the restoration, a slow but steady accumulation of capital and an extending commerce and manufacture. This economic transformation was more rapid in the western countries than in the outer European states, although its effects were felt even there. Among the leaders of the middle class the conviction was growing that they were the important figures in society and that the state should be run for their benefit. At the same time the great bankers, merchants, and manufacturers found their activities hedged about by local customs boundaries, by dis-advantageous laws of incorporation, and by mercantilist marketing regulations.[8] The freedom to speak, the freedom to move about

[7] Cf. Charles Ballot, *Introduction du mechanisme dans l'industrie française* (Paris, 1923), and Henri Sée, *La vie économique de la France sous la monarchie censitaire* (Paris, 1927), chap. ii.

[8] In Piedmont, for example, a decree of 1814 expelled the French residents who had come in during the revolutionary era. Jews who had acquired real estate were forced to put it on sale, and the Jews were again obliged to live in ghettos. Thus two of the most active trading groups, the French and Jewish merchants, were badly hit by the restoration. Moreover, the artisan guilds were restored, and the government further hindered industrial development by granting a number of monopolies. The whole matter is interestingly discussed in C. Barbagallo, *Le origini della grande industria contemporanea* (Perugia-Venice, 1929-30), II, 245 ff.

and to buy and sell, and the free choice of an occupation constituted the basis of their judgment of the worth of any government.

II. THE LOWER MIDDLE CLASS AND THE RISE OF AN INDUSTRIAL PROLETARIAT

Below these groups, which controlled the business life of the urban centers, were large numbers of small shopkeepers and craftsmen. The majority of them lived in scattered market towns which were the centers of small pockets of economic self-sufficiency. The activity of such towns was concentrated about a weekly market to which the farmers from the surrounding districts brought their produce and sold it directly to the local shopkeepers, shoemakers, and tailors. At all such markets, and at the occasional fairs which brought together traders from a wider area, all the goods bought and sold were displayed before the purchaser who satisfied himself by personal inspection of their condition and quality. This age-old economy was supplemented by an irregular exchange of goods, carried on by traveling peddlers. In many parts of Europe where the population was sparse and the towns few, the peddler supplied almost the only link between the scattered agrarian settlements and the outer world. The itinerant hawker and the stage of economic development he represented held this market until the development of the railroad altered the whole economic order.

The local café, the coffee-house, or the beer-garden brought together the tradesmen, the lawyers, and the doctors of the town and often a certain number of the farmers from the neighborhood. Here they read newspapers and discussed politics. Their growing interest in public affairs was particularly noticeable in the smaller communities of England and France where a newspaper-reading public was by 1815 already in existence. Though less marked in other countries, the beginnings of these changes could be seen also in Italy and in Germany. Elsewhere the newspaper was almost as unknown as the steam engine, and in outward appearance, at least, the life of the towns still bore the mark of earlier centuries. In Austria and the German states the return of peace produced the so-called "Era of Good Feeling"—or, as it was called later, the "Biedermeier period" —when the middle classes settled back into the enjoyment of a bourgeois comfort. But beneath this apparently unchanging surface, the revolutionary storm and the long wars that followed it had brought even to the countryside the idea and the possibility of great and fundamental changes.

Most of the craftsmen both in the larger cities and in the smaller market towns owned their own properties and maintained a certain independence. On the continent the period was a fairly prosperous one for such workers. The guilds were disintegrating, and the large factory was still rare. In parts of western Europe, the putting-out system had changed the status of some workers. Under this system the worker usually owned his own tools and worked in his own home, though by 1815 in England the capitalist entrepreneur had generally come to own the machines and even the workers' houses. Under such an industrial régime the workers, before the advent of the steam engine or the factory, had already become practically a proletarian class. The coming of the factory did no more than to make worse living and working conditions and to increase the irksomeness of the discipline imposed. Dislike of factory discipline, rather than a desire to maintain their economic independence, drove the home-workers to compete with factory-made products long after such a course had become economically ruinous. The final stages of the struggle between them and the rising factory system were marked by suffering and bitterness. The workers rioted and broke the machines in a futile effort to stop the mechanization and the concentration of industry.[9]

In a few centers in western Europe the factory stood as the symbol of the rise of a new class in European society, the industrial proletariat. This new group of wage-slaves presented a variety of serious problems which were not understood and which few thinkers or statesmen made any serious effort to grasp. The new factory system herded the workers into a common establishment where they were closely supervised and kept steadily at work. Laborers were obliged to live in quarters which they did not own and under conditions which they did not control. Before 1830 these problems appeared in only a few centers, and in certain branches of any given industry. For example, in the English cotton industry, the earlier

[9] The best accounts are still those of W. Hasbach, *A History of the English Agricultural Labourer* (2nd. imp., London, 1920), chaps. ii and iii; and J. L. and B. Hammond, *The Village Labourer, 1760-1832* (London, 1912), chaps. iii to v.

factories were for spinning and printing, and the intermediate weaving process continued to be done in cottages under the putting-out system.

Women and children were more useful than adult male workers in the spinning and printing processes where most of the work consisted of simple tasks which required little strength or skill, such as placing the cotton in the machines, tying the thread when it broke, and taking off the finished material. For this reason, the proportion of adult males in the factories remained considerably below the proportion found in the cloth industries as a whole, until the improvement of power-weaving finally drove hand-weaving from the field. As a result, the worst abuses of the early phases of the factory movement were in the exploitation of women and children, the groups least able to make effective protest. Many of the children in English factories were recruited from the larger towns where, according to laws dating from the time of Henry VIII, orphans and vagrant children could be bound out as apprentices.[10] In the new factories women and children, many of the latter no more than ten years of age, had to work from twelve to eighteen hours a day. The foremen would sometimes beat the children to keep them awake and at work. The earliest factories were seldom properly ventilated and the machines were not equipped with safety devices. Work often began as early as five o'clock in the morning and lasted until eight or nine at night with short periods for meals. The long hours weakened the resistance of the workers and contributed to the spread of disease.

Distress in the factory towns was acute.[11] Dense masses of people were shut up in melancholy streets without gardens or orchards. The towns as yet made no proper provision for sewage disposal or for water supply. Large families were crowded into miserable rooms where filth and undernourishment increased sickness, alcoholism, and prostitution, and raised the rate of infant mortality. Any crisis

10 Cf. O. J. Dunlop, *English Apprenticeship and Child Labour* (London, 1912), especially chaps. xvi and xvii, and A. E. Bland, P. A. Brown, and R. H. Tawney, *English Economic History, Select Documents* (London, 1921), 482-524.

11 "The Industrial Revolution seen in perspective may seem a gradual process, so gradual that economists rightly find the phrase incorrect. But as an experience in individual and family lives, the Industrial Revolution was sudden and its consequences sweeping." J. L. and B. Hammond, *The Age of the Chartists* (London, 1930), 20.

in trade which meant the cutting of wages or unemployment, or a bad harvest and the consequent rise of the price of foodstuffs, brought the population of the factory centers to utter destitution. Similar conditions prevailed in the mines and mining towns. The life of the workers before 1830 seems to have been peculiarly wretched in the towns and mines of central England and in the factories of Lille, Rouen, Lyons, and Mulhouse in France. The factory owners were interested in keeping wages low. The great difficulty of obtaining capital, most of which had to be saved out of the profits of the business, the necessity for improving the machinery, and the efforts to find markets taxed the resourcefulness of entrepreneurs bent only on pushing production to the utmost. To them it appeared that the rapid development of wealth in England and France was linked with the unhampered freedom of action of enterprising business men. The employing class honestly believed that they were the benefactors of their employees, and that resistance to them amounted to ingratitude. Only a few radical thinkers seem to have been aware that while the factory system was beginning to increase the national wealth more rapidly than had any earlier economic system it was almost as rapidly decreasing national well-being.[12]

In the face of oppressive working and living conditions, labor was just beginning to be conscious of its own solidarity and power. Mutual benefit societies had long been in existence in the older skilled trades, such as tailoring, printing, and carpentry. By the end of the eighteenth century these societies in most of the states of western Europe had gradually extended their common interests from social activities and insurance provisions to matters of wages, hours, and working conditions. When trade-unions began to be organized in the factories, either as mutual benefit societies or secretly as what the French called *sociétés de résistance*, it was the skilled mechanics and operatives who took the lead.

The governing classes, however, looked with great disfavor on this movement. During the revolution in France, when new privileges were being won by the middle class, the legislators proved to be interested only in ridding industry of surviving medieval

[12] A wealth of material may be found in J. L. and B. Hammond, *The Town Labourer, 1760-1823* (London, 1917), though the authors tend to exaggeration and over-emphasis.

restrictions and of the excessive governmental control which had grown up in the seventeenth and eighteenth centuries. They had abolished the half-decayed guilds and had cut down state interference in business. But the problems of the wage-earners had not concerned them, and so fearful had they been of all movements not directly controlled by the central government that they had passed laws against labor organizations. The Le Chapelier Law of 1791 in France held that "citizens of certain trades must not be permitted to assemble for their pretended common interests. There is no longer any competition in the state; there is but the particular interest of each individual and the general interest. It is necessary to abide by the principle that only by free contracts between individual and individual may the working day for each workman be fixed."[13] Other legislation completed this restriction. One article of the Napoleonic Code provided that in all circumstances "the master's word is taken both for the rate and for the payment of wages." Each worker, moreover, was obliged to carry a *livret*, a small book, in which was set down the time and place of his employment, the amount of his wages, and the conditions of his change from one employer to another. The *livret* had to be signed by the employer and by the mayor or the police. If the employer or the civil authorities refused to sign it, the worker had difficulty in finding employment. In England the behavior of the French revolutionaries had filled Parliament with a dread of all forms of popular association. As a result, Combination Acts were passed in 1799 and in 1800 making it a criminal offense for workingmen to form associations with the object of securing improvement in the conditions of their labor. A further provision prohibited similar combinations of employers against workmen, and arranged for compulsory arbitration, but these restrictions remained dead letters on the statute books.

The laws against trade-unions in France and England were not rigidly enforced, and the trade-union movement grew steadily. Since the existence of mutual benefit associations continued to be permitted by law, many labor unions hid behind this form of organiza-

[13] E. Levasseur, *Histoire des classes ouvrières et de l'industrie en France de 1789 à 1870* (2nd. ed., Paris, 1903), I, 55; see also Paul Louis, *Histoire de la classe ouvrière en France* (Paris, 1927), chap. iii.

tion, though the dues were so high that only the more skilled workers could afford to join. For a great mass of workers the only help obtainable was from charity and from state poor-relief. Private charity, both Catholic and Protestant, furnished some help by establishing soup kitchens, mutual savings banks and charity schools. The history of poor-relief in this period shows that it was badly administered and that probably it did more to keep wages low than to relieve suffering.

The only hope of the new proletarians, as they were beginning to realize, lay in developing the trade-union movement. Shut off from immediate contact with their employers, the industrial workers were being brought by the factory system into closer relationship among themselves. In the factory they found opportunity to discuss their low wages and long hours, and to form plans to force an amelioration of industrial conditions. But, in this period, the hotbeds of proletarian discontent were not always in the factories. In England, in France, and in parts of Germany the greatest restlessness seems to have been in the districts where the home-workers were rising against the introduction of factories or against the low wages paid to craftsmen competing with the factories. Theirs was a losing fight. In the 1830's the struggle ended, at least in most industries, with the victory of the factory and the disappearance of the hand-workers.

The first change in the attitude of governments toward trade-unions appeared in England. Largely through the efforts of the scholarly tailor, Francis Place, and a group of Radicals in Parliament, the government in 1824 passed an act repealing the Combination Acts. A series of strikes followed, whereupon an amending law was passed in 1825 limiting the activities of trade combinations by the common law of conspiracy. These laws of 1824 and 1825 mark the first legal recognition of the right of collective bargaining. They stand as important milestones in the history of the working classes.[14]

The early decades of the nineteenth century saw also the enactment of the first factory acts. In 1802 the English Parliament passed a law restricting the employment of children apprenticed from the workhouses to twelve hours a day, forbidding their employment

[14] Graham Wallas, *The Life of Francis Place* (4th ed., London, 1925), is a classic.

in night labor, and requiring the whitewashing of factory walls. A second factory act was passed in 1819, partly through the efforts of Robert Owen. It forbade the employment in cotton mills of children under nine years of age and fixed the working-day at twelve hours for all between the ages of nine and sixteen. The bill was attacked in Parliament on the ground that "all experience proves that in the lower orders of society the deterioration of morals increases with the quantity of unemployed time of which they have command. This bill actually encourages vice. It establishes idleness by act of Parliament."[15] During the debate on the same bill in the House of Lords, one member declared that such laws were unnecessary because questions of this type should be "left entirely to the moral feelings of perhaps the most moral people on the face of the earth."[16] In France, the governments of the period also began to show the first signs of interest in the welfare of the working classes. A law of 1803 prohibited work in manufacturing establishments before three in the morning. Other laws regulating employment in certain industries were from time to time put on the statute books. But the enforcement of all these laws was lax. That the problem was partly an international one seems to have been grasped first by Robert Owen, who in 1818 addressed a petition to the powers assembled at the Conference of Aix-la-Chapelle urging governments to fix a uniform working-day for the industrial workers of Europe. At the time the proposal was dismissed as quixotic.

The legalizing of trade-unions in England and the earliest factory legislation in both England and France represent the first reaction against the abuses of the new factory régime. Some of the delay in legislation on the new social problems seems to have been due to the inadequacy, at least in England, of governmental machinery to handle such abuses. The unreformed constitution of England possessed no means of carrying out a policy of regulation

[15] *An Inquiry into the Principle and Tendency of the Bill imposing Certain Restrictions on Cotton Factories* (London, 1818).

[16] On early labor organization and social legislation in England, see the excellent account of Sidney and Beatrice Webb, *The History of Trade Unionism* (new ed., London, 1926); also cf. A. P. Usher, *An Introduction to the Industrial History of England* (Boston, 1920), 377 ff.; G. D. H. Cole, *A Short History of the British Working Class Movement* (New York, 1927), chaps. iv and v; B. L. Hutchins and A. Harrison, *A History of Factory Legislation* (3d edition, London, 1926), chaps. ii and iii; M. D George, "The Combination Laws Reconsidered," *Economic Journal, Economic History Series*, I, 1927, 214-228.

other than that of the old local parish, county, and town. No government had at the time any experience in dealing with these problems. The English Parliament did not adopt any systematic policy of favoring the factory owners, and the worst abuses of the early stages of the factory system were due in both France and England less to any definite design for using political machinery to exploit the industrial workers than to inexperience, to indifference, and to the fact that the leading figures in the government were still largely concerned with old political and religious issues left over from the eighteenth century.

III. THE PEASANTS

The overwhelming majority of the population of every European state from Ireland to Turkey and from Spain to Russia still lived on the land. The political and intellectual movements of the time affected the peasants even less than the lower bourgeoisie or the industrial workers, yet their modes of working and living also were quietly undergoing a transformation. The old system of manorial tenure had begun to change in western Europe before the French Revolution. In England the extension of enclosures was modifying the method of land tenure and the economic status of the agricultural classes. On the continent the revolution merely hastened changes that had begun earlier. The peasant was with each decade becoming freer to rise in the world or to go under, freer to buy, to sell, and to mortgage his property, and freer to vary his methods of farming. The full results of these changes were not widely felt until after the middle of the nineteenth century, for in the country as in the towns the building of the first network of railroads, more than any other innovation, marked the division between the older economic order and the new.

The evidences of agricultural change, as of industrial change, varied greatly from country to country, and often almost as greatly from one district to another. It was still an age of economic localism, and hence generalizations are difficult. But in general it is true that, while the English peasants were losing their lands and their economic independence through the extension of enclosures, the peasants in western Europe were finding their condition improving through emancipation from a feudal status and through new opportunities for acquiring land. In nearly every state of western Europe there were roughly three classes of peasants—small freeholders, renters, and agricultural day-laborers. These categories, however, were not mutually exclusive. For example, a freeholder or a renter might on certain days of the week hire himself out as a day-laborer, or a peasant might own part of the land which he worked and might rent another part. But the tendency of the agricultural classes in western Europe to divide into these groups is clearly revealed by detailed studies of the agrarian life of the time.

The agricultural transformation in England and its connection with the contemporaneous industrial development has long been a matter of dispute among economic historians. The view has been widely held that the second phase of the enclosure movement, which began about 1750, resulted in the great impoverishment of the yeomanry, that is, of the small landowners. The large landholders were able to call a meeting of property owners in a given district and, since voting power varied with the size of holdings, they were able to secure the four-fifths vote necessary to petition Parliament to enclose the old open fields and common lands. A private act could then be passed. A board of three to seven commissioners, appointed from the local magnates, carried through the work of enclosure, usually reassigning the land in solid blocks. So the old three-field system of strip-farming, which had come down from the Middle Ages, disappeared. The small farmers soon found that they had too few acres to support themselves. Their greatest loss was the common lands on which they had been accustomed to feed their poultry, to pasture a cow, and to cut their fuel. Popular resentment against enclosures was aptly expressed in the rhyme:

> The law locks up the man or woman
> Who steals the goose from off the common;
> But leaves the greater villain loose
> Who steals the common from the goose!

Thousands of peasants were obliged to sell out to the larger proprietors and to become day-laborers, or else go to the cities to work in the factories. Even those who were able to maintain themselves on their holdings found their position more precarious than before.

Their products had to compete with those of the larger estates where improved methods were rapidly being introduced. In the period we are here considering, less than fifteen per cent of the land belonged to those who lived on it and tilled it.[17]

The cottage textile worker was bound, sooner or later, to follow the yeoman class to extinction. The cottagers who divided their time between farming and weaving were devoting themselves to forms of industry that were rapidly becoming outmoded. As craftsmen they were competing with a more efficient type of manufacture, and as tillers of the soil they could not hope to hold out against the more economical, large-scale farming. Many of them survived beyond the period here discussed, but large numbers were obliged to give up their occupation and their old way of living and to enlist in the ranks of the agricultural or industrial proletariat.[18]

The rapid growth of an unpropertied working class on the land and in the towns presented the English government with a serious social problem. The remedy first applied was that of wholesale poor-relief. The type of relief in general use at the time was that devised by a group of Berkshire magistrates who met at Speenhamland in 1795. Their program provided that wages, where they were inadequate, should be supplemented by contributions from the poor-rates, these contributions varying with the size of the family and with the price of bread. This Speenhamland plan, though never applied to the larger cities, was almost universally adopted in the country districts. Relief was distributed on a lavish scale, with the result that everywhere wages and relief became completely confused. Wages remained so low that most agricultural laborers were forced to go on the rates. Since the larger landowners preferred not to engage independent workers, lest they demand higher wages, it became hard for a worker not on the rates to find employment. The governing classes accepted the system and even praised it, be-

[17] E. Davies, "The Small Landowner, 1780-1832," *Economic History Review,* I (1927), 87-113. For the rest the reader may be referred to the leading treatments: Gilbert Slater, *The English Peasantry and the Enclosure of Common Fields* (London, 1907); Arthur H. Johnson, *The Disappearance of the Small Landowner* (Oxford, 1909), chap. v; E. C. K. Gonner, *Common Land and Inclosure* (London, 1912); J. L. and B. Hammond, *The Village Labourer, 1760-1832* (London, 1912), chaps. iii to v; W. H. R. Curtler, *The Enclosure and Redistribution of our Land* (Oxford, 1920).

[18] See especially W. Hasbach, *The History of the English Agricultural Labourer* (London, 1908), chap. ii.

cause in their opinion it averted a revolution. Wages fell in England after 1815, while prices rose. The peasantry steadily degenerated under the eyes of landowners who were doubling their incomes—landowners who denounced Cobbett as an "incendiary" because, when no one else dared, he pointed out the contrast.[19]

Even worse was the condition of the peasantry in Ireland. The landlords were mostly absentees, and the great estates were under the management of agents who were allowed a certain percentage of the income. Neither the agent nor the proprietor had any interest in the peasants beyond that of grinding the last farthing out of them. Taxes were heavy and a part of them went to support the hated Anglican clergy. The ordinary food of the Irish peasants was the potato, the yield of which from year to year was very uncertain. Famine and unrest were common, and many of the country districts were in a state of chronic anarchy.[20]

On the continent the position of the agricultural classes was improving. A movement to emancipate the peasants had begun in the eighteenth century. Many of them changed their status from serf to renter by purchasing their freedom over a period of years. They had been thus emancipated in Savoy, in Lorraine, in Switzerland, and in Baden. During the same period the peasants in France, most of whom had ceased centuries before to be serfs, were improving their status by reclaiming waste lands and by purchasing small lots of land from impoverished nobles. These slow and evolutionary changes were greatly accelerated by the French Revolution. In France itself the peasants were freed from a mass of feudal burdens, the system of taxation was readjusted to their advantage, and the internal customs boundaries were abolished. The state, by throwing a large number of confiscated estates on the market, gave the peasants better opportunities to buy land. It is true that most of the lands confiscated from the *émigrés* and the church passed first into the hands of bourgeois speculators. Nevertheless, they came eventu-

[19] The classic study of the poor-laws is that of Sidney J. Webb, *English Poor Law History* (London, 1927), I; but see also Hammond, *The Village Labourer*, chaps. vii to ix, and E. M. Hampson, *The Treatment of Poverty in Cambridgeshire* (Cambridge, 1934).

[20] A good account is that of J. E. Pomfret, *The Struggle for Land in Ireland, 1800-1923* (Princeton, 1930), chap. i.

ally into peasant hands, so that in the course of the nineteenth century the acreage became more widely distributed among the agricultural population in France than in any other country.[21] These changes of the revolutionary period were not confined to France. The states of western Germany became lands of small peasant proprietors. Feudal dues were commuted to fixed rents, and the peasant was made free to move, to buy land, and to cultivate his acres as he would. The liberation of the serfs by the French administration in western Germany was reflected during the Napoleonic wars by reforms in Prussia. Edicts of 1807, of 1811, and of 1816 abolished serfdom, and permitted peasants to buy and to sell property. They also provided that, for certain types of tenure, the surrender of a third or a half of the holding to the lord would secure the peasant full ownership of the rest. The edicts were carried out in a dilatory fashion, and the conditions of acquiring ownership proved to be so costly that only a small number of the wealthier peasants in western Prussia became landowners. In eastern Prussia the land remained in the control of the Junkers who lived in manorial style on their vast estates, exercising almost dictatorial powers over their peasants.[22]

In Spain and in the southern half of the Italian peninsula the agricultural classes lived in a wretched condition. Under the French régime feudalism was abolished and the peasants were converted, at least on paper, into one form or another of renters. But no provisions were made for allowing them to acquire land. After 1815,

[21] Cf. the three excellent studies by G. Lefebvre, *Les paysans du Nord pendant la Révolution française* (2 vols., Paris, 1924), *passim;* but see also Theodor Freiherr von der Goltz, *Geschichte der deutschen Landwirtschaft* (2 vols., Stuttgart, 1903), Part IV, secs. ii and iii; and "Recherches relatives à la répartition de la propriété et de l'exploitation foncière à la fin de l'ancien régime," *Revue d'histoire moderne*, 1928, and "Place de la Révolution dans l'histoire agraire de la France," *Annales d'histoire économique et sociale*, 1929. Cf. also M. G. Hottenger, *La Lorraine économique au lendemain de la Révolution* (Nancy, 1924), 39 ff.; and René Durand, *Le département des Côtes-du-Nord sous le Consulat et l'Empire* (2 vols., Paris, 1926). A general account is that of Henri Sée, *La vie économique de la France sous la monarchie censitaire* (Paris, 1927), chap. I.

[22] The standard account is that of G. F. Knapp, *Die Bauernbefreiung* (2nd edition, Munich, 1927), I, *passim;* but see also Werner Sombart, *Die deutsche Volkswirtschaft im 19ten Jahrhundert* (7th edition, Berlin, 1927), 27 ff., 45 ff. Among special studies may be mentioned, for conditions in western Germany, H. Aubin and others, *Geschichte des Rheinlandes* (2 vols., Essen, 1922), II, 137 ff.; for eastern Germany J. Ziekursch, *Hundert Jahre schlesischer Agrargeschichte* (2nd edition, Breslau, 1927), chaps. vi to viii, and Karl Böhme, *Gutsherrlich-bäuerliche Verhältnisse in Ostpreussen während der Reformzeit von 1770 bis 1830* (Berlin, 1902).

though the feudal régime was not technically restored, the peasantry continued for several generations in much the same condition as in the eighteenth century. In the more backward parts of the Hapsburg lands, in the Balkans, and in Russia the status of the peasants was perhaps worse than it had ever been in England and France in the Middle Ages. The agrarian conditions in Russia were about as bad as any in Europe. The whole economic structure rested on serfdom. Little industry or banking or commerce existed and no middle class stood between the nobles and the mass of agricultural laborers. The powers of the aristocracy were almost absolute. The government had come to depend on the nobles to supply recruits for the army, and to act as financial agents in collecting the taxes. This explains the encouragement given by the Russian state to the growth of the landowner's authority which went on steadily in spite of projects of Paul and of Alexander I for improving the lot of the peasants. Although it was against the letter of the Russian law, the noble often sold his serfs apart from the land, beat them as he would, and if angry sent them to Siberia or even put them to death. The serfs in Poland had been freed by Napoleon, and those in the Baltic provinces were gradually emancipated, but in neither case were they able to acquire ownership of the land. As renters they remained an agricultural proletariat.[23]

While in western Europe the legal status of the peasant was slowly changing, an important transformation in agricultural methods was also taking place. The lead in this had been taken in England in the eighteenth century, but the new methods soon spread to the continent. Root crops, potatoes, turnips, and beets were being grown in greater quantities, particularly on the larger estates, and artificial meadows of clover, lucerne, and rye-grass were introduced instead of fallow for renewing the soil. Deep-plowing, drill-sowing, machine-hoeing, and tile-draining all came into wider use. The abandonment of the wasteful three-field system, the use of new crops, and the improved methods of cultivation greatly augmented the productivity of the acreage. At the same time these improvements furnished more food for live stock, whose increase in turn

[23] A good picture of the old régime is given in James Mavor, *An Economic History of Russia* (2nd ed. 2 vols. London, 1926), I, chaps. ii to iv; and in G. T. Robinson, *Rural Russia under the Old Régime* (New York, 1932), chaps. ii to iv.

provided more fertilizer for the soil. Great advances were also made in the methods of stock-breeding. The new agriculture stood for experimentation and observation in place of ignorance and the use of old routine methods. It represented a better coöperation with nature, and a thorough working of the soil to its advantage in place of the older soil-scratching which was usually to its detriment. Wherever the new methods were introduced they made necessary the abandonment of the old three-field system, and in some regions, especially in England, the change worked to the disadvantage of the peasants.[24]

On the continent the adoption of these new agricultural methods was slow. In nearly every country, even in Russia, gentlemen farmers established large experimental farms. The writings of the English pioneers, Jethro Tull, Bakewell, and Coke, and of their German followers, Thaer and Thunen, circulated among the great continental landowners, especially in France, in northern Italy, and in East Prussia. On some of the large farms capital and science were being applied exactly as they were to industry. Gentlemen farmers, like Ridolfi and Cavour in Italy, after using the new agricultural methods on their estates, had their interest awakened to the need of a transformation of the industrial and political order. Others, like Mathieu de Dombasle in Lorraine, issued pamphlets describing their experiments in stock-breeding, in cropping, and in the use of improved machinery. The movement to improve agriculture was, however, greatly retarded by the small holdings in France and in western Germany, where the cultivators could not afford the improved machinery, and everywhere by the conservatism of the peasants and by the lack of markets for increased agricultural yields.[25]

The agricultural changes of the period, like the industrial changes, were checkered by the extraordinary fluctuation in prices due to the long wars and the sudden return to peace in 1814 and 1815. The agriculturists of every state found their markets disorganized, and north of the Alps the large landowners, who dominated all the

[24] A good brief account may be found in Norman S. B. Gras, *A History of Agriculture* (New York, 1925), chap. ix.

[25] Cf. Henri Sée, *Esquisse d'une histoire du régime agraire en Europe aux xviii⁰ et xix⁰ siècles* (Paris, 1921).

governments of the time, clamored for high tariffs to maintain their local monopolies. England, France, Russia, and some of the smaller states raised their tariffs soon after 1815 to protect domestic agricultural products. The first decade after Waterloo was marked in nearly every state by much agricultural distress due at times to bad harvests (especially in 1816-17) and again to great overproduction. During such crises, Ireland and central and southern Germany sent hundreds of emigrants to America. In England highway robbery, poaching, petty thieving, and rick-burning were so common that large sections of the countryside remained in an almost continuous state of anarchy until the reforms of the local police system in the 1830's and 1840's.

Despite all the changes noted in the life of the agricultural classes, none had worked itself out by 1830. The daily life of the peasant was still very much what it had been in the eighteenth century. Intellectual inertia, incessant manual labor, and unbroken routine marked his existence. The peasant accepted his lot and rarely questioned the organization of society. Nothing was more foreign to him than the modern idea that all must be change and progress. The peasants lived almost universally in small villages, where they shared their roofs with the live stock and poultry. The better houses had stone floors instead of dirt, glass in the windows, copper and pewter instead of wooden utensils, and some substantial cupboards and tables. Meat on the table, the wearing of leather shoes, and a cupboard full of linen, the family's pride, were the marks of an affluent family.

On the continent the medieval three-field system was still common, except in Italy where it was never prevalent. This method of cultivation, in which all had to sow and reap at the same time, was very wasteful because it used fallow to replenish the soil, and because so much land had to be set aside for paths and for fences. Nowhere were there enough animals for the farm work, for food, and for fertilizer. The farm machinery used by the average peasant was clumsy and inefficient, and the harvesting was done with scythes and the threshing with flails. The peasant was his own baker and butcher. He spun and wove his own wool and flax and repaired his own house and tools. Often he supplemented his income by making soap, wooden utensils and shoes, knives, or even toys and clocks which were exchanged with the neighbors or sold on the weekly market. He suffered from epidemics; sickness was common; doctors were rare. When schools existed at all they were poor. Few peasants could read. Local dialects, costumes, and strange superstitions, many of them centuries old, continued to be indicative of the extreme localism of country life. The chief figure in the village was the priest or the pastor. The great occasions for the whole community were religious holidays, and for the family circle marriages and funerals. The peasants showed little interest in politics except when political changes threatened to affect land tenure. Nearly everywhere they remained devoted to the church—undoubtedly one of the chief reasons for the failure of most of the revolutionary movements in the period from 1815 to 1850.

IV. CONCLUSION

In considering the social structure as a whole it becomes clear that neither the early stages of industrialism in England and France, nor the upheaval of the French Revolution had, even in western Europe, created an essentially new society. The traditional class lines had become blurred, but were not effaced. A transformation of the life of the English peasants was being effected through the enclosure movement. On the continent the French Revolution had in some states modified the legal status of the peasants and their method of landholding. At the same time, improved systems of cultivation were coming into use. Nevertheless, the great mass of the peasantry continued to follow in a routine of life in which their ancestors of the thirteenth century could easily have found a place. Indeed, Virgil's Roman peasant would have found much that was familiar: "Often doth the driver of the slow-moving ass load his back with oil-jars or with cheap apples, and, returning from the town bring back a grindstone or a mass of swarthy pitch."[26] After 1830 five years of the railroad produced more visible changes in agricultural life than had several decades of emancipation.

Eastern Europe was almost entirely an agricultural world, far behind western Europe in economic and intellectual development.

[26] *Georgics,* I, l. 273 ff.

A handful of the aristocracy in Hungary, Poland, and Russia affected French or English ideas which they often misunderstood. The economic activity of the towns had hardly changed for centuries; exports were mainly raw products; the mines were largely unworked; manufactures were rarely on a large scale; and transportation was hindered by the wretched state of the roads and by the almost total lack of canals. There was no large or widely distributed middle class interested in banking, manufacturing, schools, and newspapers. The clergy and the nobility ruled the masses with an iron hand. This striking contrast between the east and the west of Europe—a line drawn from the mouth of the Elbe to the Adriatic roughly marked the division—must always be borne in mind in any consideration of the general social, political, and cultural situation.

In western Europe the bourgeoisie was extending its economic power by improved methods of manufacture and by better means of communication. But the influence of the middle class was everywhere limited, as before 1789, by the presence of the aristocracy, the clergy, and the peasantry. The tendency of the business world to dominate all classes and to impose its philosophy of life on every social group was only beginning to appear. In some centers in England, France, and the Low Countries the suffering among the working classes was beginning to attract the attention of a few reformers, but the proletarian problem was still of only minor significance in the social situation of the time. In every state the population was increasing, chiefly because of the lowering of the death rate due to the progress of medicine, and in the towns to improved sewage and hospital service.[27]

What had changed since the eighteenth century, however, was not so much the economic and social organization of society as its intellectual outlook. The changes wrought by the French Revolution had everywhere started discussion of further changes. Men were more inclined than ever before either to defend or to question the validity of old ways of thinking and living. The philosophers

[27] Of the increase of the population there is no doubt, but authoritative writers have not yet come to any agreement regarding the explanation of this phenomenon. Among recent writings the following are particularly illuminating: G. Talbot Griffith, *Population Problems of the Age of Malthus* (Cambridge, 1926); M. C. Buer, *Health, Wealth and Population in the Early Days of the Industrial Revolution* (London, 1926); T. H. Marshall, "The Population Problem during the Industrial Revolution," *Economic Journal, Economic History Series,* IV, 1929, 429-456.

of the eighteenth century had spread the idea that change was desirable and the revolutionary era had given striking evidence that it was possible. This inspired some classes to hope for further advances and aroused others to oppose change bitterly. Moreover, the constant movements of the armies during twenty-five years of campaigning had brought the nations into closer contact with one another. This intermingling was particularly important in spreading ideas of western Europe among the intellectual classes of central and eastern Europe. Taking Europe as a whole, it is this profound difference in the intellectual climate rather than any striking economic or political change that makes the life of the period from Waterloo to the Reform Bill of 1832 so different from life as it had been before the French Revolution.

Chapter Three

THE SEARCH FOR A PRINCIPLE OF AUTHORITY

THE early nineteenth century was characterized by a strong reaction against the ideals of the Enlightenment. The French Revolution, which had delighted Kant in his old age because it enabled a great people to create its own constitution, now seemed to many to be a purely destructive movement capable of creating nothing. The Jacobins, in the name of reason, had acted most irrationally, and in the name of humanity had behaved most inhumanly. The belief in the natural perfectibility of man seemed to have led only to untold bloodshed and misery. The whole post-Napoleonic generation lay under the shadow of a great disillusionment.

Even the men who had made the revolution had grown afraid of it, afraid that they had destroyed not only the machinery of government but also the moral authority necessary for any kind of rule; afraid that they had left the road open only to anarchy or to the establishment of military dictatorship. The monarchs, the clergy, and the aristocracy—the groups which had suffered most from the revolutionary upheaval—detested its ideals most heartily. And there was after the wars a general and widespread weariness of intellectual analysis combined with an appeal to faith, to sentiment, to history, in fact to anything that ran counter to the ideals of the Enlightenment. The intellectual classes were oppressed with a sense of spiritual vacuum, the *mal du siècle,* which put its stamp on some of the greatest works of literature. Goethe's Faust—a vivid symbol of the age—found his soul dying within him after his long search for purely intellectual knowledge; he renewed his life through sentiment, dreams, and finally through action. Madame de Staël, one of the greatest literary influences of the early nineteenth century, declared in a similar strain: "I do not know exactly what we must believe, but I believe that we must believe! The eighteenth century did nothing but deny. The human spirit lives by its beliefs.

Acquire faith through Christianity, or through German philosophy, or merely through enthusiasm, but believe in something."[1] It would be hard to imagine a more complete repudiation of the attitude and ideals of the pre-revolutionary thinkers.

I. THE EMOTIONAL REACTION AGAINST THE ENLIGHTENMENT: PIETISM, METHODISM, AND ROMANTICISM

The reaction against the Enlightenment was heralded by popular religious and literary movements like Pietism, Methodism, and Romanticism. During the last decade of the eighteenth century it appeared in a more substantial form in the writings of a group of theorists who attacked revolutionary ideas in the name of tradition. Finally it found its fullest philosophic statement in the work of the German Idealist Philosophers. A study of the origins of this reaction shows that it was not merely the result of the experiences of the revolution. For over a century it had accompanied the development of modern science and philosophy, and its steady growth was symptomatic of the unwillingness of large numbers of men to accept the general conclusions of the prophets of the Enlightenment. Its earliest popular form was Pietism, which had first appeared in the Lutheran churches of Germany in the later seventeenth century as a protest against the arid dogmatism of the ruling theologians. In order to combat religious intellectualism, the leaders of the movement had endeavored to kindle the flame of Christian mysticism. They delighted in belittling human reason, which they denounced as presumptuous and irreligious. They laid great emphasis on those types of Bible study and devotional exercises which would develop a highly emotional religious outlook, and they carried their gospel to the masses by founding schools and institutions for the care of the poor and of orphans. Their missionaries went throughout Germany preaching an ardently emotional faith. Most thoroughgoing were the Moravian Brethren, one of whom in 1738 converted John Wesley to "the religion of the heart."

The piety evoked by the movement often contained an element of moroseness. On the intellectual side it encouraged a narrow out-

---

[1] Emile Faguet, *Politiques et moralistes du XIX siècle*, 2e série (Paris, 1895), 232. The same mood is brilliantly described in the opening chapter of Alfred de Musset's *Confession d'un enfant du siècle*.

look and a disdainful attitude toward public affairs and toward scientific and artistic culture. Yet the influence of the Pietists on German thought, and through Methodism on English thought, was profound. They captured the leading positions in some of the Protestant theological schools, notably at the University of Halle. The movement produced hundreds of devotional pamphlets and books, a type of literature which in sheer quantity outclassed every other form of publication in eighteenth-century Germany. The Pietistic point of view to some degree influenced the thought of Lessing, Herder, Goethe, Kant, and the other German Idealists, as well as that of Novalis and the leaders of the German romantic school. It affected the world of German Freemasonry through the spread of Rosicrucianism, a mystic doctrine that abhorred logic and science, and, in the last years of the century, attacked the whole ideology of the French Revolution. Rosicrucian ideals were especially cultivated in Berlin where the king, Frederick William II, became a devotee. Finally, much of the reaction against what was considered "the dry-rot of rationalism," as also the positive emphasis of the German romanticists on the affinity of poetry and religion, came originally from Pietism, above all from Jakob Böhme (1575-1624), the great progenitor of this movement.

The influence of Pietism on practical politics is very evident in the decades after 1800, though so diffused that it is frequently difficult to trace. It is most clearly shown in the growth of millenarianism between 1800 and 1815. In these years the belief grew in Germany and in a number of the royal courts of northern Europe that a man would be raised up in the north who would overthrow the Antichrist (Napoleon) and prepare the way for the second advent of Christ and the establishment of His thousand years' rule upon earth. One Pietist prophet, Jung-Stilling, who had a large following in the royal courts of Baden and Sweden, preached this strange gospel with especial persuasiveness. He believed that certain persons, among them himself, possessed the faculty of communicating directly with the spiritual world, and he found in a literal interpretation of the Bible vague prophecies of the downfall of Napoleon. In this he was not alone for, at the turn of the century, this type of Pietistic mysticism hung over Germany like a fog. Similar prophets were found in every social rank. Sovereign rulers and members of the highest aristocracy were attracted by their teachings. As the Napoleonic empire began to crumble conversions and visions increased.[2]

While staying at Karlsruhe in 1808, Jung-Stilling was visited by a Russian noblewoman, the Baroness von Krüdener, a strange adventuress who three years earlier had been converted by an ardent disciple of the Moravian Brethren. She came to believe that the latter days were about to be accomplished, and that she had been called by God to save the world. By 1811 she was widely known on the continent for her extravagant charities and her weird eloquence. Her appearance wherever she went—whether it was to visit a monarch or to seek out the Alsatian pastor, Jean Frédéric Oberlin, to draw up with his help an elaborate map of the Kingdom of Heaven—was the occasion for an outbreak of visions and prophecies. In June, 1815, she accomplished her ambition of meeting Alexander I of Russia, whose interest in this type of apocalyptic thought was widely known. The baroness found the tsar musing over an open Bible. For three hours she preached her strange gospel while the most powerful monarch in Europe sat weeping until at last he declared he had found peace. She followed him to Paris where for months, in a house near the imperial lodging, she conducted daily prayer-meetings. These were attended not only by the tsar, but also by a number of other monarchs and some of the best known members of Parisian society, Chateaubriand, Benjamin Constant, Mme. Récamier, and the Duchesse de Duras. The odd furnishings of her apartments, even the dials of the clocks, were draped with gray cloth during the sessions of prayer, while the baroness herself affected a kind of monastic costume. Mme. Récamier was told to make herself as plain as possible "so as not to trouble souls." The prophetess pretended to be guided in all her revelations by a mysterious mentor, "the Voice." In this strange religious atmosphere, the idea of the Holy Alliance grew to a precocious maturity.[3]

[2] See the excellent study by Hans R. G. Günther, *Jung-Stilling, ein Beitrag zur Psychologie des deutschen Pietismus* (Munich, 1928).

[3] Cf. E. J. Knapton, *Julie de Krüdener* (New York, 1939), A. Viatte, *Les sources occultes de romantisme* (2 vols., Paris, 1928), and F. Büchler, *Die geistigen Wurzeln der Keiligen Allianz* (Freiburg, 1929); the work of Knapton contains much valuable bibliographical material.

Though Pietism produced fantastic visionaries like Jung-Stilling and the Baroness von Krüdener, it was at the same time the leading influence in the thought of Schleiermacher, the greatest of modern theologians. Educated in a school of the Moravian Brethren, he went as a young man from this deeply pious atmosphere to the University of Halle. His study of Kant aroused his interest in the philosophy of the Enlightenment which served to temper his earlier Pietism. In 1796 he settled in Berlin where he became a friend of Friedrich Schlegel, Novalis, Tieck, Fichte, and Schelling. The fruit of these first years in Berlin was his *Addresses on Religion to the Educated who Despise it* (1799), his most influential work and one which marks an epoch in the history of German opinion. Appealing to those who in the name of science reject religion, he endeavored to show that a scientific culture is not irreconcilable with the religious and mystical spirit. Religion, as he defined it, is not a system of thought but an inner experience, the greatest that life may offer. Like the contemporary *Génie du Christianisme* of Chateaubriand, his writing and preaching helped to make religion and tradition respectable among the intellectual classes. Schleiermacher, however, never advocated political or religious reaction. At times he attacked both. Nevertheless, he undoubtedly helped indirectly to prepare the way in Germany for such reaction by throwing the weight of his authority against the great assumptions of eighteenth-century thought.[4]

Pietism at the same time was contributing to the growth of the religious revival in the German Catholic Church. Baader, the leading Catholic theologian, like the Pietists, was profoundly influenced by the writings of Böhme. His best known work, *Fermenta Cognitionis* (1822-1825), an attack on the fundamental position of the German Idealist Philosophers, won him a professorship in the University of Munich where he became one of the founders of a powerful German Catholic party. Although Baader never gave a systematic statement of his ideas, he started with the assumption that human reason itself can never reach the end at which it aims. Thus men are not justified in trying to throw aside the presupposi-

[4] Cf. Günther Holstein, *Die Staatsphilosophie Schleiermachers* (Bonn, 1923), Ernst Müsebeck, *Schleiermacher in der Geschichte der Staatsidee* (Berlin, 1927), and K. Pinson, *Pietism as a Factor in the Rise of German Nationalism* (New York, 1934).

tions of faith, church, and tradition. Moreover, society should possess an organic unity and every member must give up his individuality for the sake of the whole. Authority and faith, the fundamental bases of such a society, are found only in the universal Catholic Church. To make the individual independent in thought and action, and to establish a direct relation between him and the state can only lead to anarchy.

Although a reactionary in politics, Baader's views on social problems—like those of his contemporaries, Southey and Ballanche—were rather advanced. He maintained that revolutionary sentiments are due not to the faults of the government but to the poverty of the masses. The worker is enslaved by the owners of capital, and the social problem should be solved by giving the proletariat a system of representation, through which the workers might make their grievances known. Baader's influence, however, like that of Schleiermacher, was primarily on theology.[5]

English Methodism, even more clearly than German Pietism, was a revolt against the deism, skepticism, and democratic thought of the eighteenth century, although the movement produced no thinker of the caliber of Schleiermacher. Largely under the influence of Pietism, the leaders of Methodism had revived the venerable Protestant doctrine of justification by faith, and had set out "to spread holiness over the land." The movement created among the thousands who were converted to it a highly emotionalized outlook and a great preoccupation with problems of personal salvation. The Methodists propagated their faith by crude methods; their religious services often led to outbreaks of collective hysteria which would continue for days.[6] Their preaching converted thousands to a distrust of the rationalism and the republicanism of the older types of English nonconformity.

Methodist leaders found their greatest following among small shopkeepers, artisans, and agricultural laborers, though by the early nineteenth century the ideas and attitudes of the movement had permeated all the dissenting sects, as well as the Anglican Church

[5] Cf. D. Baumgardt, *Baader und die philosophische Romantik* (Halle, 1927).
[6] An example of the exaggerations which characterized the movement is that of the Methodist prophetess, Joanna Southcott, who in 1814 was the talk of London because she was promising at the age of sixty-five to become the mother of a Son of God.

itself. Like Pietism in Germany, it modified the whole intellectual outlook of the English nation. Its doctrines stressed the necessity of preserving order in society, and the need for loyalty to the public authorities. This political and social philosophy is clearly reflected in the *Statutes of the Wesleyan Body of 1792* which expressly demanded of its members loyalty and obedience to the government. "None of us," says this declaration, "shall either in writing or in conversation speak lightly or irreverently of the government. We are to observe that the oracles of God command us to be subject to the higher powers."[7] In the minds of the leaders all ideas of political or social liberalism were hopelessly compromised because those who advocated them were often atheists. In the opinion of Lecky and of other more recent historians like Halévy the influence of Methodism was one of the chief forces which spared England a revolution in the years 1789 to 1815. By supporting the existing social and political powers and by diverting attention from the problems of contemporary society to those of personal salvation, it continued to retard reform in the decades that followed.

As a current of opinion, wide in its influence but difficult to define, the romantic movement is comparable to Pietism and to Methodism. All three were emotional and, to a less extent, intellectual reactions against the prevailing attitudes and ideas of the Enlightenment. Romanticism, however, cannot be identified with any particular political or social doctrine.[8] In the early period of its development, literary romanticism was favorable to free-thought and democracy. The French Revolution had passed through its first stages before the leaders of the movement began to go over to the side of reaction. But once the current had set in, only a few isolated romantic writers of the generation who experienced the revolution,

[7] *Minutes of the Methodist Conferences* (London, 1812), I, 270. John Wesley himself was very conservative in his political views. He once wrote: "The greater the share the people have in the government, the less liberty, civil or religious, does a people enjoy. Accordingly, there is most liberty in a monarchy, less under an aristocracy, and least under a democracy."

[8] "Trust your genius; follow your noble heart; change your doctrine whenever your heart changes, and change your heart often. Such is the practical creed of Romanticism." Josiah Royce, *The Spirit of Modern Philosophy* (Boston, 1892), 173. In its wider aspects, the romantic movement contained a many-sided complex of ideas and attitudes, and the earlier stages of its history concealed the beginnings of many divergent lines of development. It should be noted that here the movement is treated in only one of these aspects and in but one period of its history.

Hazlitt in England, Mme. de Staël in France, and Goethe in Germany, escaped conversion to reaction. In the 1820's, however, the young generation of romanticists again espoused liberal ideas.

The career of Chateaubriand is typical and of special interest because his influence on French letters overshadows that of all the literary men of his generation. As a young man he was deeply influenced by the writings of Bossuet, Montesquieu, Voltaire, and above all, Rousseau. Out of the experiences of privation and exile which he suffered in the French Revolution he was converted to an ardent Christian faith, and in 1802 he published his *Génie du christianisme*. In this work, which, significantly enough, was originally called *Beautés de la religion chrétienne*, he poured out unqualified praise for the past glories of the Catholic Church, and insisted on the necessity of the return of mankind to its fold. The argument is founded on emotional conviction and the religion of the heart, borrowed largely from the confession of faith of the Savoyard vicar in Rousseau's *Émile*. Chateaubriand regarded this rhapsody as a satisfactory defense of Christianity against the contention of the eighteenth century that Christianity was a barbarous system which retarded the progress of the race. He presented it as the religion most favorable to civilization, and tried to demonstrate that the modern world is indebted to it for every improvement from agriculture to the most abstract sciences. The most positive political idea that the book contains is its defense of the papacy and its frank ultramontanism. "If there exists in the midst of Europe a tribunal which in the name of God may judge the nations and their rulers and may prevent wars and revolutions, it is the papacy. . . . If Rome understands her position she has before her the most brilliant destiny."[9]

Chateaubriand's rôle in this reverie was evidently not that of the theorist. This task, as we shall see, fell to Joseph de Maistre and to Bonald. The mission of Chateaubriand was rather to recruit the forces of sentiment through the medium of art. His new Christianity was, in the words of Georg Brandes, "a parade religion, a tool for the politician, a lyre for the poet, a symbol for the philosopher, a

[9] Chateaubriand, *Génie du christianisme*, Part IV, chap. 6. Cf. V. Giraud, *Le christianisme de Chateaubriand* (2 vols., Paris, 1925-1928) and P. Moreau, *La conversion de Chateaubriand* (Paris, 1933).

fashion for the man of the world. . . . In the seventeenth century men believed in Christianity, in the eighteenth they renounced and extirpated it, and now in the nineteenth" they looked at it "pathetically, gazing at it from the outside, as one looks at an object in a museum, and saying 'How poetic,' 'How touching.' Fragments from the ruins of monasteries were set up in gardens; a gold cross was once more thought a most becoming ornament for a fashionable lady; the audiences at sacred concerts melted into tears . . . To make the antiquated principle of authority look young and attractive they painted it with the rouge of sentimental enthusiasm."[10]

Chateaubriand, in demonstrating the truth of Christianity by the poetry of its liturgy and the melancholy eloquence of its church bells, is one of the founders of the æsthetic neo-medieval Catholicism that passed for Christianity with many of the devout during the whole nineteenth century. After the restoration of the Bourbons, Chateaubriand supported their government, though he made it clear in a widely read pamphlet, *De la monarchie selon la charte* (1816), that he believed in constitutional monarchy. At the end of the reign of Louis XVIII (1824) he went over to the opposition though he always remained an ardent ultramontane. The other French romantic writers of the Restoration resembled Chateaubriand in their political views. Lamartine began his literary career as an ardent Catholic and royalist. The early poems of Victor Hugo also contain the whole system of orthodox political and religious principles which were valid under the Restoration. But by 1830 both had veered away from the throne and the altar.[11]

The rallying of literary romanticism to reaction was even more striking in Germany than in France. The precursors of German romanticism had been prophets of an ideal of boundless liberty. No rules should bind the genius because the divine spirit spoke in him. But before the end of the Napoleonic wars nearly all the chief poets, critics, and novelists of the movement had passed into

10 G. Brandes, *Main Currents in Nineteenth Century Literature* (New York, 1901), III, 79, 85. Brandes fails to see that this generation was confronted with the problem of a religious vacuum, and that back of the tinsel there was a deep desire for belief and assurance.

11 Cf. L. Cordelier, *L'évolution religieuse de Lamartine* (Paris, 1895); P. Dubois, *Hugo, ses idées religieuses 1802-1825* (Paris, 1913); H. Girard, "La pensée religieuse des romantiques," *Revue de l'histoire des religions*, 1924, and A. Viatte, *Le catholicisme chez les romantiques* (Paris, 1922).

a mood of the blackest reaction. The reversal of their point of view is shown above all in the conversions to Catholicism. The one consistent element among these German romanticists lay in their persistent attempts to fly from reality and to construct an illusionist view of life. Their revolt, it would seem, was not against the wrongs of life, but against its prose. They began, for example, by evoking the Middle Ages in the name of fantasy, and they ended by dressing up society to look medieval in order to get poetic reality. Their intangible imagery and their strange vocabulary give one the impression that most of their passionate blows were dealt in the air.[12]

Novalis, the founder of German political romanticism, had begun as a revolutionary who announced that he was "prepared for any sort of enlightenment." He had expressed the hope that he might live to see a "new massacre of St. Bartholomew, a wholesale destruction of despotism and prisons." Yet this same poet ended by looking on the King of Prussia as a gift of providence, and, though a Protestant and a former pupil of a Moravian school, he came to defend the temporal power of the pope. In his *Christenheit oder Europa* (1799) he attacked the Enlightenment for its mechanistic and utilitarian view of the state and its ideals of natural rights, social equality, and political democracy. In the course of the argument, he extolled the spirit of Jesuitism and declared it a misfortune that the papacy no longer had the power to stop such dangerous theories as those of Copernicus. The ideal of a paternalistic and authoritarian régime, the glorification of mediæval culture, the emphasis on the religious element in civilization and the regeneration of society through Catholicism, and finally the necessity of submerging the individual in the group—all these are first brought together in German thought in the fragmentary writings of Novalis. Though primarily an artist, he gave to the more purely æsthetic and religious doctrines of the early German romanticists a political coloring.[13]

Friedrich Schlegel, the outstanding thinker of the group, made his début as an eighteenth-century rationalist, cosmopolitan, and classicist. Under the influence of Fichte and Schleiermacher, and

[12] On the psychological cast of German romanticism see the brilliant essay of Carl Schmitt, *Politische Romantik* (2nd edition, Munich, 1925).
[13] R. Samuel, *Die poetische Staats- und Geschichtsauffassung Friedrich von Hardenbergs* (Frankfort, 1925) and E. Spenlé, *Novalis* (Paris, 1933).

under the impressions of the French Revolution, he took a deep bath of romanticism wherein he rid himself of all taint of Jacobinism. He was converted to Catholicism, and spent his last years at Vienna in the circle of Metternich. Speculative reason, which was for the eighteenth-century rationalist an infallible guide, became in his eyes the chief source of falsehood and delusion. In his writings, especially in his *Philosophie der Geschichte* (1829), he frankly takes as his central concept irrationalism, or, to use a favorite expression of the period, the "Organic"; life is accepted in all its incomprehensibility in preference to what is mechanical or reducible to rational formulas. This type of romanticism was bound to support "tradition as the expression of a slow evolution ripened in the womb of time, a work not of arbitrarily deciding reason, but of mysteriously working life." Schlegel, like most of the German romanticists of this generation, idealized the old Holy Roman Empire and dreamed of a new society which should be a confederation under the pope. He saw in the German Middle Ages an epoch in which a simple faith was supreme, in which poetry found a glorious expression in the songs of the Minnesingers and in which the arts reached perfection in the work of Dürer and Peter Vischer.[14] Kings in this age may have been cruel, but they added to the pageantry of life; priests may have been superstitious, but they built cathedrals. It was a fancy-dress world whose *décor* seems made of painted plaster of Paris like much of the imitation wood and stone sculpture in the houses of the Gothic revival. Clemens Brentano, Tieck, and Kleist showed much the same tendencies. For these German romanticists there was no middle ground between wild revolt and unqualified submission.

In the world of practical affairs the most significant of the German romanticists converted to reaction was Görres, the founder of modern German journalism. Like the others he was an early admirer of the French Revolution, preaching a violent anticlerical

[14] The romantic movement in the early nineteenth century gave to the Middle Ages the same sentimental glorification that, in the eighteenth century, it gave to classical antiquity. Many of the attitudes of the literary romanticists were reflected in the Gothic revival in architecture, in the German Nazarene school of painting, and later in English Pre-Raphaelitism. There is much of interest on Schlegel's earlier career and views in Richard Volpers, *Friedrich Schlegel als politscher Denker und deutscher Patriot* (Berlin, 1917); see also F. Imle, *Friedrich von Schlegels Entwicklung* (Paderborn, 1927); Benno von Wiese, *Friedrich Schlegel* (Berlin, 1927) and R. Guignard, *Brentano* (Paris, 1933).

doctrine, and for a time he worked for the establishment of a free Rhenish republic after the French model. In 1814 he founded the *Rheinische Merkur*, to defend liberal and nationalist ideas, a journal that Napoleon called "the fifth power of Europe." The Prussian government suppressed the paper in 1816. Görres then wandered about Germany for several years and before long became a Catholic. In 1827 he joined the faculty of the University of Munich and, as an advocate of ultramontanism, was soon the center of the circle of Catholic intellectuals and politicians who laid the foundation of a Catholic political party in Germany. The same man who in early manhood had held that the past was detestable, that revolutionary France was the promised land, and that the rest of the world was the domain of slavery, now expounded views which brought him the praise of Joseph de Maistre, greatest of all theorists of the reaction in France. But Görres was consistent in at least one train of thought—he was an ardent exponent of nationalism, like many other German thinkers of his generation. He contrasted French immorality with the pure morality of the German, French free-thought with the devout faith of old German Catholicism, and the frivolous and artificial art of France with the simple and earnest folk-art of Germany.[15]

The most extreme and fantastic of the German romantics was the dramatist, Zacharias Werner. Like countless others he had been, in his youth, a devoted disciple of Rousseau. His respect for the great French master went so far that for a time he dated the year not from the first of January, but from the second of July, the date of Rousseau's death. By 1811 he had been converted to Catholicism and shortly afterward was ordained a priest. During the Congress of Vienna his fanatical sermons drew great audiences, which often included members of the congress. The pope and the executioner, he declared, were the two powers necessary to quell the rebellious spirit of unbelief and disobedience called forth by the French Revolution. Anyone who reads his extreme and almost hysterical appeals will feel some sympathy for the strictures of the great Danish critic, Georg Brandes, who remarks: "One feels as if Romanticism ended

[15] See M. Berger, *Görres als politischer Publizist* (Bonn, 1921). There is an excellent treatment of him in Georges Goyau, *L'Allemagne religieuse, le Catholicisme* (Paris, 1910), I. Book II, chap. iii.

in a sort of witches' Sabbath, in which the philosophers play the part of old crones, amidst the thunders of the obscurantists, the insane yells of the mystics, and the shouts of the politicians for temporal and ecclesiastical despotism."[16]

Still it would be a mistake to overlook the profound and far-reaching influence of German romanticism. It gave German thought a dominant position during the early nineteenth century not so unlike that held by Italian thought in the sixteenth century and by French classicism in the seventeenth and eighteenth. The thousands of French *émigrés* who lived in Germany in the time of the revolution and during the Napoleonic period took back the ideas of romanticism when they returned to their homes in 1814. Mme. de Staël's famous essay *De l'Allemagne* exerted an almost incredible influence and did more than perhaps any other book to spread the new gospel throughout Europe.[17] In the great German universities foreign students were steeped in the romantic outlook. Coleridge and Carlyle among English writers, Emerson among Americans, and a large group of scholars and writers in Russia, the Balkans, and among the Slavic peoples of middle Europe carried far and wide the ideals and literary forms of the German masters. It would be hardly too much to say that in the first four decades of the century European thought was becoming German thought.

The English writers of the romantic school never succumbed to the creed of political reaction as completely as did the French and Germans. Walter Scott, who was a Tory from the beginning, was beyond the need of conversion. He always condemned utilitarianism because it did violence to the old ties of religion, patriotism, and family loyalty, all of which he delighted in investing with the glamour of sentiment. He greatly admired Burke to whom he refers as a writer of "almost prophetic power." During the early nineteenth century, Scott's novels were probably the most widely read books in Europe; Nicholas I of Russia was fond of reading them to his Prussian wife. Their tremendous influence defies accurate estimate, but they obviously increased the taste for a romantic

[16] Brandes, *op. cit.*, II, 16.
[17] Cf. F. Baldensperger, *Le mouvement des idées dans l'émigration française* (2 vols., Paris, 1924).

view of past times, and furnished an imaginative medieval setting for the attempt of the reactionaries to resurrect the past.

The reaction was more striking among the poets. In his youth Wordsworth hailed the coming of the French Revolution. To follow its changes more closely he went to France. As the years passed, however, he turned against the movement and deplored the influence it might have on the old institutions of England, especially on the Anglican Church. He wrote poems against Catholic Emancipation, the Reform Bill, and popular education. This "lost leader" of Browning's verses was one of those who, as Hazlitt said of Southey, "missed the road to Utopia and landed in Old Sarum."[18] Southey, a second member of the Lake school, as a young man joined Coleridge in planning a communal settlement on the Susquehanna. When the French Revolution began he, too, welcomed it with enthusiasm; then, like many others of his generation, he discovered that revolutionary doctrines had not made men good, and quite characteristically he jumped to the conclusion that they had made men bad. On social questions he was more liberal, demanding juster rewards for the downtrodden working classes. But his orthodox religious and political views won him the position of poet laureate in 1813. The appointment drew the fire of the radicals—Byron makes his name rhyme with "mouthy"—and he was blamed for the apostasy of the Lake poets from the revolutionary faith.

The greatest thinker among the poets of the Lake school was Coleridge.[19] He began his career as a writer by proclaiming most of the usual doctrines of Jacobinism, the natural goodness of man, the corruption of all governments, and the consequent right of the individual to obey his inner voice against all external dictates. The violent changes of the period and his study of German romantic literature and philosophy gradually led him away from all such ideas. In later life he was recognized as the greatest conservative thinker of his generation in England, though, unlike some of the German writers, he never became an advocate of blind resistance to change. He opposed the Reform Bill though he supported Catholic Emancipation, free trade, and the early factory acts. His lament

[18] Cf. E. C. Batho, *The Later Wordsworth* (New York, 1933), for a different view.
[19] Cf. R. J. White, ed., *Political Thought of Coleridge* (London, 1938).

over a world given up to atheism and materialism, especially in his work, *The Constitution of Church and State* (1830), and his defense of the Anglican Church as the promoter of civilization not only influenced Newman and the leaders of the Oxford movement, but contributed much to the growth of the new attitude later characterized as the Victorian.[20]

It would be possible to trace some of the same currents in the thought of the romantic writers of other countries, notably of Manzoni in Italy,[21] though, as has been observed earlier, romanticism in itself did not necessarily involve any political or social program. The wide variety in romantic thought becomes clear, not only in tracing the change of outlook among writers from the eighteenth century into the early nineteenth, but also in observing the transformation in political outlook among the younger generation of romanticists. In the course of the 1820's it became increasingly evident that romanticism was beginning to rally to liberalism. The dramatic defection of Chateaubriand (1824) from the cause of the Bourbons and the growth of a more liberal point of view in the writings of Stendhal, Hugo, and Lamartine, the rise of the Young Germany movement under the leadership of men like Heine, Börne, and Gutzkow, the growing interest in the poetry of Byron, the early writings of Mazzini in Italy, the poetry of Pushkin in Russia, and of Mickiewicz in Poland, and the whole Philhellenic movement—all these developments point to a new outlook among the young generation which came to maturity after 1820.

II. THE APPEAL TO TRADITION

Throughout the long eighteenth-century attack on the Ancien Régime, no serious attempt had been made to defend this order. Its supporters either considered it strong enough to stand without apology, or, being in control, resorted to the easiest weapons of defense—force and repression. Only with the outbreak of the French Revolution were there made any substantial efforts at justification. From this body of writing, which appeared between 1790 and 1820, most of the fundamental arguments of modern conservatism have

[20] The best general treatment is by Crane Brinton, *The Political Ideas of the English Romanticists* (Oxford, 1926).
[21] Cf. P. Fossi, *La conversione di Manzoni* (Bari, 1933).

been drawn. This traditionalist theorizing, as we find it in the early nineteenth century is, indeed, far more original than the liberal thought of the same period, which simply represents a further development of the ideas of the eighteenth century.

The new philosophy of conservatism, while deriving the source of royal, aristocratic, and ecclesiastical power variously from God, from nature, and from history, was grounded in a denial of the doctrines that power was from the people and that reason alone could build a new society. All written constitutions aroused the scorn of these theorists, especially those which, like the American Constitution, embodied advanced democratic ideas. The traditionalist systems also repudiated the idea that the free life of the individual is the end of society. There are no natural rights anterior and superior to the whole social organism. The individual exists solely through society, and society can be improved only by slow degrees and in line with tradition. To Blackstone and Burke tradition was represented by the British Constitution; to Gentz and to Savigny, by Germanic institutions; to Haller, at least in part, by the institutions of Switzerland; and finally to Joseph de Maistre and Bonald, by the absolute French monarchy and, beyond that, by the Catholic Church. The writers of the school all borrowed arguments back and forth, and exerted much influence on one another.

The first thoroughgoing criticism of the principles of the revolution was Edmund Burke's *Reflections on the Revolution in France* (1790). This brilliant essay, which has remained ever since one of the most widely read handbooks of conservatism, was at the same time an ardent defense of the British Constitution, and a telling attack on the philosophy of the Enlightenment. Burke's primary appeal was to history and experience as the only satisfactory guides in statecraft. Human society, an organism of slow growth and of infinitely complex structure, may show many faults, but the behavior of the French revolutionaries proved that it is better to endure these minor ills than to fly to others that we know not of. So Burke defended the British Constitution, rotten boroughs and all, against those who would change it abruptly. "Our Constitution," he had written in 1770, "stands on a nice equipoise, with steep precipices and deep waters upon all sides. In removing it from a dangerous leaning toward one side there may be risk of oversetting it on the other."[22] Blackstone in his *Commentaries on the Laws of England* (1765-1769) had elaborated much the same point of view. Indeed, in his defense of British institutions Burke was only giving philosophic expression to the view of the governing classes in England, that the glorious Revolution of 1688 had given the British Constitution its ultimate form.

Burke criticized both the method of thought and the basic ideas of the French *philosophes*. These French spinners of logic, whose "rage and frenzy will pull down more in half an hour than prudence, deliberation and foresight can build in a hundred years," had failed to see that society is a vast organism in which the present moment is as nothing and in which the wisdom of any man or group of men or of any generation is in itself of little significance. He showed the fallacies of the whole social contract theory; "Society is indeed a contract . . . but the state ought not to be considered as nothing better than a partnership agreement in a trade of pepper and coffee, to be taken up for a temporary interest and to be dissolved by the fancy of the parties. . . . It is a partnership in all science, in all art, in every virtue and in all perfection. As the ends of such a partnership cannot be obtained in many generations, it becomes a partnership not only between those who are living, but between those who are living, those who are dead and those who are to be born."[23] Revolutions are justified only when, like the American Revolution, they are efforts to fulfill great historic traditions. The French Revolution was not legitimate because it broke with tradition and was carried through by only a small fraction of the nation and in violation of the national constitution. And, finally, the French revolutionaries stood condemned because they failed to recognize the importance of a religious basis for society.

Burke continued to write attacks on the revolution until his death in 1797. His arguments were taken up by hard-pressed monarchs, *émigrés,* churchmen, and counter-revolutionaries of all sorts. Before he died he had received the praises of George III, a gold medal from Stanislas of Poland, and congratulations from Catherine of

[22] Burke, *Works* (Oxford, 1906), II, 74. Cf. D. A. Lockmiller, *Blackstone* (Chapel Hill, 1938).   [23] Burke, *op. cit.,* IV, 106.

Russia. The *Reflections* were translated at once into French. De Maistre wrote in 1793, "I cannot tell you how Burke has strengthened my anti-democratic and anti-Gallican views."[24] Gentz made a translation into German, and in one version or another the book spread its influence across the Continent in the early decades of the nineteenth century. But the use made of his writings by the reactionaries of succeeding generations must not obscure the fact that Burke was one of the great political thinkers of modern times. Not only did he expose with unanswerable logic the fallacies and superficialities of much eighteenth-century rationalizing about the state, but he demonstrated as never before the essential complexity of political problems—above all that of liberty—and the unescapable fact that the present and the future of society cannot be separated from its past. With Burke, said Lord Acton, the authority of history was so strong that it "alone devoured all the rest of his principles, and made the first of Liberals the first of Conservatives."[25] The evolutionary approach to political and social problems is now so generally accepted that it is hard to think in other terms. In a very real sense this orientation is a contribution of Edmund Burke.[26]

Burke's principal German disciple, Friedrich von Gentz, as secretary of the Congress of Vienna and as the aide of Metternich, became the chief apologist of reaction at the Hapsburg court. Gentz began his career as a liberal publicist. "If this Revolution were to fail," he wrote soon after the beginning of the movement, "I should deem it one of the greatest misfortunes which had befallen mankind. It is the first practical triumph of philosophy. . . . It is a hope and comfort for our race, which is groaning under so many evils."[27] This conviction soon faded, and Gentz, partly for reasons of personal advancement, moved over into the reactionary camp. In 1801 he published his *Über den Ursprung und Charakter des Krieges*

[24] R. Soltau, *French Political Thought in the Nineteenth Century* (London, 1931), 19 note.

[25] Quoted from the Acton manuscripts by Robert H. Murray, *Edmund Burke, a Biography* (London, 1931), 357 note.

[26] See especially Alfred Cobban, *Edmund Burke and the Revolt against the Eighteenth Century* (London, 1929), and the monograph of Mario Einaudi, *Edmondo Burke e l'indirizzo storico nelle scienze politiche* (Turin, 1930). There is much of interest regarding Burke's influence on Gentz and Müller in Frieda Braune, *Edmund Burke in Deutschland* (Heidelberg, 1917).

[27] Brandes, *op. cit.*, II, 317.

gegen die französiche Revolution, the most important of his long series of writings attacking the principles of the revolution. Some years later he summed up his creed in words that remind one of his master, Metternich, "In an age of decay, the sole function of a states-man is to prop up mouldering institutions." Gentz insisted that there was no longer order in society because there was "too much movement, too many irresponsible wills in the world."[28] Writing in 1819 he declared that, "as a preventive measure against the abuses of the press, absolutely nothing should be printed for years. . . . With this maxim as a rule, we should in a short time get back to God and the Truth."[29] His voluminous writings furnish a running commentary on the policies of Metternich and an attempted justifi-cation of them. Curiously enough, both Metternich and Gentz were greatly interested in the new liberal economic doctrines. It was at Gentz's suggestion that Garve in 1794 made the first adequate Ger-man translation of Smith's *Wealth of Nations.*

Closely allied with Gentz was his friend, Adam Müller, also a Prussian who finally found favor at the Austrian court, where he became a convert to Catholicism and a well-known pamphleteer. Drawing on the arguments of Burke and Bonald he attacked the principles of individualism and progress in the name of authority, tradition, and the organic community. The highest realization of the individual is possible only in the Christian state under strong rulership—a state which stands for the totality of human affairs. His economic views were more original and interesting, for they were directed against the doctrines of Adam Smith who, so Müller argued, had failed to incorporate in his theory the spiritual values of life and society. Müller was less subtle than Gentz, and his writings abound in exaggeration. He asserted, for instance, that the existence of the Holy Trinity proved conclusively that any national economic system based on a single principle must be wrong. "In fanaticism," says Treitschke, "Müller excelled all the rest."[30] He was one of the most important spiritual ancestors of the National Socialism in Germany.

One of the most esteemed reactionary theorists in the German

---

[28] E. Denis, *L'Allemagne 1810-1852* (Paris, n. d.), 110.
[29] Legge, *op. cit.,* 39. Cf. A. Robinet de Cléry, *Les idées politiques de Gentz* (Lausanne, 1917).
[30] H. von Treitschke, *History of Germany in the Nineteenth Century* (London, 1916), II, 341; cf. L. Sauzin, *Adam Müller* (Paris, 1937).

world was the Swiss professor Karl Ludwig von Haller. As an official of the Canton of Bern, he had seen the power of the Swiss patricians collapse amid the storms of the revolution, and this had aroused in him a deep hatred of Rousseauism. Believing that "the legitimate rulers having been restored, we must now rest on thought that is legitimate," he published in 1816 the first of six volumes of an extended work on political theory, *Restauration der Staatswissenschaften*. Herein, after attacking the theory of the social contract, and the dogmas of natural rights and the sovereignty of the people, he set out "to reëstablish monarchy upon its true foundations, to overthrow the presumptuous revolutionary science of the godless eighteenth century, and to make the Catholic Church shine with renewed effulgence."[31] All that he really advanced in place of the hated political dogmas of the Enlightenment was a restatement of the principles of patrimonial law upon which the authority of the Bernese aristocracy had been based. Just as in former days the rulers of Bern had treated the subject lands of Aargau and Vaud simply as the private property of the little republic, so Haller founded his theory of the state solely upon the right of the stronger. The state is the property of the prince who may do with it what he will, since he is dealing only with what is rightfully his. If the people were to disappear, the state would still exist in the person of the prince, who could readily find new subjects. A further argument for absolutism could be found in the dependence of the weak on the strong, a relationship which is not artificial, but rests in nature itself. The Catholic Church, to which Haller was a convert, came in for extended praise as one of the bulwarks of the social order. The attempt to cover the whole ground of political thought gave the work a comprehensive thoroughness which made it a great encyclopædia of conservatism, particularly in Prussia, where Haller was highly esteemed by the crown prince, later Frederick William IV. Hegel, however, characterized the work as one of "incredible crudity."[32]

Of much greater depth were the writings of Savigny, for years a professor in the University of Berlin and one of the outstanding scholar-jurists of modern times. The genesis of Savigny's theories, especially as set forth in his principal work, *Geschichte des römischen*

[31] Treitschke, *op. cit.*, II, 360-361.
[32] Cf. W. H. Sonntag, *Die Staatsauffassung Hallers* (Jena, 1929).

Rechts im Mittelalter (1815-1831), was to be found in Herder's ideas of social evolution and in his own nationalistic hatred for the foreign laws introduced by the French east of the Rhine. Savigny agreed with many of the other conservative theorists in rejecting the individualism and the *a priori* reasoning that lay back of the French Revolution. Law and institutions, he held, are not made solely by legislation. They came into existence in the remote past and continue, like languages, to grow with the nations, with their beliefs, their customs, and their whole life. They are unconscious products of the spirit of the people (Herder's *Volksgeist*), and must grow slowly and organically. These views squared with the widely prevailing ideas of the German romanticists, who believed that the slow and unconscious growth of society produces results far superior to those derived from a mechanical ordering. They were at one in denying that good institutions can spring suddenly from the brain of a legislator or from the debates of an assembly.[33] The movement of German scholarship—at this time the most advanced in Europe—seemed to confirm Savigny's assumptions. Niebuhr applied the same conceptions to the study of Roman history, Bopp to comparative philology, and the Grimms to the study of literature and folk-lore. Savigny's insistence on the superiority of the state as against its individual members was also in complete harmony with the political views of the classical German philosophers.[34]

Cuoco, a follower of Vico and the most profound Italian thinker of his time, was propounding some of the same traditionalist views in Italy. Using Vico's political philosophy as the basis of his historical writing, he published in 1801 his *Saggio storico sulla rivoluzione napoletana del 1799,* an elaborate analysis of the failure of the French revolutionary movement in Italy. This failure, he believed, lay in the unhistorical attempt to apply to Italian affairs the abstract rationalist theories of the eighteenth century. The revolutionary flurries in the Italian states did not arise from the needs or impulses of the people but were promoted, with French help, by a small group of intel-

[33] Cf. S. Schultzenstein, *Savigny* (Berlin, 1930) and F. Zuřlgmeyer, *Die Rechtslehre Savignys* (Leipzig, 1929).

[34] The first work of Friedrich Stahl, *Die Philosophie des Rechts nach geschichtlicher Ansicht* (1827), reflects something of the same outlook as the writings of Savigny. Stahl's influence as a conservative religious and political theorist, however, belongs to the reign of Frederick William IV.

lectuals who had no understanding of actual conditions. Like Burke and Savigny, Cuoco was as much a nationalist as he was an opponent of doctrinaire rationalism, and his hatred of the abstract political thought of the French seems to have grown deeper with the humiliations which year after year of foreign rule imposed upon the Italian people. But he was never as reactionary in his theories as the historical thinkers of the period in England and Germany. In fact, his attacks on French liberal thought were made in the name of a liberalism in which constitutional formulas were to be reinforced by historical and traditional institutions. His belief that an improvement of the wretched conditions in the peninsula could be effected only by slow degrees led him to an interest in education and in the formation of an enlightened public opinion which he regarded as the only certain means of regenerating the Italian people. The whole Risorgimento— through Manzoni, Romagnosi, Mazzini, and Gioberti—was to feel his influence.[35]

The most thoroughgoing philosophers of reaction were the French, for in France the revolution had wrought most havoc in the old order of life. Amidst a great flood of treatises and pamphlets, defending either the Ancien Régime or the restored government of the Bourbons, there was general agreement on the importance of a monarchical and aristocratic structure for the state, though there was a sharp difference of opinion about ecclesiastical policy. Some writers were Gallican, others were ultramontane. The principal Gallican theorists, Frayssinous and Montlosier, defended the restored monarchy against the encroachments of the Jesuits, while de Maistre, Bonald, and Lamennais were ardent ultramontanes.

Frayssinous, a teacher in the Seminary of Saint-Sulpice in Paris and later minister of ecclesiastical affairs, revived the historic Gallicanism of Bossuet. His *Vrais principes de l'église gallicane* (1818) was an attack on the deism, rationalism, and individualism of the eighteenth century, combined with a glorification of the Bourbons and the church as they existed in the last centuries of the old monarchy. The work embodied the views of Louis XVIII and the moderate royalists, and of the majority of the French bishops. In 1826 there appeared a much livelier treatise presenting the same

[35] Cf. F. Battaglia, *L'opera di Cuoco e la formazione dello spirito nazionale in Italia* (Florence, 1925), and G. V. Gentile, *Cuoco* (Venice, 1927).

point of view, *Mémoire à consulter sur un système religieux et politique,* the work of the Comte de Montlosier. While showing no sympathy for the ideas of eighteenth-century liberalism, and breathing a spirit of devotion to the restored monarchy and to the Catholic Church, the author launched a bitter attack on the ultramontane policies of Charles X. The Jesuits, he maintained, by their meddling in politics were discrediting all religion; if they were allowed to continue, the hatred they were arousing would destroy the monarchy and ruin the church. For the reactionaries this type of Gallican thought was too full of reservations, and for the liberals it represented an impossible compromise. So this attempt to build a theory of church and state by an appeal to the Gallican traditions of the old monarchy proved to be as fruitless as the efforts of Louis XVIII to steer a middle course between revolution and reaction.[36]

The main current of reactionary thought in France was even more ultramontane than royalist. Its most brilliant representative, Joseph de Maistre, had been influenced in his youth by Illuminism and by the occult side of the Enlightenment. The coming of the French armies into Savoy and his life as an *émigré* changed his views, and in his *Considérations sur la France* (1796) he launched his first attack on the revolution. In 1802 he was sent by the King of Sardinia to the Russian court, where he spent thirteen lonely years of exile in the writing of a number of works, the two greatest of which were *Du pape* and *Soirées de St. Pétersbourg.* For him, as for Hobbes, the necessity of order became the first principle of politics. He could not conceive of order without an absolute authority. According to his argument—which depends not merely on rhetoric, but usually carries matters back to fundamental differences which hardly admit of purely reasonable proof—there is no public authority without religion, no religion for Europe without Christianity, no Christianity without Catholicism, no Catholicism without the pope, and no pope without absolute sovereignty. He was, like some of the German theorists, as sharp a critic of the Protestant Reformation as of the French Revolution. Especially did he loathe the revolution. It had overthrown every institution he cherished. It had tyrannized over his church, had mocked his religion, and had executed the king.

[36] Cf. J. Brugerette, *Montlosier et son temps* (Aurillac, 1931) and A. Garnier, *Frayssinous* (Paris, 1925).

And underlying the revolution was "the shameful thought of the eighteenth century," which had begun by denying religion, and which praised even good men only for what was bad in them. Like Voltaire, whom he both detested and resembled, de Maistre could see with unerring sharpness the weakness in an opponent's thought, and he showed the same genius for using and misusing history for his own ends. But he exposed the superficialities and the unwarranted assumptions of eighteenth-century rationalism, and, like Burke, helped to direct political and social thought toward important and neglected realities. His emphasis on the continuity of historical evolution, and on the interdependence of the various elements in society ultimately forced both the liberal and the radical thinkers to reëxamine their whole ideology.[37]

Closely resembling Joseph de Maistre in his type of polemic was the Vicomte de Bonald. He, too, was an *émigré* attacking the principles of the revolution. For thirty-five years he continued to build on the ruins made by this revolution a complete structure of traditionalism. His principal work, *Théorie du pouvoir politique et religieux* (1796), is a voluminous study in three volumes every statement of which is buttressed with elaborate logic. The argument proceeds with a tedious monotony, for Bonald is usually as dull as de Maistre is witty. His whole philosophy was based on a denial of two of the fundamental ideas of the eighteenth century—that human nature is good and that society is the work of man. Of the first he wrote, "We are bad by nature, we are made good by society! Those who begin by supposing that we are born good are like architects, who, about to build an edifice, suppose that the stones appear from the quarry ready cut."[38] To disprove the idea that society is a human construction he started with a new first principle: man must think before he speaks, so thought must be of divine origin, thus man and his society are the creations of God. In his main conclusions, Bonald agreed with de Maistre that all power is derived from God and that society is His work, not the invention of man. Least of all is it based on the absurd social contract of Rousseau. God has con-

---

[37] The literature on de Maistre is enormous. See Peter R. Rohden, *Joseph de Maistre als politischer Theoretiker* (Munich, 1929), and René Johannet, "Aspects récents de J. de Maistre," *Revue de Paris*, October 1, 1930.

[38] Bonald, *Théorie du pouvoir politique et religieux* (Constance, 1796), Part I, Book I. Cf. H. Moulinié, *Bonald* (Paris, 1915).

stituted kings to govern men and the church to lead them out of their inherent sinfulness. All attempts to interfere with this work are attempts to interfere with the purposes of God. Under king and bishop society should be organized as a hierarchy in which every individual from the nobility to the guilds should find his proper place. "Christian monarchies are the final creation in the development of political society and of religious society. The proof of this lies in the fact that when monarchy and Christianity are both abolished society returns to savagery."[39]

To men like Bonald and de Maistre the revolution meant only the guillotine, the nonsense of the worship of the Supreme Being, civil and foreign war, the misery of a ruined currency, and finally a crushing military defeat. They carried this fear of revolutionary principles to its very limit, and, not content with denying what Voltaire and Rousseau had affirmed, they went to the extreme of reasserting all that these two prophets had denied. Reaction and repression were for them the first needs of society. "All greatness, all power, all order," wrote de Maistre, "depend upon the executioner. He is the tie that binds society together. Take away this incomprehensible force and at that very moment order is suspended by chaos, thrones fall, and states disappear."[40] Their defense of the papacy as the final authority in society was the crown of their system of political thought. They preached a strange Christianity in which religion is justified only as a panacea for lawlessness, and a still stranger philosophy in which logical arguments are used throughout for the rejection of reason. Finally, the persistence of their appeal to external authority leaves the impression that the institutions in which they placed their faith were bankrupt in everything except such authority.[41]

De Maistre was read more widely than Bonald, although both writers had an influence not only in France, but also in Italy and Germany. Gentz, for example, regarded de Maistre even more highly than he regarded Burke. Both writers were especially esteemed

[39] Bonald, *Oeuvres* (Paris, 1864), I, 482. There is a keen analysis of Bonald's thought in Harold J. Laski, *Authority in the Modern State* (New Haven, 1919), chap. ii.

[40] Brandes, *op. cit.*, III, 101.

[41] A third theorist of the group, Ballanche, shared many of the ideas of Bonald and de Maistre, though his interest was centered in an interpretation of history that looked forward to the advent of democracy. He anticipated Christian Socialism by a half-century.

at the papal court, and their writings did more than those of any others to defend the policy of ultramontanism by which the papacy, during the whole nineteenth century, sought the restoration of its power and prestige. In France, many of the ideas of de Maistre and Bonald were given a more popular presentation by Lamennais. He was a Breton of strong character and narrow mind. Time was to show that it was his nature to take a side obstinately and to defend it with eloquent love and passionate hate. In 1817 he published the first part of an extended *Essai sur l'indifférence en matière de religion*. The book contained no new ideas, although Lacordaire said later that "its eloquence cast a spell, and invested a humble priest with all the authority once enjoyed by Bossuet." Three more volumes of the *Essai* appeared before 1824, and in 1825 and 1826 he published a two-volume work, *De la religion considérée dans ses rapports avec l'ordre politique et civil*. After a trip to Rome, he became the center of a brilliant circle which included Montalembert, Lacordaire, and Maurice de Guérin. His *Progrès de la révolution et de la guerre contre l'église* was published in 1829. Each work was more ardently ultramontane than its predecessors until in this last treatise Lamennais denounced the church for attaching its cause to the dying cause of kings. The state, he maintained, was killing the church, while the hatred of the masses for the monarchy was spreading to include the clergy. The cause of the church must be made independent of that of the monarchy. This book became the charter of Liberal Catholicism in the nineteenth century.[42]

III. RECONSTRUCTION IN GERMAN IDEALISM: FROM KANT TO HEGEL

The history of German idealism from Kant to Hegel represents the culmination of this search for a principle of authority. There was a period in the lives of Kant, Fichte, Schelling, and Hegel when they shared the general attitudes of the Enlightenment on church and state. All had welcomed the revolution. The main current of their thought, however, gradually led away from the idea of natural rights and from individualism toward doctrines that emphasized deity and the submergence of the individual in the social organism.

[42] Cf. Laski, *op. cit.*, chap. iii, and the two excellent studies by C. Maréchal, *La jeunesse de Lamennais* (Paris, 1912), and *Lamennais, la dispute de l'essai sur l'indifférence* (Paris, 1925).

All found the state necessary for normal human living, and Hegel finally justified the extension of its activities under the guidance of a monarch. But in their efforts to harmonize the conclusions of science and of free-thought with traditional religious beliefs they arrived at syntheses which faced in two directions. On the one hand they defended the liberty for which the eighteenth century and the revolution stood, and on the other they came increasingly to praise the discipline and authority necessary for its proper enjoyment. The universality and comprehensiveness of their systems make it difficult to classify them either as conservative or as moderately liberal, although the direction of this current of thought from the eighteenth century into the nineteenth was toward authoritarianism.

The beginning of this philosophical movement away from the rationalism and individualism of the Enlightenment dates chiefly from Kant's *Kritik der reinen Vernunft* (1781). Disregarding the whole superstructure of eighteenth-century thought, Kant began by examining its fundamental assumption, the universal validity of reason. In this examination he discovered that reason is only one of the elements necessary for grasping reality. Experiences of conscience, beauty, and religion are not, properly speaking, scientific or rational experiences at all. Indeed, they are quite unintelligible unless we assume that the world of experience differs from the world viewed only by science and reason. Kant definitely subordinated the abstract reasoning which the Enlightenment had deified to a moral and religious faith. His method of criticizing the eighteenth century conception of reason as an inadequate means of understanding either man or the world was carried forward, in his *Metaphysische Anfangsgründe der Rechtslehre* (1797), to an examination of the prevailing ideas of freedom and of the rights of the individual. He found a place for the freedom of the individual, but he maintained that this freedom does not lie in arbitrary action outside of all law, for such freedom is anarchy. Real freedom is to be achieved only by an authority which the individual must exercise over himself. The individual's choice of action, however, is hedged about by the ideals and standards of the group, for the individual can realize himself only in and through society. Kant attacked the type of external repression that had passed for law and order under the Ancien

Régime because it assumed that men could be treated as cogs in the social machine, whereas, as ethical beings, they must always remain ends in themselves. On the other hand, he attacked the excessive individualism he discerned in Rousseau. Thus the chief problem of modern government will always lie in harmonizing general control with individual liberty. It is largely from Kant that the German idea of *Freiheit* arose, a concept that in its development has been very different from the English ideal of *Freedom* and the French idea of *Liberté*. In its thoroughgoing analysis of the basic assumptions of philosophy as it had developed from Descartes to Locke, Kant's system has been the very pivot of modern thought.[43]

Kant's ideas were developed by his most brilliant follower, Fichte, whose dialectic subtlety was more refined, if possible, than the master's. He developed the Kantian doctrines that reason is only of partial use as a guide to truth and that personal freedom is limited by the freedom of others. For the problem of freedom for one individual cannot be solved except by a common solution for the group.[44] In Fichte's view this group was the nation. His *Grundlage des Naturrechts* (1796) and *Reden an die deutsche Nation* (1808) represent an interesting combination of the nationalist ideas of Herder and the political philosophy of Kant,[45] developed in an effort to arouse and to unify the fragmented and humiliated Germany of his time.

Schelling followed closely in the footsteps of Kant and Fichte, though he was less a metaphysician than a mystic. After welcoming the revolution he turned against it and denounced pure rationalism because it was undermining individual morality, society, and the state. He even suggested that the government should prohibit the teaching and the publication of the ideas of the Enlightenment. His interest was centered in the construction of a vast world-order in which the individual was submerged. In his later writings, Schelling

---

[43] A good study is that of Kurt Borries, *Kant als Politiker* (Leipzig, 1928).

[44] "The individual life has no real existence, since it has no value in itself, but must and should sink into nothing, while on the contrary the species [*die Gattung*] alone exists, since it alone ought to be looked upon as really living." Fichte, *Werke* (Berlin, 1845), VII, 37. Cf. X. Léon, *Fichte et son temps* (2 vols., Paris, 1922-7).

[45] The anti-individualism of Fichte's thought led him to some socialist theorizing, particularly in his work, *Der geschlossene Handelsstaat* (1800). The socialist theories of Proudhon in France, and Lassalle and Rodbertus in Germany were all founded on parts of his argument.

veered off into an obscure mysticism, and the philosophic implications of his world-vision were realized only by Hegel. The religious and the poetic quality of his writings endeared him to the German literary romanticists, to Coleridge and to Cousin. In Russia his philosophy began to have a great vogue in the late 1820's, and it contributed substantially to the growth of a mystic Slavophilism.[46]

The greatest philosopher of the early nineteenth century, Hegel, began as a follower of Kant, Fichte, and the earlier Schelling, but the progress of his thought was toward greater authoritarianism. He turned against the French Revolution earlier than Kant. "In this bloody drama," he wrote, "there melted the cloud of liberty, in embracing which the people have fallen into an abyss of misery." But Hegel was at one with his predecessors in his striving to find a compromise between the abstract rationalism and individualism of the revolutionaries, who would make a clean sweep of the past, and the no less abstract historicism of the reactionaries, who would do the same for the present. The principal statement of his political philosophy is in his *Naturrecht und Staatswissenschaft* (1821). In this work, as in others of his writings, it is evident that his theory of the state is much more fundamental to his whole system than are such theories in the systems of Kant and Fichte.

In contrast to the revolutionary doctrine that the state was an artificial creation made by a contract which brought together individuals, each of whom continued to possess his natural rights—an idea to which Kant in part subscribed—Hegel held that the state was a natural organism representing a phase of an historical world process. He denied Rousseau's belief that "man is born free and is everywhere in chains" and insisted that primitive man is always enslaved by passion, by superstition, and by armed force, and that only in the process of social evolution and only through the protection of the community does he achieve freedom. Freedom to be of any value must be freedom from caprice. A strongly organized and well defended state is neither an obstacle nor an unwarranted interference with the course of nature, but the means by which a conscious society wins a genuine freedom. The individual has his existence only as a member of the state, the power of which is derived

[46] Schelling's influence is discussed in Rudolf Haym, *Die Romantische Schule* (4th ed., Berlin, 1920), chap. iv.

not from freedom or the ability of its inhabitants individually considered, nor from the fertility of its soil, nor from the size of its
territory. Its power lies in its cohesiveness, in the unity of the whole
state, and in its active head, the monarch. By emphasizing the ruler
as the unified state in action Hegel often seems to divert attention
from his collectivist theory of state sovereignty to an apparent
identification of sovereignty with the monarch. So his system came
to fit neatly into the national needs of Prussia, of which he became
the official philosopher.[47]

Hegel combined his theory of the state with the belief that the
organization of every government should be the result of an historical evolution. Thus he agreed with Burke, de Maistre, and
Savigny that the attempt to declare a new constitution by decree was
futile. He followed Herder and Fichte in believing that every nation
has a peculiar spirit and culture through which it makes its special
contribution to world-civilization and presents a phase of the developing world-spirit. Hence, instead of applying to political and social
institutions the particular standard which happens to appeal to us
as reasonable, we must judge institutions by their history, surround-
ings, and environment. Hegel viewed all history as a vast panorama
which portrayed the gradual unfolding of the universal spirit. Ideal
"freedom" being the goal of this historic evolution, he distinguished
four stages of development: the Oriental, in which the despot alone
was free; then the Greek and the Roman, in which some men had
become free; and finally the German, in which all would eventually
be free; a vast evolutionary conception which has been one of Hegel's
chief contributions to modern thought.[48]

Hegel's comments on the specific issues of his time hardly permit
of classifying him as either a conservative or a liberal. He championed
the king of his native state of Württemberg in his struggle with the

[47] He provides expressly for war. War keeps a people from stagnation, and war must
be the sole arbiter between sovereign states. Private morality cannot apply to the state,
for states are bound only by self-determined obligations, and each state must decide
when its sovereign rights are invaded. The judgment of history is the only judgment
to be passed upon the state. It is significant that Hegel suggests nothing beyond the
state; there is no hint of a confederation of nations representing the world-spirit.

[48] Among the innumerable studies of Hegel the following recent monographs might
be mentioned: Franz Rosenzweig, *Hegel und der Staat* (2nd ed., 2 vols., Munich, 1920)
especially II, chaps. x and xi; Friedrich Bülow, *Die Entwicklung der Hegelschen
Sozialphilosophie* (Leipzig, 1920), and the excellent analysis in Victor Basch, *Les doctrines politiques des philosophes classiques de l'Allemagne* (Paris, 1927), chaps. vi.
and vii.

feudal interests and he pleaded for the extension of the jury system and for the publication of the debates of the German provincial assemblies. Just before his death he wrote an article moderately favorable to the English Reform Bill. But his liberalism was decidedly mild, a liberalism which held that while in some states a legislature was essential as a balance against the executive powers, the sovereign must make the ultimate decisions. He disliked the current liberal agitation of his time, "this particular kind of evil consciousness developed by weak eloquence. It is most insipid when it speaks of the spirit. It exhibits the greatest self-seeking and vanity when it has most on its tongue the words 'people and nation.' "[49]

Whatever may have been Hegel's intention, his vast system, with its emphasis on the historical continuity and collective nature of society, contributed to the growth of various types of political and social thought.[50] Coleridge in England, Cousin in France, and Karl Marx in Germany were all in one way or another deeply influenced by Hegelianism. Coleridge became a defender of the old order in England, while Marx in the forties evolved out of Hegel's thought much of the theology of modern socialism, and Cousin, who perhaps least understood Hegel's thought, produced a compromise liberalism of the *juste milieu* that had favor in France under the Restoration and became the official philosophy of the July Monarchy.

In conclusion, the question may well be raised as to whether the loose classification of the political and social thought of the nineteenth century as conservative, liberal, and radical is not somewhat inadequate. It is an almost hopeless task to try to define a general outlook on life, a mental state like romanticism, and it is hardly less hopeless to attempt to force the broad flow of political and social thought into a few clearly marked channels. The philosophy of conservatism was just taking form in the early part of the century; it shows all the contradictions and exaggerations of a formative period. The writers of the reaction, like most theorists, differed in their approach and often argued about mere details. They did not by any means foresee the more subtle implications of their systems. But

[49] Hegel, *Werke* (Berlin, 1854), VIII, 13.
[50] The protean character of Hegel's political thought is interestingly shown in the fact that Frederick William III of Prussia looked upon his philosophy of the state as the great support of his absolutism, whereas his successor, Frederick William IV, was equally convinced that his royal power was being undermined by this same philosophy.

this at least they had in common: they started with a profound distrust of rationalism and of all forms of undefined individualism. To be sure, their distrust of reason, analysis, and logic did not prevent them from constructing systems as complex and closely reasoned as any of those they attacked. Any one who has read Bonald or Hegel will be ready to admit that. Nevertheless, the conservative philosophy made a great contribution to the understanding of the social structure. It emphasized not only the need for political restraint and for the subordination of the individual to the community, but introduced into political thinking a certain historical-mindedness, a concept of cultural evolution which was hardly less than epoch-making.

This evolutionary and organic view of society is the basis of all social thought in the nineteenth and twentieth centuries. We cannot think of human problems in anything but their historical setting and cannot conceive of introducing changes in the existing system without reference to the past of our institutions. The phenomenal growth of historical research and writing since the time of Napoleon may perhaps be taken as an indication of a growing need as well as of a revived interest.

The general adoption of the historical approach did not in any sense bring with it the triumph of the conservative viewpoint. Indeed, the radicals soon discovered that the historical approach could be used to prove their claims just as effectively as the claims of the reactionaries. Saint-Simon, first of the great socialist writers, derived many of his basic ideas from de Maistre, while Comte, the disciple of Saint-Simon, never tired of praising Bonald, though he admitted having drawn some inspiration from Condorcet. The influence of Kant and Fichte can be traced in the growth of modern socialism. Lassalle and Jaurès both understood socialism to be a moral movement philosophically rooted in the moral teaching of Kant and in collectivist theories like those presented in Fichte's *Der geschlossene Handelsstaat*. But of all these philosophers Hegel exercised perhaps the most direct influence. His dialectic method, his conception of the philosophy of history fascinated his contemporaries. He was the guiding star of Marx in his formative years and the inspiration of countless other theorists.[51] It was something of an accident, then, that the evolutionary conception of society was first drafted into the service of reactionary thought. Not the substance, but the method was the important contribution of the conservative theorists; their emphasis on the life of the group and their historical method were of positively revolutionary importance. They dwarf completely any contributions made by liberal theorists in this same period.

[51] The later development of Hegel's ideas has been traced in the recent studies of Paul Vogel, "Hegels Gesellschaftsbegriff und seine geschichtliche Fortbildung durch Lorenz Stein, Marx, Engels und Lassalle," *Kant Studien* Ergänzungsheft No. 59 (Berlin, 1925); Paul Barth, *Die Geschichtsphilosophie Hegels und der Hegelianer bis auf Marx und Hartmann* (2nd ed., Leipzig, 1925); Julius Löwnstein, *Hegels Staatsidee, ihr Doppelgesicht und ihr Einfluss im 19 Jahrhundert* (Berlin, 1927); Rebecca Cooper, *The Logical Influence of Hegel on Marx* (Seattle, 1925), D. Chizhevskii, ed., *Hegel bei den Slaven* (Reichenberg, 1934), and A. Koyré, "Hegel en Russie," *Monde Slave*, 1936.

Chapter Four

THE CREEDS OF LIBERALISM

I. THE PRINCIPLE OF UTILITY

LIBERALISM in 1815 appeared to be a dying cause. The bloody tyranny of the French Republic and the financial anarchy that ensued had been followed by the despotic rule of Napoleon. It was small wonder that to many the events of the revolutionary era now seemed one long refutation of its philosophy. Decidedly, the principles of 1789 had passed to the defensive. Liberalism, however, had its roots in needs and ideals that had not been satisfied, and its principles were not destined to remain in abeyance. Condorcet's optimistic belief that "there will come a time when the sun will shine only on free men who know no master other than their own reason" seemed to small but determined groups like a veritable battle cry in a society where the governing classes were behaving as though 1815 were 1715. The writings of Voltaire, Montesquieu, and Rousseau began to be reprinted, and, to the disgust and horror of those who ruled Europe from the throne and the altar, the ghost of the Enlightenment stalked again. Liberalism began to rally its forces and the older liberal programs were slowly reconstructed in the light of new conditions.

This reconstruction had to proceed cautiously, for even those who were determined to block all attempts to return to the Ancien Régime were at the same time very fearful of the rule of the mob.[1] For this reason liberal thought after 1815 lacked the daring originality of the theorizing of the eighteenth century. Fearful of abstract formulas, the liberals believed in the maintenance of social order and in the necessity of limiting power to a well-defined economic group.

---

[1] Ruggiero speaks of the appearance of this fear in France as early as 1793. "The real and effective counter-revolution was now that of the revolutionaries of yesterday, the liberal bourgeoisie." G. de Ruggiero, *The History of European Liberalism* (Oxford, 1927), 83. There is an interesting account of how Mazzini's father, a Jacobin of the 1790's, became a conservative in G. O. Griffith, *Mazzini* (New York, 1932), chap. i.

Nor did they, in the early nineteenth century, have the same generalized outlook they had had in the later eighteenth century, for the revolutionary storm had carried the liberal ideals of England and France to the south and east of Europe, to lands of very different historic traditions. Hence, after 1815, liberal doctrines varied from country to country, both in emphasis and in intensity. In those states which had a long historic unity and independence, the liberals[2] centered their efforts in a struggle against the old autocracy, the established church, and the aristocracy, and strove to establish a constitutional régime controlled by the upper middle class. Among peoples who were under foreign rule or who were dissatisfied with the weakness of their governments, aspirations for national unity and freedom took first place. But, differing in importance and in the order in which they presented themselves, all of these ideals were summed up in a word understood alike by their followers and their enemies. That word was "liberty."

Much the most characteristic thinker in the transformation of the liberal thought of the eighteenth century into that of the nineteenth was Jeremy Bentham. Bentham shared the intellectual daring and the optimism of the thinkers of the Enlightenment, but he had, in addition, the practical outlook of one trained in English law. He denounced the whole idea of natural rights and described the *Declaration of the Rights of Man* as "a hodge-podge of confusion and absurdity." In all his writings he continually condemned the dogmatizing spirit of the French *philosophes,* though often he was himself almost as dogmatic. Bentham's mind was always that of a practical reformer. Where Blackstone, Burke, and de Maistre asked of every institution, "How has it grown?" and where Voltaire and Tom Paine inquired, "How does it conform to reason?" Bentham demanded quite simply, "How does it work?" He was sure that democracy would some day prevail because, as men sought their own welfare, a government by the majority would necessarily ensure the happiness of more people than any other. But any government was to him a necessary evil; its only justification lay in the political and economic liberty it allowed and in the utility of its organization in securing "the greatest good of the greatest number." Bentham

[2] At this time the liberals usually were called reformers or radicals in England, and *indépendants* in France. The word *liberal* was first used in Spain.

shared the view of Adam Smith, that enlightened selfishness is the key to social advancement. For sixty years he subjected nearly every institution to a searching analysis. Old restrictions on trade, the anomalies of the British parliamentary régime and of all the existing legal and political systems of Europe, the evils of religious restrictions, the abuses of prisons, of criminal law and of bad educational systems were all examined by this amazingly industrious and fertile mind. For every possible type of abuse he proposed some very specific remedies. "Liberty" and "Utility" were his watchwords, and practical reform his only aim. His position in the history of liberal thought is that of a great originator of social expedients.

The fact that the weakening of the power of the British aristocracy in 1832 led to neither a social upheaval nor administrative chaos was due largely to the political experiments—the reform of local government and of the civil service, of police administration, and of colonial self-government—which Bentham's disciples developed by his methods. No thinker of the early nineteenth century has left his mark on more fields of social thought. In England his ideas were spread by a group known as the "Philosophic Radicals," and on the continent by such men as Dumont, Destutt de Tracy, and Daunou. But his influence was confined to no school or country. To be the servant not only of England but of all nations professing liberal opinions was his great desire. He had correspondents in the United States, in France, Spain, Portugal, Greece, Russia, Bavaria, Poland, and Latin America; everywhere his works were regarded as textbooks of liberalism.[3] Through Bentham's writings may be traced the process by which much of the epoch-making theorizing of eighteenth-century liberalism was reduced to terms a business man of the nineteenth century could understand.[4]

The masters of commerce and industry were becoming increasingly convinced that the legal, ecclesiastical, and economic systems which had been suitable for the feudal state had lost their utility

[3] During his lifetime, Bentham's greatest influence was not in England, but in Spain—especially on Martínez de la Rosa—and in Spanish America. Before his death in 1832, forty thousand copies of his works in French had been sold in Spanish America alone. Cf. V. A. Belaunde, *Bolívar and the Political Thought of the Spanish-American Revolutions* (Baltimore, 1938).

[4] The best studies of Bentham are those of Leslie Stephen, *The English Utilitarians* (3 vols., London, 1900), I, chaps. v and vi, and of Elie Halévy, *The Growth of Philosophic Radicalism* (New York. 1928).

and would have to be revised. In this sense liberalism was essentially the creed of the bourgeoisie. Among the Slavs, Magyars, and Italians of the Hapsburg domain, and also in Russia, liberal ideas were taken up by small groups of noblemen. In Poland, Ireland, Belgium, and northern Italy some of its tenets found support among the lower Catholic clergy. But liberalism would never have assumed the forms it did without the backing of the commercial classes of western Europe, particularly of England and France. Here, as nearly always in history, political thought became the summary of an experience rationalized and universalized.

II. LAISSEZ-FAIRE ECONOMICS AND THE BOURGEOIS STATE

The erection of a free bourgeois state required first of all the liberation of business from a mass of old mercantilist regulations. Adam Smith had already dealt the classic blow to the theories underlying these regulations, and by 1815 a régime of free industrial competition had come into force in England and France. The state in both these countries had renounced all rights of interference either with the organization of production or with the relations of masters and men, except always the right of prohibiting tradeunions. In other states, however, mercantilism, as a set of economic and political doctrines and as the practice of governments, was by no means dead. In the field of economic theory, the attack on mercantilism was now carried across the continent. A French economist, J. B. Say, proclaimed Smith's gospel in a series of lucid studies, and within a few years Ricardo in England and List in Germany modified the ideas of Smith and Say to suit the developing economic conditions. All these thinkers, despite sharp disagreements in detail, were of one mind in condemning the older type of governmental regulation which they held to be ruinous to commerce and industry.

The liberal point of view, as it was understood by the leaders of business, is well set forth in Macaulay's essay on Southey, written in 1830. "Our rulers will best promote the improvement of the nation by confining themselves strictly to their legitimate duties, by leaving capital to find its most lucrative course, commodities their fair price, industry and intelligence their natural reward, idleness and folly their natural punishment, by maintaining peace, by defending property, by diminishing the price of law and by observing strict economy in every department of the state. Let the government do this, the people will do the rest." The state, in this conception, has but three functions—defense, justice, and the construction and supervision of certain public works and institutions which it can never be to the interest of a small group of individuals to maintain. Thus, as the liberals came into political power, nearly all their reforms were, in the first instance, negative. They sought to remove what they regarded as abuses, and they liberated men from disabilities through abolition, repeal, and removal of old regulations.

The state, moreover, must be controlled and directed by those who will use it to create the atmosphere in which production flourishes. In this period factory owners were just beginning to possess a power that promised to conquer the world as no Cæsar or Napoleon had ever conquered it. It looked as if progress, now that man had found its secret, was to follow a rapid and unbroken course, provided the entrepreneurs be allowed to do everything possible to speed up production. Production, to many, appeared to have even a positive moral value. "The spirit of striving for a steady increase in mental and bodily acquirements," wrote List, "characterizes a state devoted to manufactures and commerce, while in a country devoted merely to agriculture, dullness of mind, awkwardness of body, and a want of culture, prosperity, and liberty prevail."[5] The state should be efficiently organized just as business was being organized by entrepreneurs. Both should be controlled by the same group, the real people in society, the upper middle class. Manufacturers and economists found many arguments to support this view. They considered it a disgrace for a people to remain a nation of farmers and craftsmen, and, more than a disgrace, a danger, since the nation should be able to manufacture its own war equipment. Moreover, the manufacturing groups, especially in England, were angry when they saw that, by exploiting mineral wealth, they were giving huge royalties to the owners, and that, by stimulating the growth of large urban centers, they were increasing the value of agricultural products. The work of the business leaders was thus

[5] C. Gide and Rist, *History of Economic Doctrines* (New York, 1915), 273-274.

enriching the class who owned the large estates, yet the aristocracy, hostile or indifferent to these rising interests, would allow them no voice in the government. Finally, the great bankers and manufacturers were particularly irritated after 1815 because of the acute economic maladjustment which followed the sudden return of peace. More than ever before they were convinced that, if they could control the government, conditions would grow better.

Saint-Simon's famous parable, published in 1819, symbolizes this point of view. "Let us suppose," he wrote, "that France suddenly loses fifty of her first-class doctors, fifty first-class bankers, two hundred of her best merchants, six hundred of her foremost agriculturalists, five hundred of her capable ironmasters"—and so on, enumerating the principal industries. "Since these men are its most indispensable producers, the minute it loses these, the nation will degenerate into a mere lifeless body. Let us make another supposition. Imagine that France retains her men of genius, whether in the arts and sciences or in the crafts and industries, but has the misfortune to lose on the same day the king, the king's brother, the Duc d'Angoulême, and all the other members of the royal family, all the great officers of the crown, all ministers of state, all the marshals, cardinals, archbishops, bishops, grand vicars, and canons, all prefects and subprefects, all government employees, all the judges, and, in addition to all these men, a hundred thousand landed proprietors—the cream of her nobility. Such an overwhelming catastrophe would certainly aggrieve the French, for they are a kindly-disposed nation. But the loss of a hundred and thirty thousand of the best-reputed individuals in the state would give rise to sorrow of a purely sentimental kind; it would not cause the community the least inconvenience."[6] In economic matters, then, liberalism was no longer satisfied with mere toleration. It proposed to go further and to get rid of the old mercantilist regulations, to reform the old legal systems, and, finally, to allow the commercial classes to take over the control of the state. The result hoped for by the leaders of the middle class was a more productive society under their own governance.

[6] L'organisateur (Paris, 1819), Part I, 10-20.

The leaders of the middle class idealized their way of life and passed on this ideal to lower social strata. The praise given by the great factory owners in England to hard work and thrift shows the society of the early nineteenth century fostering those forms of idealism which suited its economic program. This accounts, at least in part, for the type of humanitarianism found among such groups as the Clapham Sect, and in the various societies founded in England and France for assisting the lower classes, "the deserving poor," as they were called by the British humanitarians who wished to introduce their bourgeois virtues among the masses. Besides working for the abolition of the slave trade, and later for the improvement of prisons, they were greatly interested in the establishment of schools and savings banks. The interrelation of the various currents of reform is shown in a remark of Bentham's. It would not be expected that Bentham, who held the churches responsible for the persistence of many abuses, would have had much patience with Wilberforce and his pious friends, "The Saints," yet when Bentham learned of their work in trying to abolish the slave trade, he remarked, "Well, if to be an anti-slavist is to be a 'Saint,' saintship for me. I am a Saint!"[7]

The economic aspects of Liberalism after 1815 were stressed particularly by the commercial classes in England and France, whence have come most of the ideals and attitudes of modern European liberalism. But even in countries where almost no industrial development had taken place there was the same close relationship between the ideas of laissez-faire economics and the program of political liberalism. Count Széchenyi, the founder of modern Hungarian liberalism, was deeply interested in developing industry as a part of his program for improving Hungary. In 1830 he published a book, *On Credit,* which embodied these ideas. The Italian journals after 1818 show even more clearly this faith in commerce and industry as the vivifying elements in civilization. France and England were recognized as the leaders, especially England, which one Italian periodical praised as a nation, "so industrious, commercially so active, so enterprising, in a word, mistress of the earth. Where

[7] É. Halévy, *History of the English People in 1815* (N. Y., 1924), 510.

else prevails that union of knowledge, of interests, of power of all sorts that is to be found at London, at Manchester, at Liverpool?"[8]

Such was the world of ideas in which the young Cavour grew up. In one of his early letters he wrote, "This is not the time for mathematics; one must study economics; the world progresses."[9] The liberalism of Cavour's later life was, at least in part, rooted in his belief that a better future for Italy was possible only through a free and active commerce, and through the application of science to agriculture and industry. In the same way List had, by 1818, decided that the German people could never be united and politically free until a middle class had built up its economic power and the German states had been brought together in a customs union. Even in eastern Europe the economic ideas of Adam Smith and J. B. Say, especially of the latter, spread along with the political ideals of constitutionalism. Writing in 1818 of life in St. Petersburg, Pushkin says that in the circles which produced the Decembrist movement "political economy is in fashion."[10] Say's work was, even before 1820, translated and circulated among the Greek nationalists. In 1829 Carlyle, in his *Signs of the Times*, summed up the spirit of the age from the point of view of the leaders of the rising middle class; "This age, with its whole undivided might, forwards, teaches, and practises the greatest art of adapting means to ends." The masters of this art should be given a free hand to build and to direct a better society.

III. CONSTITUTIONALISM

There arose after 1815 a growing recognition that economic rights must be guaranteed by political rights. Freedom to possess property, to follow any profession or trade, and to make new types of contract was of little value without a corresponding freedom to speak, to publish, and to influence the government through the vote. The eighteenth century had already decided that such political rights could be realized only by embodying them in a written constitution. The French Revolution, in spite of its mistakes, had furthered this idea, and there were now in every European state liberal groups in-

[8] K. R. Greenfield, "Economic Ideas and Facts in the Early Period of the Risorgimento," *American Historical Review*, XXXVI (1930), 36.
[9] A. J. Whyte, *The Early Life and Letters of Cavour* (Oxford, 1925), xii.
[10] E. J. Simmons in *Harvard Studies and Notes in Philology*, XIII (1931), 289.

terested in constitutional problems. The English Constitution was greatly admired, partly because of its conservative character, but also because many liberal business men believed that the free institutions which England had long possessed were the cause of her political and economic power.[11] The English system of government, however, could be introduced on the continent only by embodying it in a formal document. The French Constitution of 1791—issued before the revolution had turned Jacobin—the Spanish Constitution of 1812, the French Charter of 1814, and, after the revolutions of 1830, the Belgian Constitution of 1831, all served as models. They were ordinarily preferred to the American Constitution of 1787 because they provided for limited monarchies rather than for a republic.

Programs of political reform in England all centered about methods of extending the existing system. The Whigs, the traditional liberal party, possessed neither a philosophy nor a program of reform. During the Napoleonic wars, their official leaders had retired to private life. The few who remained active in politics held to the old "principles of 1688," though they were careful to show their disapproval of the various types of radicalism recently advocated by Godwin and Tom Paine and now being brought to public attention by Bentham and his band of "Philosophic Radicals." In the period between Waterloo and the Reform Bill the most influential figure among the disunited forces of English liberalism was the popular journalist, William Cobbett. While Godwin wrote monotonous books which nobody read, and while Bentham was gathering a few followers, Cobbett's views became the common property of thousands of Englishmen. Cobbett was, however, no revolutionary. He defended the crown and the House of Lords as well as most of the British Constitution, and he attacked all revolutionary methods. Furthermore, like most of the liberal theorists on the continent he did not believe in universal suffrage. "I have," he remarked, "witnessed its effects too attentively and with too

[11] The English themselves attributed their superiority to their political organization. Lady Morgan, speaking of the lack of conveniences in the better houses in Milan, wrote, with a certain smugness, "England has the best locks and hinges, as she has the best steam engines and the best navies, because she has long enjoyed the most perfect of any known political constitution!" Lady S. Morgan, *Italy* (London, 1821), I, 205.

much disgust ever to think of it with approbation."[12] Nevertheless, he did insist, with a furious sincerity, that Parliament must
be reformed and that the British Constitution must be brought up
to date. For these beliefs he found practical reasons that made a
wide appeal. The middle class would have to gain control over
the raising and expenditure of public funds, for taxes were levied
in favor of the landed aristocrats. The interest on the huge war
debt, combined with the lavish granting of sinecures and pensions,
was an intolerable burden on industry and the industrial classes.
If these burdens were to be redistributed, Parliament would have
to be reformed by redistricting the seats and by extending the
suffrage.

Addressing himself to the workers, Cobbett warned the dissatisfied elements that it was useless to break machines and to burn
ricks, but that they, too, must work for the reform of Parliament.
As a result of his agitation, the idea that political reform was a
means to social reform dominated a large section of working-class
opinion until after the collapse of the Chartist movement in the
1840's. The cautiousness of Cobbett's liberalism, in spite of the vehemence of his language, is shown in his advice to the lower classes.
He summed up his general attitude when he wrote, "We want nothing new; we want only what our forefathers enjoyed, what the
stock-jobbers, and place-hunters, and cotton-lords have taken away."
It has often been remarked that England might have been much
nearer a revolution in the difficult years that followed Waterloo had
not this fighting journalist—one of the men who might have led
such a revolution—thrown the whole of his influence on the side
of peaceful reform. His curious combination of moderation in doctrine with rashness of statement gave him the widest hearing of
any British liberal of his generation. Hazlitt said of Cobbett that
he formed "a fourth estate of himself."[13]

The attention of the liberal groups in France, in some of the
German states, and in Poland was focused on the working of the
parliamentary régime established by the new constitutions granted

[12] W. Cobbett, *Political Works*, ed. J. M. Cobbett (London, 1835 ff.), VIII, 51.
[13] There are two stimulating studies of Cobbett: G. K. Chesterton, *William Cobbett* (London, 1925); and the more detailed biography by G. D. H. Cole, *The Life of William Cobbett* (New York, 1924).

in 1814 or in the years immediately following. These new instruments of government—in every case royal grants—spoke not of the rights possessed by men in general, as had the revolutionary constitutions, but of the rights granted to Frenchmen or Württembergers or Poles in particular. This restriction reflected the determination of the monarchs to maintain the principle of the final authority of the ruler who, within the limits of his own realm, might issue whatever ordinances he chose. The ambiguity of these charters usually made them capable of several interpretations. The conservative groups intended to ignore them; the liberals were bent on enlarging or even on replacing them as soon as possible. In states where no constitutions existed, the liberals agitated to secure grants of political guarantees.[14]

The one common idea in the constitutional theorizing of the period was that all authority, whether of the monarch or of the people, must be limited. All régimes, it was argued, must be kept within the "bounds of reason and common sense," through reciprocal checks and balances between the legislative, executive, and judicial powers. This would prevent all types of tyranny. Within these limits the practical questions usually discussed were those of just how far the franchise should be extended, of exactly how much liberty was to be allowed the press, and to whom the ministry should be responsible. The desire for an English type of limited monarchy is reflected in the French expression current among liberals all over Europe, "A throne surrounded by republican institutions," and in Thiers' dictum, "The king reigns, but does not rule." After 1815 the liberal thinkers and politicians were attacking the privileges of kings, nobles, and priests, but they had no intention of turning control over to the masses. They failed to realize—or they ignored the fact—that legal rights won by one class would later become a burden on the class beneath them. Their tendency was to view their ideal of the state and of society as a final one. Like all parties in opposition, they were in fact working only for an extension of privilege.

The great prophet of constitutionalism on the continent was

[14] Cf. J. Barthélemy, *L'introduction du régime parlementaire en France sous Louis XVIII et Charles X* (Paris, 1904), and R. Oeshey, *Die Bayerische Verfassungskunde von 1818 und die Charte Ludwigs XVIII* (Munich, 1914).

Montesquieu. His prestige had suffered less than that of any other *philosophe* of the Enlightenment. By the end of the Napoleonic wars, many of his views on constitutional monarchy had found their way into the fundamental laws of European states. Liberals of the post-war period found in him the golden mean—the *juste milieu*, as Guizot and Victor Cousin were soon to name it—between the excesses of revolutionary ardor and the dangers of reaction. Montesquieu was liked above all because of his vagueness on the subject of sovereignty. He served, in this respect, as an antidote to theorists like Rousseau and de Maistre who would have absolute authority put into the hands of powers now feared by the middle class. The influence of Montesquieu was spread by a number of French writers who, in one way or another, derived their chief ideas from him: Benjamin Constant and the group known as the *Doctrinaires*, especially Royer-Collard, Guizot, and Cousin.

Constant may be taken as typical of the group. As a young man he had spent much time in England; he therefore understood the working of the British parliamentary system better than did any other continental theorist. After 1819, when he became one of the liberal leaders of the French Chamber of Deputies, he worked to introduce the English political régime into France. He was particularly interested in freeing the press, in extending the jury system, in assuring religious freedom, in developing a system of checks and balances in the government, and in decentralizing the state so as to give greater power to local organs of government. All through Constant's theorizing there is an attempt to fix the boundary beyond which the state may not encroach on individual rights. "There is," he said, "a part of human existence which is wholly beyond social control, . . . men have rights which even the totality of the citizens cannot legitimately invade." "The liberty of the individual," he insisted, "is the object of all human association; on it rest public and private morality; on it are based the calculations of industry and commerce, and without it there is neither peace, dignity, nor happiness for men." Finally, he defined liberty as "the peaceful enjoyment of private independence; the right to pursue our own ends unimpeded, so long as they do not interfere with the equally legitimate activities of others."[15] Constant had less respect for tradition than had the *Doctrinaires*, and disagreed with them in believing that the liberties provided in the Charter of 1814 were insufficient and should be extended. In economic doctrine, he was a follower of Adam Smith and J. B. Say.[16]

The liberals of Constant's own time admired his writings and found in them an arsenal of arguments against the tyranny of reactionary governments. The essentially cautious character of his liberalism is shown by his unwillingness to accept fully the idea of ministerial responsibility and by his fear of any wide extension of the suffrage. Indeed, his statement on the question of voting power may stand as a symbol of the timidity of much of the liberal thought of the period, "Those whom poverty keeps in eternal dependence are no more enlightened on public affairs than children, nor are they more interested than foreigners in national prosperity, of which they do not understand the bases and of which they enjoy the advantages only indirectly. Property alone, by giving sufficient leisure, renders a man capable of exercising his political rights."[17] Constant exerted great influence through his speeches, his public lecture courses given at the Athénée in Paris, and his widely read *Cours de politique constitutionnelle*. He carried on a wide correspondence with liberals all over Europe, and next to Bentham was the most original and the most widely read liberal thinker of his generation.

Destutt de Tracy, in his *Commentaire sur l'esprit des lois* (1811) and Daunou in his *Essai sur les garanties individuelles* (1819) agreed with Bentham and Constant that liberty lies chiefly in the power of each man to execute his own wishes, so far as his action respects the wishes of others. Destutt de Tracy's work contains a plea for various useful and specific reforms such as the wider use of the jury system, the development of a free press, and the

[15] B. Constant, *Cours de politique constitutionnelle* (Paris, 1818-1820), I, 178, 312, 317, III, 249. Much of Constant's defense of liberty resembles that made later by John Stuart Mill in his essay, *On Liberty*.

[16] J. de La Lombardière, *Les idées politiques de Benjamin Constant* (Paris, 1928) is very slight; see the more substantial study of Elizabeth W. Schermerhorn, *Benjamin Constant, his Private Life and his Contribution to the Cause of Liberal Government in France* (Boston, 1924), and the popular biography of L. Dumont-Wilden, *La vie de Benjamin Constant* (Paris, 1930).

[17] B. Constant, *Réflexions sur les constitutions* (Paris, 1814), 106. The idea of universal suffrage was discredited not only because of its connection with the Reign of Terror, but also because, through the plebiscite, it had been used as a means of facilitating the dictatorship of Napoleon.

extension of representative government by granting universal suffrage. In attacking the gospel of natural rights, and in devoting attention to the reform of specific abuses, he took a line similar to that of Bentham. The *Commentaire*, which forms only part of a vast philosophic scheme, was praised by Ricardo and by Jefferson, who translated it into English. It found readers among the Spanish and Italian liberals, and its republican implications made it a favorite book of Pestel, the leading thinker among the Russian Decembrists. Both Destutt de Tracy and Daunou, who were close friends, admired the government of the United States under which, they maintained, men enjoyed more liberty than under the British Constitution. Their influence extended not only to the liberal monarchists, but also to the few republican groups which were forming during the period.

Though they were more conservative, the French *Doctrinaires*, Guizot, Royer-Collard, and Victor Cousin, as well as the rising historical writers, Mignet and Thiers, shared many of the same political views. All were, at this time, liberal monarchists and their doctrines became more or less the official ones of the July Monarchy. Throughout the writings of Guizot and Royer-Collard runs the idea that the best government is a constitutional monarchy with a strong, able king, an honest nobility, and a liberty-loving but not revolutionary people. They believed that some constitutional compromise between monarchy and democracy could be made and that such arrangements would be permanent, whereas Constant and Destutt de Tracy shared Bentham's conviction that monarchy was only a transitional stage between absolutism and a bourgeois republic. The *Doctrinaires* disagreed with their more liberal contemporaries also as to the moral value of the state. To them the state was no merely negative organ of control, but a union for ideal ends. Their view of the state and their appeal to generalized laws of reason and history reveal the influence of the German Idealist Philosophers which began to spread in France about 1820, largely through the writing and teaching of Cousin. The *Doctrinaires* had connections also with the British Evangelicals, particularly with the Clapham Sect, and their influence may be seen in the Spanish, Italian, and Russian liberal movements. At home, Royer-Collard was heard chiefly in the Chamber of Deputies, whereas Guizot's views and those of Cousin became known through their writings and through the students who crowded their classrooms at the Sorbonne and the Collège de France. Mignet and Thiers, who belonged to a younger generation, began to have a following only at the end of the Restoration period.[18]

Constitutional theories of similar character were circulated in Spain, Russia, Poland, Italy, and in some of the German states. The Spanish liberals, of whom Martínez de la Rosa was the most able writer, read Montesquieu, Bentham, and Constant, and tried to apply their ideas to Spain. In Russia, a group of young nobles who had served in the Napoleonic wars read the same political treatises and began to plot the overthrow of the tsarist despotism. The movement there, as in Italy, contained currents of republicanism. The Poles were mostly under the influence of Constant, and a group of the liberals there were known as the Benjaminists.

The most substantial treatises on constitutionalism after those of Bentham and Constant were written by German statesmen and scholars. Rotteck, a professor in the University of Freiburg, was the leading constitutional writer in South Germany. His *Über stehende Heere und Nationalmiliz* (1816) and a *Weltgeschichte* (1812-1827) were the most important of a series of works in which he defended the ideals of constitutional government. He attacked Savigny and his school for sacrificing the present to the past, and for refusing their contemporaries the right to prepare a better future. Rotteck's views were attractively presented. As Treitschke said, "he took the word from the mouths of the well-to-do townsmen and peasants of the South, and, with invincible courage and the fervent eloquence of conviction, announced what all were obscurely feeling."[19] Until his death in 1840 he remained one of the chief figures in the South German liberal movement. Schlosser, professor of history at Heidelberg and the author of a widely read *Weltgeschichte* (1815 ff.), turned his teaching and writing into a similar denunciation of kings and nobles.

In northern Germany Dahlmann, professor at Kiel and from 1829

[18] On Guizot the fundamental work is now Charles Pouthas, *Guizot pendant la Restauration* (Paris, 1923). On Royer-Collard see Robert de Nesmes-Desmarets, *Les doctrines politiques de Royer-Collard* (Paris, 1908), and the essay in H. J. Laski, *Authority in the Modern State* (New Haven, 1919), chap. iv.
[19] Treitschke, *op. cit.*, II, 345.

to 1837 at the University of Göttingen, tried to interest the intellectual classes in the cause of constitutional monarchy. The Hanoverian Constitution of 1832 was largely his work, but the best statement of his theories is his *Die Politik, auf den Grund und das Mass der gegebenen Zustände zurückgeführt,* which was not published until 1835. The English Constitution, according to Dahlmann, is rooted in the old Germanic ideals of freedom and is, therefore, the highest form of government for all Germanic peoples. To meet the needs of the German states he proposed to liberalize the governments by giving the old medieval assemblies of estates more control over expenditure and local administration.[20] Fries, a professor of philosophy at Jena, and the author of *Vom deutschen Bund und deutscher Staatsverfassung* (1817) was the chief intellectual influence in the *Burschenschaften,* while in Prussia the outstanding liberal theorist, Wilhelm von Humboldt, gave a classic statement of the ideas of Adam Smith and Montesquieu in his *Ideen zu einem Versuch, die Grenzen der Wirksamkeit des Staates zu bestimmen* (1792, pub. 1851). After 1815 Humboldt turned to conservatism. The progress of his political thought well illustrates the general movement of Germany during this period away from liberal ideals. Many of the theorists mentioned, as well as the poet, Arndt, the statesman, Stein, and Jahn, the famous *Turnvater,* were persecuted and forced into retirement. Such liberal theories as still found expression were based on an English rather than on a French ideal of free government. Stein's statement that "in England are most purely developed and preserved the foundations of the sort of constitution toward which all European nations are striving," and Rückert's line, "O build we now a temple on Albion's example," indicate the temper of the liberal thought which survived in Germany after 1815.

IV. ANTICLERICALISM AND STATE EDUCATION

The liberals of the restoration wished not only to curb the power of absolute monarchs, and to take over the direction of society from them and from the nobles; they were also strongly opposed to the great power and influence exerted by the established churches. Their demand for religious freedom and for the limitation of the

[20] Cf. E. R. Huber, *Dahlmann und die deutsche Verfassungsbewegung* (Hamburg, 1937).

influence of the clergy in politics was by no means novel. It had been at the basis of much of the liberal thought of seventeenth-century England and of eighteenth-century France. In England, the landowners had long been Anglican, the men of commerce largely nonconformist. Since Stuart times the latter had been distrustful of a government whose courts had at every turn hampered the activities of trade and manufacture in the interest of religious conformity. The liberal tradition, therefore, involved the belief that economic, political, and religious freedom were but aspects of a single program for the emancipation of the middle class. This ideal, whose origins were English, had spread to the continent during the eighteenth century.

The revolutionary governments had carried some of these ideas into practice. The properties of the church had been confiscated not only in France but also in parts of Germany, Italy, and Spain. In most countries inroads had been made on the prerogatives of the clergy. Above all the revolution had spread the idea of the lay state, an organization without any ecclesiastical connections and one which demanded an all-absorbing loyalty from its citizens. When the monarchs returned in 1815, however, the governments again showered favors on the clergy, and during the restoration, church and state were almost everywhere in close coöperation. The problem of the relation of church and state was more acute in Catholic countries, for in the Protestant states, in Russia, and among the Christian peoples of the Balkans, the state had long before brought the church within its control, though nowhere in Europe did the church exist as a private corporation. The quarrel between clericals and anticlericals in the period after 1815 was usually centered on a number of specific issues: Should the clergy or the government control education, and marriage and divorce? and Should the church receive back all or part of its confiscated property? Then there was the further question whether or not the church should be allowed to influence the government through controlling the votes of the faithful and the actions of the administrative personnel.

The skepticism of the Enlightenment had by no means disappeared; indeed, it sometimes gave edge to the more immediately practical reasons for attacking the encroachments of the clergy. Some of the most outstanding liberals of the period were avowed free thinkers. Bentham, for example, declared that all he admired in Jesus was His humanitarianism, little of which had apparently survived in the organized churches. The various shades of anticlericalism are best revealed in France where clericals and anticlericals were most evenly matched. On the whole this anticlerical thought is surprisingly timid. Few liberals were as outspoken as Bentham. Constant was as cautious in his views on the church as he was in his constitutional theories. Like most of the liberal thinkers of his generation he disliked pretentious priests of all stripes, and he feared the new ultramontanism of Rome. But at the same time he saw in the church a curb on the violence of the masses. Hence, he supported the Napoleonic Concordat of 1801 just as he supported the Charter of 1814.

Victor Cousin represented this attitude in a philosophy of compromise which admirably suited the spirit of the age. Religion and philosophy had the same end, he declared, but religion should always have a great hold on the masses while philosophy could safely be made the guide of only the few. A group of Cousin's friends founded in 1821 the *Société de la morale chrétienne*, which in 1825 offered a prize for the best proposals on the place the church should hold in modern society. The award went to a Swiss pastor, Vinet, whose essay was based on the idea that religious liberty is the foundation of civil liberty, and that church and state must be separated. No European government at the time would have considered adopting such a program. It was only among the small republican groups on the continent and among Bentham's followers in England that anticlericalism still smacked of the bitterness of the Age of Voltaire. These radicals would have reduced all churches to the status of purely private organizations. As the elder Littré said, *"tant cru, tant payé."* The point of view of the average liberal, however, was well expressed by Béranger and Paul Louis Courier who, though they railed at the meddling of the bishops and of the Jesuits in politics, praised the simple priest and his God, whom Béranger called "le Dieu des bons gens"—a benign bourgeois deity in the sky who looks down disapprovingly on all kings, Jesuits, and Jacobins.[21] In

21 Cf. M. Brillant, "Le masque et le visage de Courier," *Correspondant*, 1925, L. Four, *La vie en chansons de Béranger* (Paris, 1930), and Lucas-Dubreton, *Béranger* (Paris, 1934).

the religious field as in the political, the liberal thinkers were everywhere searching for a middle course. The exaggerated pretensions of the priests, which often aroused the ire even of devout Catholics, would have to be curbed without destroying the church. It was a general middle-class attitude. These people went to church service after 1815, as they had never gone in the later eighteenth century, though their stricter observance was probably due less to purely religious reasons, than to their belief in the church as a bulwark of social stability.

The liberal forces came most sharply into disagreement with the organized churches on the question of education.[22] The rising middle class saw in the extension of free education a means of helping their children rise in the world, of preparing their class for self-government, and of improving morality among the lower strata.[23] The nationalist groups in Italy and Germany, and among the Slavic peoples ruled by the Hapsburg and the Ottoman governments, took up the idea that schools could be used to further a sense of national solidarity. Liberals everywhere were, therefore, interested in freeing education from clerical control and in extending it. Education, they believed, would increase industrial efficiency, improve public morality, curb mob violence, inculcate national ideals, and help the middle class to strengthen its position in society. To be effective such a system of instruction would have to be organized as a state institution, or, in the case of subject nationalities, on a national basis.

This liberal program for promoting the interests of society by state education was opposed by most of the conservative forces of the time. Especially were the established churches hostile to such reforms. Most of the governments apparently shared the view of the member of the British House of Commons who declared in a debate that education would teach the masses "to despise their lot in life instead of making them good servants; instead of teaching them

[22] The best introductions to the whole subject of education in this period are J. W. Adamson, *English Education, 1789-1902* (Cambridge, 1930), and E. H. Reisner, *Nationalism and Education since 1789* (New York, 1922).

[23] In 1792 Condorcet wrote, "A free constitution, which should not be correspondent to the universal instruction of citizens, would come to destruction after a few conflicts, and would degenerate into one of those forms of government which cannot preserve the peace among an ignorant and corrupt people." E. P. Cubberley, *The History of Education* (Boston, 1920), 515. Adam Smith had defended the extension of education as the best means for keeping the masses from being "misled into wanton opposition to government."

subordination, it would render them fractious; it would enable them to read seditious pamphlets, vicious books, and publications against Christianity; it would render them insolent to their superiors."[24] Even in France and in Prussia, where elaborate systems of state schools had been instituted before 1815, the hostility of the governing classes threatened their existence and seriously interfered with their work.

In most countries the extension of popular education depended entirely on private enterprise. The Nonconformist sects in England conducted a large number of Sunday schools—often with the open disapproval of the Anglican clergy. The lower classes were taught to read the Bible, but often other subjects were added, arithmetic, interestingly enough, coming first.[25] The work of the British Sunday schools was soon supplemented by other types of popular instruction. Bell, an English parson, and Lancaster, a Quaker, working independently developed similar systems of training large numbers of children, by the use of student monitors, to read, to write, and to figure. This system, known as the Monitorial, or Mutual System, was very cheap to operate, but it lacked thoroughness. Still, at a time when the state would do practically nothing for education it could be used to teach large numbers the rudiments of reading and writing and consequently it had a wide appeal. It was used in parts of France, where the *Société de l'instruction élémentaire* collected funds for it, though by 1830 the clericals had practically driven it out. It was introduced also into Germany, Russia, Italy, Canada, the United States, and South America. The first Bulgarian national school, opened in 1835, followed the system of Lancaster, which had been applied earlier in Greek nationalist schools in the Ionian Islands, and was extremely popular with Protestant missionaries in southeastern Europe and in Anatolia.

Wherever men were interested in liberal ideas, this interest in new forms of popular education was to be found. A dozen or more educational societies were founded in England in the first decades of the nineteenth century, while similar societies appeared in France,

24 G. M. Trevelyan, *British History in the 19th Century* (New York, 1922), 162 note.
25 This emphasis on teaching arithmetic, found in most of the early nineteenth-century school programs, together with a similar emphasis on fine penmanship, shows that the schools were, in part, regarded as training places for those who were to enter business.

usually under Protestant auspices. Bentham and Brougham in England and Guizot and Cousin in France were, during the 1820's and 1830's, the leaders in these movements. In 1828, under the guidance of Bentham and Brougham, an important experiment in higher education was instituted through the opening of University College in London. Nonconformists and freethinkers, excluded from Oxford and Cambridge, were freely admitted. The curriculum ignored theology and emphasized science and history. Indeed, the new college was pervaded almost from the start with a spirit of scientific inquiry, found at this time only in the German and Scotch universities.

Other types of schools were opened. In England the leaders of the skilled trades organized Mechanics' Institutes, which furnished educational advantages to adults. These institutions, although they received some help from wealthy Whigs and from a few Benthamites, were self-supporting. Each possessed a reading room where lectures were given and discussion groups organized. By 1823 there were enough of these institutes in Britain to make it possible to publish a *Mechanics' Magazine*. Their work was furthered, after 1827, by the Society for the Diffusion of Useful Knowledge, which furnished the institutes with a large number of books and pamphlets at a low cost. The Mechanics' Institute idea was copied in the United States and in a few industrial centers of France, though the most interesting of the French adaptations of British adult educational schemes was the Athénée in Paris. In its reading rooms lectures were given by nearly all the important liberal thinkers of the Restoration, so it became a force in the formation of liberal public opinion. Its clientèle, however, came from a higher social stratum than that represented in the Mechanics' Institutes.[26]

Finally, it should always be borne in mind that, on the idealistic side, many liberals accepted the doctrine of Locke and Rousseau, that men are made by their environment and that a change of the educational system is one of the surest ways of effecting a change in society. This ideal in education was most clearly set forth by Pestalozzi in Switzerland. He had begun his educational work in 1799 by opening a school for pauper children of his neighborhood.

[26] Cf. Dejob, "L'Athénée," *Revue internationale de l'enseignement,* 1889.

THE CREEDS OF LIBERALISM 103

Here he gradually developed Rousseau's educational ideas into a workable program. Emphasis was laid on developing the individual capacities of each child, and on trying to arouse the child's interest by utilizing the objects and the activities immediately about him as the basis of learning. His writings, especially *How Gertrude Teaches her Children* (1801), were read all over Europe. Students from every European state visited his school. Fröbel spent two years there, and Bell, Fichte, Frederick William III of Prussia, Mme. de Staël, Brougham, and Robert Owen were among his visitors. Owen's famous school at New Lanark was largely a Pestalozzian enterprise, and the same methods were introduced into the primary schools of Prussia, a country which had the oldest public-school system in Europe. To Pestalozzi, more than to any educational reformer, is due the whole movement that led to the foundation of the modern, free, secular, and vernacular school. This type of school was soon to become one of the chief organs for the propagation of nationalist doctrines.

V. ASPIRATIONS FOR NATIONAL UNITY AND FREEDOM

The French Revolution had awakened among many of the European peoples a new sense of national solidarity and a new hope for a better national future. This spirit, aroused first in France, had spread into central Europe and in the end had become one of the forces that helped to overthrow Napoleon. Yet, after 1815, many national groups in Europe found themselves living under governments which they disliked. Two of the greatest historic peoples, the Germans and the Italians, possessed no political unity, and were only beginning to be conscious of a common culture. Other groups, which had once been independent, had for centuries been under foreign rule. In the Italian and German states, in Greece, and to some extent in Hungary and Poland, nationalist ideas were part and parcel of a constitutional program. With the Irish, nationalism was primarily an economic and religious matter, while among the Czechs and southern Slavs the ideal of a national cultural rebirth was the sole basis for attacking the established régime. Among all these oppressed peoples the lesser nobility or the lower clergy, or both, took the leadership in opposing the government. In its earlier stages the growth of nationalism was not so clearly a part of a bourgeois program as was constitutionalism.

Underlying the growth of nationalist ideals in the early nineteenth century was the romantic movement, which turned the attention of literary men and scholars to the study of the folk-ways, the folk-art and music, and the folk-legends of the Middle Ages. For several generations a great deal of writing and research was devoted to reviving the interest of some national group or other in the old and indigenous civilization which, during the seventeenth and eighteenth centuries, had lain buried beneath the cosmopolitan, neo-classical, and Frenchified culture of the upper classes.

It was Herder who gave these ideas and attitudes their clearest statement and much of their theoretical justification. He believed that the nation was the indispensable basis of any sound social order. It was a creation of God, and its development was a part of a divine plan in history. Humanity would never realize its highest possibilities until every national group had come to self-realization and to the control of its own destinies. In each national organism, he argued, there is inherent a creative power, a national soul, which is the source of its culture. This soul expresses itself in history, language, literature, religion, law, and art. As Mazzini, one of Herder's greatest disciples, wrote in 1834, "Every people has its special mission, which will coöperate towards the fulfilment of the general mission of humanity. That mission constitutes its *nationality*. Nationality is sacred."[27]

Herder insisted on the necessity of studying and using the national language. "Has a people," he wrote, "something more precious than the language of its fathers? In it resides the whole intellectual wealth of tradition and religion. To take away the language of a people means to take away its only immortal property."[28] The national language must be studied in the schools, and it must be used in the government, in the church, and in all literature. Herder was not a political theorist nor was he greatly interested in practical politics. His nationalism was almost entirely of a cultural sort, and

[27] *Life and Writings of Mazzini* (London, 1891), III, 33.
[28] Herder, *Sämmtliche Werke* (Berlin, 1877-1913), XVIII, 384.

was always combined with a cosmopolitan humanitarianism. He was opposed to the forcible imposition of the culture of one people on another, and regarded national pride as "the most harmful disease in history." If each nationality would put its own house in order, humanity would then come to its fullest development, international peace would ensue, and progress would proceed apace. To the Germans he said, let us be good Germans, not because we are superior to all other nationalities, but because the unique contribution we can make to humanity is that of being peculiarly and specifically ourselves.[29]

In the next generation, the War of Liberation made his ideas popular in Germany. Görres, Fichte, Schleiermacher, the Grimms, the Schlegels, and above all Hegel took them over, frequently giving to them a narrow and local emphasis that Herder had not intended. A whole generation became conscious of its cultural ties and embraced the idea that the Germans not only had a great past, but had a still more glorious future. Fichte, in his *Reden an die deutsche Nation* (1807-8), envisaged the German spirit as an "eagle, whose mighty body, rising on strong wings, thrusts itself on high and soars into the empyrean, that it may raise itself nearer the sun whereon it delights to gaze."[30] He assured his hearers that the Germans were the only people of Europe that had preserved its nationality unadulterated; the only people that possessed a truly national language and literature; the only race worthy of the name. They were *the* people, the *Urvolk*. If they were lost, all would be lost.[31] In these stirring addresses, Fichte made the first unconditional statement in Germany of the belief that a commonwealth of learning, literature, and art is no substitute for a strong, free state, and that the political weakness of a nation threatens the very existence of its culture. Already a somewhat more exclusive and selfish national interpretation was being given to Herder's ideal. After 1800 all the German romanticists contributed to the growth of this nationalist enthusiasm, as did also the teachers of history in the

[29] Cf. R. Ergang, *Herder and the Foundations of German Nationalism* (New York, 1931).
[30] Legge, *op. cit.*, 83. Cf. Engelbrecht, *op. cit.*, pp. 9, 128-32, 159.
[31] The nationalist ardor of the War of Liberation is vividly set forth in Kleist's *Catechism* in K. Francke, *History of German Literature* (Boston, 1901), 480-481.

schools and universities. No movement since the Reformation so swept the German world as did this sentimental nationalism.[32]

Bentham was another important theorist of the cultural nationalism that characterized the period. He shared many of Herder's ideas, though he combined them with the ideals of laissez-faire economics and political constitutionalism. He believed that nationality—a common cultural tradition and purpose—was the proper basis for state and government, and, like Herder, he was opposed to the domination of one nationality by another. He urged his own government and that of France to give up their colonies because they were unprofitable and because the colonists were not Englishmen or Frenchmen. He had protested earlier against the partition of Poland and had criticized the governments of the partitioning powers. Devoted to England, he was, nevertheless, generous in his praise of the United States, and he accepted honorary citizenship in France. He himself coined a word which expresses his point of view, the word *international*.

The nationalist ideas of Bentham and of Herder—especially those of Herder—spread across Europe in the early nineteenth century. Quinet published in 1827 a French translation of Herder's most influential work, *Ideen zur Philosophie der Geschichte der Menschheit* (1784-1791).[33] It found a ready response in Restoration France where the nation, proud of the position it had had during the revolution, was now disgusted with the timid foreign policy of the Bourbons. Quinet's translation became the chief influence in the formation of the ideas of Michelet, the most influential French historical writer of the nineteenth century. Like Fichte, Michelet used Herder's ideas to justify a proud and intolerant sense of racial superiority. Another reader of Quinet's translation, and one who remained much closer to Herder's ideals, was Mazzini, the founder of *Young Italy*. Similar ideas were developing, often independently of Herder, all over central Europe. Before Mazzini began to write,

[32] On the general development of nationalism see especially C. J. H. Hayes, *The Historical Evolution of Modern Nationalism* (New York, 1931); G. F. Preuss, *Die Quellen des Nationalgeistes der Befreiungskriege* (Berlin, 1914); A. D. Verschoor, *Die ältere deutsche Romantik und die Nationalidee* (Amsterdam, 1928); the classic work of Meinecke, *Weltbürgertum und Nationalstaat* (7th edition, Munich, 1928), and H. C. Engelbrecht, *Fichte, a Study of His Political Writings* (New York, 1933).

[33] Cf. O. Wenderoth, "Der junge Quinet und seine Uebersetzung von Herders 'Ideen,'" *Romanische Forschungen*, XXII (1908).

a number of Italian literary men, Alfieri, Foscolo, Pellico, Giordani, Niccolini, and Leopardi had urged the development of an Italian culture that would bring together the intellectual classes of the whole peninsula. Leopardi wrote in 1819, "Italy has nothing to hope for unless she has books read and understood from one end to the other of the country. The recent example of other nations shows us clearly all that can be done, in our century, by truly national books, to arouse the sleeping spirit of a nation."[34]

These ideas, however, were most active among the Slavs. Herder's influence was very great, though nationalist movements were already under way before his time. In his collection of folk-songs, *Die Stimmen der Völker in Liedern* (1778-79), Herder had included a number of Slavic songs, and in many of his writings he had praised the Slavs and had predicted a great future for them. Especially had he urged the Slavic peoples to cherish their native languages, literatures, and customs. These Slavic peoples under Austrian and Ottoman rule had almost forgotten their history and their folk-literature. Their languages had been greatly corrupted. The upper classes had ceased to speak them, and few books were written in them. The clergy were frequently hostile to the native culture. The Jesuits in Bohemia, and the Greek clergy among the Serbs, Rumanians, and Bulgarians had, during the seventeenth and eighteenth centuries, burned quantities of books in the native languages.

In spite of this, Slavic philologists, historians, and men of letters began in the later eighteenth century the work of resurrecting the past. They made collections of folk-legends, poems, and chronicles, wrote grammars, and compiled dictionaries. By 1815, Herder's ideas having furnished a definite program and inspiration, there were, from one end of Slavic Europe to the other, scholars and poets who were organizing nationalist movements. They not only wrote books, but they worked to establish newspapers and schools that used the native languages. Kopitar and Karadžić among the Croats, Serbs, and Slovenes; Sofroni and Venélin among the Bulgarians; Dobrovsky, Jungmann, Kollár, Šafařik, and Palácky among the Czechs and Slovaks; Széchenyi and Kossuth among the Magyars; Brodzinski and Mickiewicz among the Poles; and finally Karamzin

---

[34] J. Luchaire, *L'évolution intellectuelle de l'Italie de 1815 à 1830* (Paris, 1906), 150.

and a group of Slavophils in Russia, all shared a more or less common set of cultural nationalist ideals.

The Czech nationalists were in closest touch with Germany, many of them having studied in the German universities. One of them, Kollár, tried to bring all these isolated national forces into contact. In fact, the only essentially new idea in these Slavic movements was his doctrine of Pan-Slavism, although it was not clearly formulated until after 1830. Kollár lamented the fact that the Serbs knew nothing of the Czechs or the Poles, while these peoples regarded the Serbs and Bulgarians as Turks. Each national group was too much occupied with local problems to realize their common destiny. The Czechs were struggling against the Austrian Germans, the Slovaks and the Croats against the Magyars, the Poles against the Russians, and the Serbs and Bulgarians against the Hellenizing policy of the Greek Church as well as against the tyranny of the Ottoman government. These oppressed Slavic peoples differed also in religion. Some were Protestants, while others were Roman Catholics, and still others Greek Orthodox. There was, then, no unifying bond of religion or language among the Slavs, not even a common enemy. Kollár urged the establishment, throughout the Slavic world, of bookstores for the spread of Slavic ideas. He believed that all educated Slavs should learn the four principal Slavic languages, Czech, Polish, Serbian, and Russian. This would give the scattered nationalist groups hope, encouragement, and a sense of a common destiny, even though they would inevitably remain disunited politically and religiously. Since his ideas were generally accepted only by his own people, Pan-Slavism remained largely a Czech nationalist movement. For several generations, this ideal of cultural nationalism was the basis of the liberal faith and of liberal agitation throughout central Europe. It usually contained, however, an admixture of the ideas of laissez-faire economics and of constitutionalism.[35]

Nationalism became during the nineteenth century one of the

[35] The best account is that of A. Fischel, *Der Panslawismus bis zum Weltkrieg* (Berlin, 1919); but see also H. Oncken, "Deutsche geistige Einflüsse in der europäischen Nationalbewegung des neunzehnten Jahrhunderts," *Deutsche Vierteljahrschrift für Literaturwissenschaft und Geistesgeschichte*, VII (1929), 607-627; A. Skene, *Entstehen und Entwicklung der Slawisch-nationalen Bewegung in Böhmen und Mähren im neunzehnten Jahrhundert* (Vienna, 1893); M. Murko, *Deutsche Einflüsse auf die Anfänge der böhmischen Romantik* (Graz, 1897).

deepest currents of political thought and action. Among the theorists only the ultramontanes and the socialists seem in any important degree to have escaped its influence, and in the latter part of the century even the socialists embraced some of its ideals. But the influence of nationalist thought was, even in the period considered here, no monopoly of the liberals. Burke, Savigny, Haller, most of the literary romanticists, and the German Idealist Philosophers showed its influence, and, though they deprecated the use of nationalist propaganda by the forces opposed to the throne and the altar, they often found it a useful support to their own doctrines.

Chapter Five

THE FIRST YEARS OF PEACE 1815-1820

I. THE SETTLEMENT OF 1815

WHATEVER may have been the theories of government current at the time, the practical control of the political world in 1814 and 1815 was in the hands of the monarchs and their advisers, especially those of England, Austria, Russia, and Prussia. But the sudden collapse of the Napoleonic empire in 1814 found these allied powers with only partially-laid plans for the reconstruction of Europe. All efforts had so long been turned to fighting "the Usurper" that almost no attention had been given to the questions that would arise after his overthrow. The confusion of aims would have been even greater had not Castlereagh, the British foreign minister, succeeded in drawing together the four great powers in the Treaty of Chaumont (March, 1814). This treaty restated certain decisions already arrived at—the establishment of a confederated Germany, the division of Italy into independent states, the restoration of Spain to the Bourbons, the independence of Switzerland, and the enlargement of Holland—and provided further that the alliance now formed should continue for twenty years after the war had ceased, and that the powers should make a final settlement in a future peace congress. Besides uniting the great powers—England, Austria, Russia, and Prussia—for the final struggle with Napoleon and laying down some of the bases of a final peace, the Treaty of Chaumont became the corner stone of the European Alliance which was to determine the balance of power for several decades.

The general provisions of the Treaty of Chaumont were confirmed in the first Treaty of Paris in May, 1814, by which the four great powers, together with Spain, Portugal, and Sweden, made a formal peace with France, and restored, with slight modifications, the French frontiers of 1792. Finally, the powers arranged for the holding of a congress in Vienna to round out a general peace settlement.[1] Before the meeting of this congress the only points on which the four principal allied powers agreed were that they themselves should settle all important matters, that neither France nor the smaller states should do more than to acquiesce in their final decisions, and that the congress itself should only give a formal ratification to agreements previously made. The treaty carefully avoided the thorny subject of the final disposition of Saxony and Poland. At the time no one seems to have realized how deep were the differences among these allies, and through what a series of bickerings, recriminations, and threats the negotiations were to proceed. During the summer of 1814 conferences among the allied statesmen were held in Paris and London, but little progress was made.

The gathering in Vienna in the autumn of 1814 brought together six monarchs, the Emperors of Austria and of Russia, the Kings of Prussia, Bavaria, Württemberg, and Denmark, and representatives from all the minor states of Europe, together with a host of miscellaneous hangers-on and fortune-seekers.[2] The real work of the Congress was done by Castlereagh (whose place was taken in February, 1815, by the Duke of Wellington), Metternich, Alexander I, and Hardenberg, and to a less extent by Talleyrand after he had wormed his way into the councils of the others. Metternich had the constant aid of his secretary, Gentz, while Hardenberg usually acted for Frederick William III. Alexander preferred to keep matters in his own hands, though he constantly received advice from his large staff, from Stein on German affairs, from Czartoryski on those of Poland, from Capodistrias on the Balkans, and on many other matters from the Corsican, Pozzo di Borgo, from the German Nesselrode, and his old tutor, the Swiss Laharpe.

Some important decisions were formulated in committees appointed from time to time for some special investigation, such as

[1] This congress was not, strictly speaking, to be a peace congress, because peace had already been made by the *first* Treaty of Paris, in which the issues between France and the Allies had been settled. The state of war had ceased both in fact and in law, and France could now claim representation with the other powers as a regular member of the European states-system. Herein the situation differed from that of 1919.

[2] No appreciable difference would have been made in the final settlement if a large majority of these representatives had failed to appear. They gave the congress a picturesque setting and they seem to have enjoyed greatly the endless round of balls and entertainments furnished by the almost bankrupt Austrian government and by the nobility.

those on Switzerland, Italy, the slave trade, the German Confederation, diplomatic precedence, international rivers, and statistics of population. The ministers of the great powers met nearly every morning for an informal conference in Metternich's apartments. From time to time the three sovereigns of Austria, Russia, and Prussia met to review the matters that had been previously discussed by their ministers. Besides these meetings, innumerable private conferences were going on at all hours. The representatives of the smaller states were consulted only at such times and on such terms as suited the representatives of the great powers. The Austrian government maintained an elaborate spy system. Letters were opened, wastebaskets were searched by servants in the government's pay, and people in all ranks of society were used to collect bits of information. Some of the other governments maintained secret agents in Vienna. The net result of all this spying is hard to estimate, though its final influence seems to have been slight.[3]

If any statesman took the leading rôle in the negotiations, it was Castlereagh. He usually provided the plan of action and then calmly set about procuring its acceptance. His consistent aim was, as he said later, "not to collect trophies, but to bring back the world to peaceful habits." He represented a government that, for economic reasons, was anxious to have Europe return to peaceful conditions as soon as possible. England was then, as she was after the World War, more heavily burdened with debts than any other state, her public finance was in disorder, her warehouses were bursting with manufactured goods waiting for the reopening of continental markets, and her people were suffering from great economic distress.

As soon as the diplomats had gathered at Vienna, a lively discussion arose as to how the congress should be organized. Metternich insisted that the representatives of the four great powers should keep all matters in their own hands as originally arranged. Talleyrand, with the backing of Spain, Bavaria, and some of the German states, at once began an intrigue to prevent this. But the result of months of negotiation on this question of organization resulted in the failure ever to constitute a congress, for Talleyrand dropped the matter as soon as he found he could gain more by direct nego-

[3] This aspect of the congress is interestingly exposed in A. Fournier, *Die Geheimpolizei auf dem Wiener Congress* (Vienna, 1913).

tiation with the representatives of the great powers. So the important
decisions were all made by the four great powers, to which group
Talleyrand was admitted in January, 1815. The attention of the
whole of Europe was, in the meantime, focused on Vienna. Every
group and every interest from Spain to Russia thought it saw opening before it the opportunity to realize its hopes. Liberals and nationalists, political and religious reactionaries, and all the rulers
from the pope to the most petty German princeling, seem to have
deluded themselves into believing that the congress would reconstruct society according to their hearts' desires.[4]

Certain matters had been decided by earlier treaties; others were
still to be settled—above all, the final disposition of Saxony and
Poland. The long negotiations over this knotty problem nearly
brought the powers to war. Alexander kept his troops in Poland
because, in spite of earlier promises, he was determined to hold the
country and to carry through his program of reconstituting old
Poland as a Russian dependency. In this plan he had secured the
backing of the King of Prussia, who had agreed to relinquish the
Prussian part of Poland if Alexander would work for the annexation of Saxony to Prussia. Both Metternich and Castlereagh opposed
the plan, principally because they felt that the aggrandizement
of Russia and the advance of the Muscovite frontier to the west
would upset the balance of power in Europe. International adjustments could best be guaranteed by strengthening the central part
of the continent against France on the one hand and against Russia on the other. Here, finally, the intervention of Talleyrand and
the mediation of Castlereagh, who continued his efforts to keep
peace among the peacemakers, was to bring a compromise. In January, 1815, Castlereagh, Talleyrand, and Metternich signed a secret
treaty of alliance which bound their governments to furnish con-
tingents for a common army in the case of a Russian or a Prussian
attack. This new alignment forced both Russia and Prussia to withdraw from their former positions. The diplomats then proceeded
to strike a balance. Prussia got about two-fifths of Saxony, and Rus-

<hr />

[4] On the diplomacy of the years 1809-1815 and on the Vienna Congress, cf. C. S. B.
Buckland, *Metternich and the British Government, 1809-1813* (London, 1932), C. K.
Webster, *The Foreign Policy of Castlereagh, 1812-1815* (London, 1931), and the first
volume of H. von Srbik, *Metternich* (Munich, 1925).

sia was allowed to reconstitute part of the old Polish state as the new Kingdom of Poland.

The rest of the agreements took several months of further negotiations. On the ninth of June, a Final Act, a kind of codification of the work of the congress, was signed by nearly all the powers both great and small. Holland received the Austrian Netherlands and Luxemburg; Genoa and part of Savoy went to the Kingdom of Sardinia, and Prussia was given lands along the lower Rhine—all with the idea of erecting a series of strong bulwarks which would prevent an attack by France on the peace of Europe. This establishment of Prussia on the Rhine, which ultimately made her the national champion of Germany against France, proved to be the most important territorial change made by the congress. In Germany Prussia received Swedish Pomerania in addition to part of Westphalia, two-fifths of Saxony, and territories in the Rhineland; Hanover was enlarged, and the other states were carved up to suit the wishes of Austria and Prussia. A loose German Confederation of thirty-nine states, the *Deutscher Bund,* was created under the presidency of Austria. In Italy, besides the enlargement of the Kingdom of Sardinia, the Bourbons were restored to Naples, though only after the congress broke up, just as shortly before they had been restored to France and Spain. The Papal States were returned to the pope; Lombardy and Venetia went to Austria to compensate her for the loss of the former Austrian Netherlands, which she did not want anyway; and in northern and central Italy three small duchies, Tuscany, Parma, and Modena, were placed under Austrian princes. Thus, in both Germany and Italy Austria held the dominant influence. Switzerland was guaranteed her independence and neutrality, an arrangement which proved the most durable achievement of the congress. Norway was taken from Denmark and joined to Sweden, which in turn gave Finland to Russia. By the terms of the first Treaty of Paris England received Cape Colony, Heligoland, Malta, Ceylon, Mauritius, and islands in the West Indies. Later she received a protectorate over the Ionian Islands. At Vienna she secured from the powers agreements for opening certain rivers to navigation and for abolishing the slave trade; termination of the traffic in slaves was an uncompromising demand of the British

Evangelicals and Non-conformist groups who, through their fanatical zeal and their insistence that most of the peace negotiations be subordinated to this reform, not only greatly endangered the acceptance of their own program but seriously interfered with Castlereagh's efforts at Vienna.[5]

Such was the most important international settlement between that of 1648 at Westphalia and that of 1919 at Paris. It was the fashion of the liberal historians of the nineteenth century to denounce the decisions of the Congress of Vienna.[6] Since 1919, however, it has become clear that the diplomats called together at the close of a general European war are so bound by earlier agreements and by the exigencies of the moment that they cannot build a New Jerusalem. They are fortunate if they are able even to reconstruct an old order. In 1815 neither the statesmen nor the peoples of Europe had any thorough understanding of the vague principles of nationality and democracy. Moreover, there was, at the time of the Vienna Congress, a widespread distrust of these revolutionary ideas. It is as incredible that the statesmen of 1815 should have made them the basis of a reconstructed Europe as that the delegates at the conference of 1919 should have revamped Europe in accordance with the precepts of communism. After the overthrow of Napoleon the diplomatists quite naturally resorted to the familiar ideas of the balance of power and to the notions of legitimacy, and tried to fuse them into some sort of compromise that would guarantee Europe a period of peace. Whatever may be said against them, they were, most of them, reasonable, fair-minded, and well-intentioned. These qualities were most strikingly revealed in their treatment

[5] Cf. W. E. Dubois, *The Suppression of The African Slave-Trade to the United States* (Cambridge, 1896), and R. Coupland, *The British Anti-Slavery Movement* (London, 1933).

[6] In this they were preceded by Gentz who, at the time, said, "The Congress has resulted in nothing but restorations which had already been effected by arms, agreements between the great powers of little value for the preservation of the peace of Europe, quite arbitrary alterations in the possessions of the smaller states, but no act of a higher nature, no great measure for public order or the general good which might compensate humanity for its long suffering or pacify it for the future." Klinkowström, *Oesterreichs Theilnahme an den Befreiungskriegen* (Vienna, 1887), 540. Characteristic of the liberal point of view of the middle of the nineteenth century is Cavour's statement, "Resting on no principle, neither that of legitimacy, nor of national interests, nor of popular will, taking account neither of geographical conditions, nor of general interests, this august assembly, acting only by right of the strongest, erected a political edifice without any moral foundation." *Revue nouvelle*, May 1, 1846. Compare this with the view of a textbook written originally before the World War: C. D. Hazen, *Europe since 1815* (New York, 1923), I, 8-9.

of France and in the general absence of rancor in their decisions. Patriotic Frenchmen sometimes claim that it was as hard for France to lose territories like Belgium, which had been occupied for twenty years, as it was for Germany to give up large slices of territory in 1919, but the disinterested outsider can hardly accept the comparison. The fact is that reasonable Frenchmen were generally satisfied with the first Treaty of Paris, and that even after the imposition of the harsher terms of the second treaty Europe enjoyed nearly a half-century of peace on the basis of the Vienna settlements.

While the Congress was still in session, Napoleon had escaped from Elba, and on March 1, 1815, had landed on the south coast of France. Without firing a shot or shedding a drop of blood, he had marched northward, and within twenty days had reëstablished himself on the French throne. He began at once to negotiate with the allied powers but they would have nothing to do with him. The plenipotentiaries of England, Russia, Prussia, Austria, and some of the smaller powers proclaimed him an outlaw and pledged themselves "not to lay down their arms until Napoleon is rendered wholly incapable of again disturbing the peace." The allied armies were hastily reassembled. Early in June, 1815, Napoleon pushed north into Belgium to defeat the English army under Wellington before Blücher and the Prussians arrived. Though at first successful at Ligny on June 16, 1815, his plan failed and he was overwhelmed two days later at Waterloo. Driven back to Paris, he abdicated on June 22, fled to the coast, and delivered himself into the hands of the English.

The entrance of the allied forces into Paris brought the plenipotentiaries together again. After prolonged and often embittered negotiations, they signed, on the twentieth of November, the second Treaty of Paris. France was obliged to restore most of the works of art taken by Napoleon, to agree to pay a heavy indemnity, and to support an allied army of occupation until it had been paid. Her boundaries were reduced to the limits of 1790, and it was due only to the moderating counsels of Castlereagh, Wellington, and Alexander that she was not compelled to cede Alsace-Lorraine and lands along the northern frontier. On the same day another agreement was signed by the four great powers which bound them in a

Quadruple Alliance to maintain by armed force the arrangements of Chaumont, Vienna, and Paris for twenty years, both in regard to the territorial boundaries and to the exclusion of Bonaparte and his dynasty from the throne of France. An attempt of Alexander to embody in this treaty a provision that would oblige the signatories to intervene in France to maintain Louis XVIII and the Charter of 1814 was rejected by Castlereagh. His contention, which remained fundamental in his point of view until his death in 1822, was that England could not guarantee any more than the general settlement of boundaries. She would not intervene in the internal affairs of any state except in one case—the possibility of a Bonaparte returning to power in France. The treaty called also for periodic meetings of representatives of the four powers, "for the purpose of consulting upon their common interest and for the consideration of the measures most salutary for the maintenance of the peace of Europe." The ascendancy of the great powers in general European affairs was herein for the first time clearly set forth, and along with this the principle of a European concert and the idea of diplomacy by congresses and conferences.

Two months before this Tsar Alexander had presented the various European monarchs with a draft of the Holy Alliance.[7] This curious document, in which Baader and Mme. de Krüdener had a hand, stated that the rulers of Europe would in future regulate their acts in both domestic and foreign affairs according to the benign principles and precepts of the Christian religion. Castlereagh referred to the document as a "piece of sublime mysticism and nonsense," and most of the other statesmen were equally contemptuous. It is only fair to say, however, that the so-called Holy Alliance was for Alexander only a makeshift, a mere fragment of a much larger scheme for the reconstruction of Europe in accordance with advanced principles. The tsar had made an effort to gain a hearing for his plans at Vienna, but the practically-minded statesmen of the powers regarded him as either a dangerous Jacobin or a clever schemer with ulterior motives. So Alexander never got beyond the acceptance of the preface of his program. The Holy Alliance in itself was a perfectly innocuous if somewhat pompous document.

[7] Cf. H. Schraeder *Die dritte Koalition und die Heilige Allianz* (Königsberg, 1934).

It was signed by all the monarchs of Europe with the exception of
the regent in England (who, however, sent an approving letter),
the Ottoman sultan, and the pope. The sultan was not asked to
sign, while Pius VII replied to the invitation with the tart remark
that "from time immemorial the papacy had been in possession of
Christian truth and needed no new interpretation of it."[8]

The Alliance had no direct influence on affairs, for "charity" and
"love" are not capable of being stated in diplomatic terms. The
powers of the Quadruple Alliance pursued a conservative and repressive policy in the years following the peace, so that the contrast
between high-sounding principles and actual practice quite naturally produced in the minds of the peoples of Europe the suspicion
that their rulers were hypocritically leagued against them. In the
popular mind, the Holy Alliance remained for a half-century confused with the Quadruple Alliance.

The representatives of the powers, having sent Napoleon to St.
Helena, having redrawn the map of Europe, and having provided
the machinery for perpetuating their territorial settlement, returned
to their own capitals to occupy themselves with the domestic
situation.

II. THE REACTION IN ENGLAND

In the overthrow of Napoleon the British navy and British sub-
sidies had played a major rôle, but the celebrations over Waterloo
had hardly passed before it became evident that victory in a modern
war is little more profitable than defeat. The high prices obtained
for foodstuffs during the wars suddenly collapsed and the English
countryside, which not so long before had been famed as the land
of roast beef and plum pudding, was now peopled by wretches—as
Cobbett describes them—"in ragged smock-frocks with unshaven
faces, with a shirt not washed for a month and with their toes
peeping out of their shoes." The misery of the agricultural classes
was increased by the bad harvests of 1815 and 1816. Within a few
years half the population in many parishes was on the poor-rates.
In the factory towns thousands were thrown out of work, and even
for the employers, with markets fluctuating and uncertain, the strug-

[8] E. F. Henderson, *Short History of Germany* (New York, 1917), II, 326.

gle for survival was desperate. Banks and commercial companies went to the wall by the hundreds. At the same time taxes were very heavy because the state was burdened by a larger debt than ever before incurred by any nation. As a result of this maladjustment thousands in the towns and on the land were on the verge of utter destitution and the whole country was filled with discontent.

Unusual statesmanship was needed to meet these difficulties, but the government was directed by men who, though they had carried the country to final victory in the long struggle with France, had nothing in their training which fitted them to handle the widespread distress and discontent. In their view the successful conclusion of the wars had invested the whole existing social and political system with a halo of sanctity. They looked upon those who advocated any measure of reform as dangerous firebrands. In contrast with the governments of most of the continental states, that of England was without an adequate police force. The ministers, falling into clumsy methods of military repression, depended for information not on competent detectives but on the tales of private spies and on agents provocateurs. The larger towns were, for the most part, still dominated by little oligarchies, seldom public-spirited and often corrupt, while the country districts, and those that were country one year and town the next, were under the rule of squires whose idea of governing was merely to enforce the old laws in the old ways.

Like the civil administration, Parliament was in the hands of a closed caste which was at the time directed by the Tory party. The long danger of French invasion had enlisted on its behalf all the patriotic sentiment exploited by the Whigs in the days of Louis XV. George III had strengthened this Tory reaction by a policy of granting large numbers of peerages. As a result, the official Whig leaders had gone politically to sleep in their country seats, and their party had almost ceased to exist. After 1815 it suffered not only from numerical weakness, but also from internal disunion. The Grenvillite group seceded in 1818 and in 1822 joined the opposition. The few outspoken radicals in the party, like Admiral Cochrane and Sir Francis Burdett, indulged in such extravagant language that they only dragged the whole party into further disrepute. But for the energy of one Whig member, Henry Brougham, the opposition in Parliament would, for a time, almost have disappeared.[9] The Whigs, however, even if they had been in power, might have shown as little understanding of conditions as did the Tories, for in the unreformed Parliament, where both parties represented only the upper classes, neither side showed any fundamental disagreement with, or even any great dislike for, the other. Knowing that some day the turn of the political wheel would put them into office the "outs" usually guarded themselves in their attacks on abuses which sooner or later might benefit them. Until 1822 the most conservative wing of the Tory party dominated Parliament. The leading figures in the Cabinet, Liverpool, the prime minister, Castlereagh, the secretary for foreign affairs, and Eldon, the lord chancellor, had no program after 1815 except that of repressing all internal dissent. At the same time they implored the country to enjoy "the blessings of peace and order." This Tory domination was made possible not only by the success of the party in concluding the wars, but also by the great wave of popular discontent which swept through the lower classes of the nation and frightened the aristocracy and the bourgeoisie into accepting this policy of repression.[10]

As neither the Tories nor the Whigs showed any understanding of the social misery that was growing in the land, the agitation for reform fell into the hands of groups of radicals outside Parliament. These radicals had no common organization or program, though nearly all of them shared the idea that the road to improvement lay through a reform of Parliament. Before 1820 neither Bentham nor Owen, who had little interest in political reform, had found much of a following. Far more influential were individuals like Cobbett and groups like the Hampden Clubs. These organizations had been founded by Major Cartwright before the end of the wars. Their membership, though small, was widely distributed through the larger towns. Their program centered chiefly on the need of reforming the House of Commons where, as Cartwright had said, one found nothing but "idle schoolboys, insignificant coxcombs, toad-

[9] Cf. A. Aspinall, *Lord Brougham and the Whig Party* (Manchester, 1927).
[10] Cf. F. J. C. Hearnshaw, *Conservatism in England* (London, 1933).

eaters, gamblers, public plunderers and hirelings."[11] After 1816 the
dues of these societies were reduced to one penny a week, and their
program was broadened by the inclusion of a demand for universal
manhood suffrage. The local organizers of these radical groups,
which resembled the secret liberal societies in many continental
countries, borrowed the tactics used by the Methodists. There was
the same plan of local organization with trifling dues, the same
open-air meetings conducted in a highly emotional atmosphere, and
a similar paid service of itinerant preachers. During the years 1816
to 1819 most of the public gatherings that so outraged the authorities
were organized by members of these societies.

Even more influential in arousing public opinion were a number
of free-lance reformers, first among whom stood Cobbett, the greatest
of all English popular journalists. Cobbett's close first-hand knowledge of actual conditions among all layers of the population and his
deep sincerity gave point to his violent invective. In 1816 he began
to get out an edition of his *Political Register* for two pence, and so
for the first time in history put a newspaper within reach of the
lower classes. Farmer and mill-hand, in cottage and tenement, read
in its columns of the unfairness of the law courts, of the game laws,
and of the electoral system, of the abuses of taxation, and of the millions of pounds poured out by the state to the holders of sinecures;
the last-named abuses were the chief causes of popular discontent
in the period. Cobbett advised his readers, however, to stop using
violence and urged them to join the Hampden Clubs and to work
peaceably for the reform of Parliament. Although his economics
were often wild and his insight limited, of all the authors of the
movement that finally aroused the Whigs to action and later brought
about the Reform Bill of 1832, he was the most powerful. Henry
Hunt and Thistlewood stand out beside him as the two best known
agitators among the popular leaders of discontent. Hunt was a forceful mob-orator; Thistlewood, the chief figure in the Cato Street Conspiracy of 1820, was a violent demagogue.

By 1816 the full force of unemployment and high prices began to

[11] John Cartwright, *Legislative Rights of the Commonalty Vindicated* (London, 1777),
xii. Bentham's friend, Place, said of the same régime that it was "a perpetual cheat,
a fraudulent game of fictitious honors and real emoluments, a continual practice of
pompous meanness." J. H. Rose, *The Rise and Growth of Democracy in England* (New
York, 1898), 41.

be felt. An epidemic of violence and bread-rioting in the towns, of strikes in the mining districts, and of incendiarism in the country broke out all over England. The radicals tried to give this discontent a political program by holding public meetings. The indifference of the Tory ministry to the distress, combined with an unwillingness to differentiate between reasonable demands for parliamentary reform and mere mob-violence, was first shown at the time of a series of outdoor assemblies held at Spa Fields, near London, in the autumn of 1816. In one of these meetings Hunt, in a fiery speech, denounced the system which taxed bread, beer, clothing, and the other common necessities of life and which used the proceeds to pension "the fathers, brothers, mothers, sisters, cousins, and bastards of the borough-mongers."[12] Everything passed off peaceably, except for the looting of a few bakeshops in the evening. In December a second large meeting was addressed, before Hunt's arrival, by Spence, one of the most violent of all the radical agitators. A small group of men, after hearing the speech, rushed off, seized a gunsmith's shop, killed its proprietor, and paraded noisily through Cheapside. The outbreak was given wide publicity in the papers, and was used by the ministry to frighten the upper and middle classes.

These meetings and an attempt on the regent's life led to the appointment of secret parliamentary committees in 1817 to examine, not the causes of discontent, but the activities of the reform societies. The committees in their alarmist reports alleged that a traitorous conspiracy was under way, that it was proposed to seize the Bank of England and the Tower of London, to arouse the army to mutiny, and to effect a general Jacobin revolution. The evidence had been furnished chiefly by a disreputable informer named Castle whom the government was using also as an agent provocateur. As a result of its investigation, Parliament forbade all public meetings, suppressed all societies not licensed by government officials, and suspended the Habeas Corpus Act (until March 1, 1818). The country was swept with an hysterical fear; one magistrate refused to sanction a mineralogical society on the pretext that the study of such a subject led to atheism. The courts tried a number of rioters and supposed conspirators and instituted suits against offending

[12] London *Times*, November 16, 1816.

newspapers which, in some cases, resulted in heavy sentences and, in others, in dramatic acquittals. Public meetings ceased for a time and discontent was driven underground. Cobbett went to America, whence he began to write home of the glories of a republic with no established church or titles, no "long-sworded and whiskered captains . . . no hangings and rippings up," and "no Wilberforces, think of that! no Wilberforces!"[13]

The newspapers and the periodical press, however, continued to present a grave problem to the ministry. Great periodicals, like the Whig *Edinburgh Review,* and most of the sixteen London dailies, as well as the principal provincial papers, had such large incomes from advertising that they were beyond being bought by the government. The *Times,* an independent paper, the Whig *Morning Chronicle,* and even the Tory *Morning Post* were given to plain speaking, though they always seemed pale in comparison with Cobbett's *Political Register.* The press remained the only effective outlet for criticism of the existing régime.[14] Many editors and newspaper owners were haled into court for jury trial, but the state's case often failed because the prosecution labeled all criticism as treason. Since the penalty for treason was usually death, juries refused to convict. During all the discussion of discontent great stress had been laid by the government on the irreligious character of the radical propaganda and in 1818 Parliament presented its solution of this problem by granting a million pounds to build more churches.[15]

The repressive legislation of 1817, combined with the improvement in trade conditions and an abundant harvest, brought a lull in the agitation for reform. Nevertheless the election of 1818 returned thirty more Whigs to Parliament. This indicated that the governing classes were by no means as unanimous in their support of repression as the ministry imagined. A moderate opposition was growing both within the Tory ranks and among the Whigs. It was still very timid and its chief efforts were directed not toward the delicate problem

---

[13] G. H. D. Cole, *The Life of William Cobbett* (New York, 1925), 226.

[14] The use of the steam press after 1814 and of the cylinder press after 1827 greatly decreased the cost of publication. As the newspapers became big businesses, however, heavy investment in plant made them more cautious, and pamphlets and handbills did more than the press to bear the brunt of the fight against the government.

[15] This action was attacked in Bentham's *Church of England Catechism Examined,* in Byron's *Manfred,* Shelley's *Alastor* and *Revolt of Islam,* and in the pages of Leigh Hunt's *Examiner.*

of parliamentary reform but toward such questions as the reform of public finance and of criminal law. This new opposition was responsible for the passage of the first Factory Act in 1819 and for the resumption of specie payments, the latter step being largely due to the efforts of the young Peel and of the economist, Ricardo.

Another economic flurry in 1819 brought on a wave of unemployment and a revival of radical agitation. The ministry still continued its old policy of carrying on from day to day, repressing all opposition outside Parliament and piously hoping for things to get better of themselves. The economic depression of 1819 proved to be far less severe than that of 1815-1817, but the political crisis became more acute. During a series of strikes among the cotton workers in northern England, which continued for several months, a number of agitators began to organize groups of the dissatisfied, and to hold public meetings. Their language was often violent but their program called only for repeal of the Corn Laws and reform of parliamentary representation. On these points the manufacturers and the workers were in agreement, though the millowners, fearing violence, still played into the hands of the Tory ministry.

Some of the radical agitators formed a plan to hold mass meetings in the larger cities of the North and the Midlands at which unofficial representatives to Parliament were to be elected. An outdoor gathering, held at Birmingham in July, 1818, and attended by about 25,000, elected Sir Charles Wolseley "legislative attorney and representative" of the city. The government thereupon issued orders that no more such meetings should be held. But at Manchester the radicals had already decided to follow the example of Birmingham, and a public meeting had been called for the sixteenth of August. A number of the men who were to take part in it underwent some preliminary drill, in order that they might move on to the field with military regularity. Banners with various inscriptions were prepared to decorate the processions. The authorities, however, had been vigilant; troops had been moved to Manchester and special constables had been enrolled. The entire country was in a ferment of expectation.

On the appointed day about 60,000 men, women, and children had gathered in St. Peter's Fields when Henry Hunt rode up in a carriage. He mounted the speaker's stand; the vast multitude became silent. But he had hardly begun his address when a squadron of cavalry suddenly started to force its way toward the platform. The vast throng fell into a wild panic and began to rush away. In ten minutes the field was cleared; the ground was left strewn with the wounded, and with hats, shoes, walking sticks, and torn banners. Eleven people had been killed, and several hundred hurt. A howl of anger and disgust arose throughout the length and breadth of England. To make matters worse the regent and Lord Sidmouth, the home secretary, without waiting to make inquiries, sent their congratulations to the local authorities. For this victory of the government over their fellow citizens the radicals at once coined the name, the Battle of Peterloo. The memory of it long endured; as Carlyle said, "This is what the poor Manchester operatives, with all the darkness that was in them, did manage to perform. They put their huge, inarticulate question, 'What do you mean to do with us?'"[16]

In spite of protests from the Common Council of London and other highly placed bodies, the ministry was again able to play upon the fear of the upper classes. In November Parliament discussed and passed the Six Acts, the most repressive laws Great Britain had known for generations. In the long debates memories of the French Revolution cropped up repeatedly. Was the government, asked the ministers, to imitate the weakness of Louis XVI and his government and go along idly while the throne and the altar perished as they had in France? The Ultras in France and the reactionary statesmen in Germany, Spain, and Italy were all, at the time, using the same language. Of the Six Acts, the first forbade the practice of military exercises by unauthorized persons; the second provided for the speedy trial and drastic punishment of all offenders against public order; the third empowered the magistrates to issue warrants for the search of arms in private houses; the next authorized the seizure of seditious or blasphemous libels and the punishment of their authors; the fifth restricted public meetings to those called by government officials and prohibited all gatherings held to examine complaints against church and state; and the last subjected all publications below a certain size to the heavy stamp duty already levied on newspapers. All, except the third and fifth, were designed to be

[16] T. Carlyle, *Past and Present*, chap. III, Cf. F. O. Darvall, *Popular Disturbances and Public Disorder in Regency England* (Oxford, 1934).

permanent. Wellington wrote of the Six Acts to Pozzo di Borgo, November 25, 1819, "Our example will render some good in France as well as in Germany, and we must hope that the whole world will escape the universal revolution which seems to menace us all."[17]

Lord Grey and Lord Holland denounced the Six Acts in Parliament, the latter declaring that the laws already on the statute books were sufficient to prevent disorder, and that the new powers now given to the state were liable to serious abuse. Above all, he insisted that public meetings are "a vent, comparatively innocuous, of that discontent which if suppressed might seek refuge in conspiracies." Gradually the opposition was being forced to take a stand. A Whig motion in the House of Commons calling for an inquiry into the Peterloo affair secured a hundred fifty votes. The majority, however, still backed the ministry. It was little wonder that by 1819 thousands of Englishmen were deeply convinced that the governing classes were in league against their welfare.

III. THE RETURN TO BOURBON RULE IN FRANCE AND SPAIN

If an old and established government like that of England found peace as beset with difficulties as war, it is little wonder that the new régime in France faced still more perplexing problems. Lack of experience in handling a parliamentary government and the rancorous hatreds created by the revolution made continuity of policy nearly impossible. Indeed, the revolution had created such a fundamental cleavage in French society that until 1870 it proved impossible for any régime to maintain itself longer than two decades. The Restoration in France was inevitably an age of extremes. Ultramontanes and atheists, absolutists and democrats, men who had joined the camp of the émigrés at Coblenz and men who had sat in the Convention met in the Chambers and in society. Many of them seemed more ready to begin the revolution all over again than to try to live in peace.[18]

The sudden collapse of the Empire in 1814 found both the French and the allies still undecided as to who should succeed Napoleon.

[17] Wellington, *Dispatches, Correspondence and Memoranda* (London, 1867), I, 87.
[18] Cf. P. de La Gorce, *La Restauration, Louis XVIII* (Paris, 1926), a good introduction.

A small Bourbon faction in France was making spasmodic attempts to communicate with allied headquarters where, however, decision was for a long time delayed because of conflicting views. In the meantime Bordeaux declared for the old royal family. Largely on the insistence of Castlereagh and Talleyrand the allies finally agreed to accept the Comte de Provence as Louis XVIII. Soon, under the inspiration of the ever-ready Talleyrand, the Senate, the Municipal Council of Paris, and other official groups voted for the return of the Bourbons as the best guarantee of peace. In the midst of the general distress and discouragement in France, the allies sent Napoleon to Elba and Louis returned from England.[19]

At once everyone began to wonder what the new king would do. The French people showed little enthusiasm for these forgotten Bourbons, whose very names the press of the Empire had been forbidden to mention. Before the new monarch arrived, his brother, the Comte d'Artois, and a group of returning *émigrés* were trying to get control of the situation. Fully realizing the danger of their counter-revolutionary designs and desiring to curb their ardor, as well as to satisfy the tsar, Louis XVIII issued a proclamation shortly after landing in France. In it he promised not to disturb anyone for his opinions, and agreed to grant a constitution. This charter, he promised, would assure the payment of the public debt, freedom of the press and of religion, equality before the law, and would guarantee full property rights to those who had purchased national lands during the revolution. This Déclaration de Saint-Ouen seems to have had a reassuring effect on everyone, except the circle of the Comte d'Artois.

The new monarch entered Paris in May, 1814, and took up his residence at the Tuileries, where the servants busied themselves sewing the royal coat of arms on the carpets and chairs over the tops of the Napoleonic eagles. After a few days of deliberation the Constitutional Charter was drawn up by a committee of former ministers, senators, and deputies of the Empire. The document, which, according to the secretary, was thrown together like the text of a comic opera, embodied the promises made in the Déclaration de Saint-Ouen. It guaranteed the land settlement of the revolution, and the

[19] Cf. E. J. Knapton, "Some Aspects of the Bourbon Restoration of 1814," *Journal of Modern History*, 1934.

continuance of Napoleon's autocratic system of local administration, his codes, his Legion of Honor, and his educational system. For the central government it established a parliamentary order similar to that of England, a régime which, as time showed, fitted ill with the highly centralized and authoritarian administrative system of the empire. The monarch was to share the direction of the government with a Chamber of Peers nominated by himself, and with a Chamber of Deputies elected for five years on a very restricted franchise. The document was vague and contradictory on important points, above all on the matters of ministerial responsibility, control of the press, the method of holding elections, and the right of the king to issue ordinances. The preamble, quite in the spirit of the Ancien Régime, announced that the Charter was the monarch's gift to France, while the document itself was dated "in the nineteenth year of our reign." Only usage and experience could reveal what the Charter would mean. The mass of the population was apathetic toward these changes. The French, like the other peoples of Europe, seemed to be willing to accept anything that would assure a return of peace.[20]

During the first Restoration (1814-15) the only active and organized party in France was that of the ultra-royalists, commonly known as the Ultras, headed by the Comte d'Artois. He established himself in the Pavillon de Marsan in the Tuileries, and his circle at once became a kind of invisible government. Artois prided himself on being surrounded by men who had never served any of the revolutionary governments and who, out of devotion to their monarch, had stayed out of France or had lived in seclusion for a quarter of a century. The Ultras wished to turn over the whole Napoleonic administrative machine to men of ardent royalist connections (the two Napoleonic institutions they approved of were the police and the prefects), to return to the émigrés all property that had not been sold, to indemnify the others, to subject the press to a severe censorship, and to abolish the Napoleonic Université de France.

In 1814 and 1815, Ultra agents went about the provinces securing support for their program from the municipal councils. The exaggerated statements made by these extremists and by some of the

[20] Cf. P. Simon, *L'élaboration de la charte* (Paris, 1906).

higher clergy, especially their extravagant threats that the government might take back the clerical and noble lands sold during the revolution, aroused the peasants and brought serious discredit on the new régime even before it was under way. Other ill-timed acts on the part of the government itself aggravated the situation. To save money the army was greatly reduced, and many Napoleonic officers were put on half-pay. These disgruntled soldiers were soon scattered all over France, sowing hatred against the Bourbons. In Paris the allied agents, the Duke of Wellington and Pozzo di Borgo, were meddling in French affairs. Louis XVIII and the new order seemed nowhere to find friends.

When Napoleon returned from Elba in March, 1815, he was accepted by the army as preferable to the Bourbons. In nearly every town, as he moved northward toward Paris, he was greeted with tales of the popular dread of a restoration of the Ancien Régime, and with bitter denunciations of the priests. Louis XVIII fled to Lille and then to Ghent and Napoleon easily reëstablished himself. But he soon discovered that he could not hope to remain in power unless his government were liberalized. He was under the ban so far as the allied powers were concerned and in France he faced the hatred of the clergy and of many of the nobility and the apathy and fear of the middle classes. He could only hope to hold his position by again rousing the old revolutionary ardor of the masses. Forced to act quickly he called in Benjamin Constant to prepare, in imitation of the Bourbon Charter, an "Additional Act to the Constitutions of the Empire." The document, the sixth constitution France had known since 1789, provided for a responsible ministry, jury trial, and freedom of the press. This makeshift was presented to the French people through a plebiscite in which only a million and a half bothered to vote. France was evidently weary of constitutions, and uncertain, too, of the desirability of this latest régime. Napoleon's destiny, however, did not depend on what the French thought of him for he was soon overwhelmingly defeated by the allied powers and forced to abdicate.[21]

Louis XVIII returned in July, 1815, to a situation of great complexity and uncertainty, but at once he showed his renewed de-

[21] Cf. H. Houssaye, *1815* (new ed., 3 vols., Paris, 1912) and E. Le Gallo, *Les cent jours* (Paris, 1923).

termination to maintain a régime that would "heal the wounds of the revolution." His enemies, especially the Bonapartists, made fun of this gouty old gentleman who had arrived "in the baggage of the allies." But Louis proved to have unexpected judgment and courage. Rich in the patience acquired in weary years of exile, he showed a surprising willingness to make concessions and even to use men like Talleyrand and Fouché whom he personally despised. Yet despite all his efforts a White Terror broke out in the provinces. Because of the ease with which Napoleon had returned to power, the Ultras were able to convince many people that a great plot was on foot to overthrow the newly established government.

The whole country was in a state of hysteria. At Orleans, a mob burned a large portrait of Napoleon in one of the principal squares, and then took bayonets and smashed a bust of him. A group of infuriated royalists at Carcassonne butchered a live eagle caught in the mountains. Mobs in the Vendée and in the south of France murdered men who had been prominent in the revolution, and the local authorities did not venture to intervene. Not content with butchering their victims, the royalists went further and insulted the corpses. Marshal Brune, a brave Napoleonic officer, was struck down at Avignon; at his burial the coffin was broken open and his body tossed about and cast into the Rhone. The king, in order to mollify the Ultras, ordered the trial of a number of the officers who in 1815 had gone over to Napoleon. Apparently he hoped that some of the more prominent ones would escape. When an industrious prefect captured Ney in the provinces, Louis exclaimed, "This is a piece of stupidity that will cost us dearly." Brought back to Paris, Ney was tried by the Chamber of Peers, declared guilty of treason and shot. A number of other Napoleonic officials were imprisoned and executed by the government.

In the midst of this wave of royalist reaction, the first elections for the new Chamber of Deputies were held. The nobility and the upper middle class, the only groups which had the right to vote, were so anxious for peace that they returned a majority of Ultras. In a moment of amiable enthusiasm Louis XVIII called it the *Chambre Introuvable,* an expression he must have regretted later. The first result of the election was the resignation of the provisional

Talleyrand-Fouché ministry and the formation of a cabinet of moderate Royalists under the Duc de Richelieu (1815-1818). Included in it were the Duc Decazes, a personal favorite of Louis XVIII, and a group of men who backed the monarch's program of trying to steer a middle course between reaction and revolution.

The new ministry soon found itself blocked by the Ultra majority in the Chamber of Deputies. The Ultras hated Louis XVIII, whom they dubbed the "crowned Jacobin" and "King Voltaire." They set about embarrassing him and his ministers in every way possible. The more intransigent Ultras proposed to abolish the Université de France and demanded an immediate restitution of the *biens nationaux*. They did succeed in abolishing divorce, in banishing a number of men prominent in the imperial régime, in muzzling the press (few sessions of the Chambers during the Restoration passed without some changes in the press-laws and the electoral system), and finally in passing a law setting up special courts to try persons suspected of treason. These *Cours Prévôtales* soon became notorious for their high-handed methods, which seriously interfered with the king's policy of conciliation. Suspected persons were arrested and held for weeks without trial; semi-military methods of procedure were used, and fines and terms of imprisonment were imposed in wholesale fashion. Some of the worst judicial abuses took place in Grenoble, where an outbreak in the garrison was brutally put down.

All over the country business was disorganized as a result of the sudden end of the wars, but the declaration of Baron Louis, the minister of finance, that the new government would recognize the debts of the Empire, held out the hope of better conditions. But during the years 1816 and 1817 the economic situation was very bad, both in the towns and in the country districts. The harvests were as meager in France as elsewhere in Europe. The food required by the 150,000 men in the allied army of occupation forced up prices in the eastern departments even above those in the rest of France. In some districts the population was starving. In the midst of this growing distress and uncertainty, the behavior of the *Chambre Introuvable* only aggravated the situation. On the advice of the allied powers, who feared that its Ultra policy might provoke a revolution, Louis XVIII dissolved it by royal decree in September, 1816.

The next four years, from 1816 to 1820, were, from the political angle, the calmest of the Restoration. New elections returned a Chamber of Deputies of a more conciliatory stripe, and in both chambers the king and Richelieu had the backing of a majority of moderate royalists. What were to become the great political parties of modern France were just beginning to gather their forces, though as yet no regular party organizations had come into existence. At the extreme right of both houses sat the Ultras, while at the extreme left were a number of determined liberals. Both these groups disliked the Charter and would have been glad to modify or abolish it, but the Ultra opposition was, before 1820, the more effective. Its members employed nearly any means to discredit the king and the ministry. In the sessions of the *Chambre Introuvable* they had defended the Charter against the king, insisting that its terms required the monarch to choose his ministers from the leading parliamentary group (the Ultras). Then, hoping that the peasants would show a greater enthusiasm for their program than did the upper middle class, the Ultras in 1816 demanded a wide extension of the suffrage. The Liberals jeered at these champions of divine right who were now mouthing the phrases of British Whiggism. As one wit put it, the Ultras were "entering into the spirit of the Charter as the Greeks entered the Trojan horse." After 1816 the Ultras of the Right and the Liberals of the Left on occasion joined hands to embarrass the Center and the ministry, for, as the Ultra journal, the *Drapeau Blanc*, said, "Better a Jacobin than a Ministerialist!"[22]

The combination of the Ultra Right and the Liberal Left was not yet strong enough to prevent coöperation between the king, the ministry and the Center. In 1817 the ministry carried through the Chambers a new electoral law extending the vote to 88,000 (out of a population of thirty millions), and a law providing for a renewal each year of a fifth of the membership of the lower house. It also carried through a reorganization of the army along more democratic lines, and, by paying off the indemnity to the Allies, obtained the liberation of the occupied territory. The arrangement for the payment of the indemnity of seven hundred million francs and the

[22] Cf. J. Barthélemy, *L'introduction du régime parlementaire sous Louis XVIII, et Charles X* (Paris, 1904), and F. B. Artz, "Les débuts des partis modernes en France, 1815-1830," *Revue d'histoire moderne*, 1931.

reception of France into the Quintuple Alliance at the Congress of
Aix-la-Chapelle were largely the work of Richelieu. The Ultras
pushed their plan to discredit him even to the point of urging the
allied powers to continue the military occupation of France. This
action, together with a disagreement with the king on electoral
policy, led Richelieu to resign in 1818; Louis XVIII then reformed
the ministry under Dessoles and his favorite, Decazes. A more
liberal press law was passed in 1819, and the new electoral law
brought into the Chamber of Deputies a number of more outspoken
Liberals, like the Abbé Grégoire, some of whose sayings, as "Kings
are in the moral order what monsters are in the physical," had made
his name widely known throughout France.

The sessions of the Chambers in 1818 and 1819 grew steadily
more acrimonious. Embittered Ultras, like La Bourdonnaye, and
Liberal firebrands, like Manuel and Foy, rose on the slightest pretext to refight the battles of the revolution. Even Constant, who
believed in the Restoration compromise, was now veering to the
Left. At no time in modern France have fundamental principles
of government been so thoroughly debated as in these legislative
sessions of the Restoration. The deeper implications of the debates
were most effectively embodied in the lofty discourses of the moderate royalist, Royer-Collard. Through all the discussions ran a
conflict as to whether the social, educational, and administrative
settlement of the revolution should be continued and broadened,
or narrowed, or even destroyed. The debates in the lower house
were printed in the official *Moniteur* and commented on in the
ultra-royalist *Quotidienne* and *Drapeau Blanc*, in the more moderate *Journal des Débats*, and in the liberal *Constitutionnel*, which for
a time had the largest circulation of any newspaper in Europe.
Although newspapers were relatively expensive, the reading public
in shop, café, and at the fireside followed the parliamentary war
with lively interest. This world of newspapers and politics offered,
comparatively speaking, a new experience for the French people
who now, for the first time, were making an extended experiment
in representative government. In this lies the great importance of
the Restoration in the political history of modern France. By 1819
the return of prosperity and the conciliatory attitude of the king

were gradually winning the trading classes and the peasants to the support of the new régime.

While Louis XVIII was showing such remarkable shrewdness in reëstablishing the Bourbon monarchy in France, his cousin, Ferdinand VII, was rapidly driving Spain toward revolution. The Spanish monarch reëntered his kingdom in March, 1814. The enthusiasm of the mass of the Spanish people who had been fighting for years for his return greeted him at the frontier: everywhere he was acclaimed as the "well-beloved" and the "long wished-for." This soon convinced him that, during the long struggle with Napoleon, he had become the living symbol of the national ideal, and that now he could have a free hand in settling his accounts with the handful of liberals. In 1814 it would not have been possible to convince the masses that he had fawned on his jailer, Napoleon, and that he had even congratulated Joseph Bonaparte on his accession to the throne of Spain. On the tenth of May, soon after he reached Madrid, prominent liberals in the city were arrested, and hurried off to prison amidst the jeers of a mob that yelled, "Long live the absolute king, long live the Inquisition, down with the Freemasons!" The next morning the city was placarded with a royal proclamation dissolving the Cortes and announcing, "Not only do I refuse to swear to observe the Constitution [of 1812], or to recognize any decrees of the Cortes, but I declare Constitution and decrees alike null and void, today and forever."[23]

Ferdinand then proceeded to reëstablish the Inquisition, to return the ecclesiastical and feudal property that had changed hands since 1808, and to restore the seigniorial rights and jurisdictions of the nobles in twenty-five thousand villages in Spain. For this he received the enthusiastic support of most of the aristocracy and the clergy. Foreign books and newspapers were seized at the frontiers, while in Spain itself the government permitted the publication of only two newspapers. An English traveler in Spain said of these newspapers, and much the same could have been said of the press in the Austrian Empire and in the Italian states, that they contained nothing but reports of the weather and "accounts of miracles wrought by different Virgins, lives of holy friars and sainted nuns,

[23] H. B. Clarke, *Modern Spain* (Cambridge, 1906), 33.

romances of marvelous conversions, libels against Jews, heretics, and Freemasons, and histories of apparitions."[24]

In making all these changes, Ferdinand was not only restoring the pre-revolutionary power of the monarchy, the nobility, and the church; he was going back to an even older system of governing that nullified all the reforms of the eighteenth century. After 1814 he ruled partly through a group of ministers and partly through a court camarilla, one member of which had formerly been a water-carrier and another a porter. He played one group against another; he allowed no one to remain for long either in the ministry or in the palace clique, and dismissal was usually accompanied by exile or imprisonment. Between 1820 and 1830 he had thirty ministers. The Duke of Wellington protested against these policies, and Louis XVIII, in refusing the proffered help of a Spanish regiment after Napoleon's escape from Elba, showed his disgust with Ferdinand's behavior.

This scandalous régime, which the young American scholar, George Ticknor, characterized as a "confusion of abuses," did nothing to relieve the economic distress of the exhausted and poverty-stricken people which had fought so bravely against the French invaders. All the public services were neglected, commerce and industry were ruined, the treasury was bankrupt, and the army and navy went unpaid and underfed. Seville, Cadiz, and the other commercial cities were full of merchants ruined by the long wars and by the revolt of the Spanish colonies in the New World. As a result, the upper middle class grew increasingly restless, and the liberal party which had framed the Constitution of 1812, though it represented only a small minority of the population, began to reorganize its forces and to conspire against the government. Discontent spread in the army, whose officers had been brought into contact with French liberal ideas during the wars, and in the larger ports, where the economic depression was worst. The rapid growth of secret societies and the increase in membership of the Masonic lodges, as well as a series of small outbreaks between 1815 and 1817,

[24] J. Bowring, *Observations on the State of Religion and Literature in Spain* (London, 1820), 8.

showed that the restored monarchy was resting on the weakest of foundations.

IV. THE HAPSBURG DOMINATION IN MIDDLE EUROPE: THE AUSTRIAN EMPIRE AND THE GERMANIC CONFEDERATION

From the Baltic to Sicily the destinies of Middle Europe were in the control of the Hapsburgs. Throughout all these lands the fall of Napoleon had been welcomed with enthusiasm; on the return of peace the mass of the population in every state settled back into acceptance of the existing order. To them the governments did not seem despotic; they had no sense of oppression, such as the British and to some extent the French people would have felt had they been living under Hapsburg rule. The censorship of the press and the arrest of a few students or conspirators passed unnoticed among the rank and file. But among small groups of students and army officers, among members of the lesser nobility and the commercial classes there was dissatisfaction and conspiracy.

Although the discontented elements differed in their projects of reform, all were agreed in their hatred of Metternich. Through the next decades they developed such a portrait of him as a tyrant and even a monster that it has now become difficult to estimate him with any degree of fairness. It has already been pointed out that Metternich's whole policy was centered in his devotion to the imperial house he served, and that out of its needs he elaborated a general European program of conservatism. In the delicately balanced Hapsburg system, the German, Italian, Slav, and Magyar lands were all geared into the central dynastic wheel in such a way that the introduction of democratic institutions or the recognition of national entities anywhere could easily upset the Hapsburg machine everywhere. The task of holding together such a federated empire, made up of half the races and religions of Europe, presented problems of administration practically unknown in London or Paris. Metternich was by aptitude and training a diplomat rather than an administrator, and after 1815 he was inclined to rely too exclusively on diplomacy for the support of the existing system. Whatever one may think of him, however, he was not a mere fanatic of order; indeed, this eighteenth-century gentleman, who to the end of his life loved to read Voltaire, was not a fanatic of anything. His failure, in the long run, lay in the fact that he could think of no way of preserving what was except by preserving it as it was.

The internal condition of the Austrian Empire, which lay at the center of the Hapsburg domains, had been little affected by the Napoleonic wars; the population accepted the government's censorship and its paternal rule. The provinces of Austria, as well as the outlying sections of the empire inhabited by Czechs, Slovaks, Magyars, Rumanians, and Croats, had local diets which were constituted in the medieval fashion of estates. They met rarely and for brief sessions; that of Hungary had no meeting from 1812 to 1825. They possessed no real power.[25] Throughout the empire there was practically no middle class, only nobles and peasants. The strongest parts of the government machine were the police and the army. The administration carefully distributed the latter; Hungarian regiments garrisoned Lombardy and Venetia, German soldiers were sent to Bohemia, and Croats defended Hungary. The central administration at Vienna, in striking contrast to that at Berlin, was not coördinated. There was no regularly organized ministry; each department went its own way or rusted in its groove. Metternich tried to improve this administrative chaos, but failed to make way against old privileges and vested interests.

In the German world outside Austria the princes drifted back into an eighteenth-century way of living. Heine effectively characterized the little German despotisms of the time: "When I was at the top of the St. Gotthard Pass, I heard Germany snoring. . . . She slept peacefully under the protection of her thirty-six monarchs. In those days, crowns sat firmly on the princes' heads, and at night they just drew their night caps over them, while the people slept peacefully at their feet." The thirty-nine German states, following the arrangements made at Vienna, were now united into a federated *Bund* under the presidency of Austria, though only a part of the Austrian Empire and a section of Prussia were included. In the Assembly of the Confederation the King of England was represented for Hanover, the King of Denmark for Holstein, and the

25 The Emperor Francis said of them, "I have my estates, and if they go too far I snap my fingers at them and send them home."

King of Holland for Luxemburg. The loosely organized *Bund*, together with the great personal prestige enjoyed by Metternich, especially in Berlin, enabled the Hapsburgs to dominate the Germanies more effectively than at any time since the Thirty Years' War. In 1816 the representatives of the princes met for the first time in a Diet at Frankfort. It soon became evident that this aristocratic body, directed from Vienna and helpless without a real executive, an army, or a system of local administration, was not the unifying and democratic assembly of which German patriots had dreamed during the War of Liberation. Small groups of liberals and nationalists were not slow in starting agitation against the whole arrangement. Decade by decade their clamor increased. In 1847 Prince Hohenlohe called the Diet "the bed in which Germany has slumbered for thirty years." Earlier Görres had said that the *Bund* gave the German people "an unlimited right of expectation."[26]

Within the various German states the promises of constitutions, made in the heart of the last conflict with Napoleon and embodied in Article XIII of the Federal Act, were only in part fulfilled. The Grand Duke of Saxe-Weimar was the first to grant a written constitution, and between 1818 and 1820 the rulers of Bavaria, Württemberg, Baden, and Hesse-Darmstadt took similar action. This was done in part to show their defiance of Austria and in part to get more enthusiastic support from the new districts added to their states by the Congress of Vienna. These constitutions, like the French Charter, were all royal grants; none recognized the sovereignty of the people. The suffrage was limited to a small group of wealthy landowners, and the administrative bureaucracy, as in France, often interfered in the elections.

All over the German world the liberals were waiting to see what Prussia would do. In May, 1815, Frederick William III had promised his people a constitution, but month after month passed and no such document was forthcoming. Behind the scenes in the royal court at Berlin a bitter quarrel was raging between Hardenberg, who had originally urged the monarch to grant a constitution, and an absolutist group led by Prince Wittgenstein, the agent of Metternich. Finally, in 1817, the Prussian monarch announced the creation of a Council of State, and it became evident that the project of a constitution had, for the time being, been abandoned. No action was taken toward the establishment of a central parliamentary order until 1823. Great was the disappointment of the German liberals and nationalists who, having hoped that Prussia would take the lead, now looked to the south and central German states, rather than to Austria or Prussia, as the home of liberty and progress.

But Prussia was compensated for her loss of prestige in other ways. The Council of State, made up of princes of the royal house, heads of the army, departmental chiefs, and nobles from the various provinces, brought the scattered districts of Prussia under one central administration. With the help of a university-trained bureaucracy, which was just coming into use, the government in some measure redeemed a reactionary policy by developing the best administrative efficiency in Europe. Modern Prussia has been made not by legislators, but by the honest and capable administration of bureaucrats and soldiers. Public finance, the army, the educational system and, after 1818, the tariff régime were greatly improved. Between 1815 and 1866 the extension and improvement of the civil and military administration of Prussia did far more for German unification than did any other force.

A cartoon of the time of the War of Liberation showed the German people dragging their frightened princes out from under the table, setting them on their feet, and urging them to fight the usurper. Now the liberals complained that, although it was the German people who had defeated Napoleon, it was only these same cowardly princes who were profiting by the peace settlement. The universities became the chief centers of this discontent. Students returning from the wars in 1815 began to organize societies, *Burschenschaften*, to improve student morality, to break down the older types of local patriotism, and to stir the youth of the land with nationalist ideals. The leaders of the movement corresponded with each other and created a loose central organization for these societies, which by 1816 had members in sixteen German universities.

The most active of these student groups was at Jena, where the indulgence of the Grand Duke of Saxe-Weimar allowed the members to discuss and to publish freely, and to parade with their picturesque "Teutonic costumes" and their black, red and gold banners, the colors of a volunteer corps of the War of 1813. The Jena society in 1817 arranged a gathering of all the *Burschenschaften* at the Wartburg Castle, to celebrate the fourth anniversary of the Battle of Leipzig and the tercentenary of Luther's *Theses*. On October 17 about four hundred students from twelve universities assembled. Luther's "Ein' feste Burg" was sung, speeches were made by professors from Jena and by a number of students, Luther and Blücher were praised, and the students were urged, in very general terms, to dedicate their lives to the "holy cause of union and freedom." In the evening one group formed a torchlight procession and marched to a hilltop opposite the castle. There, about a great bonfire, more speeches were made and several books, among them Kotzebue's *German History*, a pamphlet by Schmalz, Haller's treatise, and the *Code Napoléon*, together with a corporal's cane, a wig and other symbols of tyranny were thrown into the flames. It was all a rather juvenile escapade, but the effect produced on the German world was great, for it was the first public protest against the settlement of 1815.[27]

The *Burschenschaft* at the University of Giessen contained a small group of republicans led by Karl Follen, a brilliant student of law. He preached a mystical doctrine of republicanism and tyrannicide and even talked of assembling a mob on the battlefield of Leipzig and proclaiming a republic. In March, 1819, Karl Sand, a young and mentally unbalanced theological student and a follower of Follen, murdered the dramatist, Kotzebue, an agent of Alexander I of Russia. Shortly afterward a student in Nassau made an attack on the head of the government there. During his trial, Sand maintained that he had had no accomplices and that he had carried through his deed unaided. In spite of all efforts of the prosecution, no evidences of a general plot could be discovered. Sand was con-

[27] Cf. W. Oncken, *The Wartburg* (Berlin, 1907), chap. ix, and H. Kühn, *Das Wartburgfest* (Weimar, 1913).

demned to death. At the execution some of the spectators dipped their handkerchiefs in the assassin's blood, and carried them away as relics.[28]

Metternich made capital of all this, and used the occasion to tighten his grip on the German states, especially on Prussia. The year before, at the Congress of Aix-la-Chapelle, he had found an opportunity to impress on the Prussian king, as well as on the tsar, the threat of revolution that hung over Europe. After the murder of Kotzebue, he called together representatives of the nine principal German states. They met at Carlsbad in August, 1819. While the British Parliament was considering the Six Acts, the German diplomats drew up a series of decrees. These were presented to the Diet at Frankfort on September 20 and this body, which had dragged out discussion of the Federal Act for more than four years, now ratified Metternich's Carlsbad Decrees in less than four hours.[29] The decrees provided that the *Burschenschaften* and the gymnastic societies established by Jahn be dissolved, and that inspectors for each university and censors for the press be appointed, both of which provisions strengthened the power of the secret police. At a conference of representatives of some of the German princes held at Vienna in 1820 a so-called Final Act was agreed upon. The resistance of the governments of Bavaria and Württemberg to the growing power of Metternich made it impossible to force them to withdraw their constitutions. Nevertheless, Metternich now obtained from all the governments an agreement limiting the subjects which might be discussed in the Chambers. All the delegates recognized the right of the federal organs to intervene in any state where the legislature dared to assert its supremacy over the monarch.

The conference at Carlsbad in 1819 had created a Federal Commission at Mainz to study the discontent in the Germanies and to keep the governments informed. This commission continued to

28 There is a good study of Follen and the *Burschenschaft* movement in G. W. Spindler, *Follen* (Chicago, 1917).

29 This method of getting action by calling together representatives of the principal states had not been provided for in the Federal Act, and it represented a constitutional change in the Confederation which had important effects later on. Metternich was here applying to the German problem the same method he was using in Europe; i.e., government by diplomatic conference.

function for nearly eight years, and, though it was never able to discover any organized plot, it instituted proceedings against 161 individuals of whom forty-four were acquitted. Metternich was convinced that the secret societies all over Europe, and especially those in Germany and Italy, had an effective central organization in each country as well as an international bureau. Neither assumption has ever been proved. A few radicals, above all an Italian exile, Buonarroti, who lived in Geneva, dreamed of such an international liberal organization. They corresponded and conspired to further the idea, but without any important results.

At the conferences called at Austria's behest between 1817 and 1820, Metternich succeeded in frightening the tsar, the King of Prussia, and the monarchs of most of the German states. After 1819 the persecution of liberals increased. In Prussia, Jahn was imprisoned, Arndt lost his position at the University of Bonn, and Görres fled to Strasbourg. Spies were sent to hear the sermons of Schleiermacher, Stein was watched by the police, and Börne was forced to flee from Hesse-Darmstadt. By 1820 it was clear to German liberals that both Austria and Prussia, the two states which could force through a program of German unification, were hostile to liberty. The great hopes raised by the War of Liberation were not to be realized easily.

V. THE HAPSBURG DOMINATION IN MIDDLE EUROPE: THE ITALIAN STATES

Much the same situation existed in Italy as among the German states. There was a similar apathy and indifference on the part of the masses and the same disappointment and restlessness in higher circles of the population. But discontent was more widespread than in Germany. Italy had suffered less and gained more from the changes made by the French Revolution than either Spain or Germany. For nearly two decades the Italians had had excellent codes of law, a fair system of taxation, a better economic situation, and more religious and intellectual toleration than they had known for centuries. At the same time, the populace had been surprised to see how easily the temporal power of the pope could be abolished and their monarchs driven into exile. Everywhere old physical, economic, and intellectual barriers had been thrown down and the Italians had begun to be aware of a common nationality.[30]

The last years of the Empire, with the theft of art works, the Continental Blockade, the heavy taxes, and the conscription, had made Napoleon's imperial rule as hated in Italy as it was elsewhere. Hence his overthrow was widely acclaimed. When it became evident, however, that Austria would use all her powers to restore the Ancien Régime, Italian liberals at once protested. The peace settlement was made at Vienna without any consideration whatever for Italian hopes. It doomed Italy to remain, until 1860, the mere "geographical expression" of Metternich.[31] Over the whole peninsula lay the shadow of Hapsburg domination. Austria's influence in Italian affairs had grown steadily through the eighteenth century, and the settlement of 1815 simply completed the process. Austria ensured her control by her dynastic connections with the reigning Italian families,[32] by a treaty with Naples and another with Tuscany, and by the use of the secret police of all the Italian states who were obliged to report to the Austrian authorities. As the system worked out, the secret police of the various states, coöperating with that of Austria, functioned as a sort of Hapsburg administrative system from one end of the peninsula to the other. This political police aroused a profound abhorrence among the Italians. The irritation created was precisely of the kind which the patriots could most effectively use. The dark machinations of the political spy could be set off most effectively against the life of the shining young patriot-hero who was caught in the subtle toils of the police and was delivered over to a martyr's fate of prison, exile, or death.

In the individual states, the governments set up by the returning rulers combined the worst features of the old order and of the French rule, the obscurantism of the former, and the political police

[30] The two most useful studies of the Italian situation are A. Luzio, *La massoneria e il risorgimento italiano* (2 vols., Bologna, 1925) and K. R. Greenfield, *Economics and Liberalism in the Risorgimento, 1814-48* (Baltimore, 1934).

[31] Napoleon from St. Helena judged the situation with more shrewdness than Metternich. "Italy is surrounded by the Alps and the sea; and, isolated between her natural limits, she is destined to form a great and powerful nation. Rome will be chosen as the capital." Contessa Martinengo-Cesaresco, *The Liberation of Italy* (London, 1895), 3.

[32] The wife of the King of Piedmont was the cousin of the Austrian Emperor, as was also the Duke of Modena. The Duke of Tuscany was his brother, Marie Louise of Parma his daughter, and the Queen of Naples his aunt.

and the foreign control of the latter. Some French institutions were abolished; those that remained lost their effectiveness because of the policies of the restored rulers. In the south, including three-eighths of the peninsula, was the Kingdom of the Two Sicilies. The monarch, Ferdinand I, an ignorant reactionary like his nephew, the King of Spain, was bound by a secret treaty with Austria not to introduce liberal reforms. At Metternich's bidding he abolished the Constitution which, in 1812, the British had helped introduce in Sicily, and which Ferdinand had promised to observe. He restored many of the monastic lands, invited in the Jesuits, and reconstituted the Holy Office. His chief minister, Canosa, summed up the royal theory of government when he remarked that "the first servant of the crown should be the executioner." The police, though unable to curb the worst brigandage in western Europe, committed such atrocities on liberals that the representatives of England and Russia protested. The lower elements of the population were miserably poor and sunk in superstition, laziness, and filth. They remained strongly royalist and clerical and after 1815 were frequently used by the government against the middle class liberals.

In the Papal States conditions were not much better. Consalvi, who had served the papacy so well at Vienna, tried to introduce reforms in local administration, but he could make no headway against the Zelanti, the reactionary party at the papal court. So he turned his efforts to furthering the European interests of the Holy See. All the innovations introduced by the French, from law courts to vaccination, were abolished, priests filled all the public offices, and "the images of the Madonna again began to roll their eyes." Brigandage was nearly as bad as in the Kingdom of the Two Sicilies. The police spent much time in hunting down "a class called thinkers." At times there were in Rome, besides many political prisoners, as many as three thousand suspects confined to their houses between sundown and sunrise. The general administration of the Papal States was so wretched that in 1821 the powers issued a common note of complaint against the abuses. Characterizing the situation with much foresight, the Piedmontese ambassador wrote, "It is only reasonable to suppose that, if the present state of things continues in Rome, some fundamental crisis will take place. The most probable outcome is that the great city will become merely an ecclesiastical capital, retaining only the shadow of imperial power."[33]

In the rest of the Italian states a fairly honest administration was combined with political tyranny and repression. The ablest monarch among the rulers of the four duchies, Modena, Parma, Tuscany, and Lucca, was Francis IV of Modena. He was a treacherous and ambitious man, who was regarded by the liberals as a sort of Cesare Borgia. After his restoration he spent his best energies intriguing to gain more power in the peninsula. Although he was generous in his treatment of the poor, he feared and persecuted the middle class. In Tuscany, the Hapsburg Archduke Ferdinand III and his chief minister, Fossombroni—whose dictum was "Tomorrow, tomorrow—dinner will spoil, the state will wait"—returned to the political methods of eighteenth-century despotism. The government gave shelter to refugees from the Romagna and Naples; it permitted the publication after 1820 of the *Antologia,* a liberal literary review; and allowed the Florentines to send help to the Greek insurgents. Florence was the only Italian city where the dramas of Alfieri and Niccolini could be played. Still, the archduke's government irritated the people by maintaining an elaborate system of spies, and amused them when, on the discovery of Giotto's portrait of Dante beneath the whitewash on the walls of the Bargello, it had the colors altered lest they suggest the revolutionary tricolor. Commerce and manufacture flourished under a laissez-faire régime, and the easy-going Tuscans seem to have been reasonably contented.

In the Kingdom of Piedmont Victor Emmanuel I and his staff returned to Turin wearing powdered wigs, and the monarch soon instituted a general clearing-out of much that the French had introduced. As in Lombardy and Tuscany, the Jesuits were excluded, and the secular clergy were controlled by the state. In a certain old-fashioned honesty and efficiency of administration, and in the attention paid to the army, the Kingdom of Piedmont resembled Prussia. Yet the young Cavour, living in Turin, a "city half-barracks and half-cloister," found his native land "an intellectual hell." Economically the country prospered, profiting especially from the annexation in 1815 of the great port of Genoa.

[33] *Cambridge Modern History,* X, 109.

The richest and the best administered section in all Italy was the Lombard-Venetian Kingdom, a territory which conferred on its possessor the strategic keys to the peninsula, the four great fortresses of Mantua, Verona, Peschiera, and Legnago, known as the Quadrilateral. In spite of some traces of local self-government, the two provinces were ruled directly from Vienna. The Austrian government built excellent roads and bridges and introduced the best system of state education that existed anywhere in Italy. These advantages, however, could not hide the fact that the Hapsburg rule, in matters of policing, taxation, and tariff policy treated the provinces like conquered territories. The censorship was so severe that even the works of Dante had to be expurgated. Metternich reminded the inhabitants that "the Lombards must forget that they are Italians." Milan had the most cultivated aristocracy and the most prosperous middle class in Italy. In these circles the rule of Austria became very unpopular. Here Pellico, the poet, and Conte Confalonieri founded in 1818 a liberal literary magazine, *Il Conciliatore,* whose existence was cut short by the authorities in 1819. From Sicily to the Alps Italy, like Germany, was ultimately ruled from the Hofburg in Vienna.

As the whole life of the Italian people had been more deeply affected by the changes of the French Revolution than that of the Germans or Spaniards, it was natural that after 1815 the hatred of reaction should be more widespread. This dissatisfaction took different forms, each of which in turn contributed to the freeing of Italy. Among the intellectuals in the north the nationalist propaganda of a group of literary men began to take root. During the revolution Alfieri, the father of modern Italian patriotic literature, had used his dramas to denounce all forms of arbitrary government and had preached the ideal of a free and united Italy. Although he died in 1803, his influence increased, and many a Carbonaro knew by heart long passages from his tragedies. In the next decades a series of novels and plays and poems by Foscolo, Berchet, Pellico, Manzoni, Niccolini, Giordani, and Leopardi emphasized the value of literature as a means of arousing a new spirit of national unity among the Italian people.[34] Through the influence of these men

[34] Cf. R. Huch, *Confalonieri* (Leipzig, 1922), and I. Origo, *Leopardi* (Oxford, 1935).

Dante and Machiavelli were reprinted and became living forces in the movement. Foscolo's novel, *Jacopo Ortis* (1802), is typical of this new romantic and nationalist literature. Just as Kollár was, a few years later, to address the Slavs, so Foscolo in his story lamented that the Italians in their little states regarded each other as foreigners, whereas they were really one people with a common destiny. The movement took deep hold of the rising generation; Mazzini, Cavour, and Garibaldi all found Foscolo's novel the most inspiring reading of their youth. Few of these literary men were members of the Carbonari, though Pellico joined the sect and took part in the conspiracy that produced the Revolution of 1821. He and several others suffered exile or imprisonment. Their ideas of the glories of Italian culture and their hope for a brighter national future spread in the universities. The results were seen after 1820 when the universities began to furnish to the nationalist movement its thinkers and writers.

The only organized opposition to the existing order, before 1831, took the form of secret societies. During the Napoleonic period groups which resembled the *Tugendbund* in Germany had been organized against "the Usurper." These organizations, like the liberal associations in Spain, and after 1821 in France, were often recruited in part from the membership of the Freemasonic lodges. Originally the lodges had been favorable to Napoleon, who had used them to stabilize his régime. But in the later days of the Empire they had turned against him. From the Freemasons the liberal secret societies borrowed their complicated system of organization, their ritual of initiation, and certain signs and passwords. The lodges and the secret societies, after 1815, usually maintained friendly relations, though most of the conspiring was done in the secret political associations. The earliest of these was the Carbonari of Naples, founded before 1810. Gradually similar groups were formed in the other states, the Federati in Piedmont, the Guelfi in Bologna, the Adelphi in Lombardy. Before the downfall of Napoleon these societies had been strongly clerical and opposed to the French régime, but after 1815 they became liberal and nationalist in purpose. Thousands flocked into these organizations. There were between fifty and a hundred thousand members in the Kingdom of the Two

Sicilies alone in 1820. This large membership included some criminals and adventurers, but the majority was made up of doctors, lawyers, students, overtaxed small proprietors, civil and military officers who had served under the Napoleonic régime, and some of the lower clergy.

These groups corresponded with each other, though they had no central organization, as the governments believed. Beyond a hatred of Austria and of tyranny in general, they had no common program. In Sicily the secret societies wanted the expulsion of the Neapolitans; on the mainland the Neapolitan groups plotted for the establishment of a constitutional régime; in the Papal States the conspirators hoped for a government by laymen; and in Piedmont they wished to introduce a constitution. Some were liberal monarchists; others were republicans. As Mazzini pointed out later, their great weakness lay in their failure to think and plan in terms of the whole peninsula. Despite their poor organization and the lack of a common program the secret societies were able in 1820 to start a revolution in Naples and in 1821 in Piedmont. By that time discontent was wide and deep, and, as time was to show, neither police vigilance, nor the galley, nor the gallows was able to stamp it out. Persecution only fanned and scattered the smoldering flame.[35]

[35] The great regeneration of Italian life that was beginning to get under way was not comprehended in the north of Europe. Ranke, Lamartine, Byron, and other travelers shared Metternich's view that the Italians had no future. In 1818 Shelley wrote to Godwin, "The modern Italians seem a miserable people, without sensibility or imagination or understanding."

Chapter Six

THE CRISIS OF 1820

BY THE end of 1819 liberalism seemed a lost cause. The Six Acts in England, the Carlsbad Decrees in the Germanies, and the repressive measures used by all governments had driven resistance underground; as a result, the surface of political life from Lisbon to St. Petersburg bore the appearance of profound calm. But the year 1820 had hardly opened before a series of revolutionary disturbances broke out. In Spain and Portugal, in some of the Italian states, and eventually in Greece the revolutionaries overthrew the existing order; even in England and France attempts were made upon the lives of members of the government. Within a few years a serious revolt broke out in the Russian army. "On Andes' and on Athos' peaks unfurled," wrote Byron, "the self-same standard streams o'er either world!"

The conservative forces were convinced that the revolutionaries of every country were united and were working together through the Freemasonic lodges. This was not the case, however. The Freemasons, as such, had no political program beyond the one idea of religious liberty. Hence in the countries which allowed such freedom the Freemasons showed little or no hostility to the government. In Catholic countries, because of the opposition of the clergy, the Freemasons were forced to work in secret, and were inevitably more or less opposed to the government. The membership included more intellectuals and more military men, fewer members of the wealthy bourgeoisie and no government officials. In France, Spain, Italy, Poland, and Russia the Freemasonic lodges and the secret societies often coöperated. The conservatives, though, suffered from a number of illusions—that the Freemasons throughout Europe were united in a common political front against all governments, that

149

the Freemasons and the secret societies were everywhere working in the closest coöperation, and finally that there was for all the secret societies a single organization directed from Paris. The monarchs of Europe were united, and they jumped to the conclusion that their enemies must be.[1]

Of the series of disturbances that broke out, those in England and France were of a less dangerous nature than the revolts in southern Europe. In England the Six Acts had embittered the radicals to a point where some of the hotheads were willing to resort to assassination. The aged and insane George III died on the twenty-ninth of January, 1820. Less than a month later Thistlewood and a band of radical associates were arrested for hatching a plot to get rid of the whole Tory ministry. A dinner was to be the occasion for the carrying out of the conspiracy. The assassination of the ministers was to be followed by the seizure of sufficient cannon to overcome the London populace and to occupy the Bank of England; then a provisional government was to be set up. An agent provocateur had supplied the plotters with arms, had pointed out the most opportune time and place for the attempt, and, finally, had brought in the police. The result was that the conspirators, who met in a house on Cato Street, were surprised in the midst of their preparations. They resisted the police and killed the first constable who entered the place. In the confusion the leader and fourteen of the conspirators escaped so that, at the time, only three were arrested, but Thistlewood and several others were captured the next day. Brought to trial on a charge of treason, all were sentenced to death. Thistlewood and four others were executed on May 1 and the rest were forced to leave the country. This affair, together with the suppression of a political riot near Glasgow, on April 2, prejudiced the liberal cause in England and for the time seemed to justify the arbitrary measures of Lord Liverpool's Tory cabinet. The popular reform movement was crushed only to reappear ten years later at the time of the agitation that preceded the reform of Parliament in 1832.

A week before the discovery of the Cato Street Conspiracy, the Duc de Berri, the nephew of the French king, was assassinated as

[1] Cf. G. Weill, "Buonarroti," *Revue historique*, 1901.

he was leaving the Opera House in Paris. The act was the work of a fanatic, Louvel, who had plotted without accomplices. He had planned to cut off the hopes of the royal family for an heir, as it was now assumed that the king's other nephew, the Duc d'Angoulême, would never have children. All the pent-up fury of the Ultras broke loose, and in the Chamber of Deputies a member demanded the resignation of Decazes, the head of the ministry, whom he accused of being an accomplice of the assassin. The Ultra press openly blamed Decazes for the crime and spoke of the knife that had killed the Duc de Berri as a "liberal idea." In vain Decazes affirmed his innocence, and proposed a more severe censorship and a new electoral law. The royal family, especially the Comte d'Artois and the Duchesse d'Angoulême, clamored for his dismissal. Louis, complaining that the Ultras thought only of exploiting his grief, finally agreed to part with his favorite, who was made a duke and sent as minister to London. The king then called back the Duc de Richelieu, who formed a new ministry.

For the Ultras the assassination of the Duc de Berri had, as one of the Liberals said, "something providential about it, and he was now more useful to them than his living presence would have been." It brought about a change such as had not occurred in French politics since 1815, and entirely upset the compromise policy of Louis XVIII. Hitherto the moderate royalists had hoped that, with the backing of the king, they might reconcile liberalism with the monarchy, but Louvel's crime had made such a middle course impossible. Henceforth moderate royalism was a losing cause and within a few years there were just two factions in France, the Ultra and the revolutionary. The new ministry under the Duc de Richelieu initiated a more reactionary policy by reëstablishing a severe censorship over the press and by altering the electoral laws so as to throw the balance of power into the hands of the larger landed aristocrats. The royalists rejoiced when on September 29, 1820, the Duchesse de Berri gave birth to a son, the Duc de Bordeaux, thus assuring the continuance of the dynasty.

The growing reaction on the part of the government led to a rapid increase in the membership of secret societies in France, all of which, because they had a centralized organization on the model of

the Neapolitan Carbonari, came to be known as the French Carbonari. Most of the members were recruited from the ranks of the
army, though some professional men and well-to-do peasant-
proprietors joined, the latter, as in Italy, because they feared the
government might force them to give up the lands of the church
and the nobles which they had acquired as a result of the revolution. By 1822 there were branches of a centralized secret organization in thirty-five departments. The conspirators directed all their
efforts toward overthrowing the Bourbons, though they had no common proposal for replacing them. Some were Bonapartists, others
were Orleanists, and a small faction were republicans. Victor Cousin,
the philosopher, Thierry, the historian, Dubois and Jouffroy, who in
1824 founded the *Globe*, and Bazard, later one of the founders of
the Saint-Simonian School, were among the members.[2]

The French secret societies, like corresponding organizations in
Spain, Italy, Germany, Poland, and Russia, made no serious attempt to affiliate the mass of the peasants or the working classes of
the towns. In the years 1821 and 1822 the societies produced a series
of plots, chiefly in the garrison towns; all failed miserably. At La
Rochelle four young sergeants, who refused to answer all questions,
met their death so heroically that they have ever since been regarded
by French radicals as the outstanding political martyrs of the Restoration. The high social and political position of some of the conspirators, among them the redoubtable Lafayette, deterred the government from conducting a thorough investigation of the whole movement. Although the Ultras in France and the Tories in England, as
well as Alexander and Metternich, regarded this conspiring as very
dangerous, it never proved to be a serious menace to the Bourbon
régime. The failure of the plots led to the break-up of most of the
French secret societies by 1822.[3]

These flurries in England and France failed to gain the attention
that would have been given them earlier, because a more serious
revolt in Spain was now focusing the interest of all governments.
Since the return of Ferdinand in 1814, the dislike of his rule had

[2] Cf. G. Weill, *Histoire du parti républicain en France, 1814-70* (2nd ed., Paris,
1928).
[3] Cf. A. Calmette, "Les carbonari en France sous la Restauration," *Révolution de
1848* (1913-14).

grown steadily, especially in the army, where the men suffered from poor rations, wretched barracks, and insufficient pay, and among the merchants of the large ports, whose trade had been ruined by the revolt of the colonies. The royal government had most to fear from the army, not only because of this acute discontent but also because the long wars against Napoleon had created a resourceful body of officers used to taking things into their own hands. During the rest of the nineteenth century they were, on a number of occasions, to start rebellions, issue pronunciamentos, and take over the government.

When Ferdinand returned to his throne in 1814 he had found that the revolt of the colonies in America made the financial recovery of the government nearly impossible. Unable to acquire the revenues he needed from Spain itself, and unable likewise to get help from Russia or any of the other powers, he had deepened his determination to subdue the rebellious colonies.[4] Early in 1820, when a contingent of the army was ready to start from Cadiz to fight the revolting colonists in America, two military detachments proclaimed the Constitution of 1812.[5] At first the rising met with little success. The revolutionary forces lacked military equipment and the population remained apathetic. In order to arouse the people and to procure supplies for the revolutionary troops, Riego, the commander of one of the revolutionary detachments, marched his men through central Andalusia. Failing to obtain support from either the civilian population or the military garrisons, he disbanded his forces in the mountains. The outbreak seemed to be over.[6]

Suddenly, however, news reached Madrid that, while the southern rebellion was fading out, a veritable revolution was spreading in the north, and that Corunna, Oviedo, Saragossa, Valencia, and Barcelona had proclaimed the Constitution of 1812. At Madrid it-

---

[4] Cf. A. F. Zimmerman, "Spain and its Colonies, 1808-1820," *Hispanic American Historical Review* (1931).

[5] This document was to play a leading rôle in the Portuguese and Italian revolutions of 1820 also. It provided for a government by a single-chambered legislature elected by a limited suffrage. It gave to the monarch only a suspensory veto. The most conservative provision stipulated that Catholicism was to be the religion of the state. The greatest weakness of the constitution, however, was that it did not represent the needs or wishes of the country but was the work of a handful of liberals from the larger commercial cities.

[6] There is much new material on the Spanish Revolution in J. Sarrailh, *Martinez de la Rosa* (Bordeaux, 1930), Villa-Urrutia, *Fernando VII, rey constitucional* (Madrid, 1922), and E. Astur, *Riego* (Oviedo, 1933).

self, where mobs began to sing revolutionary songs in the streets, the king and his camarilla were in dismay. Early in March Ferdinand saw that he would have to yield, and on the seventh of the month he announced in the official gazette that the Cortes would be convened at once. He accepted a provisional government of liberals, which organized a national militia, and set July as the time for the meeting of the Cortes. On the eighth of March the king issued a decree in which he announced, "I have decided to take the oath to the Constitution promulgated by the Cortes of 1812." There was great rejoicing in the larger towns; the names of great squares were changed to "Plaza de la Constitución"; revolutionary juntas were formed; liberals, some of whom had been in prison since 1814, were released, while others returned from exile. On the ninth of March Ferdinand took the oath to respect the Constitution.

The liberals now began to show both their inexperience and their lack of unity. When the Cortes met, the *moderados*, who were anxious to avoid an open conflict with the king and the church, held a majority of the seats. Their program, part of which was enacted into law, was condemned by the extremists on both sides. The resentment of the conservatives was aroused by the abolition of some of the religious orders and the confiscation of about two-thirds of the church lands, by changes in the laws of inheritance, and by the amnesty to those who had followed King Joseph Bonaparte. At the same time, the immunity granted to those army officers who had resisted the liberal forces, the curbing of the activity of revolutionary patriotic societies, and the restrictions on the press angered a younger group of radicals, the *exaltados*, who leaned toward republicanism and who found the older liberals, "the men of 1812," too moderate. The division in the Cortes between the *moderados* and the *exaltados*, neither of whom had any real backing in the country, grew more marked after a visit which Riego made to Madrid in August.

The military hero of the revolution was fêted by the radical clubs. Impressed by this adulation, he threatened, for a time, to establish a kind of dictatorship over the Cortes. The ministry forced him to leave the capital and to return to the army, but the partisans of Riego expelled the friends of the government from the Freemasonic lodges, and established new Masonic centers, known as *comuneros*, a name given to the Castilian insurgents of 1520. By 1822 this society numbered ten thousand members. The split was fatal for the *moderados* and for the ultimate success of the revolution. Affairs moved in a vicious circle; each excess of the extremists provoked repressive measures from the ministry; each repressive measure made the radicals more violent. They insisted that the conquests of the revolution were being taken back piecemeal by its pretended friends. Crowds surged through the streets singing the "Hymn of Riego," a song composed for the hero's troops, and roaring out the popular phrase, *"Tragala, perro!"*—"Swallow it[the constitution], you dog!"

Outside the capital local government practically disappeared. While the Cortes debated, confusion grew. The finances were in complete disorder, the army dwindled almost to nothing, yellow fever raged through the southeast, and by 1822 a French army of observation (soon to become an army of intervention) was concentrated along the Pyrenees. The Cortes was completely discredited, and the king and the reactionary party began to hope. The elections of 1822 assured the radical wing, the *exaltados*, of a majority. Riego was chosen president of the new Chamber which, owing to a provision in the constitution, contained no members of the Cortes of 1820. Martínez de la Rosa and a group of *moderados* were chosen by the king to form a ministry. Refusing to accept this cabinet, the Cortes forced its resignation, and the monarch, who was now merely biding his time until the powers should intervene, chose a ministry of *exaltados*. The action of this new Chamber outraged the moderate liberals and the Catholic masses, and helped to strengthen the counter-revolutionary party.

The reactionaries had set up a royalist regency at Urgel which was actively preparing to aid the European powers who were on the point of intervening. A manifesto of this regency, dated August 15, 1822, and signed by the Archbishop of Tarragona, denounced both the Constitution of 1812 and the Cortes, and called upon the Spanish people to liberate "their captive king." The revolutionary government forced the leaders of the regency to flee to France, but the secret plotting of the royalists continued. Throughout the provinces there were continual clashes between royalists and radicals and a state of civil war prevailed. The growing danger of foreign intervention drove the Cortes to ever more radical measures. The efforts of the British ambassador to moderate its ardor and to get it to provide for a second chamber, a project earlier favored by some of the *moderados*, met with no success. On account of the split in the liberal forces, the reactionaries were slowly gaining the upper hand when the threat of a French invasion led the Cortes to remove itself and the king to Seville on the twentieth of March, 1823. On April 7, a French army under the Duc d'Angoulême crossed the frontier, and the doom of the revolution was sealed.

The overthrow of despotism in Spain had provoked a somewhat similar movement in Portugal. When the royal family fled to Brazil in 1807, the government was put in the hands of a regent, though from 1809 to 1820 the real ruler of the country was the English soldier, Marshal Beresford. His honest but severe rule was distasteful to the upper classes who were, at the same time, dissatisfied with the idea of seeming to be only a dependency of Brazil. In 1820, when Beresford went to Rio de Janeiro to consult John VI, and to procure from him greater powers for repressing the growing discontent, a revolt broke out in Oporto. As in Spain, the army took the lead; a revolutionary junta was formed, and the English officers were driven out. Other towns having revolted, a provisional government was established in Lisbon, and the timid regent was forced to accept it. The new government demanded the return of the monarch from Brazil and called a national assembly to draw up a constitution. In four months this document was completed. Following the model of the Spanish Constitution of 1812, it abolished the last relics of feudalism, guaranteed the equality of all citizens and the freedom of the press, and established a single-chambered legislature as the governing body of the state. When this assembly met it suppressed the Inquisition, abolished some of the religious orders, and confiscated part of the church lands.

The king returned to Portugal in 1821, leaving his eldest son, Dom Pedro, as regent in Rio de Janeiro. Arrived in Lisbon, John VI agreed to accept the new order; in October, 1822, he swore allegiance to the new constitution. The leading men in Brazil, in the meantime becoming indignant at the high-handed attitude of the revo-

lutionary government in Lisbon, forced Dom Pedro to proclaim
the independence of Brazil and to accept the title of emperor. This
sudden loss of Brazil, though not officially recognized by the Portuguese government until 1825, brought discredit on John VI and
the revolutionary régime in Portugal. The queen, her second son,
Dom Miguel, and a group of nobles forced the monarch to dissolve the assembly and revoke the constitution. The king, however,
was far from being pleased to find himself in the hands of his wife
and son and their absolutist followers. Though he abrogated the
Constitution of 1822, he appointed a junta to draw up a new charter
establishing parliamentary government after the English model.
Dom Miguel and his absolutist followers continued to quarrel with
the government. It took the united action of the powers to hold
the monarch on the throne, and the intervention of England in 1826
and 1827 to maintain even the semblance of a parliamentary régime.
The term anarchy best describes the general condition of the country.

During these same years the revolutionary movement was sweeping over Italy. On July 2, 1820, soon after the news of the successes
of the Spanish liberals reached the Kingdom of the Two Sicilies, a
revolt broke out in the garrison at Nola. A few days later a small
band of troops marched to the headquarters of General Pepe, a
high-spirited officer whom the king had offended and who had
plotted in 1819 to kidnap him. They offered Pepe the leadership
of the revolution. He hesitated, but when he heard that the Carbonari of the neighboring districts were joining the revolt, he threw
in his lot with the insurgents. In the beginning the uprising was
directed more against Austrian influence in the army—the com-
mander-in-chief, Nugent, was an Austrian—than against domestic
tyranny. The king was aware that the army, which had remained
loyal to Murat to the end, would be of little use against the insurgents. So he yielded to the demands of a delegation of Carbonari,
who waited upon him at the royal palace, and proclaimed the
Spanish Constitution of 1812, the actual provisions of which seem
to have been unknown. A provisional committee under the regency
of the king's son took over the government. Political prisoners were
liberated, the special military courts which had been used for political
oppression were abolished, and the press freed. Agreeing to these

changes, Ferdinand assured Pepe, whom he had made head of the army, that he would have granted a constitution earlier had he only known there was a general desire for one![7] The Carbonari organized a great procession to celebrate their triumph. Priests with rosaries and swords at their belts and carrying red, white, and green banners led the host. Doctors, lawyers, teachers, and soldiers followed. Orators harangued the crowd, and the ancient city of Naples seemed to renew its life. The revolution had been accomplished with almost ludicrous ease.

When the news of these sudden changes reached Sicily, the army in some of the garrison towns proclaimed the Spanish Constitution, but the other factions, reaffirming the Sicilian Constitution of 1812, refused to coöperate with the revolutionary government on the mainland. A civil war broke out in Palermo. Only after the provisional government had sent an army to take the city did the Sicilians yield. Thus the Neapolitan government not only received no help from the Sicilians, but was obliged to keep a garrison of six thousand men in the island.

Parliament met in Naples in October, 1820. The majority of the deputies, like those in the Spanish and in the Portuguese assemblies of the same year, were moderates, chosen almost exclusively from the lower nobility and the professional classes. Only seventeen out of the seventy-two deputies were members of the Carbonari. The Parliament did indeed represent the intellectual élite of its generation, but the deputies were inexperienced and were, like their fellows in Spain and Portugal, hampered at the outset by the Spanish Constitution of 1812, which gave great opportunity to the extremists. Some of the moderates, as in Spain, proposed the introduction of a second chamber, but the extremists opposed it furiously. Parliament failed, in every case, to work fast enough to

[7] On July 13 he took the following oath: "I, Ferdinand of Bourbon, by the grace of God and by the Constitution of the Neapolitan monarchy, King of the Two Sicilies, swear in the name of God and on the Holy Evangels that I will defend and preserve the Constitution. Should I act contrary to my oath and contrary to any article in this Constitution, I ought not to be obeyed; and every act by which I contravened it would be null and void. Thus doing, may God aid and protect me, otherwise may He call me to account." Then, uplifting his eyes he uttered this brief prayer: "Omnipotent God, who with Thine infinite gaze readest the soul and the future—if I lie or intend to break this oath, do Thou at this instant hurl on my head the lightnings of Thy vengeance." Again he kissed the Holy Book, and, turning to Pepe, who stood near, he said meekly, "General, believe me, this time I have sworn from the bottom of my heart." E. Poggi, *Storia d'Italia dal 1814 al 1846* (Florence, 1883), I, 262-263.

suit the radical element in the army and in the Carbonari societies and so, from the very beginning, it was threatened at one and the same time by the reactionary intriguing of the king and by the revolutionary plotting of the radicals. The mass of the population, in the meantime, remained indifferent. While the various revolutionary groups dickered among themselves, the Neapolitan king, now in communication with Metternich, was planning the overthrow of the revolution. In January, 1821, he left for Laibach to confer with Metternich, having solemnly promised the assembly in Naples before his departure that he was going to see the allied statesmen "in order to obtain the sanction of the powers for the newly acquired liberties" and that he would do everything to leave his people "in the possession of a wise and free constitution." His Parliament, with even more naïve faith than that which the Spanish Cortes had placed in their king, allowed him to go. In the meantime, an Austrian army was being assembled in Lombardy.

The disturbances in Naples led to revolutionary flurries in the Papal States, though the police kept them from going further than the planting of liberty trees. But the sparks were flying northward. In March, 1821, a revolt broke out in Piedmont. This rising was the work of a group of aristocrats and intellectuals, as well as of army officers; its aim was not only to establish a constitutional government but also to expel the Austrians and to unite the whole of Italy under the House of Savoy. The conspirators hoped to be able to persuade the heir to the throne, Charles Albert, a youth of twenty-two, to place himself at the head of the movement. For a time he seems to have intended to coöperate, but his loyalty to his father and uncle finally overcame his burning hatred of Austria. He changed his mind, informed the conspirators that they must not count on him, and then notified the minister of war of the plot. The leaders attempted to prevent the rising, but their messengers arrived at Alessandria too late to forestall the seizure of the citadel by a band of soldiers and citizens. When the news of the outbreak reached the liberal leaders in Turin, they made a half-hearted effort to carry out their original plans. They demanded the Spanish Constitution of 1812 and a war against Austria. Victor Emmanuel, a ruler of greater decision than was shown by his fellow monarchs

in Spain, Portugal, and the Two Sicilies, not wishing to start a
war with Austria, promptly abdicated in favor of his brother, Charles
Felix, and turned over the government to a regency under his
nephew, Charles Albert. The young regent proclaimed the Spanish
Constitution of 1812, subject to the approval of Charles Felix who,
on his arrival in Turin, rejected everything that his nephew had
done. Charles Albert had in the meantime left Turin, and on his
uncle's orders had exiled himself to Florence. The revolutionaries,
under the command of Santorre di Santarosa, continued to hold the
loyalty of a part of the army, though it was evident that, even without foreign intervention, the movement was destined to fail.[8]

II. THE EUROPEAN ALLIANCE AND THE CRUSHING OF THE REVOLUTIONS, 1818-1823

The epidemic of revolution in Spain, Portugal, and Italy, together
with a revolt of the Greeks against the Ottoman government which
broke out in 1821, taxed to the limit the diplomatic resources of
the European Alliance. Until 1820 the Alliance had worked successfully. The attempt to govern Europe by conference, begun during the last years of the wars, for a time took the form of an ambas-
sadorial committee in Paris, of which the Duke of Wellington acted
as head. Its primary function was to watch over France, especially
to arrange the payment of the war indemnity and to supervise the
army of occupation—the first international army that had ever
existed in time of peace. By the beginning of 1818, after the ambas-
sadorial conference had set definite sums for the payment of war
damages to the various powers and the French government had
arranged for the final payment, the allied governments deemed it
time to call a general conference to confirm these agreements and
to decide on their future relations with France.[9] Such a conference,
the first to be called in time of peace, met at Aix-la-Chapelle in 1818.
The rulers of Austria, Russia, and Prussia were present, and, in addi-

---

[8] On the situation in Piedmont, cf. N. Rodolico, *Carlo Alberto* (Florence, 1931), and
B. Allson, *La vita di Pellico* (Milan, 1933).

[9] Between 1815 and 1818 there had been sharp difference of opinion among the powers.
Alexander was anxious to gain the favor of some of the lesser states. Russian diplomats
were flattering the French ministry and a similar policy was being undertaken by the
Russian representatives in Spain and Naples. This annoyed Castlereagh and Metternich,
who feared that Alexander might form an alliance with the Bourbon states in the hope
of being able then to force his wishes on England and Austria.

tion, Metternich, Hardenberg, Nesselrode, and Capodistrias. Castlereagh and Wellington represented England. The Duc de Richelieu,
though not formally admitted to the conference, was present on
behalf of France. Alexander had wished to call representatives of
some of the smaller powers, but the opposition of Castlereagh and
Metternich forced him to abandon the project.[10]

After extended bickerings, a secret agreement, signed in November, 1818, renewed the Quadruple Alliance to guard against France
again becoming dangerous. France was invited to join a Quintuple
Alliance which was "consecrated to protect the arts of peace, to
increase the internal prosperity of the various states, and to awaken
those sentiments of religion and morality which the misfortunes
of the time had weakened."[11] Projects of disarmament, the first ever
seriously discussed among European statesmen, were considered by
the powers at the request of Alexander, but mutual jealousies prevented the question being brought up again. The tsar then proposed
the formation of an international army to guarantee the frontiers
and the existing governments of Europe. The idea was rejected
brusquely by Castlereagh, more suavely by Metternich. Another of
Alexander's suggestions was that a general union against revolution
be undertaken by the sovereigns who had signed the Treaty of
Vienna. At first no one bothered to gainsay him. Castlereagh moved
cautiously because all of his decisions had to be presented to Parliament, where his policies had already been attacked for their
supposed docility to Russia. One speaker had even painted a lurid
picture of Cossacks encamped in Hyde Park awaiting orders to
overawe the House of Commons! At the same time, Canning and
other members of the British cabinet were raising objections to
England's entanglements in continental affairs. Naturally, then,
Castlereagh opposed this scheme of Alexander "to provide the trans-
parent soul of the Holy Alliance with a body," and he obtained
the help of Metternich in blocking it.

In spite of his efforts to unite the monarchs against revolution,
Alexander still maintained his liberal ideas. He dreamed of realizing them by first fixing all kings firmly on their thrones, and then

10 On the whole subject cf. C. K. Webster, *The Foreign Policy of Castlereagh, 1815-22*
(2nd ed., London, 1934), a masterful study.
11 G. Weill, *L'éveil des nationalités et le mouvement libéral* (Paris, 1930), 31-32.

forcing them to grant constitutions on the model of the French Charter. The interference of the great powers, he insisted, was to be constructive and not merely repressive. The constitutions granted would emanate from the royal will and would reconcile all peoples to their rulers. The whole scheme was utterly chimerical, and Castlereagh and Metternich were determined to thwart its realization. Eventually the two pacified Alexander by agreeing to a vague formula about "moral solidarity." That the Alliance survived was again largely due to the skill and patience of Castlereagh.[12] In spite of the opposition of some members of the cabinet and of Parliament, and the difficulty of making terms with the tsar, whom he rightly considered "half a madman," he had kept in existence the system of diplomacy by conference. France had now been admitted to a position among the great powers and the Alliance had been strengthened.

Certain important details of the European situation had been left unsettled at the Aix Conference, and these were passed on to a conference of ministers which met at Frankfort in 1819. They agreed on a treaty which was mainly concerned with minor territorial adjustments in the German Confederation and in Italy. With the break-up of this conference at Frankfort (the Council of Ambassadors had been terminated after the conference at Aix-la-Chapelle), Europe was left for the first time since 1814 without any central representation. The relations among the members of the Alliance continued to be strained chiefly because of the intrigues of Alexander; his agents were again active in Italy, in France, in Spain, and in Germany. In Spain and in the Germanies they were backing the reactionary monarchs; in Italy and France, they were favoring the liberals. Metternich, who was always inclined to believe the worst rumors about the tsar, received a report that Laharpe, Alexander's former tutor, had presided over a meeting of the Carbonari at Bologna. Exactly what Alexander intended it is impossible to discover, though the allied governments were justified in believing that much of his meddling was planned to strengthen Russian influence in the affairs of western Europe. The tsar's intrigues were

---

[12] For the first time in history the press was represented at a political conference; the *Times* and the *Morning Chronicle* sent special correspondents.

a menace to the balance of power quite different from those dangers that were soon to arise from revolutionary disturbances, but on many occasions they caused Metternich and Castlereagh fully as much worry.

The Cato Street Conspiracy in London, the assassination of the Duc de Berri in Paris, and then the outbreak of the Spanish Revolution gave Metternich and Alexander a great fright, and in the end brought about a rapprochement between them. Nevertheless, when the tsar proposed a conference to consider these matters, Metternich, desirous of keeping both Castlereagh and Alexander in line, hesitated to declare himself. Standing by his policy of nonintervention, Castlereagh declared his hostility to this Russian proposal. He insisted that the Alliance had been made against France, and that it was "never intended as a union for the government of the world or for the superintendence of the internal affairs of other states."[13] The chief British objection to intervention in Spain, however, was the fear that this might lead eventually to intervention against the revolting Spanish colonies where England was developing a very lucrative trade.

When word reached Metternich of the outbreak of revolution in Naples, he was greatly shocked. Although he had earlier agreed to Castlereagh's veto on intervention in Spain, he realized that the rising in the Kingdom of the Two Sicilies directly threatened the whole Hapsburg system in middle Europe. He varied his metaphors from "conflagrations" and "torrents" to "earthquakes," and he quietly began to lay his plans to intervene. Since Austria had a treaty with the Neapolitan king, her action there did not involve the other members of the Quintuple Alliance. Alexander, nevertheless, continued to insist on the necessity of calling a conference, and Metternich began to yield because, much as he feared and distrusted the tsar, he now needed his general moral backing. For Metternich realized that, if he could show clearly that Russia and

[13] C. K. Webster, *The Foreign Policy of Castlereagh, 1815-1822* (2nd ed., London, 1934), 238. This famous Cabinet Memorandum of May 5, 1820, setting forth the doctrine of non-intervention, merely stated more bluntly the British position since 1815. Castlereagh concluded by saying, "We shall be found in our place when actual danger menaces the system of Europe, but this country cannot and will not act upon abstract and speculative Principles of Precaution." H. Temperley, *The Foreign Policy of Canning, 1822-1827* (London, 1925), 16.

the other powers were on his side, Austria would be in a much stronger position to fight revolutions in both Germany and Italy. It had finally come to the choice between acting alone, as Castlereagh entreated him to do, or of bringing the Alliance into the affair. A compromise was finally struck; a conference was to meet at Troppau, and the rulers of Russia, Austria, and Prussia agreed to attend. The British cabinet consented to allow Lord Stewart, the English ambassador at Vienna, to be present as an observer; he was, however, given no power to act. France also agreed to send an observer. The Alliance had been preserved, but in the course of the negotiations England had all but withdrawn.

The conference at Troppau, which opened on October 29, 1820, was really a conference of the three eastern powers, Russia, Austria, and Prussia. It marked the beginning of that great cleavage in European politics which became clearer as the nineteenth century progressed. Alexander now assured Metternich that his former liberalism had all been a mistake. "So we are at one, Prince, and it is to you that we owe it," the tsar said; "you have correctly judged the state of affairs. I deplore the waste of time, which we must try to repair. I am here without any fixed ideas, without any plans; but I bring you a firm and unalterable resolution. It is for your emperor to use it as he wills. Tell me what you desire, and what you wish me to do, and I will do it."[14]

Metternich, who dominated the conference, still strove to keep the general question of revolutions, Alexander's favorite theme, out of the discussions. Eventually he found that he could not get the tsar's permission to invade Naples without some general statement on this subject.[15] So on November 19, 1820, a famous protocol was drawn up. It consecrated the principle of intervention in the following words: "States which have undergone a change of government, due to revolution, the results of which threaten other states, *ipso facto* cease to be members of the European Alliance, and remain excluded from it until their situation gives guarantees for legal order and stability. If, owing to such alterations, immediate danger

[14] W. A. Phillips, *The Confederation of Europe* (2nd ed., London, 1920), 206.
[15] Alexander was now searching the Scriptures and finding in the stories of Nebuchadnezzar and of Judith and Holofernes, and in the Epistles of St. Paul, divine lessons applicable to the existing perils.

threatens other states, the powers bind themselves, by peaceful means, or if need be by arms, to bring back the guilty state into the bosom of the Great Alliance."[16]

Castlereagh was much occupied with internal difficulties in England which threatened to bring on the overthrow of the Liverpool cabinet. But on January 19, 1821, he issued a carefully prepared protest in which, while admitting the right of Austria to act in Italy, he condemned the claim that the Alliance had the right to put down revolutions anywhere. The protest was published in the British newspapers and discussed in Parliament. In the meantime, the conference had been adjourned to Laibach so as to be nearer the scene of disturbance.

The adjourned conference, which met the second week of January, 1821, had somewhat more of the character of a general congress than that at Troppau owing to the fact that all the Italian princes were represented. Its discussions were practically confined to Italian affairs, and it was finally arranged that Austria should send an army into the Kingdom of the Two Sicilies. Attempts were again made, though without success, to persuade England and France to enter an open agreement with the other powers. Before the congress adjourned word was received of the outbreak of a revolt of the Greeks against their Ottoman masters. The matter was discussed, but Alexander, though anxious for intervention in Spain and Italy, regarded the Balkans exclusively as a field of Russian action and wished to keep Metternich out. No decision was reached. The tsar and Metternich, however, did agree that a conference should be held in Italy the next year for the purpose of discussing what action should be taken in regard to the revolution in Spain and the revolt in Greece.

Austria now had a free hand to deal with the revolution in Naples, though it was only with the greatest difficulty that Alexander was dissuaded from accompanying the Austrian army. Having defeated General Pepe and the Neapolitan army at Rieti, the Austrian troops marched into the kingdom in March, 1821. They met with little resistance. Colletta, the minister of war, and General Pepe worked furiously to whip their forces into shape. But the revolu-

16 W. A. Phillips, op. cit., 208-209.

tionary army was badly equipped and poorly disciplined, and a considerable part of the troops were still in Sicily restoring order. Ferdinand, who stayed well out of danger in the rear of the Austrian army, issued manifestoes in which he called on his faithful subjects to receive the forces of his allies, not as enemies but as friends come to protect them. He threatened with death and confiscation all who resisted. On March 23, without another blow, the Austrians entered Naples. Ferdinand reëstablished his despotism and called back Canosa as his chief minister. General Pepe and the poet, Rossetti, with a few other revolutionary leaders fled into exile; others were thrown into prison. The barbers in Naples busied themselves with cutting off the telltale locks and beards of the frightened Carbonari. The revolution ended as suddenly as it had begun.

The Austrian army then pushed northward to extinguish the uprising in Piedmont. The revolting forces under Santarosa were defeated by the Austrian and Piedmontese troops at Novara, April 18, 1821. The leaders fled to Genoa; some of them embarked for Spain where the revolution was still successful. An Austrian army of occupation of 12,000 was kept in Piedmont until September, 1822. Count Confalonieri, Pellico, the poet, and the leaders of the liberal forces in Milan were seized and sent to the Spielberg fortress in Austria. In the other Italian states, especially in Modena, liberals were hunted down; many were cast into prison or put to death. The pope, in September, 1821, issued a Bull against all secret societies, warning the faithful against doctrines which "seem smoother than oil, but are naught but arrows which perfidious men use to wound those who are not on their guard. They come to you like sheep, but they are at heart only devouring wolves."[17] About two thousand Italians left the peninsula in the year 1821, followed by about the same number during the next few years. The exiles scattered to England, Switzerland, Holland, Spain, Corsica, and Greece where all, with the exception of those who fled to England, were watched by the police and often treated with great indignities. Few were the families in the upper and middle classes in Italy which had not to tremble for the safety of one of their members. Austria

[17] W. R. Thayer, *The Dawn of Italian Independence* (Boston, 1899), I, 293.

was now more powerful than ever in all parts. Thus faded the vision of liberty which had passed like the phantom of a dream over the Italian world.

After the conference at Laibach, whose procedure had greatly exasperated England, Metternich changed his tactics and began again to cultivate the favor of Castlereagh. In Spain, in the Americas, and in the Near East the interests of Austria and of England did not conflict. Indeed, both governments feared the activities of the tsar in these areas. A great duel was at the time going on at Constantinople between the representative of Russia, who was pushing toward a war with Turkey over the Greek question, and the British ambassador, who was trying to prevent such a conflict. In western Europe a similar struggle was taking place between Alexander's minister, Capodistrias, who favored military intervention, and Metternich who, having secured the full coöperation of Castlereagh, insisted that the Greek Revolt must be allowed to burn itself out "beyond the pale of civilization." The Austrian chancellor plied the tsar with arguments to prove that the unrest in Turkey did not differ essentially from that elsewhere in Europe and that the Greek insurgents, like any others, were rebels against legitimate authority. Faced with the alternative of offending the pro-Greek sentiments of the Russian people or of bringing down in ruin the whole edifice of his international program, Alexander chose the former.

In the autumn of 1821 Castlereagh and Metternich had an interview at Hanover. Castlereagh, who had strengthened his position at home, agreed to attend a conference of the powers to be held the next year in Italy. The question of the Greek Revolt dragged on, though England, by getting the Ottoman government to promise reforms, averted the threatened war between Russia and Turkey. The Greek insurrection was for the time being allowed to continue without interference. Long negotiations among the powers over what was to be done with the revolting Spanish colonies in America had likewise brought no decision. Much more pressing were the affairs of Spain. At Laibach the tsar had declared that Spain was the nest of all revolutions, "the tribune to which all the revolutionists of Europe have recourse, as to a vehicle from which they can disseminate their pernicious doctrine."[18]

Metternich, having kept the tsar in the Alliance, and having again got on good terms with Castlereagh, hoped that some joint action regarding the Spanish Revolution would be taken at the forthcoming conference in Italy. Before it met, Castlereagh, worn out by overwork, committed suicide, and was succeeded at the British foreign office by George Canning. This "malevolent meteor," as Metternich was to call him, was far less interested than Castlereagh in maintaining the Alliance. Canning's ignorance of continental affairs, his desire to find markets for British manufactures, and his belief that England's interests were often on the side of revolution rather than against it, gave him an outlook different from that of his rival and predecessor. On the other hand, Canning's readiness to further the dissolution of the Alliance by the gradual withdrawal of England was simply a variant of Castlereagh's fear that, in certain eventualities, the Alliance would "move away from England" without her having quit it. The Duke of Wellington was sent as England's delegate to the Congress at Verona. He took with him for his direction the elaborate memorandum prepared by Castlereagh before his death.

The subjects which, according to this British cabinet paper, were to come up for discussion, were wide in their range. There were the Turkish-Greek question, the problem of Spain and the fate of the Spanish colonies, the affairs of the Italian states, the perennial subject of the suppression of the slave trade, and, finally, the situation arising from a ukase of the tsar closing the Bering Sea and the adjacent American waters to all but Russian ships, against which both England and the United States had protested. With respect to Spain, England was again to preserve "a rigid abstinence from any interference in the internal affairs of that country."

When the congress met, October 20, 1822, the Greek question had reached a temporary settlement, but the Spanish problem, which had grown more acute, and in which the French were now proposing to intervene, stood in the foreground. The congress brought together a large number of rulers and statesmen, and Metternich,

[18] C. K. Webster, op. cit., 343.

fearful of intrigue and recrimination, hastened to push matters toward a quick decision. The tsar was anxious to use his large army to intervene in Spain. France now had an ultra-royalist ministry which was more willing than the preceding cabinet to listen to Ferdinand's frantic appeals for aid, and believed that a little military glory would help the Bourbon cause at home. It had sent an army to the Pyrenees, ostensibly to prevent the plague from spreading into France, but really to watch political developments in Spain. The French representatives at Verona, Chateaubriand and Montmorency, following their private convictions rather than their instructions, began to clamor for the right of the French army to intervene in Spanish affairs. After some negotiations, Austria, Russia, and Prussia agreed to recall their ambassadors from Madrid and to lend France their moral support. A French army was to proceed against the revolutionary government. These negotiations aroused the British cabinet to anger. Canning sent instructions that, if there was a determined project to interfere by force or by menace, then, "come what may," England would not be a party. On October 30, 1822, Wellington communicated this news to the congress. It fell like a bombshell and marked England's withdrawal from the Alliance. Canning's comment was, "Things are getting back to a wholesome state again; every nation for itself and God for us all."[19]

At the beginning of 1823 identical notes from Russia, Austria, and Prussia ordered Spain to modify her constitution, and threatened punishment in case of refusal. The revolutionary government flatly denied the right of foreign powers to interfere in any way in Spanish affairs. Thereupon the French army, which was ready to enter the country, crossed the Pyrenees (April 7, 1823) and moved on Madrid. A regency was set up to rule the country until the king could be freed. At once it began the work of "purification" by throwing hundreds of constitutionalists into jail and condemning many of them to death. The revolutionary government was moved from Seville to Cadiz where finally, by the end of September, 1823, the Duc d'Angoulême and his French troops stormed the Trocadero

[19] Cf. E. Beau de Loménie, *La carrière politique de Chateaubriand, 1814-1830* (2 vols., Paris, 1929).

fortress, ended the resistance of the Spanish revolutionaries, and freed the king.

Before he was liberated, Ferdinand had signed an agreement with his ministers promising to all who had taken part in the revolution "pardon complete and absolute without any exception whatever." But, like his relative in Naples, he broke all his promises when he was again in power. Liberals by the thousands were driven into exile; thousands of others were imprisoned; hundreds were tortured and executed. Louis XVIII and the Duc d'Angoulême protested, but in vain. Fortunately Angoulême was able to help some of the deputies and members of the government in Cadiz to escape. On the other hand, the governments of Austria, Russia, and Prussia urged the king to leave no trace of constitutionalism. The admonition was unnecessary, for the restored monarch was proceeding with savage ferocity. The same mob which a few years before had acclaimed Riego now shouted for the king when their former idol was dragged, with savage pomp, in a basket at an ass's tail to one of the principal squares in Madrid. There he was hanged and cut into five parts which were sent to be publicly exposed in the five towns where he was best known. The revenge taken by the restored monarch in the towns and cities of Spain was more bloody and revolting than that taken by any reactionary government in nineteenth-century Europe. The result was far from peaceful, for the king's brother, Don Carlos, now started a fanatical clerical movement and the wretched country entered on a long period of internal anarchy.[20]

The Congress of Verona marked the end of the alliance that Castlereagh had forged in the troubled years of 1814 and 1815, though no one at the time fully realized the fact. During the period after 1822 repeated efforts were made to revive it. In every case, England prevented its resuscitation. When the French army invaded Spain in 1823 Canning was furious, and turned to America to take his revenge. Among the Spanish colonies England had been building up a valuable trade, and, now that tariffs were being raised against British goods all over the continent, these South American

[20] Cf. Geoffroy de Grandmaison, *L'expédition française d'Espagne en 1823* (Paris, 1928), J. Sarrailh, *Le contre-révolution sous la régence de Madrid* (Bordeaux, 1930) and Villa-Urrutia, *Fernando VII, rey absoluto* (Madrid, 1931).

markets seemed all the more valuable. After the victory of the French forces in Spain, Canning feared that a concerted effort might be made to force the revolting colonies back under the yoke of the mother country.

He found that this view was also held by President Monroe, who, on the advice of his secretary of state, John Quincy Adams, had in 1822 recognized the new Spanish-American republics. After some negotiations in London, however, the American government decided to act alone. In December, 1823, Monroe, in a famous message to Congress, declared that the Americas were henceforth closed to European colonization or intervention. The knowledge that England had designs on Cuba and that Russia was seeking to get recognition of claims along the Pacific coast had convinced the American government that it was time for the United States to take a positive stand. At the same time, Henry Clay's continual appeals in behalf of a republican system in both the Americas, always with an eye to the recognition of the new South American states, had prepared the country to support the president.[21]

The first challenge to the European Alliance by an organized state came then from the New World. Monroe's message was praised by the leading English journals and lauded by Brougham in the House of Commons. In France, it called forth the praises of Lafayette and of some of the leading liberals. The governments of the continental states, however, were displeased, though none of them took it with sufficient seriousness to protest.[21] Canning was disappointed that Monroe's action had not been taken jointly with England, but he was pleased because it blocked the program of the other powers. In 1825 England recognized the independence of Colombia, Mexico, and Argentina, and Canning, not averse to stretching the truth, boasted, "I called the New World into existence to redress the balance of the Old."

In the questions of Portugal, and of the Greek Revolt, Canning, a past master at arousing the nationalist enthusiasm of the British and the liberal sentiment of Europe, was to carry England still further away from the eastern powers, Austria, Prussia, and Russia.

[21] Weill, *op. cit.*, 73. Cf. C. K. Webster, *Britain and the Independence of Latin America,* 2 vols. (Oxford, 1938).

Thus, the first serious experiment in international government ended in failure. It was not, however, without some far-reaching results; it introduced the idea of coöperation among a group of powers and of personal conference among a number of statesmen, and it established the idea of common interests among the nations. Unluckily there never grew out of the alliance any real machinery to prevent the great catastrophe that closed the nineteenth-century epoch.

III. THE TWILIGHT OF ALEXANDER'S LIBERALISM AND THE DECEMBRIST REVOLT, 1815-1826

The strange and often contradictory rôle that Alexander was taking in general European affairs he was also playing in his own empire. His earlier liberalism had been largely a matter of vague phrases and cloudy aspirations. Only when he had been confronted with revolution abroad and discontent at home was he forced to formulate a definite program for his liberal ideas. The formula on which he finally settled was one which held that, while every monarch should grant his people a constitution, none should be exacted from below by the people. As his friend, Czartoryski, said, "Alexander wants everyone to be free on condition that everyone will obey him blindly!" Much of the tsar's behavior can be explained only on the assumption that a strange education and a tragic early experience made him intellectually and emotionally unbalanced, especially in later life. Metternich once shrewdly remarked that in the character of Alexander there was always some element lacking, but that it was impossible to tell in advance just what the particular element would be.

In Finland, after 1815, the tsar allowed the constitution that had existed under the Swedish régime to continue, with himself as grand duke. The Finnish state retained its own laws and courts, its own administrative system directed by a native senate, its own army, coinage, and postal system. The government personnel was entirely non-Russian. Russians were not even allowed to settle in Finland without permission from the local authorities. The aristocracy of the country and the upper bourgeois classes in the towns were Swedish and Lutheran. Swedish was the official language, though a Finnish nationalist movement, which proposed to substitute the native language, was under way. The constitution provided for meetings of a diet, but none was called until 1863. Finland, in the reigns of Alexander and Nicholas, remained prosperous and fairly contented under Russian rule, though in Finland, as in Poland, Alexander's experiment in the self-government of a dependent nation brought him much criticism from his own people.

A much more striking example of Alexander's desire to pose as the great patron of liberalism was the constitutional régime he granted to a section of the Polish people who, after 1815, lived under the Russian government.[22] The constitution, chiefly the work of Prince Adam Czartoryski, allowed the Poles to maintain an army of 40,000 men and a Polish administrative personnel. The Code Napoléon was left in force, and the constitution guaranteed liberty of speech, freedom of the press, free right of association, and special protection for the Catholic Church. Legislative power was vested in a Diet composed of a Senate, named by the tsar as king, and a Chamber of Deputies elected by the most liberal franchise in Europe. The Diet was to meet every two years for a session of thirty days; its debates were to be public. As a whole, the constitution was the most advanced instrument of government that existed anywhere on the continent.

When put into practice, however, the new régime showed many imperfections. The Diet had no control over the army, which was kept under Russian command. The tsar, as King of Poland, could prorogue, adjourn, or dissolve the Diet at will; he alone could propose laws. To make the new constitutional order still more unworkable Alexander never allowed the Diet to discuss the budget. As his viceroy in Poland he appointed not Prince Adam Czartoryski, who was regarded by the Poles as the logical candidate, but the aged and ineffectual General Zajacek. The real power, however, was in the hands of the tsar's brother, the Grand Duke Constantine, and the Russian agent, Novosiltsev. Constantine, who was given command of the army, had married a Polish noblewoman and seems to have liked the Polish people, but he soon made himself hated

[22] The Congress Kingdom of Poland, established by Alexander, included only about 127,000 square kilometers. There were nearly 500,000 square kilometers of former Polish territory that were directly under Russian rule, where the population enjoyed none of the privileges granted to those who lived under Alexander's constitution.

as a martinet. Novosiltsev was appointed by Alexander as "Commissioner for the Kingdom," a position not provided for in the constitution which in practice tended increasingly to make the liberal provisions of the new régime an illusion. Both Constantine and Novosiltsev interfered at every point in the administration; every week the latter sent a secret report to the tsar.[23]

From the very beginning difficulties arose. Instead of forming a civilian national guard, Constantine created a police force directly under his own command. He threw out many of the higher officers of the regular army and replaced them with his own appointees; he also began to spend on army equipment enormous sums which the impoverished country could ill afford. A session of the Diet was called in 1818. In his opening speech Alexander intimated that he intended to annex Lithuania to the new Congress Kingdom and also that he expected to introduce a constitutional government in Russia. Both suggestions furthered the growth of discontent among the Polish population outside the new kingdom. This speech, made by the tsar to the Polish Diet on March 27, 1818, marks the culminating point of his liberalism; thenceforth reactionary tendencies began to prevail. In 1820 a second session of the Diet was held. Alexander attended in a mood compounded of mysticism and irritation. The year before, the Russian historian, Karamzin, had warned him that the restoration of Poland would lead to the dismemberment of Russia and that, since Poland had been conquered by the Russians, its affairs should be controlled entirely from St. Petersburg. Many of the Russian aristocrats at court were insisting on the same ideas, and were doing all they could to prejudice the tsar against his liberal experiment in Poland.

In the session of 1820 Alexander lectured the Diet on being "carried away by the seductions too common in our day." Led by the deputies from Kalisch and the brothers Niemojewski (one of whom in 1831 published a Polish translation of Constant's *Réflexions sur les constitutions*), the opposition complained of the bad administration

---

[23] Alexander said of the position of Constantine and Novosiltsev in the Polish government, "Alongside the liberal principles that a monarch believes he should adopt, he ought to establish corresponding means of repression. I have given the Poles a constitution, but along with this I have created such organs of repression as will make the Poles understand that they must not go beyond a certain limit." Cf. Pingaud, "Alexandre I, roi de Pologne," *Revue d'histoire diplomatique*, XXXIII.

ILLUSTRATIONS

1. TRAVEL BY STAGE-COACH IN THE EARLY NINETEENTH CENTURY
Boilly

2. LIVERPOOL AND MANCHESTER RAILWAY, 1831. THE STATION WHERE HUSKISSON
WAS KILLED

3. London Stock Exchange

4. Machines for Printing Cotton Cloth

Wellington   Nesselrode   Gentz, Humboldt
      Metternich
Hardenberg   Castlereagh   Labrador   Talleyrand

5. THE CONGRESS OF VIENNA
by Isabey

6. Talleyrand   7. Alexander

8. Metternich
by Thomas Lawrence

9. Castlereagh
by Thomas Lawrence

10. BARONESS VON KRUDENER

11. LOUIS XVIII
by Gérard

12. Francis I of Austria
by *Thomas Lawrence*

13. FRANCE REVIVING THE BOURBON LILIES, (turning her back on Napoleon and military glory)

15. CARICATURE OF THE CARLSBAD DECREES, 1819

14. KARL LUDWIG SAND

16. EARLY NINETEENTH CENTURY LABORATORY
The Royal Institute in London, (the youthful Faraday assisting Davy)

17. LENOIR'S MUSEUM OF MEDIAEVAL AND RENAISSANCE ART—PARIS

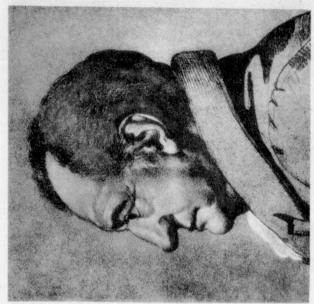

20. WALTER SCOTT
by David Wilkie

21. FIRST PERFORMANCE OF HUGO'S *HERNANI*

22. THE COTTAGE
by Constable

23. THE BAY OF BAIAE
by Turner

24. WHEN THE MORNING STARS SANG TOGETHER
by *William Blake*

25. THE OATH OF THE HORATII
by Louis David

26. THE RAFT OF THE MEDUSA
by Géricault

27. THE MASSACRE OF CHIOS
by *Delacroix—Salon of 1824*

28. THE VOW OF LOUIS XIII

by *Ingres—Salon of 1824*

29. Faust and Mephisto

30. GERMAN NAZARENE SCHOOL
Annunciation by Carolsfeld

31. NEUBRANDENBURG AT SUNDOWN

32. PARIS
by Canova

33. CLASSICAL REVIVAL—CHURCH OF SAN FRANCESCO DI PAOLA AT NAPLES

34. CLASSICAL REVIVAL—PROPYLAEA, MUNICH
Designed by von Klenze

36. GOTHIC REVIVAL
"A Villa in the Thirteenth Century Style"

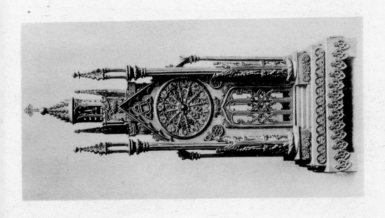

35. GOTHIC REVIVAL—CLOCK

37. Charles Fourier

38. Idealized View, Owenite Community—1823

40. FRIEDRICH LIST

39. LAMENNAIS—1818

41. HEGEL IN HIS STUDY—1828

42. CARICATURE OF LOUIS XVIII'S INTERVENTION IN SPAIN—1823
(Emperors of Austria and Russia at the Left)
by Cruikshank

43. Coronation of Charles X in the Cathedral of Rheims

44. GEORGE CANNING
by Sir Thomas Lawrence

45. Flag Presented to the Polish Revolutionaries of 1830 by the
Young Men of Boston

46. Liberty Guiding the People in 1830
by Delacroix

47. REVOLUTION OF 1830 IN PARIS

48. Coronation of Otto I in Athens

and of the censorship, instituted in 1819. Nearly every bill presented
to the Diet was rejected. The tsar hastened to close the session, and
had it not been for the intervention of the British ambassador and
of Pozzo di Borgo, he would then and there have abrogated the constitution. In the administration the liberal, Potocki, who was developing an excellent school system and was improving the new
School of Engineering and the new University of Warsaw, was
replaced by a reactionary. Other arbitrary replacements followed,
for all of which Novosiltsev was chiefly responsible, though he often
had the coöperation of the Polish Jesuits and some of the Polish
bishops. Public finance, however, was in 1821 placed in the hands of
a Polish noble, Lubecki, a very competent financier who put the
public funds in order and through wise administration stimulated
in an extraordinary fashion the growth of commerce and industry—
the one happy chapter in the history of the Congress Kingdom. It
was chiefly owing to Lubecki that the foundations were laid for that
industrial development which afterward made Russian Poland the
great manufacturing center for the whole empire.

The hostile attitude of the tsar toward the Polish Diet and the
increasing interference of Constantine and Novosiltsev in Polish
affairs with the purpose of emasculating the constitutional régime,
as well as the older desire of the Poles to see their former state reconstituted, led to the formation of secret societies in the army. The most
important of these was the National Patriotic Society, founded at
Warsaw in 1821 by Major Lukasinski. The organization was copied
from that of the Neapolitan and French Carbonari; the members
knew only their local head, who was part of a vast secret network.
With the help of the police in Paris and Berlin, the organization
of the National Patriotic Society was discovered. Lukasinski and
several other leaders were arrested, and were condemned in 1821 to
sentences of hard labor.[24] The same hostility to the tsar's régime
was also manifested in the third session of the Diet in 1825, though
Alexander refused to admit the leader of the opposition to the
sessions. After a few meetings the Diet was dismissed; the tsar then

[24] Owing to the reticence of Lukasinski during his trial, the secret Patriotic Society
continued its work. In 1823 it was in touch with the secret societies in Russia, though no
agreement was reached.

issued an Additional Act which suppressed the provision of the constitution making the sessions of the Diet public.

The reactionary policy of the Russian government in the new Polish kingdom and the memory of the former Polish state aroused a nationalist movement among the Poles who lived within the Russian state and who had hoped in due time to be incorporated in the Congress Kingdom. The center of this agitation was the new University of Vilna, founded in 1813, where a group of students organized societies originally intended to improve student morals but later devoted to nationalist propaganda. The most important of these was the Philomathians, whose membership included the youthful Adam Mickiewicz, destined to be the greatest of Polish literary masters. These student societies showed the influence of the German *Burschenschaften*, Polish students having come into contact with the movement of the Universities of Berlin and Königsberg. The nationalist ideas of Herder were spread among the youth of Poland through the writings of Brodzinski, a professor of Polish literature in the University of Warsaw, especially through his *Über die Klassizität und den Romantismus* (1818), which glorified Polish national traditions and the artistic and intellectual possibilities of Polish culture.

The students protested publicly against the failure of the Russian government to incorporate in the new kingdom all the Poles under Russian rule and also against the current Russian policy of depriving them even of their existing rights. In 1824 the government, at the instigation of Novosiltsev, arrested the leaders of the Philomathians and transported them to Russia or Siberia, where some were forced into the army. The same year several of the most eminent professors, including the great Polish historian, Lelewel, were dismissed and the university placed under close surveillance, the police being ordered to watch the students and the faculty "in class, at church, in their dwellings and everywhere else." When Alexander died in 1825, the hopes of Polish freedom were rapidly vanishing.[25]

[25] In the Final Act of Vienna it had been stipulated that "the Poles subject to Prussia, Russia, and Austria will receive a system of representation and national institutions organized according to the type of political existence that each of the governments to which they belong will judge convenient and opportune to grant them." Neither the Austrian nor the Prussian government fulfilled these promises. On the contrary, they ruled the Poles allotted to their governments with more severity than they had used earlier. Especially in Prussian Poland, an active policy of Germanizing the schools and the administration was undertaken. The little Republic of Cracow, with 103 square

After 1815 Russian affairs occupied Alexander far less than international concerns; the last ten years of his reign form a rather melancholy chapter in Russian history. The Napoleonic Wars had made
Russia one of the leading European powers and the tsar, aware of
the fact and proud of it, liked to spend much of his time in western
Europe hobnobbing with kings and statesmen. Whenever he returned to Russia, he seemed preoccupied and generally weary of
life. The obscurantism that had marked his actions since his conversion in 1812 now descended more than ever upon him, clouding all
his decisions. Although he frequently announced to his family his
intention to abdicate, he found it easier to allow things to drift.
The administration of the state fell increasingly into the hands of
the brutal Arakcheiev and after 1822 that of the church was influenced by Photius, a fanatical monk and a strange holy man, who
wrote in the third person a life of himself describing in detail his
combats with devils. Arakcheiev faithfully did everything that he
could to please Alexander, and went to all lengths to humor him
and to keep the Russian people from making any disturbance that
would jar his nerves. After the tsar's fright over a minor disturbance
in one of his favorite regiments in 1820, which Arakcheiev falsely
made Alexander believe was a revolt, it became nearly impossible
to communicate with the emperor except through his favorite. It
was Arakcheiev's passion for detail and his undeniable ability as an
administrator that made it possible for the tsar to turn over to him
the whole management of the Russian state. All the bright hopes of
reform that had marked the beginning of Alexander's reign now
gradually vanished, and the government fell more and more into
the hands of officials who employed "every sort of knavery, trickery,
fraud, and embezzlement."[26]

Arakcheiev, seeing that the tsar was now indifferent, frustrated
the numerous proposals for social or political reform in which Alexander had earlier interested himself. It was through the same agency
that Alexander introduced a system of military colonies, which in

miles and 90,000 inhabitants, on the other hand, had its own self-government, and the
Poles who lived under it were more contented than those who lived under the governments of Russia, Prussia, and Austria. These governments had also promised to bring
all the parts of old Poland into a free-trade area. This promise was likewise left unful-
filled.

    [26] V. O. Kluchevsky, *A History of Russia* (London, 1931), V, 164.

the last years of his life did most to make him hated in Russia. As early as 1815, he had become convinced that the army should be established in agricultural communities scattered over the land, a plan he seems to have got from the work of a French officer, Servane, published in 1810. In these villages the soldiers would live with their families under the most severe discipline. The scheme was instituted to save money—the army was using about a third of the total revenue—and to improve the morale of the troops, though neither result was obtained.

By 1825 nearly a third of the army had been placed in these colonies. The discipline, which was extended to the peasants living in the neighborhood, became increasingly severe. The whole population of these military villages was put under a rigorous drill; even the children had to wear uniforms. Revolts broke out, but Arakcheiev put them down with savage brutality. In the matter of religion, too, the government became more repressive after 1815; the Jesuits were expelled and the activities of the Bible Societies were restricted. The universities were placed under the direction of one of Alexander's closest friends, Prince Golitsin. After 1822 many professors were dismissed, and orders were issued to those who remained that they were to base all their teaching on the ideas expressed in the Holy Alliance, even to the point of demonstrating in the mathematics courses the moral significance of the triangle as a symbol of the Trinity. This reactionary policy was extended to the secondary schools and went far to undo the excellent educational program that Alexander had earlier instituted. Finally, Photius, the tsar's religious adviser, was even able to persuade Alexander to dismiss his old friend, Prince Golitsin.

The policies of the tsar after 1815 disappointed many of the upper classes who had hoped that he would fulfill his earlier promises of liberalizing the government. There was disgust, too, over the fact that Metternich seemed to be influencing Alexander to pursue policies contrary to the interests of Russia, especially in keeping the tsar from helping the Greek revolutionaries. Some were angry that the Poles should have privileges denied to the Russians. The long wars and the army of occupation kept in France from 1815 to 1818 brought large numbers of Russian officers into contact with western

European ideas. On their return to Russia they saw more clearly
than ever before the evils of their own government, and they began
to consider reforms. As early as 1814 a group of officers had founded
a secret society, reorganized in 1816 as the Union of Salvation, the
leading figure of which was Colonel Paul Pestel, a brilliant young
officer who had lived for a time in Dresden. Its statutes, like those
of the Polish Philomathians and the German *Burschenschaften,* were
modeled on the statutes of the *Tugendbund.* In 1818 its name was
changed to the Union of Welfare. The chief result of its efforts at
reform was the introduction into a few regiments of the Lancastrian
system for the teaching of reading.

In 1820 the society was disbanded, but soon three societies of a
more revolutionary character took its place. The Society of the
North, under the direction of Muraviev, Prince Trubetskoi, Nicholas
Turgeniev, who had studied at the University of Göttingen, and the
poet, Ryleiev, proposed to make Russia into a federated, liberal
monarchy and to free the serfs. The Southern Society, under Pestel,
who had become much more radical, planned a centralized republic
which, when established, would not only liberate the serfs but
would also grant them lands. The third secret society, the United
Slavs, with a more restricted influence, was likewise republican in
outlook. Its program included a design to unite the Slavs of Russia,
Poland, Bohemia, and Croatia. The directors of these societies, most
of whose membership was recruited from the young noblemen in
the army, represented the intellectual élite of their generation. They
were, however, far more interested in discussing the theories contained
in their programs than in preparing a plan to realize them. They
read the writings of Beccaria, Montesquieu, Rousseau, Bentham,
Destutt de Tracy, Constant, and the liberals of the west, they
studied the American and Spanish constitutions, and followed with
an all-absorbed interest the movements of the secret societies everywhere, so far as they were able to find out about them. The Northern
and the Southern Societies could not agree on many points, but
they differed above all on the methods to be employed in accomplish-
ing reform. Pestel believed in the use of assassination and other violent means, while the leaders of the Northern Society had no
sympathy with such tactics. An attempt to get a promise of coöpera-

tion from the Polish secret societies failed. Alexander knew about the existence of the societies, but at first he did nothing to stop their growth. They annoyed him, but he said, "I have shared and encouraged these errors, it is not for me to treat them with severity." In 1822, however, he ordered the closing of the Freemasonic lodges, with which some of the members of the secret societies had affiliations.

On December 13, 1825, Alexander died at Taganrog in the Crimea where he had gone with his wife in search of rest and health. He had intended that his younger brother, Nicholas, should succeed him. Constantine, the first in line of succession, had agreed to this, and in 1823 a statement of the decision had been deposited in the hands of several government agencies. But Nicholas, who was unwilling to assume power without a declaration from Constantine, proclaimed him emperor at St. Petersburg, while Constantine in turn, proclaimed Nicholas tsar at Warsaw. Nicholas refused to take the throne without a formal declaration from his brother. Constantine declined to make such a definite official statement, writing, at the same time, in a private letter to Nicholas that he had long ago given up all idea of reigning. As a result, the throne remained vacant for nearly three weeks. In this interval, the Society of the North, thinking the time ripe, hastily completed plans for a revolt in the garrison at St. Petersburg. Their intention was to force the Senate to convoke an assembly of national representatives to discuss the question of the disputed succession, the details of which none of the conspirators knew. Prince Trubetskoi was to act as dictator. One of the conspirators, a close personal friend of Nicholas, warned him that to save his life he had better abdicate. This warning enabled the government to be prepared.

Arrangements were finally made for Nicholas to mount the throne without the formal consent of Constantine. On the day the troops were to take the oath of loyalty, December 26 (whence the name of the whole movement, the *Decembrist Revolt*), the leaders harangued the men of the Moscow regiment. They told the astonished soldiers, who had not been taken into the plot, that the crown belonged not to Nicholas but to Constantine, and started the cry of "Long live Constantine, long live the Constitution," which the men thought was the name of Constantine's wife. For a few minutes it would have been possible to kill, or at least to seize, Nicholas. But the leaders of the conspiracy failed to act. They had no definite plan; each expected the other to decide and waited for someone to take the lead. All through a day of bitter coldness, without food, and without any knowledge of what the uprising was really about, the common soldiers in the revolting regiment waited patiently for orders from the rebel leaders. None came. Toward evening loyal troops were brought in, and firing on the rebellious soldiers, they crushed the revolt. In January 1826, the Southern Society led by Sergei Muraviev started a rebellion, which was also quickly put down.

The Decembrists never had any chance of success, for their project was the adventure of only a small group. But Nicholas had been given a terrible fright—the specter of revolution haunted him to the end of his days—and he grossly exaggerated the danger, though at the same time he failed to grasp its full significance. Hundreds were arrested in the capital and in the provinces, though only a hundred and twenty were finally tried. Nicholas examined many of the prisoners himself. Most of the leaders bore themselves with dignity and made no secret of their intentions and plans. None were allowed to appear at their own trials, and sentences were pronounced without any defense being permitted. Five of the leaders, including Pestel and Ryleiev, were executed, and the others sentenced to penal servitude or exile to Siberia. "The trial," says Mirsky, "was the first act of a reign that made inevitable and irremediable the cleavage between the monarchy and the best part of the nation and sealed the fate of the Romanovs. It created the legend of the Decembrists which, in Russia, was more effective than anything in raising the moral and poetic prestige of the revolutionary movement and in giving it an almost religious sanction."[27]

The emperor, however, was so impressed with the abuses in the government that he ordered a summary of the facts and opinions of the conspirators to be made. "It is necessary," said this document, "to grant definite and positive laws, to reëstablish justice through more rapid court proceedings, to improve the moral education of

[27] D. M. Mirsky, "The Decembrists," *Slavonic Review*, IV (1925), 403; cf. A. Mazour, *The First Russian Revolution* (Berkeley, 1937), an excellent study.

the clergy, to aid the impoverished nobility, ruined by loans made by the credit associations, to revive commerce and industry, to further education in accordance with the status of the pupils, to improve the condition of the farmers, to abolish the humiliating sale of human beings . . . in short, to rectify the innumerable disorders and abuses."[28]

As a result of the Decembrist Revolt and the investigation that followed, Nicholas I, while talking vaguely of reform, turned at once to the creation of the Third Section, a new type of political police which became a terrible implement of espionage and oppression. During the next years he gave up the earlier practice of using the Russian nobility to govern and introduced so many Germans into the administration that one of the highest Russian nobles appealed to the tsar "to be promoted to be a German." Some reforms were to be made—the reorganization of the central administration, the codification of the laws, some improvements in the status of the peasants, especially of those who lived on the crown lands—but his reign as a whole was later characterized by Herzen as "the plague zone which extended from 1825 to 1855," and by Michelet, who said, "Russia is only an administration and a whip, the administration is German, the whip is Cossack!" This was the only aspect of his rule that was to be known in western Europe.

IV. THE FIRST REVOLUTIONARY WAVE OF THE NINETEENTH CENTURY—A FAILURE

The failure of the Decembrist Revolt completed the triumph of the powers of the Holy Alliance over the scattered forces of Liberalism. Only the Greek Revolt, the fate of which was still undecided, kept alive the Liberal ideal. Everywhere else reaction was again the order of the day. All the revolutions that took place between 1820 and 1825 had been the work of small groups in the armies; only in England was the political unrest directly traceable to economic distress. In the continental states discontent had become acute because the officers were dissatisfied with the cutting-down of the military forces and the replacing of the men who had served during

[28] P. Miloukov, Seignobos, et Eisenmann, *Histoire de Russie*, 2nd ed., (Paris, 1935), II, 732.

the Napoleonic wars by officers of a more legitimist stripe. The secret societies, which had been the instruments of the revolutions, never recruited large numbers of civilians; the mass of the population remained apathetic or hostile. The revolutionaries of 1820 were, as one Pole said of the Decembrists, "a generation without fathers and without sons."

The lack of competent leaders, the cheap mysteries and rites, the vague purposes of the secret societies, and the excesses committed by the more unprincipled members, all tended to discredit conspiracy before it came into action and to hasten its dissolution as soon as it began to operate. The inexperience of the revolutionaries was so great that, after the old governments in Madrid, Lisbon, and Naples had been overthrown, their attempt to erect a new order broke down before any army of intervention marched in. The failure, though complete, was not ignoble. As Ryleiev, expressing the ideal of many of the liberals of his generation, said, "I am certain we shall perish, but our example will remain. Let us offer up ourselves for the future liberty of our fatherland!"[29]

[29] P. Miloukov, "La place du décembrisme dans l'évolution de l'intelligence russe," *Le monde slave*, (1925), 341. London and Paris were filled with exiles from the Revolution of 1820-5. One Italian exile wrote in 1823, "London is peopled with exiles . . . constitutionalists wanting a single chamber, constitutionalists wanting two chambers, constitutionalists on the French model, and others on the Spanish or American models; generals who were deposed . . . presidents of parliaments that had ceased to be . . . and a swarm of journalists, poets, and men of letters. London is the Elysium . . . of illustrious men and of heroes who have failed." *Times Literary Supplement*, 20 Nov. 1937.

Chapter Seven

THE RISE OF A NEW GENERATION

WHILE the frightened kings and statesmen were busy extinguishing the embers of revolution, a new generation was coming of age. By 1824 the majority of the European population had been born since the outbreak of the French Revolution, and so had taken no active part in the movement. Men of this new generation had not yet risen to the highest positions of church and state, but in the 1820's they were to be found in large numbers in business, in the professions, and in the lower ranks of the political and ecclesiastical administration. This younger generation, which had known the bitter conflicts of the revolution only in childhood, found many of the stock political and intellectual formulas of their elders tiresome and meaningless; they began to overhaul the entire inherited ideology of both revolution and reaction. Gradually the fear of bloody revolt and the horror of war were evaporating; the new generation believed that peace and calm could be purchased only by sacrifices too costly for the individual and the nation. New schools of republicanism, Bonapartism, socialism, and Liberal Catholicism appeared, while in the Philhellenic movement romanticism formed an alliance with liberalism. Furthermore, the years of peace that followed Waterloo, the first Europe had known for over a quarter of a century, offered extraordinary opportunities for the development of the arts and the sciences.

I. THE BEGINNINGS OF NINETEENTH-CENTURY SCIENCE AND SCHOLARSHIP

The social transformation which had accompanied the political upheaval of the revolutionary era had changed the life of the scholar. During the eighteenth century learning had been supported chiefly by private wealth or by patronage, but after the wars England was the only important state where this practice persisted. In France, Germany, and Scotland state institutions were becoming the centers of research.[1] Paris, though, was still the greatest of all; the best scientific work in Europe was done in the Collège de France, the Faculté des Sciences, the Muséum d'Histoire Naturelle, and the École Polytechnique. By the end of the 1820's the German universities were developing laboratories and their scholars were beginning to publish important studies. The mathematical teaching and publication of Gauss at Göttingen and the chemical work of Liebig, who was trained in Paris under Gay-Lussac and who in 1826 opened his famous laboratory at Giessen, mark the beginning of an extraordinary development of scientific work in German universities.[2]

Scholars, however, still lacked adequate means of making their results known to each other. Often the same discoveries, made in several places at about the same time, would lie buried in the transactions of some local body. A German, Crelle, began in 1826 to publish a mathematical periodical and in the next two decades new journals were established for the other sciences. The different departments of knowledge gradually became more specialized and the associations of scientists came to be international rather than local. At the same time, the development of German Idealist Philosophy, with its attempt to bring all creation into a single system, forced a separation of philosophy and science. More rapidly than ever before, science, with its varied and independent methods, was establishing its freedom from a philosophy which attempted to cover all things with a vague and nonquantitative formula. The interaction between science and industry, too, became more important than it had been. During the eighteenth century, the growth of new industrial techniques, whereby old industries were transformed and new industries created, had furnished impetus to private investigators. But the first quarter of the nineteenth century marks the beginning of the modern period, in which scientific research and formulation lead the way for invention. Engineering, the application of theoretical science, became pos-

[1] Mme. de Staël wrote of the scholars of Germany: "They are continually discovering new districts in the vast region of antiquity, metaphysics, and science. What is called study in Germany is truly admirable, fifteen hours a day of solitude and labor during years on end appear to them a natural mode of existence." Mme. de Staël, *De l'Allemagne,* Part I, chap. xiv. Southey declared, "there is now more intellectual activity in Germany than in any other country in the world." G. Ticknor, *Life, Letters and Journals* (Boston, 1877), I, 136.

[2] The best introduction to the history of science is J. D. Dampier-Whetham, *History of Science* (2nd ed., New York, 1930).

sible, and with it came rapid mechanical advances that transformed society.

The main outlines of exact quantitative science were taking shape. Dalton established the definite combining weights in chemistry; and in 1815 Avagadro, an Italian scholar, proposed the famous hypothesis which fixed the relation between atom and molecule and completed the quantitative basis of chemistry, though the significance of the formulation was not appreciated until later in the century. Gay-Lussac, a Frenchman, Berzelius, a Swede, and Liebig, a German, perfected methods of exact analysis on which future investigation was to depend. Berzelius introduced the present chemical symbolism. "So great had been the progress in chemistry that a chemist of 1831 would feel more at home with the chemistry of 1931 than with that of 1781."[3] Two Frenchmen, Fourier and Sadi Carnot, in the 1820's laid the foundations for the mathematical handling of heat transformations essential for thermodynamics, a work fundamental for steam engineering. Fresnel established in 1818 the wave theory of light which, with the work of Fraunhofer on the spectrum lines, represents the beginning of modern optics and spectroscopy.

Electricity and magnetism had for a long time attracted interest as scientific curiosities, but their obvious importance for chemistry and for the investigation of living matter now aroused interest in their quantitative aspects. Volta had made possible the battery and the measurement of electric currents. The discovery of the influence of an electric current on a magnet by Oersted, of circuits on each other by Ampère, together with the careful measurement of these effects by Ampère and Weber were other decisive steps. Davy and Faraday in England founded electro-chemistry. Ohm managed to find a stable source of current in the thermoelectric couple and

[3] E. J. Holmyard, *Makers of Chemistry* (Oxford, 1931), 25. The progress in science becomes even more remarkable when one considers the laboratories of the time. Wöhler describes Berzelius' laboratory at Stockholm: "As Berzelius led me into his laboratory, I was, as it were, in a dream, doubting whether it was really true that I was in this famous place. Adjoining the living-room, the laboratory consisted of two ordinary chambers with the simplest fittings; there was neither oven nor fume chamber, neither water nor gas supply. In one room stood two ordinary work-tables; at one of these Berzelius had his working-place, the other was assigned to me. On the walls were several cupboards with reagents. In the middle of the room stood the mercury trough and glass-blower's table. The washing place consisted of a stone cistern having a tap with a pot under it. In the other room were the balances and other instruments. In the kitchen, where the food was prepared by the severe old Anna, cook and factotum of the master, stood a small furnace and the ever-heated sandbath." E. J. Holmyard, *op. cit.*, 241-242.

worked out the exact relations of potential, resistance, and quantity of current, thus establishing the principal electric measurements and their fundamental relations. Mathematics, in the work of Fourier and Gauss, kept pace with the needs of the new knowledge.

Parallel to these new conceptions in physics and chemistry, striking advances were being made in geology and biology. Geology was a new science whose progress was beset with all sorts of fantastic preconceptions. Among a number of works published at this time, that of Lyell, an Englishman, stands out as the most important. By close observation of geological processes at work in his own day, he reached the conclusion that the long operation of similar processes was sufficient to explain how the earth had assumed its present form. These conclusions, embodied in his *Principles of Geology* (1830), and the similar views of other geologists were immediately attacked by those who held the theological explanation of creation. In biology the controversy between mechanism and vitalism entered a new phase because of the work of the organic chemists who were beginning to make the products of living matter in the laboratory. Wöhler in 1828 produced urea in his laboratory; other artificial preparations hitherto found only in living matter were soon evolved. In 1827 Baer, by discovering the mammalian ovum, overthrew the old theory that every egg contains the complete animal in miniature, and thus created modern embryology. Gall did fundamental work on the structure and physiology of the brain, though he was also responsible for many myths of heredity and brain localization.

In the field of natural history Lamarck's speculations led to a famous dispute in the French Académie des Sciences between Cuvier and Saint-Hilaire. Cuvier, taking the orthodox side, maintained that his opponent's hypothesis of the unity of all species was a limitation of the absolute liberty of God who might create independently of any law of nature. In defending the Biblical doctrine, he was much praised by the theologians of his time, but the future belonged to Saint-Hilaire, though not until twenty years later was his hypothesis taken up by Darwin and given an adequate inductive basis.[4] On the day the news of the July Revolution reached Weimar, Goethe chanced to meet his friend, Eckermann, and asked him whether he had heard

---

[4] Cf. J. Vienot, *Cuvier 1769-1832* (Paris, 1932).

the exciting news from Paris. When Eckermann began to discuss
the political situation, Goethe replied that what he had in mind was
this scientific quarrel whose significance he considered far greater
than that of any political upheaval. The greatest result of all these
scientific changes was the further growth of the belief that there
was a general scientific method that could be applied in all fields
of human activity. It was now more possible than it had been in
the eighteenth century for men to say that ultimately all problems
could be solved by science. The ecclesiastics began a violent attack
upon this new faith, this independent source of truth.

The humanities—archeology, philology, and history—made extraordinary progress during this period. The conviction was growing that the only sound approach to an understanding of the present
was through a study of the past; that the true explanation of political,
religious, linguistic, and juristic ideas and usages lay in history.
Archæologists continued the slow work of unearthing the past and
of studying it critically. Improved facilities of travel enabled scholars
to visit ancient sites; at the same time governments spent large sums
in extending and improving the museums. Friedrich Schlegel, approaching the study of Indian history through Sanskrit philology,
showed the influence of the civilizations of India on those of the
west. In 1822 Champollion, after studying the material collected by
Napoleon's expedition to Egypt, devised a method of reading hiero-
glyphics and so unlocked the secret of the history of Egyptian civilization. Societies for Oriental studies, like those formed in the eighteenth
century by the Dutch in Java and the British at Calcutta, were organized in Paris in 1822 and in London in 1823.

The study of the culture of Greece and Rome, which in the
eighteenth century had been greatly advanced by the excavation of
Pompeii and by the critical writings of Winckelmann and Wolf,
was rapidly furthered in the first quarter of the nineteenth. Ludwig
I of Bavaria, in 1812, brought the pediment sculptures of Aegina to
his new Glyptothek at Munich; a few years later the Louvre acquired
the Venus of Melos. In 1816 the English government bought the
Parthenon sculptures, which Lord Elgin had transported from
Greece, and installed them in the British Museum. The reinterpreta-
tion of Greek history dates from the work of Böckh on Athenian

economic life and that of his pupil, Otfried Müller, on the history of Aegina. Through their writings a realistic view of Greek civilization became for the first time possible. Rome attracted archæologists even more than Greece. The best work again was done by German scholars, aided by a succession of Prussian ambassadors at Rome, Wilhelm von Humboldt, Niebuhr, and Bunsen. Niebuhr's *Römische Geschichte* (1812-1832) was the first scientific account of the early history of Rome. His work had a great influence on all later historical study, for, besides showing the value of a close examination of documents and inscriptions, he had grasped the truth that in writing the early history of a people emphasis must be placed on political and social institutions rather than on events. His view ranged prophetically over the future of archæological studies; in 1829 he foretold that Nineveh would be the Pompeii of Middle Asia and that a Champollion would arise for Assyrian studies.

The romantic movement did a great deal to revive interest in the art of the Middle Ages. First Horace Walpole in England and then, after 1800, Chateaubriand in France, Scott in England, and the Schlegels and their circle in Germany prepared the way. After 1815 the governments of England, of France, and of the German states began extensive restorations of medieval monuments, a work of preservation in which France took the lead. The completion of the half-finished Cathedral of Cologne became a national project to which Germans of all faiths contributed. During the Empire Lenoir had gathered from churches damaged during the revolution a magnificent collection of medieval sculpture which he exhibited in Paris and which was visited by scholars and amateurs from all over Europe.[5] The collection was broken up in 1816 and the monuments returned to their original places, but soon the great state museums of Europe for the first time began to exhibit medieval art. The Louvre opened a gallery of Romanesque and Gothic sculpture in 1824, and three years later the superb collection of German primitives assembled by the Boisserée brothers was bought by the King of Bavaria for the Pinakothek at Munich.

Closely connected with the development of ancient and medieval

[5] Cf. Courajod, "L'influence du musée des monuments français sur le développement de l'art et des études historiques," *Revue historique*, 1886, and F. Rücker, *Les origines de la conservation des monuments historiques en France 1790-1830* (Paris, 1913).

archæology was the growth of philology. In Napoleon's time Paris had become an important center for the study of foreign languages; Rémusat published studies of Chinese linguistics and Sylvestre de Sacy put the study of Arabic on a scholarly basis. Burnouf, one of their students, brought out in 1826 a work on Hindu philology which continued the work of Friedrich Schlegel; in 1829 he began the publication of the first substantial study on the languages of Persia. Linguistic studies were pursued with an almost religious enthusiasm in the German universities. The brothers Grimm, who had studied at Marburg with Savigny, the historian of Roman law, were resurrecting the whole of the German past—folk-lore, law, religion, and social institutions—by an extended research into old Teutonic literature and legendry. Their enthusiasm carried them to the mystic belief that there was a superior folk-wisdom contained in the old Germanic stories and legends, and in the end they did much to breed an overweening nationalism. They also influenced the German literary movements of the first half of the nineteenth century; Tieck, Uhland, Arnim, Brentano, and others among their contemporaries owed much of their inspiration to the enthusiasm for every part of the life-story of the German peoples which the Grimms were creating. Another German scholar, Bopp, founded comparative philology by publishing in 1816 a work which showed the similarities of Sanskrit, Greek, Latin, and Germanic conjugations. Raynouard, a French scholar, pointed out the same resemblances in the Romance languages, while a Dane, Rask, proved the relationship of Latin, Greek, the Germanic languages, and one of the Slavic dialects. At the same time, a German scholar, Creuzer, founded the study of comparative mythology.[6]

The years 1789 to 1815 had brought more dramatic changes than the preceding two or three centuries, and had given to all men a new sense of the movement of history.[7] This, in turn, contributed to a brilliant renaissance of historical scholarship and writing. After 1815 vast collections of documents were gathered in state libraries, museums, and archives; the most fundamental of them were edited

[6] Cf. H. Pedersen, *Linguistic Science in the Nineteenth Century* (Cambridge, 1931), and Karl Francke, *Die Brüder Grimm* (Dresden, 1899).

[7] An excellent survey of the history of historical writing in the nineteenth century is G. P. Gooch, *History and Historians of the Nineteenth Century* (2nd edition, London, 1913).

and printed. The great German patriot and reformer, Stein, when driven from public life, devoted himself to inaugurating an extended series of documents of German history, the *Monumenta Germaniæ Historica*, with the motto, *"Sanctus amor patriæ dat animum."* The first volume, edited by Pertz, appeared in 1826 but the series is not even now complete. The work was so admirably done that the *Monumenta* have long since become the model for countless similar publications. In France, the Bourbon government founded the École des Chartes (1821) for the training of archivists and librarians, and the reorganized Académie des Inscriptions et Belles Lettres undertook to continue a number of series of important publications begun under the Ancien Régime. Quantities of historical memoirs and documents were published; during the fifteen years of the Restoration nearly three hundred volumes of historical texts were brought out. The best editing was that directed by Guizot, who in 1833 started the great collection of *Documents inédits sur l'histoire de France.*[8]

The writing of history was deeply affected by romanticism, by the growing influence of the idea of social evolution, and by nationalist ideals. The historians of each nation, partly through the use of documents but more by a glowing literary style, followed in the path of Walter Scott and Chateaubriand and tried to evoke a living picture of the great ages of past national glory. In Germany, Stenzel treated the Franconian emperors and Raumer the Hohenstaufens. Voigt wrote a prose epic of the conversion and settlement of Prussia by the Teutonic Knights, while Luden, in a long career of teaching and writing, ranged over the whole history of the German Middle Ages. In France, Barante published an extended narrative of the history of the Dukes of Burgundy, in order that people might "see the fifteenth century instead of hearing it described." Fauriel, in a work on early French history, contended that, in the formation of medieval civilization, the Celtic element was more important than the Frankish. Michaud described the glories of the French in the age of the Crusades, and Raynouard, drawing a vivid picture of the troubadours, proclaimed the supremacy of French

[8] Cf. D. Doolittle, *The Relations between Literature and Medieval Studies in France from 1820 to 1860*, (Bryn Mawr, 1933).

among the Romance languages. Augustin Thierry, a more gifted
stylist, wrote a dramatic account of the Merovingian period and,
in a later work, of the age of the Norman Conquest. The leading French master of "historical resurrection" and of nationalist
idealism, however, was the young Jules Michelet. He began as a
student of philosophy under Cousin, but his reading of Vico and
Herder turned him at an early date to historical studies. In 1833
he published the first volume of his *Histoire de France*, in which
romanticism and nationalism are fused in a great literary masterpiece.[9] The same patriotic and romantic spirit characterized the
historical work of Karamzin in Russia, Lelewel in Poland, Cantù
in Italy, and Palácky in Bohemia.

Many historical works were written primarily from the liberal
point of view. In the German universities professors like Rotteck at
Freiburg and Schlosser at Heidelberg turned their historical teaching and writing into a long attack on the evil ways of kings and
nobles. Sismondi, a Swiss, in an excellent history of the Italian
city-states of the Middle Ages, tried to prove that no state can become or remain great without liberty. The Englishman, Hallam,
though a conscientious scholar, wrote his remarkable survey of
medieval history and his account of the development of the British
Constitution from the point of view of the Whiggism of the 1820's.[10]
In the course of the same decade Mignet and Thiers in France began
the historical defense of the French Revolution, and Guizot, the
ablest of all historical apologists for liberalism, reinterpreted all history as the story of the rise of the middle class. According to Guizot,
the development of the educated bourgeoisie has always been
synonymous with human progress. In modern times, the upper
middle class has supported the arts and sciences, and is now working
to hold the balance between absolutism and Jacobinism. The ground
won by the middle class in the revolution must never be surrendered
either to the forces of autocracy or to the mob. The political doctrines
embodied in Guizot's writings gave his works an enormous vogue
in the middle of the nineteenth century.

[9] Cf. Introduction to C. Jullian, *Historiens français du XIXᵉ siècle* (Paris, 1897),
Augustin Thierry, *Thierry* (Paris, 1922), and G. Monod, *Michelet* (2 vols., Paris, 1923).
[10] Cf. T. P. Peardon, *The Transition in English Historical Writing, 1760-1830* (New
York, 1933).

The introduction of a more scientific method into historical studies was chiefly the work of Niebuhr and Ranke. Niebuhr, as we have seen, applied the canons of classical philology to the study of the early history of Rome and so placed modern historiography on a scientific basis. Ranke, a younger man, elaborated a similar method for modern history. In a work published in 1824, he recommended a careful study of documents and an objective approach as the first requirements of the historian whose ultimate aim should always be to see the past *"wie es eigentlich gewesen."* He founded the first historical seminar in 1833; his teaching, even more than his writing, determined the course of modern historical scholarship for a century, and is still authoritative.[11]

II. A NEW ROMANTIC GENERATION IN LITERATURE AND THE ARTS

Goethe, Chateaubriand, and Wordsworth were still writing during the restoration, but their places were soon to be disputed by a new generation of romantic poets and novelists. This younger group continued the denunciation of the rationalistic and academic canons of eighteenth-century classicism, and, like the earlier romantic generation, demanded the right of free, imaginative expression. For their subjects they still turned to the Middle Ages, to nature, or to their own emotions, in a word, to anything which the writers of the Enlightenment had abhorred. More than ever before the names of Shakespeare, Dante, and Cervantes—so unmistakably great in defiance of all the rules of Aristotle—were being invoked to tie up the movement with that of the Renaissance and to endow it with a glorious ancestry. As complex as ever, romanticism continued to produce results contrary to those which appeared inevitable. But it was evident after 1815, and especially after 1820, that the movement was turning away from a defense of the throne and the altar to nationalist and liberal ideals.[12]

By 1820 the greatest days of German romanticism were over. Novalis and Kleist were dead, E. T. A. Hoffmann and Tieck had already published their more significant works. The aged Goethe,

---

11 Cf. H. Oncken, *Aus Rankes Frühzeit* (Gotha, 1922), and E. Simon, *Ranke und Hegel* (Munich, 1928).
12 Cf. P. Van Tieghem, *Le mouvement romantique* (2nd edition, Paris, 1923), an admirable introduction.

until his death in 1832, held court in Olympian grandeur at Weimar. Here he received visitors from every country in Europe; from France, Benjamin Constant, Victor Cousin, and the sculptor, David d'Angers; from England, a British publisher bearing a posthumous letter from Byron; from Poland, Mickiewicz; from Denmark, Oehlenschläger; from Russia, Zhukovsky. Kollár, the young Slovak poet, brought him his collection of Slavic songs; Quinet sent his translation of Herder, Delacroix his lithographs of the Faust story, and Berlioz his score of the *Damnation of Faust*. Goethe still maintained an interest in the poetry of his younger contemporaries; he read their penetrating critical treatises—a field in which the German romantic movement was easily the richest in Europe—and he found much of value in the collections of folk poetry that they were publishing. But his sympathies were no longer with the movement; "Classic," he declared, "is that which is healthy, romantic that which is sick."

In the 1820's Lenau, Wilhelm Müller, Rückert, Eichendorff, Chamisso, and Mörike continued the great tradition of German romantic lyricism, and in Vienna Grillparzer brought out his first drama. Heine published his earliest collection of verses in 1822, followed in 1827 by his famous *Buch der Lieder*. His brilliant lyric gift renewed all the old themes of German romanticism, the love of nature in all her moods, the fascination of old folk-tales, and the glorification of the spontaneous emotions of the heart. After the Revolution of 1830 he went to Paris and began to attack the forces of reaction, clericalism, the Holy Alliance, and royal absolutism. In his enthusiasm for liberty and for the rights of man, he carried into German literature the attitudes of Byron. A similar point of view was expressed in the early critical writings of Ludwig Börne; he and Heine and Gutzkow became in the 1830's the leaders of *Young Germany*.

In England, where Scott was now pouring out his historical romances, a new generation of romantic writers was coming of age. Keats returned to the Elizabethans for his inspiration, and though he died at twenty-five, he enriched the language with some of its finest lyrics. His friend Shelley, "a man of talent and honor," as Byron said, "but crazy about religion and morality," was an ardent atheist and democrat. His *Prometheus Unbound* (1820) enshrined the old Jacobin doctrines in one of the greatest poems in the English language. The new orientation of English romanticism is even more strikingly shown in the poetry of Byron.[13] In *Childe Harold's Pilgrimage*, in *Cain*, and in *Manfred*, as well as in many other poems and dramas, he announced a gospel of boundless liberty. In England before his departure in 1816, and afterward on the continent, he took up the cause of the underdog. "I have simplified my politics," he declared, "into a detestation of all existing governments." He spoke of the cause of oppressed nationalities as "the very poetry of politics"; everywhere he made political discontent and revolt romantic.[14] Newspapers, periodicals, and memoirs of the time are filled with his name, and his poems were translated into a dozen languages. His heroic death in Greece in 1824 canonized him as a martyr of liberalism and made his name a rallying cry of the dissatisfied in every state in Europe.

The French romantic school of the 1820's lagged behind that of England and Germany. Mme. de Staël's *De l'Allemagne* (1813) and a translation of Wilhelm Schlegel's study of the drama (1814) —works that influenced the romantic movement in every country— and Sismondi's *Littératures du Midi de l'Europe* (1813) brought French literature strongly under foreign influences.[15] These new currents were discussed after 1823 in a number of literary circles (*cénacles*). A new journal of opinion, the *Globe* (1824), began to sponsor romantic ideals, and in a series of literary manifestoes by Stendhal, Sainte-Beuve, and Victor Hugo (whose *Préface de Cromwell* attracted the widest attention) a new literary canon was evolved. Meanwhile the early poems of Lamartine and Alfred de Vigny, the first historical novels of Merimée, Balzac, and Hugo, and the plays of Dumas and Hugo had aroused the reading public to a high

---

[13] Cf. D. L. Raymond, *The Political Career of Byron* (New York, 1924).

[14] As one Italian poet wrote, "I never saw the falls of Niagara, nor have I seen a volcano, though I have witnessed great storms and lightning has struck near me. Nothing, however, could equal the emotions I had in reading the verses of Byron; ancient and modern wisdom, God set beside Satan and appearing pale by comparison. For years I have been able to see or to think of nothing save through Byron!" P. Hazard, "L'âme italienne de 1815 à 1830," *Revue des deux mondes*, April 15, 1910, 880.

[15] Cf. I. A. Henning, *L'Allemagne de Mme. de Staël et la polémique romantique* (Paris, 1929); P. Gautier, "Les deux Allemagnes de Mme. de Staël", *Revue des deux mondes*, 1930; F. Baldensperger, "A la recherche de l'esprit européen avec Mme. de Staël," *Occident*, 1930, and Jean-R. de Salis, *Sismondi 1773-1842* (Paris, 1932).

pitch of excitement. All the forces of classicism in the schools and
the press opposed the efforts of the younger men. Nowhere in Europe
did the war between classicism and romanticism become so dramatic.
It finally came to a battle in 1830 when the classicists tried to drive
Hugo's *Hernani* off the stage of the *Comédie Française*. All the
young poets and novelists joined in the fray, their ranks being
swelled by Delacroix, Berlioz, and their followers. The romanticists
won their cause just a few months before the political liberals defeated the royal troops in the street fighting of July, 1830. By this
time the romanticists had discovered that their Bourbon rulers did
not resemble Charlemagne or St. Louis, and that their *émigré*
aristocracy had little of the glamour of old-time chivalry. Chateaubriand, suffering from this sentimental disappointment, as well as
from the shabby treatment given him by the king, had deserted the
Bourbon cause as early as 1824.[16] Gradually the younger men identified their literary aspirations with the political ideals of democracy,
for, as Hugo declared, "Romanticism is liberalism in literature."[17]

The romantic movement, as it spread from Germany, England,
and France across Europe, deeply affected the subject matter and
the style of every national literature from Portugal and Spain to
Russia and Scandinavia. After 1820 new romantic works began to
appear in large numbers among all these peoples, almost all of them
in a strongly nationalistic key. In northern and eastern Europe the
influence of German romantic ideals was most clearly marked,
though these ideals were often spread by Mme. de Staël's *De
l'Allemagne*. The Émigration and the movement of armies during
the revolutionary period, the growth of travel literature and of the
periodical press—especially the circulation of the *Edinburgh Review*
and the *Westminster Review* in England, the *Augsburg Gazette* in
Germany, and the *Globe* in France—and, finally, the hordes of exiles
created by the revolutions of 1820 and 1830 helped to stimulate a
literary exchange among the nations, which became fully as characteristic of the time as the growth of nationalist and liberal ideas
in literature. In every country poets and dramatists and novelists
were turning for their subjects from the life of the Gallicized upper

[16] Cf. F. Baldensperger, "Les années 1827-1828 en France et au dehors," *Revue des
cours et conférences*, 1928.
[17] Cf. J. Marsan, *La bataille romantique* (Paris, 1912).

classes to that of the common people, especially to their traditional customs and national legends. This romantic nationalism which was spreading across Europe was still almost entirely of a cultural type, but it created an atmosphere exceedingly favorable to the development of the exaggerated political nationalism so characteristic of the later nineteenth century.

In Norway, Sweden, and Denmark, collections of old legends and poems were made and an original romantic literature appeared in the poetry of Tegner and Geijer in Sweden and of Oehlenschläger in Denmark. Zhukovsky introduced the romantic themes in Russia and in the 1820's the young poet, Pushkin, a friend of the Decembrists, wrote his first verses, remarkable for their combination of stylistic perfection and fervid romantic sentiment.[18] His great historical drama, *Boris Godunov,* was composed in 1825, and between 1822 and 1831 he worked at the various parts of his masterpiece, *Eugen Onegin,* a long, narrative poem which bore many traces of the Byronic influence. What Pushkin accomplished in creating modern Russian literature was being done for Poland by the young Lithuanian liberal, Mickiewicz. In his *Conrad Wallenrod* (1828), a stirring Byronic tale of medieval life, he produced a great national epic of the Polish people.[19]

Among the Czechs and the Magyars, romanticism evoked a glowing picture of the past and preached the necessity of reviving a sense of national solidarity through literature. Kollár's *Slava's Daughter* (1824), a tale of the Czech people, and the early writings of Kisfaludy and Vörösmarty in Hungary derived their poetic inspiration and their nationalistic ideals mostly from German romanticism.[20] In Italy, Milan was the center of romantic innovation. Here was published, in 1818 and 1819, the *Conciliatore,* a political and literary journal like the *Edinburgh Review,* in whose pages Pellico attacked Boileau and the French classic tradition. The new romantic currents found brilliant expression in the poetry and fiction of Manzoni and in the verses of Leopardi, though the strongest

[18] Cf. E. Simmons, *Pushkin* (Cambridge, 1937), and O. J. Falnes, *National Romanticism in Norway* (New York, 1933).

[19] Cf. E. Krakowski, *Mickiewicz* (Paris, 1935).

[20] Cf. G. von Farkas, *Die ungarische Romantik* (Berlin, 1931), G. Kornis, *Ungarische Kulturideale, 1777-1848* (Leipzig, 1930), and the admirable biography of Kossuth by O. Zarek (London, 1936).

advocacy of Italian nationalism was to be found in the work of the lesser figures, Berchet, Rossetti, Niccolini, and D'Azeglio. In nearly all countries the romantic historical novel, inspired by the models of Scott and Chateaubriand, had a tremendous vogue. In sheer quantity this type of nationalistic romantic writing over-shadowed all other literary types in this period.

The fine arts experienced a similar reaction against the classicism of the eighteenth century. Painting, and to a less extent architecture and sculpture, sought out new modes of expression. The fight be-tween classicists and romanticists waxed particularly hot after 1820. The classicists held that there was a universal type of beauty which was the same for all countries; the romanticists retorted that beauty differed from century to century and from nation to nation. The classicists insisted, further, that painting should concern itself chiefly with the representation of the human figure and that form and composition were of first importance; the romanticists often turned to natural landscapes for their favorite subjects and conceived every-thing in terms of light and color. When the romanticists finally triumphed, it was evident that they had borrowed much from their rivals; their differences now seem less marked than they imagined.

The earliest manifestations of the new romantic style of painting were in England and Germany where academic canons had less hold than in France.[21] Greater freedom in the handling of light and color and movement appeared first in the work of the portrait painters, especially in the later portraits of Sir Thomas Lawrence, and then in the paintings of a group of very original landscape artists, which included Constable, Bonington, and Turner. The work of these painters, while it derives somewhat from that of the Dutch and the French landscapists of the seventeenth century, struck an essentially new note. Its freshness and vitality were due in part to an earlier development of English water-color painting. Many of the landscapes of Bonington and Constable were first rapidly sketched in water-color directly from nature. Turner formed his style through learning to paint in the same medium. With its deep feeling for the beauty of the English countryside, the art of these

[21] Cf. H. Focillon, *La peinture au XIXᵉ et XXᵉ siècles* (2 vols., Paris, 1927-28), and L. Réau, *L'art romantique* (Paris, 1930).

men resembles in mood the poetry of Wordsworth. Their contribution to the technical development of modern painting lay in their handling of color; the paint was often put on in smears, dots, and scrapings of the palette knife. The effect was vibrant and alive, far removed from that produced by the smooth, shiny surfaces of much eighteenth century painting. Outside most of the currents of his time was the painter, engraver, and poet, William Blake, an artist of the highest imaginative power who overburdened his designs with a strange, apocalyptic symbolism.

The German painters were deeply influenced by the æsthetic theories of the literary movement, especially by the writings of Wackenroder, Tieck, and Friedrich Schlegel.[22] A group of young artists, reacting against the classical canons of Winckelmann, foregathered in Rome, where they formed the Nazarene School. In the city of martyrs and popes, the Veit brothers, the Schadow brothers, and Overbeck became Catholics, while Cornelius, the ablest of the group, though born a Catholic, underwent conversion to a more mystic faith. The school revived the style of Dürer and of the Italian primitives, and in the name of religion attacked all the technical progress that had been made in painting since the sixteenth century. Returning to Germany—Cornelius reigned successively at Düsseldorf, Munich, and Berlin—they covered the walls of churches and public buildings with vast historical and allegorical frescoes. Like the paintings of the English Pre-Raphaelites of the next generation, their work is literary in its interest; by turning painting into an instrument for the expression of theories, they ended in an academism more lifeless than that against which they had earlier revolted. The most gifted of the German landscape painters was Friedrich, whose simple and powerful manner was evolved largely by himself. None of his paintings was made directly from nature; the subjectivity of his style often gives his work an eerie effect quite like that of some of the poetry of German romanticism.

The most significant school of romantic painting was the French. During the Empire the great collections gathered in the Louvre revealed to the rising generation of art students the glories of Rubens

[22] Cf. J. B. C. Grundy, *Tieck and Runge, a Study of the Relationship of Literature and the Fine Arts in the German Romantic Movement* (Strasbourg, 1930).

and the Venetian painters who, like Shakespeare in literature, had achieved superb expression without a knowledge of classical rules. With the return of the Bourbons, David, the high priest of classicism, was banished to Brussels, and within a few years English portrait and landscape painting began to be exhibited in France. The road was opened for the development of new ideals of beauty, and the younger men gradually threw off the academism of their teachers. The first outstanding achievement of the new style was Géricault's *"Le Radeau de la Méduse,"* exhibited in the Salon of 1819, a painting full of movement and color and an open defiance of the tinted bas-reliefs that often passed for paintings in the work of the school of David. In the Salon of 1824 Delacroix's *"Scène des Massacres de Scio"*—called by his detractors the "Massacre of Painting"—was hung opposite the classical *"Vœu de Louis XIII"* of Ingres, a follower of David. This same Salon included also some excellent English landscape paintings, which strengthened the position of the French romantic painters even more than did their own work.[23]

A veritable war now raged between classicists and romanticists. The classicists accused their opponents of "painting with a drunken broom"; the romantics turned up their coat-collars when they passed a classical painting lest they catch cold! In the schools, especially through the influence of the Académie des Beaux Arts, Raphaël, David, and Canova continued to be held up as models and the classical cause was brilliantly supported by Ingres. His work, though often deficient in color and mechanical in composition, was, through its matchless drawing, a continuing comment on the chief weakness of the romantic painters. More quietly a revolution was taking place in French landscape painting. Michel, during the Empire, had begun to paint landscapes as he saw them; then came the great influx of English influences and, in the Salon of 1824, Corot and Huet exhibited their first works. Their position was soon strengthened by the Barbizon School which during the July Monarchy made French landscape painting the greatest in Europe.[24]

In the fields of sculpture and architecture, classicism held its own

[23] The Salons of 1824, 1863, and 1904 are the three great events in modern painting. The first featured the work of the English painters and Delacroix; the second, that of the impressionists; and the third was a retrospective exhibition of the work of Cézanne.
[24] Cf. L. Hautecoeur ed., *Le romantisme et l'art* (Paris, 1928).

until the 1840's. The Italian, Canova, occupied in sculpture the place earlier held in painting by David. Many of his oversized nudes with their slick surfaces and their lifeless muscles give the appearance of having been modeled from cadavers. Among his followers were the Dane, Thorwaldsen, Pradier and Bosio in France, and Schadow and Rauch in Germany. David d'Angers, a friend of Hugo and Sainte-Beuve, left nearly five hundred medallion portraits of his contemporaries. Not until after 1830 did sculpture, as shown by the work of Barye and Rude in France, begin to break away from the lifeless classicism of Canova. In architecture Rome was the great school for a classic, international style. Students flocked there from all countries and Roman buildings were pastiched by Percier and Fontaine in Paris, Schinkel in Berlin, and von Klenze in Munich; even in Russia every great public building or church had to be crowded behind or put inside a row of heavy columns.

The beginnings of the Gothic revival were to be seen in England in a number of pseudo-medieval country houses and churches which were covered with meaningless turrets, crenellations, and pinnacles.[25] After 1815 the taste for Gothic bric-a-brac and furniture began to spread from England on to the continent. The products of this growing craze were often mixed with other incongruous elements. At his country home, La Vallée aux Loups, which was originally a small brick house, Chateaubriand built a portico supported by two columns of black marble and two caryatids of white marble, "for," he said, "I remembered that I had passed through Athens." At one end of the house he added "simulated battlements." The amazing vulgarity of it all never seems to have struck Chateaubriand's generation. The electicism of nineteenth century art was already under way.

Music, in its technical development the youngest of the arts, was easily swept along by the romantic tide. Germany was still the center of musical development; there were to be found the best orchestras and choirs, the most intelligent audiences, and the belief among poets and literary critics that music was the highest of the arts. Over the world of German music towered still the figure of

---

[25] Cf., besides K. Clark, *The Gothic Revival* (London, 1929), M. Trappes-Lomax, *Pugin, a Mediaeval Victorian* (London, 1932), and P. Yvon, *La gothique et la renaissance gothique en Angleterre* (Caen, 1931).

Beethoven, whose style, in its development and enrichment, shows most clearly the transition from classicism to romanticism. Beethoven, however, was now nearing the end of his work, and the ablest of the younger men was the young Viennese composer, Schubert. He died (1828) only a year after Beethoven, but left some remarkable instrumental works and over six hundred songs. By his settings of the poems of Goethe, Rückert, Uhland, Heine, Müller, and other romantic poets, in which the text is given fully as much place as the music, he practically created one of the great forms of modern music. The legacy of Beethoven and Schubert fell to the young Mendelssohn and later to Schumann. In 1821 Weber, the creator of modern German opera, presented *Der Freischütz* in Berlin; two more operas, *Euryanthe* and *Oberon*, which inspired Wagner's early style, show Weber's remarkable growth in richness of expression. Like the romantic poets and scholars, he was deeply interested in the ancient art and legendry of the German people, and in his scores he used, with much effectiveness, melodies in the style of the folk-song. With a great career before him, he died (1826), like Schubert, still a young man.

The striking advances made in musical style in Germany were taken up in France by Hector Berlioz who, according to Théophile Gautier, formed with Hugo and Delacroix "the trinity of French romantic art."[26] His *Symphonie fantastique* (1830), written with a descriptive program, shows his extravagant romantic emotionalism, and, in the handling of the orchestration, his unusual originality. Berlioz and Weber developed orchestral parts for instruments earlier neglected—horns, trumpets, clarinets, and bassoons—and, like the romantic painters, achieved a variety and color in their effects largely unknown to their classical predecessors. Preferring the opera-comique style of Boïeldieu, Hérold, Adam, and Auber, and the Italian grand opera style of Rossini, the public was indifferent to Berlioz' work. At the close of the 1820's the violinist, Paganini, and the youthful Hungarian pianist, Franz Liszt, were developing new violin and piano techniques which made possible for the first time

[26] Cf. A. Boschot, *Berlioz, une vie romantique* (Paris, 1919), F. Baldensperger, *Sensibilité musicale et romantisme* (Paris, 1925). C. Laforêt, *La vie musicale aux temps romantiques* (Paris, 1929), J. Tiersot, *La musique aux temps romantiques* (Paris, 1930) and R. L. Evans, *Les romantiques français et la musique* (Paris, 1934).

the adequate presentation of the works of the masters and in turn revealed new musical resources for the composers. The appeal of music, as of literature, was now less to the aristocracy and the wealthy patron and more to the intelligent and cultivated public. The audiences outside Germany, however, still preferred the florid Italian style of opera, concert, and church music, and entertainers of the type of Rossini, Donizetti, and Bellini found it easier to make a living than did the great composers of the period. Thousands sang the airs of Rossini's *Barber of Seville* (1816) and *William Tell* (1829), and of the operas of Bellini and Donizetti but few knew the work of Beethoven, and practically all were wholly ignorant of the compositions of Schubert, Weber, and Berlioz.

III. THE REVIVAL OF LIBERALISM

The failure of the revolutionary movement of 1820 led liberals to redefine their ideals and to consider new programs of reform. In England, in both the Tory and the Whig parties younger and more liberal leaders were coming to the fore; especially the apparently defunct Whig party was being galvanized into new life. This changing orientation of liberalism, however, was most clearly shown in France, where the failure of the French Carbonari in the years 1821 and 1822 convinced the opponents of Bourbon rule that they should abandon their secret intriguing and should openly defend the Charter of 1814 against all royal encroachments. The leaders, Guizot and Victor Cousin, who had earlier seen the value of such tactics, were now more heeded. They made the *Globe* an effective organ for the expression of their ideals. From its inception in 1824, the editors appealed to the younger generation. Jouffroy published in its pages in 1825 a manifesto for French youth, *Comment les dogmes finissent,* in which he announced, "A new generation is growing up. It has listened and it has understood, and already these youths have passed their elders and seen the emptiness of their doctrines." These neo-liberals had no clearly defined program; their chief contribution was their penetrating criticism of all existing political systems. The keen analysis of ideas found in the *Globe* gave it a general European circulation; it furnished Goethe, as he said, "much to think about three times a week." Gradually its adherents broke up into different groups; some of the younger men, like Mignet and Thiers, continued the defence of the Charter and of constitutional monarchy, though with a less detached attitude; others became republicans, Liberal Catholics, or followers of the new Saint-Simonian School.

Republicanism and Bonapartism, which harked back to the very régimes which the older liberals regarded as nightmares, were beginning to find more followers in all ranks of the population, not only in France but here and there all over Europe.[27] Admiration for the republican ideal was inspired by the success of the United States, by a revival of interest in the writings of Rousseau, and by a new interpretation of the French Revolution in French historical writing. In 1818 Mme. de Staël published her *Considérations sur la Révolution française* in which she praised the Constitution of 1791, though she was careful to differentiate this early phase of the revolution from those which followed. Six years later, Mignet, in his *Histoire de la Révolution française*, the first adequate treatment of the movement, showed that it was not an accidental convulsion, and that its work was not purely destructive. Still more favorable were the ten volumes of Thiers' *Histoire de la Révolution française*, published between 1823 and 1827. Sainte-Beuve remarked later that this work had the effect of the "Marseillaise" and made one love the revolution. No important new theorist of republicanism except Mazzini, who was as yet unknown, appeared during this period, but the republican implications of Destutt de Tracy's *Commentaire sur l'Esprit des Lois* (1811) helped to revive the older republican ideals. Since it was impossible to dwell on the idea of popular sovereignty without realizing its logical possibilities, there were by 1830 currents of republican thought in nearly every European state. Republicanism was particularly strong among the students in Paris, many of whom took part in the street fighting of the July Revolution. As the press could not in any country outwardly advocate such theories, it is impossible to estimate the strength of the movement.

[27] Quinet, as a youth during the Restoration, chanced to come across a book on the revolution which he found filled with strange, new words, like Girondists and Jacobins. "A single word," he said, "had now replaced all the others, the word 'Terror.' I had to have a dictionary for each line, so completely had the language of the Revolution ceased to be a living language." E. Quinet, *Histoire de mes idées* (Paris, 1858), 75-76. Cf. G. de Ruggiero, *History of European Liberalism* (Oxford, 1927).

The growth of Bonapartism is still harder to define.[28] In France it spread from the army and still more from the former soldiers of the Empire, now forced into retirement, into various classes of the population. It gathered force from a flood of memoirs, some of which came from Napoleon's circle at St. Helena, that Promethean background which his foes had unwittingly furnished for the closing scene of his career. After his death in 1821, literary men like Béranger, and towards 1830 Victor Hugo and Stendhal, began to praise Napoleon, while during the whole of the Restoration quantities of cheap lithographs and imperial bric-a-brac were being sold among the French people. From all these sources the legend was arising of a Napoleon who was a supporter of religion, the champion of the principles of the French Revolution, a lover of peace, and the symbol of French national glory. By a deliberately eclectic process, part of his career was brought into prominence, and the rest of it was discreetly relegated to obscurity. Thus in France Bonapartism came to be mingled vaguely with republicanism, with patriotism, and, finally, with romanticism. The rule of Napoleon, which had seemed so tyrannical at home, had been regarded as revolutionary abroad. In Poland, Italy, Germany, and Spain the basis of this vague Bonapartist enthusiasm lay not so much in an understanding of Napoleon's achievements as in the liberals' remembrance of him as the enemy of their hated and despised masters and, after 1815, of the ideals of the Holy Alliance.

It was in the years after 1820, when republicanism and Bonapartism were beginning to take root among the people here and there in Europe, that the leaders of business and banking grew more disaffected. Weary of war and economic chaos, they had welcomed the return of peace in 1815, but now, as prosperity returned, their dissatisfaction with the repressive policies of the governments grew apace. The ideas and political activities of bankers like Laffitte and manufacturers like Ternaux in France, of business men like Huskisson and Brougham in England, and of economists like Ricardo and List show very clearly the growing strength of the alliance between business interests and liberal political principles during the 1820's.

[28] The significance of the Bonapartist movement has been variously estimated. A good introduction is J. Deschamps, *Sur la légende de Napoléon* (Paris, 1931).

In Italy this identification of capitalist interests and liberal ideas was combined with a strong nationalism. The group which in 1818 had founded the *Conciliatore* in Milan believed that to achieve a strong and united Italy it was first necessary to regenerate the country economically and culturally. The *Conciliatore* was given up in 1819 under the persecutions of the Austrian government, but many of its ideas were revived in the *Annali Universali di Statistica*, directed, after 1827, by Romagnosi. The *Antologia*, founded in Florence in 1821 in imitation of the *Edinburgh Review*, proposed "to make Italy know itself, to bring before Italians a national and not a municipal ideal." In all these reviews, but especially in the *Annali*, the articles, which covered a wide range of subjects, stressed the need of better roads and canals, free ports and the removal of tariff barriers, steam navigation, insurance companies, modern banks, uniform systems of weights, measures, and coinage, agricultural societies, model farms, public schools, and a national literature and intellectual culture. The movement brought together young nobles and business men of a generation excluded from the political scene except on the few occasions when they rushed in only to make martyrs of themselves. The different currents of Italian liberal thought in the 1820's are interestingly shown in the fact that while Mazzini wrote his first essay for publication on the patriotism of Dante, Cavour wrote first on model farms. Back of all this propaganda, however, was the idea that once the social, economic, and intellectual conditions of Italy were improved, a political regeneration would be inevitable.

The drift toward liberalism in the course of the 1820's was not only affecting new peoples and new layers of the population; its ideals began to infiltrate even the Catholic Church. Without wishing to change its religious dogmas, some Catholic leaders hoped to get ecclesiastical support for the freedom of the press and of education and for liberating oppressed nationalities. O'Connell united the Catholic forces of Ireland to work for Catholic Emancipation; in Belgium the Comte de Mérode and others were having striking success in rallying the Catholics against the rule of the King of Holland. These two instances of the church turning against the established government, and disgust with the ultra-Catholic policies

of Charles X in France, converted Lamennais to the idea that the
church was making a great mistake in attaching its cause to the
dying cause of kings.[29] His *Progrès de la Révolution et de la lutte
contre l'église* of 1829, written with all the eloquent power of his
earlier works, was a call to the French Catholic Church to desert
the hated Bourbons and to ally itself with the rising forces of democracy. "Instead of trembling before liberalism," he said, "let us
Catholicize it!" This bold doctrine found little acceptance at the
time, but in the fall of 1830 Lamennais and a group of his followers,
which included Montalembert and Lacordaire, began to publish
L'Avenir, a journal which in the next two years attracted attention
all over Europe. With a motto of *"Dieu et Liberté,"* it championed
freedom of conscience, freedom of the press, disestablishment, and
universal suffrage—a program completely in contradiction to papal
policy. "We belong," said Montalembert, "to a new generation whose
motto is to love freedom more than anything else in the world, and
the Catholic religion even more than freedom."[30]

Philhellenism, the most striking movement in European opinion
in the years following the downfall of Napoleon, is the clearest
indication of the revival of liberalism.[31] After the outbreak of the
Greek Revolt in 1821, its earliest sympathizers in western Europe
were scattered groups of liberals in Germany, France, and England.
At a time when it was impossible to cry "Long live Liberty," those
who were disaffected were quick to see the advantages of shouting
"Long live the Greeks!" Committees began to be formed to collect
funds to help these insurgent Christians, the descendants of the
race of Plato and Pericles, who, despite all the principles of the
Holy Alliance, were so valiantly fighting for their freedom. As the
movement gathered force, literary romanticists, like Chateaubriand
and Hugo in France, Uhland and Müller in Germany, and Byron
and Shelley in England, helped to fan the flames.

The war, which Metternich regarded with cold disdain, "appealed
to every fiber of the romantic nature. It was heroic, it was dazzling

---

[29] The literature on Lamennais is very extensive; cf. especially F. Duine, *La Mennais*
(Paris, 1922), and V. Giraud, *La vie tragique de Lamennais* (Paris, 1931).

[30] R. Soltau, *French Political Thought in the Nineteenth Century* (London, 1931), 83.

[31] The best introduction to Philhellenism is in A. Stern, *Geschichte Europas, 1815-
1871* (new edition, Stuttgart, 1913), II.

with Oriental color," and, being a struggle between the Cross and the Crescent, it recalled the Crusades and the Middle Ages.[32] Moreover, to a generation trained in classical studies, the cause of the race of Pericles became a holy cause. "We are all Greeks," wrote Shelley. "Our laws, our literature, our religion, our arts, have their roots in Greece. But for Greece, Rome would have spread no illumination with her arms and we might still have been savages and idolaters." In the heat of this Philhellenic excitement, romanticism was deserting its earlier alliance with the throne and the altar and was embracing the ideals of liberty. The kings of Württemberg, Bavaria, and France, as well as the pope, contributed money. Reactionary governments like the Prussian were obliged to let the propaganda and the collection of funds go on. Even in America Greek committees were formed and the cause was praised by President Monroe and by Daniel Webster. Eynard, a philanthropist of Geneva, became the collecting and distributing agent for the contributions that streamed in. The pressure became so strong that finally the governments of England, France, and Russia broke away from the reactionary program of Metternich and intervened to help the Greeks. The significance of Philhellenism lay in the fact that, while reaction still prevailed in domestic affairs and while the memory of interventions in Italy and Spain was still fresh in men's minds, a general European public opinion was reborn and was permeated by a great liberal ideal.

IV. THE RISE OF SOCIALISM

At the extreme left of the liberal forces were a number of isolated thinkers who were developing some of the doctrines of modern socialism. They believed that only the upper and middle layers of the bourgeoisie had been benefited by the overthrow of the old order. They saw that there was arising, as a result of the extension of the factory system, a class of wage-slaves for whom the new régime was more oppressive than the old. The commercial crises of 1815, 1818, and 1825 brought acute sufferings to these factory-workers and showed more clearly than ever before the abuses of the new industrialism.

[32] A. Guérard, *Reflections on the Napoleonic Legend* (New York, 1924), 29.

The period after Waterloo began with the economic doctrines of laissez-faire in full possession of the field. Slowly there appeared, first in the writings of Sismondi in France and of the Ricardian Socialists in England, then in the work of Robert Owen, Fourier, and the Saint-Simonian School, a criticism of the abuses of private property which developed into schemes of full-fledged communism. Some of this early pre-socialist and socialist theorizing was in harmony with the tenets of liberalism. Owen and Fourier, for example, set up an ideal of individual happiness and "the greatest good of the greatest number." All were strenuous in their defense of personal liberties in religion, education, and the press. They went beyond the liberals, however, in retaining the great faith in human nature which was the basis of the gospel of Rousseau, and the belief in progress which had inspired the *philosophes*. Moreover, they differed from the liberals in their general indifference to political reform. A better society, they believed, was to be built, not through the ballot box but through a complete reorganization of the methods of production and distribution. These social radicals of the early nineteenth century worked independently.[33] Even when they knew of one another's theories, they usually disagreed.

Sismondi noticed that, while the total national wealth in England and France was rapidly increasing, the workers were sinking into greater wretchedness. In his *Nouveaux principes d'économie politique* (1819) he attacked Say's identification of the national wealth with national welfare. "The earnings of an entrepreneur," he wrote, "sometimes represent nothing but the spoliation of the workers."[34] He stopped short of socialism and did not look for an overthrow of capitalism; his remedy for the exploitation of the workers was government regulation. He was, nevertheless, one of the first thinkers to maintain that the Industrial Revolution was dividing modern society into two classes, the capitalists and the proletariat, and that the intermediary ranks would tend to dis-

[33] Useful surveys of the history of socialism are M. Beer, *Allgemeine Geschichte des Sozialismus* (2 vols., Berlin, 1922-23), and H. W. Laidler, *History of Socialist Thought* (New York, 1927).
[34] Sismondi, *op. cit.*, (2nd edition, Paris, 1827), I, 92. Cf. M. Tuan, *Sismondi as an Economist* (New York, 1927).

appear. A group of his followers in France, Fodéré, Villeneuve-Bargemont, and Buret, supported his theories with elaborate statistical studies, which were used later by Louis Blanc and Pierre Leroux as an arsenal for an assault on the whole capitalist order.

In England similar criticisms of the abuses of the new industrial order were being made by some of the radical contemporaries and disciples of Ricardo.[35] Ricardo was an orthodox follower of Smith, but in his systematic analysis of land, labor, and capital, society stood revealed not as a community with common interests, but as an unstable combination of warring elements in which the interests of one part were often opposed to those of another. Especially in his emphasis on the part played by labor in creating value and on the social nature of rent, Ricardo forged implements that the Radicals—Charles Hall, William Thompson, and Thomas Hodgskin—were not slow to use. Most of their work was done in or around 1825, a year of depression, when the Owenite idea of coöperation was beginning to absorb the interest of a part of the working classes. The influence of Owen as well as that of Ricardo is evident in the writings of these so-called Ricardian Socialists. Hall viewed the entrepreneur as a lender of capital at usurious rates to producers (workers). As a result, there was arising an irreconcilable conflict between two classes, the one enriching itself through exploitation, the other aspiring toward a just reward for its labor. Hodgskin, a friend of Francis Place and an advocate of trade-unions, was one of the founders of the London Mechanics' Institute and the editor of the *Mechanics' Magazine*. His *Labor Defended against the Claims of Capital* (1825), like Thompson's *Inquiry into the Principles of Wealth* (1824)—the most original work of the school—was directed toward proving the injustice of unearned income. Both writers insisted on what Marx was later to call "the labor theory of value." These Ricardian Socialists did not work out a doctrine of state socialism, any more than did the followers of Sismondi in France. They did, however, clearly show the injustices of the economic system as it then existed.

The real founder of British socialism was Robert Owen. He was not an obscure writer like the other radical theorists of the time,

[35] Cf. H. L. Beales, *The Early English Socialists* (London, 1933).

but one of the most successful manufacturers in Europe. For that reason his ideas attracted wide attention not only among the workers but also among the governing classes. All his doctrines were based on the belief, which he never tired of repeating, that men are made by their environment. To improve the environment the most urgent need was to get rid of profit and to substitute coöperation, thus reducing "all that gives rise to that inordinate desire for buying in the cheapest market and selling in the dearest." His own age, though disturbed by his attacks on Christianity and his views on marriage, was interested in his great social exhibition, New Lanark in Scotland. Here, out of a miserable factory town, he created a model community. Cleanliness, order, and comfortable homes gradually replaced filth and wretchedness. All children between the ages of five and ten years were sent to school, the hours of labor were reduced from seventeen to ten a day, and a store was opened where the workers could buy at little more than cost. Owen tried to effect reforms through Parliament, but, being only partially successful, he later attempted to found other communities like New Lanark. The perfect community, he believed, would consist of from 500 to 3,000 people settled on a tract of from 1,000 to 1,500 acres. Its members would carry on various occupations so that it would be, as nearly as possible, self-sufficing. He believed in private property and in machine production, but both should be used to promote human welfare. Coöperative communities might be established by private individuals or by the state, and, as they multiplied, might be united until finally the whole world came within their embrace.

Tories like Lord Liverpool, Evangelicals like Wilberforce, and economists like Ricardo denounced Owen's plans, but his books— the New View of Society (1813) and The Book of the New Moral World (1820)—and his achievement at New Lanark brought him a following among the workers. He helped to found, in 1831, the National Union of the Working Classes, an organization that tried to bring together all the British trade-unions. This proved to be less enduring than his influence on the growth of coöperative stores, of which there were, by 1831, three hundred in Britain. His indictment of the social order for its waste and injustice and its crises of unemployment, and his emphasis on the value of education and the possibilities of social well-being are both reflected in the later history of British education, trade-unionism, and social legislation.[36]

Fourier, though a man of totally different experience and temperament, was elaborating somewhat similar ideas in France. He attacked the social evils which resulted from competition, speculation, and the profit system. Society was totally maladjusted for the proper development of man's nature, to the understanding of which Fourier thought he possessed the secret. Like Owen he did not aim at a reorganization of society from the center, but at the creation of small co-partnership communities, *phalanges,* which, if increased in number, would slowly produce a complete social transformation. Membership in these communities was to be entirely voluntary; indeed, in all his schemes, Fourier was so anxious to give the individual free development that he is sometimes classed as an anarchist. Capital was to receive four-twelfths, labor five-twelfths, and "talent" (management) three-twelfths of the income. He differed from Owen in emphasizing agriculture and handicrafts rather than manufactures as the main concerns of his ideal community. The promotion of the worker to the rank of a property owner by giving him a stake in the community would remove the ancient antagonisms of master and servant and would free men from the necessity of doing uncongenial work. Like Owen he never aimed at the abolition of property, but at a juster coöperation of capital and labor and at the creation of a new type of social environment. There is much of the utterly fantastic in his writings, but buried in them, especially in his *Nouveau monde industriel* (1828-29), there is a great deal of profound insight.[37]

Far better known in France were his contemporaries, the Saint-Simonians. Saint-Simon, the founder of the school, after an extraordinary career in war, politics, and business, spent his later years in criticizing the social order. In a series of confused essays, but especially in his *Du système industriel* (1821) and *Nouveau Christianisme* (1825), he developed the idea that the old social and economic order, which was "Christian and feudal," was giving way to an industrial order. This new society would not be used by a

[36] Cf. G. D. H. Cole, *The Life of Robert Owen* (2nd. ed., London, 1930).
[37] Cf. E. S. Mason, "Fourier and Anarchism," *Quarterly Journal of Economics,* 1928.

few men to exploit their fellows, but all would join together, under
the direction of scientists, engineers, and industrialists, to exploit
nature.[38] Although the main emphasis of Saint-Simon's thought was
laid on the necessity of developing industrial production, out of
some of his ideas a group of his followers, among them Enfantin
and Bazard, evolved a system of communism.[39] The leaders of the
Saint-Simonian School attacked the whole fabric of laissez-faire
economics and declared that society must control the machinery
of production as well as the distribution of wealth. To accomplish
these revolutionary changes they depended, as did all their radical
contemporaries, on persuasion, not on violence. The passing of laws
would abolish inheritance and would gradually arrange the taking-
over of private property by the state. Everything would thus eventually
come under government control. Men would work in coöperation, and the state would see that rewards would go "to each according to his capacity . . . and according to his works."[40]

Among these scattered and isolated radical theorists, only Robert
Owen attracted much public recognition or aroused an interest
among the industrial workers, for, prior to 1830, it was only in England that a large working class had become sharply separated from
the rest of society. The debates in the English Parliament and in
the French Chambers showed that the governing classes had no conception of the extent of social misery or of the nature of the new
social problem that industrialism was creating. Even a fiery liberal
like General Foy, though he could make the French Chamber of
Deputies ring with his denunciations of the king and the Jesuits,
always regarded the discussion of these new social ideals as a tire-

[38] Cf. Saint-Simon, a special number of *Revue d'histoire économique et sociale*, 1925.

[39] Auguste Comte, for a few years the secretary of Saint-Simon, drew most of the
ideas of his *positivism* from the teaching of his master, though this influence belongs
entirely to a later time. Like his master, and indeed like nearly all the theorists of the
time on both conservative and liberal sides, he worked out an elaborate interpretation of
history to prove the necessity of his ideas. In the first half of the nineteenth century
no theory of art, literature, politics, or society seems to have been possible without an
appeal to history. These appeals, which were used in almost infinite variety, were usually
to some historical past that never existed as the Hegels, the Comtes, the Hugos, and
the Schlegels conceived it. Cf. H. Gouhier, *La jeunesse de Comte et la formation du
positivisme* (Paris, 1933).

[40] The clearest statement of the doctrine of the Saint-Simonians is in Bazard and
Enfantin's *Doctrine de Saint-Simon, Exposition, Première Année, 1829*. The school
broke up in 1832, though its influence continued. Cf. S. Charléty, *Histoire du Saint-
Simonisme* (2nd. ed., Paris, 1931), H. R. d'Allemagne, *Les Saint-Simoniens* (Paris,
1930).

some interruption of the real business of government. The political life of the period from Waterloo to the Reform Bill was, in general, characterized by a continuation of the animosities that had been aroused by the French Revolution. The conservatives continued to base their political action on the Christian theory that human nature is evil and that it could best be directed toward salvation by authority and the church, while the liberals maintained, in part, an eighteenth-century belief that human nature is good, but that it would always find its best guidance among the captains of industry and commerce.

Chapter Eight

THE DISINTEGRATION OF THE RESTORATION, 1820-1830

I. THE DECLINE OF TORY DOMINATION IN ENGLAND

By 1820 militant radicalism in England had been suppressed. But the ministry, because of its repressive policy, was in disrepute. The events which tipped the balance of public opinion against it and prepared the way for its reorganization were connected with the attempt of the cabinet to obtain a divorce for George IV.[1] The new king, though a clever man, had made himself contemptible by his debauchery and by his shameless treatment of friends and relatives. In 1795 he had married Caroline of Brunswick; within a year they had separated. For a time the princess lived in seclusion in England, but in 1814 she moved to the continent. On George IV's accession to the throne, she returned to take her position as queen. The king would have none of her and persuaded the ministry to institute divorce proceedings.

Although Caroline was a frivolous and unattractive woman whose conduct had not been discreet, the public championed her cause with indiscriminate enthusiasm. From her landing in England to her arrival in London, crowds everywhere acclaimed her. For several months there were popular demonstrations in her honor and against the king and the ministry. Lord Brougham defended her in the divorce proceedings before the House of Lords, where the king produced a number of paid witnesses from the continent. The divorce was passed by the House of Lords, but with a majority of only nine votes. The cabinet now found itself more nearly in collision with the whole nation than had any government since the days of George III and Lord North. Afraid of the results, the ministry did not dare carry the case to the Commons for final decision. At

[1] Cf. W. D. Bowman, *The Divorce Case of Queen Caroline* (London, 1930), Shane Leslie, *George IV* (London, 1926), E. B. Chancellor, *The Regency Rakes* (London, 1925), and, by the same author, *Life in Regency and Early Victorian Times* (London, 1927).

George IV's coronation, Caroline tried in vain to get into Westminster Abbey. Less than a month later the dilemma was cut short by her death, but the scandal had weakened the position of the cabinet more than had its repressive measures at home or its entanglement with the Holy Alliance abroad. The elections of 1820, however, made it possible for the ministry to maintain itself a while longer.

Gradually the pressure of the more moderate groups that demanded reform began to make itself felt. Bentham's *Radicalism not Dangerous* (1820) showed clearly that changes in the existing social and political order could be made without violence, and even without serious disturbance. His ideas were defended in Parliament by Hume, and by the wealthy and democratic member from Westminster, Sir Francis Burdett. Outside Parliament, they were held by growing numbers of business men and bankers who could in no wise be considered revolutionaries. At the same time both the old parties, the Whigs and the Tories, began to break up into factions. Some of the Whigs rallied about a new leader, Lord John Russell, a member of one of the great noble families and a liberal of the highest respectability. From the Tory ranks there now came to the front a less reactionary group—the economist, Robinson, after 1823 the chancellor of the exchequer, Huskisson, whom Canning was soon to make president of the board of trade, Canning himself, who had withdrawn from the cabinet in 1820 because he disagreed with his colleagues on the matter of the king's divorce, Lord Palmerston, who announced that it was time to abandon "the old, stupid Tory party," and the brilliant young capitalist, Robert Peel, who, though an enemy of Canning, was dissatisfied with the traditional Tory policies.

In 1822 the suicide of Castlereagh brought Canning into the cabinet as secretary for foreign affairs and as leader of the House of Commons; Peel became secretary for home affairs, and Huskisson joined the cabinet soon after. The accession of these three and of several others caused a change of policy in the Tory ministry of Lord Liverpool as decisive as if an entirely new cabinet had been formed. Canning, the leader of these dissenting Tories, was convinced of the danger of delaying necessary changes; with the aid of some colleagues who shared his opinions, he began to project reform. It was soon evident that the economic and political outlook of these new Tory leaders was very different from that of the squires and country parsons who composed the majority of the party.

The first break in the policy of repression that had prevailed since 1815 was the passage of a series of acts (1822-1829) reforming the criminal code by reorganizing court procedure and abolishing one hundred penalties which involved a death sentence. Before these reforms were made, over two hundred offenses were punishable with death; picking a pocket and stealing as little as five shillings from a shop were capital crimes. Juries were unwilling to convict— of 655 persons indicted for shoplifting between 1805 and 1807, 103 had been sentenced to death, but in no case had the penalty been inflicted. The result of this wretched lack of law-enforcement, as Bentham and others had long been insisting, had been the steady increase of crime. With more enforceable laws on the statute books and with a new police force established by Peel in 1829, the British administration of justice became the best in Europe. Peel also abolished the government's use of agents provocateurs and tried to break the long connection of Tory rule with repression. It was, however, the humanitarian aspect of these legal changes which appealed to the popular imagination and which, during the next two decades, led to the passage of a series of similar reforming acts. At the same time Canning, though following Castlereagh's foreign policies more closely than he would openly acknowledge, made a great appeal to public opinion when he led England away from the European Alliance. He denounced the French government for intervening in Spain, and championed the cause of national self-determination. He not only refused to take part in a congress of the powers that contemplated the suppression of the revolts in the Spanish colonies, but began at once to urge the government of the United States to coöperate with England in preventing European intervention in South America.

Under Huskisson's aggressive leadership and with the full support of the laissez-faire economists, who were now at the height of their fame, public finance was thoroughly reorganized and the initial steps were taken toward breaking down the mercantilist system which still bound British commerce. Huskisson was an experienced parliamentarian—he sat in the House of Commons continuously from 1796 to 1830—and he had a better understanding of the whole business life of his time than any other member of Parliament. This first-hand knowledge of the rapidly changing economic situation, together with his talent for lucid exposition of economic principles and his willingness to back all commercial undertakings, accounts for the immense respect in which he was held by the financial and business leaders. His unusual foresightedness was especially evident in his insistence on the necessity of developing Britain's colonial empire, in a period when none of the leading statesmen of either party had any conception of its value or future importance. Under his direction, laws were carried through Parliament which removed the restrictions of the Navigation Acts from the shipping of all countries that maintained no restrictions on British shipping. Furthermore, the duties were sharply reduced on certain raw materials greatly needed by manufacturers, like silk, wool, and iron, on other commodities not produced in the United Kingdom, such as wines and coffee, and even on a few manufactured products, like cotton, linen, and woolen cloth. These moves in the direction of free trade were less important in themselves than in establishing a precedent which rendered further alterations inevitable. It was only the severe industrial crisis in 1825 that prevented further changes for several years.[2]

In 1824 the Combination Acts were repealed. Huskisson and Peel had been converted to the idea of abolition by the evidence gathered by the master-tailor Francis Place, an ardent Benthamite. They had obtained the help of Hume, a radical member of Parliament and a close friend of Bentham and James Mill. Place picked the witnesses whom Hume brought before a parliamentary committee, and furnished such a mass of data on the injustices inflicted on the workers by their employers that Parliament repealed the acts.[3] Once the workingmen were allowed to organize, a series of strikes followed, with some violence and injury to property. A new law was

[2] Cf. A. Brady, *Huskisson and Liberal Reform* (Oxford, 1928).
[3] "The act of 1824 is the first case of the impartial application of the doctrines of laissez-faire even when they benefited the workmen as against the master." G. M. Trevelyan, *British History in the 19th Century* (London, 1922), 201.

therefore passed in 1825 forbidding combinations of workingmen for any purpose other than that of securing the regulation of hours and wages. The use of violence or even of intimidation of any sort was strictly forbidden. Thus, while the principle of trade-union organization continued to be recognized, any really effective action on the part of the industrial proletariat was declared illegal. In this unsatisfactory position the workers remained for more than forty years.

The years 1820 to 1825 were marked by a great improvement in economic conditions in Britain. Prosperity was returning on the continent and, on the other side of the world, the whole American hemisphere was opened to commercial intercourse. England, situated between, acted as the great clearing house. "Nearly all property has risen greatly in value," wrote one observer, "and every branch of industry is thriving. Agricultural distress has disappeared; the persons employed in the cotton and woolen manufactures are in full employment; on all sides new buildings are in progress, and money is so abundant that men of enterprise find no difficulty in commanding funds."[4] The value of exports rose from £48,000,000 in 1820 to nearly £70,000,000 in 1830; during the same period the import of wool increased from less than 10,000,000 lbs. to over 32,000,000; and the number of cotton spinners rose from 66,000 to over 135,000. The phenomenal industrialization of modern England, retarded by the wars, was now rapidly proceeding.

The rate of development was at first too fast. Wild financial speculation, especially in South American investments, that had had no parallel since the days of the South Sea Bubble, brought on a financial crisis in 1825-26. Within five days, in December, 1825, a hundred twenty-two banks suspended payment. Riots broke out in the manufacturing areas, looms were smashed, and much property destroyed. The prolonged drought in the summer of 1826 added to the general distress, but no radical agitators appeared to assume the leadership of the masses, as in 1816 and 1817. The difference between the attitude of the public during this crisis and its earlier attitude was indeed striking; few now talked politics, but everywhere men discussed

[4] J. A. R. Marriott, *England since Waterloo* (New York, 1927), 75.

banks, paper money, free trade, and the abolition of the Corn Law.[5] Gradually the worst effects of the crisis passed off, trade picked up, prices rose, and the steadfast behavior of Canning and Huskisson restored confidence in the government.

The reforms instituted after the reorganization of the Liverpool ministry in 1822 were creating growing friction between the new and more liberal members and the older Tories in the cabinet. In Parliament and in the press the more reactionary members continued to command the backing of the clergy and the landed aristocracy, while the progressive wing was supported by the commercial classes, especially by the bankers and the new "captains of industry." The ministry was held together only by Lord Liverpool's skill in reconciling the differences between the factions; but a stroke of apoplexy in 1827 forced his retirement, and upset the balance. After some negotiations Canning became prime minister, several Whigs were brought into the cabinet, and three of the prominent Tory members, Wellington, Eldon, and Peel, resigned. Canning himself was almost completely taken up with foreign affairs, particularly with the Greek War of Independence. He died within a few months of his appointment, August 8, 1827. His reputation rests primarily on his foreign policy, the bases of which, however, had been prepared by Castlereagh. Canning's abilities as a diplomatist were combined with a talent for showmanship which captivated public opinion and with a skill at political maneuvering that made him a widely suspected and well-hated man, even among those who recognized his talents and the strategic importance of following him.

Early in 1828 the Duke of Wellington, a stiff-necked conservative, succeeded to the headship of the ministry. He promptly dropped the Whig members and brought back the old Tories; soon even the liberal Tories resigned and before the end of 1828 the cabinet was again as reactionary as it had been before 1822. But Wellington proved to be a prime minister without political ambition. Once he saw the tide moving in a certain direction he yielded to it without fear of criticism or dread of inconsistency. In this opportunism he was urged on by Peel, who, though a convinced Tory, disagreed

---

[5] While Lord John Russell was predicting revolt, Greville wrote in his diary, "So great and so absorbing is the interest which the present economic discussions excite that all men are become political economists." Greville, *Memoirs* (London, 1875), I, 81.

with the policies of the old-fashioned die-hards in his party. The first important act of his ministry was the repeal of the Test and Corporation Acts which, since the reign of Charles II, had required every holder of a civil or military office to receive the sacraments according to the rites of the state church. These acts had not been enforced for a century, but they galled the pride of prominent Dissenters, and, against the wishes of many in the cabinet, they were now repealed by Parliament.

The same year an effective breach was made in the agricultural monopoly maintained by the Corn Laws, the ark of the Tory covenant. The Corn Law of 1815, which practically excluded foreign grain, had not brought the expected prosperity to the agrarian classes; it hampered foreign trade and it kept the prices on farm products so high that strong opposition was aroused among the industrial leaders and the workers in the towns. Although the law had been repeatedly attacked in Parliament, only slight modifications were made. Canning and Huskisson believed that, since only a third of the population lived on the land, industrial interests should be favored, not only because of the unfairness of the existing arrangements but also because they were convinced that the future prosperity of England was to be built on her commerce and manufacture. But when, in the hard times of 1826, Canning tried to induce Parliament to modify the law, the Duke of Wellington secured a defeat of the proposal in the House of Lords. Now that the duke was prime minister, a group in the cabinet forced him to carry through Parliament an act which allowed grain to be imported at any time, though it fixed a sliding scale of duties which made the tariff high only when the price of English grain was very low. Just as Huskisson's legislation had initiated the movement toward free trade in raw materials and manufactured products, so the new Corn Law of 1828 marked the first important move toward free trade in agricultural products. In both these matters England was a number of decades ahead of the continental states.[6]

The Wellington ministry was suddenly confronted with a problem far more difficult than that presented by the Corn Laws. The whole

[6] Cf. D. G. Barnes, *History of the English Corn Laws, 1660-1846* (London, 1930), and C. R. Fay, *The Corn Laws and Social England* (Cambridge, 1932).

question of Catholic Emancipation was suddenly brought to a head
by the election to Parliament of Daniel O'Connell, head of the
Catholic Association in Ireland. This was, to be sure, but the latest
phase of an issue that had occupied Parliament for several decades.
Between 1791 and 1793 a series of acts had removed many Catholic
disabilities, even allowing the Catholics of the United Kingdom to
vote in parliamentary elections.[7] But certain disqualifications remained: no Catholic could sit in the Parliament at London, nor
become a sheriff, nor rise to the highest positions in the state, the
army, or the bar. Pitt had intended to remove these restrictions, but
the opposition of George III had killed the project and had forced
Pitt's resignation in 1801. The question continued to be raised in
Parliament, though it proved impossible to carry through the House
of Lords a bill removing the last disabilities.

It was O'Connell's Catholic Association which had now finally
forced the issue.[8] This union of Irish Catholics, founded in 1823,
was suppressed by the government in 1825 as "an unlawful combination," but was immediately reorganized as an educational and
charitable society. After a few years it was again allowed to conduct
political propaganda. Its rapid growth in membership was due not
only to O'Connell's ability as a leader and to the reduction of dues
to a penny a month, but to the increase of misery in Ireland. The
population was very dense, and much of the income of the peasants
went to absentee English landlords. In the towns the rapid development of English industry was ruining Irish manufactures. Ireland
was a land of poverty, ignorance, and bitterness, where the government put down all manifestations of discontent as though the country
were a conquered province. Amidst this distress and unrest the
Catholic Association worked steadily, being careful to keep all its
proceedings peaceable and aboveboard. The lists of members were
available to all who wanted to see them, all meetings were open to
the public, and anything that resembled conspiracy was scrupulously
avoided. In 1828 O'Connell's election to Parliament forced the Wellington cabinet to face the situation. The election had been marked
by no disorder. The voters, led by the priests, had gone quietly to the

[7] The technicalities of these laws are complicated; cf. F. W. Maitland, *Constitutional
History of England* (Cambridge, 1908), 519-520.
[8] Cf. D. R. Gwynn, *The Struggle for Catholic Emancipation* (London, 1928).

polls and cast their ballots, all in the most approved legal fashion. So orderly a demonstration in Ireland was convincing evidence of the thoroughness and effectiveness of O'Connell's organization. Everyone was amazed.

The Lord Lieutenant of Ireland informed the government that, much as he abhorred the idea of "truckling to the over-bearing Catholic demagogues," it would not be possible permanently to refuse legally elected Catholics the right to sit at Westminster. George IV tried to prevent the introduction of the question into Parliament, but the ministry offered its resignation, whereupon the king backed down. Peel defended an Emancipation Bill in the House of Commons and Wellington bluntly recommended it to the Lords as an alternative preferable to civil war. "I must say," he declared, "that if I could avoid by any sacrifice whatever even one month of civil war in the country to which I am attached, I would sacrifice my life in order to do it." He then proceeded to force the bill through the House of Lords as he had driven the French out of Spain. The bill passed and Catholics became eligible for all but a very few offices in the United Kingdom. For the first time in English history a political association had compelled Parliament to pass a measure into law. The reaction of O'Connell's success upon English politics resembled that of the success of the American Revolution; what Irishmen had done, certainly Englishmen could do.

Wellington and Peel (of whom O'Connell said "his smile is like a silver plate on a coffin") lacked the good sense to allow the new law to stand as an act of reconciliation. Having given rights with one hand, they proceeded to withdraw privileges with the other. Emancipation had been won by the votes of small Irish freeholders. In revenge the franchise was now so raised that the Irish electorate was reduced from 200,000 voters to 26,000. In Ireland this new move was regarded as an attempt to cancel the effects of emancipation; consequently, the Emancipation Act did little to allay discontent.

Neither the king nor the ministry survived much longer. George IV died on June 26, 1830, and was succeeded by his brother, who took the title of William IV. The accession of a new king called for a parliamentary election, and soon the whole kingdom was in a state of excited preparation for an election that was certain to be fought mainly on the issue of parliamentary reform.

II. THE GROWING ESTRANGEMENT BETWEEN THE MONARCHY AND THE NATION IN FRANCE

The assassination of the Duc de Berri and the subsequent dismissal of Decazes sealed the doom of Louis XVIII's attempt to harmonize liberalism and royalism. The king, now more gouty and weary than ever, was no longer able to resist the pressure of his own entourage, especially that of the charming Mme. du Cayla, an agent of the Ultras, who took Decazes' place as the chief royal favorite. To lead the ministry, the king recalled the Duc de Richelieu, who at once carried through the Chambers a law temporarily restricting the liberty of the press. No journal could be founded without the government's consent, no single issue could appear without the censor's permission; the government might suspend publication for six months and, under certain circumstances, suppress a journal completely. Richelieu then set about the preparation and enactment of a new electoral law which, when finally passed, established two kinds of electoral colleges, the *collèges d'arrondissement* and the *collèges de département*. All citizens paying a direct tax of three hundred francs were allowed to vote in the first, which had the right to elect two hundred fifty-eight deputies. The twenty-five per-cent of these electors who paid the highest tax—about twelve thousand voters—was allowed to vote a second time in the *collèges de département*, which elected the remaining one hundred seventy-two deputies. The president of each electoral college had to be chosen by the central government and the voters had to write out the ballots in his presence and hand them to him unfolded.

This Law of the Double Vote greatly increased the power of the government to influence elections and assured the political domination of the landed aristocracy. The administrative bureaucracy established by Napoleon was now filled largely with royalists favorable to the government, which used these administrators to manipulate elections and to interfere with the working of the parliamentary régime, established by the Charter. This situation helps to explain why the ministries were able to keep themselves in power in spite of the steady growth of opposition among the mass of the people.[9] As a result of these events of 1820, the royalist reaction, started in 1814-15, but suspended from 1816 to 1820 when more moderate policies prevailed, was now again under way. It was destined to last with only a slight interruption until 1830, when it culminated in a new revolution.

The first elections held under the new electoral law returned so many Ultras that the majority of the deputies found Richelieu too lukewarm a royalist. He was forced to resign and early in 1822 a cabinet was formed under the Comte de Villèle, who remained head of the ministry until 1828. This shift to the Right in the years 1820 to 1822 led to a series of revolutionary plots on the part of the French Carbonari; but their attempts to start insurrections all ended in failure. The easy success of the French troops in Spain in 1823 reconciled the army with the dynasty. As the strength of the secret societies had been drawn largely from the army, the immediate danger of an overthrow of the Bourbon régime disappeared.

In the Chambers, Villèle was pushing toward the realization of the Ultra program. A new law was passed by which all cases of attack on the policies of the government by the press were to be tried without a jury; the same law also made the mere "tendency" of an article to "bring about a breach of the public peace" a punishable offense. The École de Droit was closed and reopened only after twelve professors had been dismissed; the École Normale was reorganized as the École Préparatoire; the name Collège Royal was substituted for the name Lycée; Guizot, Cousin, and Villemain were dismissed from their teaching positions; and the direction of the Université de France was given to a bishop, Frayssinous. These measures were not passed without debate in the Chambers, liberal opponents like Manuel and Foy making up in vehemence what their party now lacked in numbers. In the debates on the Spanish War, Manuel denounced "this monkish crusade against liberty," whereupon his dismissal from the Chamber of Deputies was voted. He refused to leave and had to be dragged out by the police; the other deputies of the Left followed him. New elections were held early

[9] Cf. F. B. Artz, "The Electoral System in France 1815-1830," *Journal of Modern History*, 1929.

in 1824; the government went to extraordinary lengths in employing the prefects and other administrative officials to manipulate the voting; even the clergy were used as government electoral agents. The machinery worked perfectly and the liberals found their numbers in the Chamber reduced to fifteen out of a total of four hundred thirty. Encouraged by his success, Villèle arranged for a law (May, 1824) setting aside an earlier regulation which provided for the annual partial renewal of the Chamber of Deputies, and assuring the continuance of this *Chambre Retrouvée*, as the Ultras called it, for seven years. In the midst of this reaction Louis XVIII died, September 16, 1824.

The accession of Charles X at last gave the Ultras hope of fully realizing their program.[10] The new king, though a man of great personal charm, was a reactionary of the purest stripe. At the beginning of the Restoration, Louis XVIII, who greatly distrusted his brother's judgment, once remarked that the fate of the monarchy depended on whether he survived the Comte d'Artois.[11] Artois had always looked on the Charter as a temporary concession. Early in his brother's reign he had expressed his hope for an early return "to the natural order of things." Now, at the age of sixty-seven, he was not likely to change his ideas. Villèle remained at the head of the ministry and continued with unusual success his work of keeping the public finances in order and of maintaining an efficient direction of the political administration. Though a man of some capacity as a political manager, he was not able, as were Canning and Peel, to control the more reactionary members of his party.

In 1825 the king was crowned at Rheims. The ritual seemed to belong to the age of St. Louis. At the end of the great ceremony the bells pealed, the organ played a triumphal march, and a flock of doves, let loose among the vaults, fluttered about in a cloud of incense. To make the spectacle complete, the king, on the morning after the coronation, mounted a white horse and in the midst of a brilliant retinue rode to the Hôpital de Saint-Marc. There the chief

[10] For the reign of Charles X a good introduction is P. de La Gorce, *La Restauration, Charles X* (Paris, 1928).

[11] As Sorel says, "Charles X had all the qualities for gaily losing a battle or for gracefully ruining a dynasty, but none needed for managing a party or reconquering a country." A. Sorel, *L'Europe et la Révolution française* (Paris, 1885-1904), II, 173.

physician of the royal household awaited him at the head of a band of more than a hundred persons afflicted with scrofula. Charles, after a short prayer, set himself to the task of curing them by the royal touch. Those who saw the events at Rheims, though they may have heard the king take the oath to defend the Charter, may well have imagined that the revolution and Napoleon had been but unimportant incidents in the history of France, even the memory of which would soon be effaced. The extreme irritation of the liberals was expressed in Béranger's poem, *"Le sacre de Charles le Simple,"* which at once caught the popular fancy, and cost its author nine months' imprisonment.[12]

With the outward glory of the monarchy restored, the Villèle ministry wanted to secure the inner substance as well. The government was soon occupied with its program of undoing, so far as possible, the work of the revolution. This was to be accomplished by a general social and religious reorganization of France; the power of the nobility was to be reconstituted by indemnifying the *émigrés* and by enacting a law of primogeniture; the power of the church was to be restored through the reëstablishment of the religious orders and the return to the church of its traditional control of education. In 1825 the ministry carried through the Chambers a bill to indemnify the *émigrés* to the amount of a billion francs. The money was raised by lowering the rate on government bonds from five to three per cent, which greatly angered the banking and industrial groups who held these securities. Still more resentment was aroused among all classes when they saw *émigrés*, who had fought with foreigners against the French armies, rewarded handsomely out of the public treasury. The Law of Indemnification was in itself a salutary measure, for it settled, once and for all, a thorny question, but at the time it was misunderstood by all parties and its immediate result was a wave of liberal indignation.[13]

The same year (1825) a law was passed making the crime of sacrilege, the theft of sacred objects from churches, punishable by death. In defending this Law of Sacrilege in the Chamber of Peers,

[12] Cf. J. P. Garnier, *Le sacre de Charles X et l'opinion publique en 1825* (Paris, 1927).
[13] The indemnification of the French nobles in relation to the whole social and political situation is discussed in great detail by A. Gain, *La restauration et les biens des émigrés* (2 vols., Nancy, 1928).

Bonald said that it "merely sent the criminal before his natural judge," but the mass of the people saw in this provision for putting the secular arm at the service of religion a step toward the return of the Ancien Régime.[14] Paul Louis Courier said of the growing use of religion to enforce political reaction, " 'Go and teach all the nations' said the Master, but it is not written, 'Go with the police and teach'!"[15] Projects were also presented for the reëstablishment of the Law of Primogeniture, and for a law—called by Peyronnet the "Law of Justice and of Love"—which made the censorship even more severe.[16] Both bills failed to pass. When the public learned of their failure, Paris was illuminated and cries of "Down with the Ministry," and "Down with the Jesuits"—the first rumblings of revolution—were heard in the streets. The Villèle cabinet like those which had preceded it, was fiercely attacked from two sides; a group of Ultras on close terms with Charles X were impatient with the ministers for not moving more rapidly toward the restoration of noble and clerical privileges, while the liberal leaders of the Left were exerting every effort to stop the reaction from going further. The cause of moderate royalism had failed and it was becoming increasingly clear that the only alternatives were return to the Ancien Régime or revolution.

The hardest drive of the ministry was directed against the Université de France, the Napoleonic institution most hated by the Ultras. Afraid to overthrow it entirely, Villèle had begun in 1822 to attack it piecemeal. By 1824 he had succeeded in expelling the most outstanding liberal teachers and had placed the whole educational régime under the direction of Frayssinous.[17] Under this ecclesiastical administration the primary instruction in France was placed in the hands of the local bishops, and in all secondary schools (collèges royaux), laymen were, wherever possible, replaced by priests. The government also allowed the petits séminaires, where priests

[14] Cf. Montmorillon, "Au soir de la Restauration, la loi du sacrilège" Revue des études historiques, 1932.
[15] F. B. Artz, France under the Bourbon Restoration (Cambridge, 1931), 163.
[16] Talleyrand said of the bill, "It is not French because it is silly!" It was at this time that the Abbé Liautard, a prominent Jesuit, urged the king to allow in France only one newspaper, which should contain short articles written by government officials, and stock and weather reports.
[17] Cf. A. Garnier, Frayssinous, son rôle dans l'université sous la restauration (Paris, 1925).

received their elementary training, to admit lay students who had no idea of taking orders. Thus, side by side with the state Université, and organized with the purpose of subverting it, a system of clerically controlled secondary schools was brought into existence. Seven of the *petits séminaires* were directed by Jesuits, though legally the Order had no right to exist in France. The growing evidence of clerical influence in all departments of the government seems, in the years 1822 to 1830, to have aroused more opposition to the Bourbon régime than did any of its political policies. As one of the newspapers said, "The present period will be hard to explain to our descendants. One talks now of nothing but bishops, priests, Jesuits, convents, and seminaries!"[18] "The great error of the Bourbons," wrote Cournot, "as well as of the royalist party and the clergy during the Restoration was to compromise both the monarchy and religion. The French have loved and still love Catholicism and royalty, but what they have never liked has been religion put to the service of politics, or politics put to the service of religion."[19]

In the face of this reaction, fear and resentment spread rapidly among the masses, above all in the country districts where the peasants had in the earlier years of the Restoration shown little interest in politics. Since 1822 liberal leaders had based their resistance to the government on the Charter. Conspiracy had been given up, and in lectures, in speeches, and in the press they had proclaimed the advantages of living under a free constitution. They had denounced all official action which seemed to undermine the fundamental instrument of government which Louis XVIII had granted and which Charles X had sworn to uphold. With great astuteness and with much show of legality, the liberal leaders used Bourbon precedent to attack the Bourbon in power. In the name of Louis XV, who had driven the Order out of France, they attacked the Jesuits, and against all ultramontane tendencies they evoked the Declaration of Gallican Liberties of Louis XIV. Despite the repressive laws of censorship, much of this liberal criticism found its way into the press. The few liberals left in the Chamber of Deputies after the elections of 1824 kept up the fight, and the *Moniteur*, the

[18] Artz, *op. cit.*, 160.
[19] Cournot, *Souvenirs* (Paris, 1913), 129.

official journal, published their biting attacks on the ministry. Reports appeared also of civil cases in the courts in which a liberal judge or lawyer attacked the policies of the government or the church. The liberal cause received support from the Royal Court of Paris, which considered itself the successor of the old Parlement; a number of press cases brought to it ended in dramatic acquittals. Other courts followed suit and the government found it increasingly difficult to secure convictions in cases involving the freedom of the press. Other criticisms were embedded in historical and literary articles and reviews. Everywhere it was evident that the opposition was growing stronger. The fight was kept up most effectively in the press by the *Constitutionnel* and the *Journal des Débats*, and by the anticlerical and antiroyalist pamphlets of Paul Louis Courier and the popular songs of Béranger. The French Academy added its voice of protest against the government's press policy. The Chamber of Peers, which contained a number of Napoleonic nobles, proved to be less reactionary than the lower house. In the case of a number of important laws it put up a stubborn resistance to the program of Villèle. It amended the Law of Sacrilege so as to make it harmless, and, to the delight of the opposition, the peers rejected the Law of Primogeniture and the press "Law of Justice and of Love." Even some of the most ardent defenders of royalism were now deserting the king and the ministry. Chateaubriand, who had been summarily dismissed by Villèle and Louis XVIII "like a domestic servant," had gone over to the opposition in 1824, and was attacking the government in the pages of the *Journal des Débats;* the old *émigré*, Montlosier, though an ardent believer in royalty, in 1826 launched a violent attack on the Jesuits and the ministry which supported them. The Congrégation and the Jesuits, he asserted, dominated the ministries; they could count on a hundred five deputies; they were spreading their propaganda everywhere. In answering Montlosier's attacks, Frayssinous, the minister of ecclesiastical affairs, acknowledged the presence of the Jesuits in France, in spite of the laws prohibiting them. The liberals at once made great capital of this avowal.

By 1826 it was evident that the nation and the monarchy were

moving in opposite directions; the monarch was preparing to establish a despotism while the nation was drifting toward revolution.
Charles X continued to aggravate the situation. He appeared in
religious processions on the streets of Paris, especially in 1826, at
the time of the celebration of the papal jubilee. The same year,
as he was reviewing the National Guard, he was greeted with cries
of, "Down with the Jesuits!" and "Down with Villèle!" Whereupon,
at Villèle's urging, he ordered its disbandment. The Guard was the
pride of the French middle class—the wits of the time called the
members, *les épiciers janissaires*—and this summary action of the
king made him very unpopular in Paris. The guardsmen were
allowed to keep their arms, of which they were to make effective
use three years later in the street fighting of the July Revolution. In
the Chambers Villèle's majority was waning. Sure, however, that
new elections would favor him, he induced the king to dismiss the
Chamber, which still had four years to run, and to call for new
elections.

The ministry again sent a circular to every prefect instructing him
to inform all officials that they must vote for the government's
candidates and do all in their power to influence others to act likewise. The clergy loudly denounced the liberals and urged the faithful to vote for devoted royalists. The liberals, in turn, organized
political meetings, and conducted propaganda. The *Société des amis
de la liberté de la presse,* founded under the presidency of Chateaubriand in June 1827, collected funds to pay the fines of liberal newspaper owners. In July a liberal political society under Guizot's direction, *"Aide-toi, le ciel t'aidera,"* (Heaven helps him who helps
himself), was organized to spread liberal ideas and to force prefects to stop manipulating and falsifying the electoral lists. As a
result of its efforts the eligible electors in France were increased
from 67,400 to nearly 83,000. Some of the great bankers and manufacturers, like Laffitte and Ternaux, angered by the recent class
legislation in favor of the church and the nobility, gave their backing
to the new society. Men of business were henceforth arrayed with
Napoleonic veterans and liberal idealists against the whole existing
régime. Everywhere the public was aroused as it had not been since

1815. The elections took place in an atmosphere of feverish excitement.[20]

When the votes were counted, it was discovered that the opposition had won a majority of sixty in the new Chamber. Villèle and the king were both deeply disappointed. When Charles X bluntly asked him, "Have you a majority?" Villèle was forced to acknowledge that he had not. He tried to approach the Left, but the financial situation was so bad that his reputation as an administrator, which might have helped him once again to overcome a crisis, was now undermined. For five years Villèle, himself a partisan neither of clericalism nor of reaction, had tried to please the Ultras without making himself too offensive to the liberals. Now he found himself despised by the liberals and rejected by the king and his circle. After some hesitation, he handed in his resignation on January 3, 1828. When he went to take his leave of the Duc d'Angoulême, the latter, with his customary ineptitude, said to him, "Well, you have become too unpopular!" Whereupon Villèle replied, "God grant that it is only I!" Metternich, on learning of the elections and the fall of Villèle, wrote, "France is lost; the institutions she possesses do not suit her, and they will fall to pieces. . . . For France there is nothing but the Republic or the Empire. . . . It is possible that France may have to pass again through confusion to arrive at order."[21]

The king, who had parted with Villèle only with the greatest reluctance, turned to a moderate royalist, Martignac, to form a new ministry. Accepting the commission to take over the government, Martignac tried to reconstruct the moderate royalist party that had maintained the upper hand in the Chambers from 1816 to 1820. This move soon met with the hostility of the king and the Ultras, and with the still greater hostility of all the factions of the Left. Evidently the new ministry was not to command a majority for long. Cousin, Guizot, and Villemain were again allowed to teach, a number of Ultra prefects were dismissed, and a more liberal press law was voted. But the only important accomplishment of the short-lived Martignac ministry (1828-29) was the Ordinances of 1828. The first, directed against the Jesuits, withdrew the right to teach from

[20] Cf. P. Thureau-Dangin, Le parti libéral sous la restauration (2nd ed., Paris, 1888).
[21] Metternich, Memoirs (New York, 1881), IV, 434.

all nonauthorized religious orders; the second restricted the number of lay students who might enroll in the *petits séminaires*. The bishops made a vigorous protest and the Ordinances were denounced in pastoral letters and from the pulpit. The clergy proclaimed that an age of persecution had begun and spoke in the same breath of Julian the Apostate, Marat, and Martignac. The violence of their language was so extreme that the pope ordered them to moderate their attitude, though the king secretly encouraged them.

Martignac next prepared a plan for the reform of local government, a proposal that had been discussed for nearly fifteen years. According to this project the town and the departmental councils, instead of being appointed by the king, should be locally elected. Martignac was interested chiefly in changing the town councils, but the interest of the liberal opposition was centered on the reform of the departmental councils, through which it hoped to curb the influence of the prefects. In the Chambers the controversy turned on the question as to which law should be brought up first, and in the debates Martignac was attacked furiously from both the Right and the Left. His attempt to command a moderate royalist majority ended in failure and, despised and neglected by the king, he was obliged to resign in August 1829. Charles X had evidently been trying to prove that nothing would please the Chambers and that all attempts to reconcile royal with constitutional government were doomed to failure, as indeed, from his point of view, they were.[22]

Charles X now determined to defy the Chambers, a stand which had not been taken since Louis XVIII maintained Richelieu in power against the will of the majority in the *Chambre Introuvable*. He recalled Polignac from England, where he had been French ambassador, and, in the teeth of an overwhelming majority in the Chambers, made him head of a new ministry. Son of a favorite of Marie Antoinette, and a prominent royalist intriguer against Napoleon, Polignac had returned to France after the fall of the Empire. In 1816 he was one of the two members of the Chambers who had refused to take the oath to the Charter, and he was widely known as one of the most prominent members of the Congrégation. Polignac was probably the most hated Ultra in France; his

[22] Cf. E. Daudet, *Le ministère Martignac* (Paris, 1875).

very name was a battle cry. Not until August 1829, did he succeed in bringing a cabinet together. It was a strange collection, which included La Bourdonnaye, the noisiest and most boastful Ultra in the Chambers, and General Bourmont, who had betrayed Napoleon in 1815. "Coblenz, Waterloo, 1815," as one liberal journal declared, "squeeze, press the ministry as you like, you will wring from it nothing but national dangers and humiliations!" In choosing Polignac and the rest of the ministry, Charles made it clear that he was no longer trying either to maintain the appearance of constitutional rule above all parties or of rule in accordance with the wishes of the majority. The king and a small party were now on the verge of establishing a despotism. The Ultras openly discussed a royalist *coup d'état*, citing in justification Article 14 of the Charter, by which the king was granted the right to issue ordinances when the country was in danger. They extolled the action of Louis XIV, who had arrived booted and spurred and whip in hand to reprimand the *Parlement de Paris!* The nation, however, was getting ready for a revolution. In December, 1828, the young Cavour wrote, "The coming year will be very interesting. In France the two parties are about to come to a decisive struggle, and it is probable that the dregs of the Villèle administration and the counter-revolutionary party will be completely beaten by the true defenders of civilization. The course of events will drag all Europe in its train."[23]

III. THE UNDERMINING OF HAPSBURG POWER IN MIDDLE EUROPE

The Carlsbad Decrees and the crushing of the Italian revolutions in 1821 tightened the hold of the Hapsburgs on every court in central Europe from Naples to Berlin. Within the Confederation some of the South German states, under the leadership of King William of Württemberg, kept up their resistance to the policies of Metternich and of Frederick William III of Prussia, who usually worked in close coöperation with him. To make trouble for Metternich, the King of Württemberg granted his people a constitution a few weeks after the publication of the Carlsbad Decrees. In 1820 an anonymous pamphlet, the *Manuscript from South Germany,* written under the direction of King William, condemned the decrees and

[23] A. J. Whyte, *The Early Life and Letters of Cavour* (Oxford, 1925), 26.

proposed the formation of a South German Confederation consisting of Bavaria, Württemberg, and Baden, which should be independent of all Austrian and Prussian influence. Other attacks on these two great powers followed, and in 1823 William sent a circular dispatch to some of the German rulers protesting vigorously against the interference of Austria and Prussia in the internal affairs of the lesser states of the Confederation. Metternich thereupon demanded that Württemberg recall Wangenheim, her principal representative at Frankfort. When King William refused this demand, Austria and Prussia promptly withdrew their envoys from Stuttgart. At the request of the Mainz Commission, the Diet ordered the suppression of the leading journal in the Württemberg capital. William was forced to back down completely, Wangenheim was recalled, the press was censored, and the Württemberg government assented to the renewal of the Carlsbad Decrees in 1824. Gentz hailed these changes as a greater victory for "the principles of sound government" than the French overthrow of the Spanish Revolution.

Metternich was now at the height of his influence in the Germanies; none of the federated states dared defy the wishes of Austria. The Diet at Frankfort met during only four months of the year and its activities were directed largely by Metternich's agents. Repression was, more than ever, the order of the day. Those rulers who had granted constitutions were obliged to curb all liberal agitation in their assemblies; in every state the press was severely censored, and the universities, in which the *Burschenschaften* had been secretly revived, were put under surveillance. Large numbers of liberals were kept in prison, and even suspected foreigners were held; in 1824 Victor Cousin, while making a sojourn in Germany to study the work of the Idealist Philosophers, was arrested in Saxony and later detained for six months in Berlin. The régime in Prussia after the death of Hardenberg in 1822 became nearly as repressive as in Austria. Metternich's agent, Prince Wittgenstein, became the leading figure in the government. No attempt was made to fulfill the promise of 1815 to grant a constitution, though in 1823 provincial estates to look after local affairs—road building, poor-relief, and tax-assessment—were established for the eight provinces of Prussia. Great improvements were made in the organization of the Prussian army and in local administration, and the system of taxation and public finance was reconstructed. Politically, however, all the states of the Confederation stagnated until they were aroused by the clarion call of the July Revolution in Paris.

At the very time when the rulers of the German states, terrified by the specter of revolution so cleverly evoked by Metternich, were surrendering their political powers to the Austrian chancellor, Prussia was taking the lead in the organization of a customs union which ultimately brought together all the Germanies except Austria. In 1815 the sudden opening of German markets to cheap British manufactures had aroused German industrial leaders to the need of a complete reform of the tariff regulations. The economist, List, summed up the situation: "Thirty-eight tariff walls impede internal commerce with much the same effect as if every limb of the human body were tied up so that the blood could not circulate. To go from Hamburg to Austria or from Berlin to Switzerland, ten states must be traversed, ten customs duties paid. . . . Most discouraging is this state of things for men who want to work and trade. With envious eyes they gaze across the Rhine where a great nation can trade freely from the Rhine to the Pyrenees, from the Dutch frontier to Italy without meeting a single customs-house officer."[24]

Many German bankers and business men were now convinced that German manufactures had to be protected, smuggling curbed, the cost of tariff collection reduced, and that, inside the Confederation, trade had to be facilitated by the abolition of many local customs boundaries.[25] The movement for tariff reform began in Prussia in 1818 when, through the influence of the Prussian finance minister, Maasen, the internal customs boundaries which divided one Prussian province from another were abolished and a uniform tariff, low enough to make smuggling unprofitable, was established against the rest of the world. The other German states looked on Prussia's policy with the greatest suspicion. At the Vienna Confer-

[24] A. Birnie, *Economic History of Europe* (2nd ed., N. Y., 1931), 72.
[25] The hindrance to trade caused by the lack of uniform commercial legislation in the German states is shown by the fact that the publication of a new work of Goethe's demanded the making of arrangements with thirty-eight states to prevent pirating and to secure publication rights. Cf. W. O. Henderson, *Zollverein* (Cambridge, 1938).

ences they tried pressure to force the Prussian government to abandon it. But in a few years several tiny states enclosed by Prussian territory joined the system. By 1828 a large free trade area had been formed under Prussian leadership in North Germany. Similar unions were established between Bavaria and Württemberg and between Saxony and Hanover.

After long negotiations, which lasted until 1833, the *Zollverein*, a customs union, was formed by seventeen states with a population of twenty-six million people. Austria consistently refused to join. The constitution of the union provided for an annual assembly representing all member governments; no changes could be made without unanimous consent. Among the states in the union there was to be free trade; the proceeds of the duties collected were to be divided among the governments in proportion to the population; all raw materials required for industry were to come in free, and on manufactured products the tariffs were to be moderate. The results of the *Zollverein* were of wide-ranging significance. For the first time the greater part of Germany became an economic unit; means of communication were being rapidly developed, and soon the volume of trade and manufacture showed remarkable expansion. Its influence, however, was not limited to the economic field. "The *Zollverein*," wrote Bentham's friend, John Bowring, in 1840, "has brought the sentiment of German nationality out of the regions of hope and fancy into those of positive and material interests . . . The general feeling in Germany towards the *Zollverein* is that it is the first step towards what is called the Germanization of the people. It has broken down some of the strongholds of alienation and hostility. By a community of interests on commercial and trading questions it has prepared the way for a political nationality."[26] The Prussian state by this important service qualified itself for the political leadership of Germany and accustomed the German states to coöperate without Austria. The *Zollverein* was a menace to the Confederation in that it sacrificed political union under Austria to the new economic union under Prussia. It did as much as any other movement of the early nineteenth century to prepare Germany for unification under Prussian leadership.

[26] J. Bowring, *Report on the Prussian Customs Union* (London, 1840), 17.

The Austrian Empire was a complicated structure; the racial elements were so diverse that no bureaucratic cement could bind them into a stable edifice. It held together only because of the ignorance of the masses and because one national force neutralized another. "My peoples," said Francis I, "are strange to each other and that is all right. They do not get the same sickness at the same time. In France if the fever comes all are caught by it. I send the Hungarians into Italy, the Italians into Hungary. Every people watches its neighbor. The one does not understand the other and one hates the other. . . . From their antipathy will be born order and from the mutual hatred, general peace."[27] The local estates, which met from time to time, gave no trouble to the emperor and were of no value to the people. In the bureaucratic administration there continued to prevail the systematic ineptitude already noted. The business of the state was carried on through a large number of chancelleries, courts, and offices each of which paralyzed the others. In 1826 a prolonged quarrel broke out in the highest court circles between Metternich and Kolowrat, who had made himself indispensable through his knowledge of public finance. The unedifying rivalry of the two men seriously hampered the efficiency of the administrative system. The emperor's principle of government, it was said, was to give no service its full reward, no department its complete development, no man his proper rôle. Every force was discouraged lest it should grow too strong.

The whole Austrian conception of government was purely negative: "Govern and change nothing" was the final dictum of Francis I. Both the emperor and Metternich were aware that they were defending a losing cause, and Francis once inadvertently told a Russian diplomat, "My realm is like a worm-eaten house; if one part is removed, one cannot tell how much will fall." Vienna, the capital from which the Hapsburgs directed the affairs of all Middle Europe, was the gayest of cities, but the swarm of spies that watched its inhabitants prevented any independence of thought. A government that believed that men can read themselves into criminals censored everything. For the intellectual classes it was a depressing environment. "In all the higher branches of knowledge with the

[27] O. Jászi, *Dissolution of the Hapsburg Monarchy* (Chicago, 1929), 82.

exception of the exact sciences there is," says one writer of the time, "not a single praiseworthy literary achievement; journalism throughout the whole glorious empire is null, the clever heads discouraged, under suspicion, very often exposed to the most stubborn persecutions in consequence of slanderous denunciations. . . . Such writers as Gibbon, Robertson, Hume, are partly forbidden and all the geniuses of Germany (Goethe, Schiller, Herder, Lessing, Jean Paul) are totally or partly suppressed."[28]

Among the subject nationalities in the Austrian Empire restlessness was on the increase as nationalist ideas began to penetrate eastward. In the eighteenth century the native languages and literatures of the Czechs and Magyars were in grave danger of dying out. Latin and German were the languages of government and of common intercourse among cultivated people all over the Empire. The highest nobility had intermarried with the German aristocracy of Austria and had been won over to German customs and ways of thinking. Only among the common people were the native languages kept alive; the upper classes were often no longer able to speak or read them, and almost no books were published except in German. The attempt of Joseph II to carry still further this process of Germanization finally stimulated a national consciousness among certain groups of intellectuals. Then had come the revolutionary upheaval, which scattered new ideas and aroused new aspirations among all subject nationalities. Among the Magyars the national revival dates from the linguistic reforms and the writings of Kazinczy, who first created an interest in Magyar literature. Soon a group of younger men, Katona, the Kisfaludy brothers, Vörösmarty, and Kolcsey, were writing poems and plays which portrayed the glorious episodes in Hungarian history. These men created a literary language and style and raised Magyar literature to a position of European importance. In the 1820's the movement attracted the attention of the Hapsburg government; the works of Kazinczy were burned by the hangman and the author was imprisoned in the

---

[28] Jászi, op. cit., 78. Quite characteristic of the attitude of the government was the remark of Gentz to Robert Owen when the latter was trying to convince the Austrian government of the need of reforms. "We do not desire to have the masses well off and independent. How could we rule over them?" V. Bibl., Der Zerfall Österreichs (Vienna, 1922), I, 157.

Spielberg. The government forbade the production of some of the plays of Katona.

During the long period of Hapsburg rule, the Magyars had maintained their medieval local assemblies, but no general diet for the whole Hungarian kingdom was called between 1812 and 1825. In 1821 Metternich sent orders to Hungary calling for recruits for the war in Italy, and demanding further that taxes be paid in coin instead of in paper money. Since the central Diet had always had the right to fix the number of soldiers to be furnished to the Hapsburg army and the right to control taxes, these demands aroused some of the Magyar magnates to a high pitch of anger. The new orders from Vienna were resisted by the local assemblies and protested against by the Magyar landowners, till finally, in 1825, the Hapsburg government called a meeting of the national Diet.

When the Diet convened the lead was taken by Count Széchenyi, a young Magyar noble who now for the first time dared to address the assembly, not in the conventional Latin, but in Magyar. The opposition to the Austrian government was so strong in the Diet of 1825 that the emperor was obliged to agree to observe the laws, to raise no taxes without the consent of the Hungarian Diet, and to call it at least once in three years.[29] From this time on Széchenyi took the lead in directing the national revival. Like Confalonieri and some of the other Italian reformers of the period, he had traveled widely in western Europe and was a great admirer of England. He was convinced that Hungary needed not merely political reforms, but a complete intellectual and economic regeneration, for her backwardness, he believed, was due more to the Magyars themselves than to the policies of the Hapsburg government. He devoted a year's income from his estates to the founding of a national academy (1822) and was the leading influence in the establishment of a national theater (1837). To keep the nobles in their own country and to bring them together to discuss public affairs, he founded a club in Budapest and introduced horseracing. He started the first insurance company in Hungary, helped to organize a system of steam navigation on the Danube, and later carried through the building of a suspension bridge connecting Buda and Pesth. In 1830

---

[29] Metternich complained that in this Diet of 1825 he had "encountered all those things on which during my whole public life, especially in the last ten years, I have made war."

he wrote in his book, *On Credit,* "We can do nothing about the past, but we are the masters of the future. Let us not bother ourselves then with vain reminiscences, but let us unite in a firm, patriotic union so that our native land, which is so dear to us, may bring forth finer blossoms. Many think Hungary has been; for me, I like to believe that she will be!"[30]

Among the Slavs of the Empire, the Czechs, Slovaks, Serbs, and Croats, the agitation for national regeneration was more purely literary and cultural.[31] When Joseph II refused to be crowned King of Bohemia and forbade the use of Czech in the schools of Bohemia and Slovakia, the anger of the intellectuals was aroused as it had not been for centuries. To mollify the protestants, the emperor in 1792 established a chair of Czech literature in the University of Prague. But by trying to kill the Czech language, which was already dying a natural death, the Austrian authorities simply helped to rejuvenate it. Soon after 1800 a number of Czech scholars began to publish philological studies of the language. Little was known at the time about any of the Slavic languages; as late as 1827 Šafařik wrote to Kollár that the Serb and Bulgarian tongues were more closely related to the Turkish than to Polish or Czech! In 1792 the Scientific Society at Prague sent an ex-Jesuit, Dobrovsky, to Sweden to search for Czech manuscripts which had been carried off during the Thirty Years' War. From Stockholm Dobrovsky went to Finland, St. Petersburg, and Moscow to study old Slavic texts. On his return to Prague, he became the acknowledged leader of a national cultural movement which aimed at the resurrection of the whole history of Slavic culture. Much of his inspiration was derived from Herder, who had predicted a great future for the Slavs.[32] Dobrovsky himself was primarily a scholar rather than a propagandist. He wrote mostly in Latin and German.

A group of Dobrovsky's friends in 1818 founded the Czech

[30] F. Eckhart, *Introduction à l'histoire hongroise* (Paris, 1928), 100.

[31] The best general work is that of A. Fischel, *Der Panslawismus bis zum Weltkrieg* (Berlin, 1919).

[32] In his *Ideen zur Philosophie der Geschichte der Menschheit,* Herder wrote of the Slavs, "You, now deeply sunk, but once industrious and happy people, will finally awake from your long, listless slumber, and having shaken off the chains of slavery you will enjoy the possession of your picturesque lands from the Adriatic Sea to the Carpathian Mountains, and from the Don to the Moldau, and in them you will celebrate your ancient festivals of peaceful industry and trade." Herder, *Sämmtliche Werke* (Berlin, 1877-1913), XIV, 280.

National Museum, to which Goethe, Kolowrat, and Metternich contributed—Metternich probably because he thought the movement might help to deepen the antagonism between Slavs and Magyars in Slovakia. Another Czech scholar, Jungmann, through his translations of Milton, Goethe, and Chateaubriand, and his own original writings, first made the movement popular. During the first fifteen years of the century he was the soul of the cultural life of Bohemia. By the time Dobrovsky died, in 1829, a new Czech literature had come into existence, owing to his inspiration and that of Jungmann. The new enthusiasm for Czech antiquities ran so high that several of the younger men forged medieval Czech poems which were long believed to be genuine and which contributed greatly toward arousing interest in the movement.

Among the ablest of these younger followers of Dobrovsky and Jungmann—Kollár, Šafařik, and Palácky—the first two went to Germany to study. Here they came in contact with the ideals of the *Burschenschaften* (both were present at the Wartburg Festival), and with the writings of the German romanticists. By the time they began to write, the Magyar nationalist movement in Hungary was arousing vigorous protests among the Slovaks, who were living under Magyar rule and who had made a feeble beginning at starting a national literature in the eighteenth century. Kollár and Šafařik were Slovaks by birth but they threw in their forces with the closely related Czech movement. During the 1820's the Czech and Slovakian nationalist movements merged. From 1829 to 1848 a whole series of dictionaries, histories, philological studies, editions of folk-poems, translations of great foreign works, and original poems and prose writings appeared.[33]

Kollár's impassioned sonnet sequence, *Slava's Daughter*, which when finally completed consisted of nearly six hundred sonnets, did more for the revival of Czech culture than any other work. The prologue is typical of much of the fervid nationalist writing of the early nineteenth century and reflects the almost religious worship of

---

[33] Šafařik's chief works were his *History of the Slavic Languages and Literature*—in German (1826), and his *Slavic Antiquities*—in Czech (1837); Palácky was best known through his *History of Bohemia* (1836 ff.), of which there appeared in turn first a German, then a Czech version.

the native culture. The passage reflects the tendency of cultural nationalism to evolve into racial hatred. For Kollár, as for many other Slav writers, the Germans from whom they derived their training and their ideas became the cultural oppressors: "Here before my tear-laden eyes stretches the land once the cradle, now the tomb of my people. From the banks of the Elbe to the plains of the Vistula, from the foamy waves of the Danube to the Baltic the harmonious sounds of the Slavic language once resounded. But hatred has suffocated them. Who committed this terrible crime? Shame on you, Germany! Your hand is soiled with the blood of this crime. . . . My eye searches for Slavs on Slavic land and finds none. They were the first to awaken life in the north; they taught men to venture forth on the sea and look for rich coasts beyond the waters; they tore metals from the bowels of the earth; they taught laborers to break the soil with a plow and bring forth golden harvests. And what has been your reward for all these good deeds and lessons, my people? A perfidious neighbor has slipped into the house and thrown heavy chains around the neck of the sovereign; the gods themselves have fled; only the earth has remained true: the forests, the rivers, the walls of the villages and towns have not denounced their Slavic names; but the spirit is gone."[34]

Kollár later took up the ideas of several Polish and Slovakian thinkers of the eighteenth century who had emphasized the common history and destiny of the Slavic peoples and who had dreamed of founding a Pan-Slavist movement. He tried to arouse a sense of solidarity among all the Slavic peoples of Europe. He urged cultivated Slavs to learn the Czech, Polish, Russian, and Serb languages, to read and study each others' books, and to coöperate in common movements. His ideal is expressed in one of his essays, "What art thou? A Russian. What art thou? A Serb. What art thou? A Pole. No, my children, unity! Let your answer be, I am a Slav!"[35]

In other parts of the Austrian Empire nationalist movements were just beginning. Among the Rumanians of Transylvania Maior's *History of the Romans in Rumania*, printed in Rumanian in 1812, and Radilescu's *Rumanian Grammar* of 1828 mark the beginnings

[34] E. Denis, *La Bohême depuis la Montagne Blanche* (Paris, 1903), II, 149-150.
[35] T. Capek, *The Slovaks of Hungary* (New York, 1906), 18; see also the anonymous article, "Kollár and Literary Panslavism," *Slavonic Review*, VI.

of a Rumanian national revival. Along the Adriatic coast the Napoleonic rule had called into being a sense of national consciousness among the Croats, the Slovenes, and the Serbs. Before the fall of the Napoleonic Empire, Obradović, a Serb born in southern Hungary, had organized the schools of the new Serbian state, and had used the language of the Serb peasants in his writings. His influence on the growth of Serbian national consciousness both in the Austrian Empire and beyond its borders, was profound, and he is justly considered the creator of modern Serb nationalism. In 1815 Karadžić, a Serb, published a volume of Serbian folk-songs, followed in 1818 by a Serb-German-Latin dictionary, and in 1820 by a Serb grammar. Karadžić had received a thorough philological training at German universities. His work was admired by Goethe and the Grimms. German learned societies honored him with their membership, and the great German historian, Leopold von Ranke, cultivated a close professional friendship with him. Karadžić made a large number of reforms in spelling and raised the Serb vernacular to the status of a literary language. Making extravagant claims for his nation, "the greatest people of the planet," he announced that its culture was five thousand years old, and that Jesus and the Twelve Apostles were Serbs. A Serbian journal was published in Vienna between 1813 and 1822, and in 1826 a group of Hungarian Serbs founded a literary society, the *Matitsa*.

Among the closely related Croatians the national movement went back to the seventeenth century, when the Republic of Ragusa was a center of Slavic studies.[36] During the Napoleonic period a priest named Vodnik wrote a series of odes evoking the past glories of the Slovenes and Croatians, and Kopitar published the first Slovene grammar (1808). By 1825 the movement had progressed so far that one of the Croatian delegates to the Hungarian Diet could declare, "Croatia and Slavonia are not subject but associate kingdoms which existed long before Hungary and have Hungary not as a mother but merely as a sister."[37] The same ideas were frequently expressed

---

[36] Cf. B. Skok, "L'importance de Dubrovnik dans l'histoire slave" *Monde slave*, 1931 and B. Unbegaun, *Les débuts de la langue littéraire chez les Serbs* (Paris, 1935).

[37] Seton-Watson, *The Southern Slav Question and the Hapsburg Monarchy* (London, 1911), 28. Cf. the two works by H. Wendel, *Aus dem südslawischen Risorgimento* (Gotha, 1921), and *Der Kampf der Südslawen um Freiheit und Einheit* (Frankfort, 1925).

in the local Croatian Diet. During the 1830's a brilliant journalist, Ljudevit Gaj, started a movement which he called Illyrianism, and which aimed at the union of the Southern Slavs of the Austrian Empire—the Serbs, Croats, and Slovenes. These new national movements, to which should be added the agitation among the Austrian Poles, presented a new and very serious problem for the Hapsburg monarchy, though as yet only the nationalism of the Magyars had any political importance.[38]

The failure of the revolutionary uprisings of 1820 had deepened the hold of the Austrian government on the Italian states. For a time the Hapsburgs had their armies of occupation at Naples, Turin, and Ancona. Their agents and spies were at work everywhere; as Giusti put it, the Italians "ate Austria in their bread." In some places, however, the local princes, though still ready to appeal to Vienna in time of revolution, tried to resist Austrian interference. Piedmont and the Papal States frustrated her attempt to form a postal league; Charles Felix of Piedmont and the King of Naples successfully maneuvered to get the armies of occupation withdrawn, and in 1823 Leo XII was elected pope against the wishes of Vienna. Beneath the surface there was constant intrigue, especially on the part of the Duke of Modena, who hoped to enlarge his state at the expense of Austria and of Piedmont, and who even approached the Carbonari with the idea of getting their help in carrying out his schemes. Within all the Italian states the sternest repression prevailed; the rulers reformed no abuses but held more stubbornly than ever to their policy of treating every murmur of dissent as a crime.

The Carbonari, continuing their secret agitation, plotted against the local governments and interfered where they could with the activities of the Austrian secret police. They were particularly active in the Papal States, where the government, after Consalvi's death in 1824, became both weaker and more corrupt. In the Romagna the administration was so bad that it was commonly said, "The Turks would be better!" Brigandage flourished as never before. In many

[38] Little about these nationalistic movements was known in western Europe. When, in the reign of Louis Philippe, the minister of public instruction prepared a report urging the creation of a chair of Slavic languages in the Collège de France, he based some of his remarks on the idea that Serbian was spoken in Bohemia!

cases the Carbonari and the brigands worked together. The papal government tried the use of terror, but sporadic outbursts of law-enforcement with wholesale executions and imprisonments only increased the anarchy. In the Kingdom of Naples conditions became worse than ever after the death of Ferdinand in 1825, for the new king, Francis I, was more brutal and treacherous than his father had ever been. The government was left to royal favorites, while the king lived with his mistresses, heavily guarded and in hourly dread of assassination. In 1828 a revolt broke out, but the government easily suppressed it, beheaded the leaders and hung their gory heads in front of their own houses. The Neapolitan state, with its prisons full, its civil and ecclesiastical offices in the hands of the most venal administrators, its towns swarming with spies, and its provinces infested with outlaws, would have burst asunder had not the threat of Austrian intervention been ever present.

In the northern part of the peninsula economic conditions had improved steadily since 1815. But there was as little political freedom as there was in the south. The Hapsburg administration was honest and efficient in Lombardy-Venetia and the government at Vienna did all it could to distract the populace by supporting the theater and the opera and by treating the people to public entertainments. The Kingdom of Piedmont, since the failure of the revolution in 1821, was ruled with an iron hand by the narrow-minded Charles Felix. Typical of his rule was the regulation which required all university students, among whom was the young Mazzini, to attend mass regularly and to go to confession once a month. Tuscany was the only haven of freedom; there the *Antologia,* Vieusseux's famous reading room, and the theater furnished some outlet for Italian nationalist and liberal aspirations. Many of the great romantic literary works were published in Florence, and romanticism had, as Pellico said, become "synonymous with liberalism." Milan was also an important publishing center, but there, in the Italian city most alert to the economic movement of the time, the reformers took up a program of economic rather than political regeneration. The new intellectual movements were evidences of a slow spiritual awakening. The younger leaders held aloof from plots and insisted that the Italians must first be regenerated culturally and economically.

Cavour and Mazzini were already watching the movement of ideas and events and preparing themselves to become the leaders of the next generation. They were already convinced that before Italy's independence could be achieved a majority of the Italian people must come to desire such freedom and must be strong enough to use it.

IV. THE DECAY OF THE OTTOMAN EMPIRE AND THE WINNING OF SERBIAN AND OF GREEK INDEPENDENCE

The disintegration of the Ottoman Empire had gone on at an accelerated pace throughout the eighteenth century. The whole administrative system had fallen largely into the hands of the Phanariot Greeks of Constantinople who, with the Greek patriarch and the higher Greek clergy, ruled the Christian peoples of the Balkans for the sultan. In order to maintain their privileged position, the Greek hierarchy did everything in its power to obliterate all traces of the old Serbian, Bulgarian, and Rumanian national cultures; it destroyed manuscripts and books that were not Greek and forced the use of Greek in all church schools. For these reasons the other Balkan Christians hated the Greeks quite as much as they did the Turks. The Ottoman exploitation of the Christian peoples of southeastern Europe, galling as it was, had never been uniform or very thoroughgoing. The Turks had left to the Serbian and Greek rural and urban communities general control over purely local concerns, which were dealt with by native councils and assemblies; as a result neither of these peoples ever lost entirely the experience of self-government. During the eighteenth century, as the Turkish rule became more inefficient and more oppressive, some of the Greek and Serb peasants of independent spirit became brigands. Both the Greek *klephts* and the Serbian *heyduks*, although they robbed both Christians and Moslems, were regarded with patriotic approbation by the common people because they made private war on the Turkish régime. In the wars of independence the brigands proved to be good fighters against the Moslems.

In the outlying parts of the Ottoman Empire the sultan's government had only the loosest hold; in Egypt, Muhammad Ali, and in Albania, Ali Pasha of Janina had virtually repudiated the authority of the sultan. In Syria, Arabia, Tripoli, Tunis, and Algeria, as in Serbia, the local Mohammedan authorities followed orders from Constantinople only when it suited their own plans. Throughout the empire the highest officials, both Turkish and Greek, used their positions to amass private fortunes; the entire administrative régime, when it functioned at all, was hardly more than one of organized brigandage. The great Moslem landowners in the Balkans, who had made their economic and social position hereditary, defied the Ottoman officials and were as much the enemies of the sultan's government as they were the oppressors of the subject Christian peoples. The attempts of Selim III (1789-1807) and of his nephew, Mahmud II (1808-1839) to reform the whole Ottoman government were met by the stubborn resistance of the Moslem landowners and of the religious leaders under whose guidance there rallied all the forces that had anything to lose by innovations. Mahmud II persisted, but his efforts did not begin to bear fruit until after the destruction of the Janissaries in 1826, and then it was too late to prevent the liberation of the Serbs and the Greeks. The weakness of the Ottoman government in the early nineteenth century was well summed up in a remark made by the French ambassador to Chateaubriand on the occasion of his visit to Constantinople in 1807; "To make an alliance with Turkey is the same as putting your arms around a corpse to make it stand up!"[39]

In 1804 a new era began in Balkan affairs. Heretofore the chief enemies of Turkey had been Austria and Russia, both of which had long been planning a partition of the Ottoman Empire; now, for the first time, one of the Christian nationalities under Turkish rule rose in revolt and maintained itself. The Serbs were a backward, agricultural race, ground down by the Turkish administration, the great Moslem landowners, and the Greek bishops, but among the people the memory of Serbia's former greatness had been kept alive in song and legend. At the end of the eighteenth century a number of Serbian scholars had begun to revive interest in the national history and literature, and after 1766, when the old Serbian patriarchate of Ipek was abolished and the whole Serbian church directly organized under the Greek patriarch at Constantinople, the lower

[39] H. Bérenger, *Chateaubriand* (Paris, 1931), 136.

clergy had become active in arousing a national feeling. The most influential of these scholars, Rajić, Obradović, and Karadžić, found a haven in southern Hungary where they could publish their writings.[40]

This national renaissance was not, however, the immediate cause of the Serbian rising of 1804. Exasperation over the high-handed conduct and heartless plundering of the Janissary garrison at Belgrade drove the neighboring peasants to revolt. The members of the famous Janissary corps were no longer recruited from the Christian peoples and had long since lost the marvelous discipline for which they were once noted. They were now allowed to marry and to engage in trade, and had become a privileged corporation which terrorized even the sultan. To rid himself of their meddling, he garrisoned the most unruly of them in the provinces. In Serbia the large Mohammedan landowners joined with the native leaders in protests to the sultan against their ruthless and arbitrary administration. Thereupon the sultan threatened the Janissaries; if they continued in their ways, he would send a force against them, "not of Turks, but of men of another faith and another race." Concluding that this could mean only the Serbians, the Janissaries began to murder some of the more prominent Serbs. This, in turn, aroused the native population to action.

Among the Serbian peasantry were many men who had learned how to fight in the wars of the later eighteenth century between Austria and Turkey. It was from this group that the outraged people chose an able and fearless chief, a hog merchant, Kara (Black) George. Under his direction, the Janissaries were driven into the citadel of Belgrade and into several other fortresses. The Serbian rebels still considered themselves loyal to the Ottoman régime, but, flushed with victory, they made ever-increasing demands on the Turkish government. The sultan had given his tacit approval to the insurrection; but now, refusing to treat with the Serbs, he sent an army against them. The war then entered its second phase and became one for Serbian autonomy. The Serbs were at first very successful, but the fighting dragged on until 1813 when, at the end of

[40] Cf. G. Yakschitch, *L'Europe et la resurrection de la Serbie, 1804-1834* (2nd edition, Paris, 1913); V. Stajić, "The Centenary of the Matica," *Slavonic Review,* 1928, and D. Subotić, "The Serbia of Prince Miloš," *ibid.,* 1924.

the Russo-Turkish War, the Ottoman government was again in a position to concentrate its attention on the rebels. Turkish armies invaded Serbia from three sides; Kara George, seeing the hopelessness of further resistance, fled to Hungary, and the revolt collapsed.

The Turks took a terrible vengeance on all Serbian families connected with the revolt. Native leaders who had stood aloof became convinced that the Turks were determined to kill off a large part of the Serbian population. They had their choice between a new revolt or extermination. So on Palm Sunday, 1815, Miloš Obrenović, the most prominent leader left in Serbia, raised the standard of revolt. Like Kara George, he could neither read nor write, but he subscribed to two Austrian newspapers and a French one which his secretary read to him regularly; thus he acquired a good understanding of European affairs, and in the second Serbian Revolt proved himself a leader of extraordinary resourcefulness. Some of the leaders of the first revolt hurried back from Hungary and within two years, without foreign help, the Serbs triumphed over the Turkish rule. The part of the Serbian people who lived about Belgrade sent representatives to a national assembly and this body elected Miloš hereditary prince. Unhappily for Serbia's future, Miloš allowed Kara George, whom he accused of having poisoned his brother, to be murdered in 1817, and so started a bloody feud which lasted nearly a century. In 1826, by the Convention of Akkerman, Serbia was promised local autonomy under a Russian protectorate, and in 1829, by the Treaty of Adrianople and in future agreements made between 1830 and 1834, Miloš's title of hereditary prince and the right of the Serbs to organize their own national church were recognized. Moslem landowners were compelled to sell out and withdraw from the country. Except for an annual tribute paid to the Ottoman government and the right of the Turks to keep troops in some of the fortresses, Serbia was free to govern herself.

The Serbian Revolts had attracted little attention in western Europe, but when in 1821 the statesmen of the Quintuple Alliance in session at Laibach heard that the Greeks were in revolt against their Turkish masters, it was realized almost immediately that here was a European problem of major proportions. From then until the freedom of Greece was guaranteed in 1829, no political question was more widely discussed in the chancelleries and in the press of Europe. The events of 1821, which were such a surprise to Metternich and the statesmen of Europe, had been long preparing. During the eighteenth century many changes had taken place among the Greeks of the Ottoman Empire. In the Turkish administration they had gained control of important positions, thereby increasing their fortunes and their influence. Much of the commercial activity of the Near East, especially in the regions that border on the Black, the Ægean, and the Ionian seas, was in Greek hands, and after 1774 Greek-owned ships had been allowed to carry the Russian flag. During the French Revolution, when the French merchantmen were driven from the Mediterranean, Greek captains, sometimes carrying the Turkish and sometimes the Russian colors, had built up a flourishing trade in grain and other commodities.

It was the Greeks in the Ægean islands and in all of the great ports of the Mediterranean from Marseilles to Odessa who had profited most by these commercial and political opportunities. They sent their sons to study in French, German, and Italian universities where they came in contact with the ideology of western Europe, especially with the French liberal thought of the *philosophes*. At home they organized schools and secret societies and patronized the nationalist writers who were trying to arouse the Greek people. The mass of the peasants on the mainland of the Greek peninsula, though they were of the same race and spoke the same language, seemed, in their poverty and their cultural backwardness, to belong to a totally different nationality. The misunderstandings that inevitably existed between these peasants on the one hand, and the cultivated islanders and the Greek scholars and philanthropists on the other, became much more sharply defined in the course of the War of Independence.

The Greek merchants in the Mediterranean ports and on the islands founded a series of excellent schools, and in Chios they established a university.[41] From these centers was spread a knowledge of the writings of Rhigas, of Koraes, and of a number of other nationalist propagandists. Rhigas, a Vlach who had been inspired

[41] Cf. S. T. Lascaris, "Un institut littéraire à Corfu sous Napoléon," *Revue des études napoléoniennes,* 1925, and H. Pernot, "Coray," *L'Acropole,* 1933.

by the ideals of the French Revolution, provided the cause of Greek freedom with a body of stirring patriotic poetry; his execution by the Turks in 1798 made him a martyr of Greek freedom. Koraes, who spent most of his life in Paris, was primarily a scholar. In his introductions to new editions of the Greek classics he advocated an extended series of linguistic reforms which would bring the modern Greeks again in contact with their glorious literary heritage.[42] Words of Turkish, Albanian, and Slavic origin were thrown out, and a new language evolved which was a reasonable compromise between classical Greek and the contemporary language of the common people. Most of the reforms advocated by Koraes were put into use in the Greek schools and in books and newspapers. Ultimately his influence affected the whole of modern Greek culture.

From a number of learned societies, inspired by the writings of Rhigas and Koraes, came the members of the revived *Hetairía Philikè*, a secret society reorganized in 1814 at Odessa, the purpose of which was the expulsion of the Turks from Europe and the resurrection of the Greek Medieval Empire.[43] It grew steadily; after the headquarters were transferred to Constantinople in 1818, the membership came to include almost all Greeks of importance. In 1820 there were over one hundred thousand enrolled. The society spread propaganda, collected funds, and bought military supplies. The *Hetairía* placed its hopes in Russia, especially in one of the

---

[42] In 1801 Koraes wrote: "The seeds of learning, which today are tended and cultivated throughout Europe, first sprang from the soil of our native land; but, alas! whilst strangers plant and prune them, whilst they rise into spreading trees, and others collect their fruits, we alone have forgotten that our fathers were the first to rear them. Increase, then, your diligence to enlighten your country, and to recall the ancient honours of your race. Remember that you are the representatives of the Homers, and the Aristotles, of the Platos, and Demosthenes, of the Thucydides, and Sophocles, whose labours achieved the greatness of Greece; whose names were revered when living, and whose memory has survived decay. You are now the instructors and teachers of your country, but the time is fast approaching when you will be called on to act as its lawgivers. Unite, then, your wealth and your exertions in her behalf." J. E. Tennent, *History of Modern Greece* (London, 1845), II, 528.

[43] Some of the clauses of their oath, which resembles those of the Italian and French Carbonari, were, "I swear that I will nourish in my heart irreconcilable hatred against the tyrants of my country, their followers, and favourers; and I will exert every method for their injury and destruction. . . . Last of all, I swear by thee, my sacred and suffering country,—I swear by the long-endured tortures,—I swear by the bitter tears which for so many centuries have been shed by thy unhappy children,—I swear by the future liberty of my countrymen,—that I consecrate myself wholly to thee; that henceforth thou shalt be the scope of my thoughts, thy name the guide of my actions, thy happiness the recompense of my labours." J. S. Comstock, *History of the Greek Revolution* (New York, 1828), 143.

tsar's chief ministers, Capodistrias. He was a native of Corfu, one of the Ionian Islands which were under the enlightened rule of the English. Capodistrias, however, refused to accept the headship of the society. In 1820 a general in the Russian army, Prince Alexander Ypsilanti, son of one of the Greek *Hospodars* of Moldavia, became its leader.

The *Hetairía* planned a revolt for 1825, but when the leaders saw that the Turkish forces were occupied in what appeared to be a losing conflict with Ali Pasha of Janina, the rebel Albanian who had built up a state in Epirus, they decided to act at once. On March 6, 1821, Ypsilanti, crossing the Pruth, declared that his expedition was "sanctioned by a great power," which could only mean Russia, and called on the Rumanian people to rise against the Turks. But the Rumanians, who hated the Greek clergy and their Greek governors, the *Hospodars*, refused to have anything to do with the cause. Ypsilanti, however, was able to seize Jassy and part of Moldavia. He moved on to Wallachia where a peasant rising, led by Tudor Vladimirescu, threatened the power of the Rumanian landlords. Realizing the danger, the latter quickly made terms with Vladimirescu, and turned their efforts to helping the Turks defeat Ypsilanti and his Greeks. Ypsilanti foolishly had Vladimirescu put to death, which increased Rumanian resistance to his cause. Tsar Alexander, now quite under Metternich's domination, denounced the expedition and refused all help to the revolutionaries. The Greek Patriarch of Constantinople was obliged by the sultan to excommunicate the insurgent leader. Hard pressed by the Turkish troops and left without any support either from Russia or from the Rumanians, Ypsilanti fled to Austria, where he was thrown into prison. The enterprise collapsed. The only important result of the whole incident was that the Ottoman government in 1822 replaced the Greek *Hospodars* with native Rumanian princes, who acted thereafter as governors for the Turks. From this change the Rumanians date the beginnings of their movement for national independence.[44]

Barely a month after Ypsilanti crossed the Pruth, another and more

[44] The most useful works on the Greek Revolution are the older work of G. Finlay, *History of Greece* (new ed., Oxford, 1877), VI and VII, and the monograph of C. W. Crawley, *The Question of Greek Independence* (Cambridge, 1930).

serious revolt, also engineered by the *Hetairía*, broke out in the Morea. With wild fury the Greek peasants turned on the Turkish population and murdered all who could not take refuge in the walled towns; from the beginning the war was marked on both sides by horrible butchery. By May, 1821, the Turkish rule in the Morea was at an end.

Meanwhile, the Turks had begun to make reprisals. On Easter Day the Greek Patriarch of Constantinople and three Greek archbishops were hanged in their sacred vestments. After the bodies had hung for three days outside the archiepiscopal palace, they were thrown into the Bosphorus. This aroused the Greeks all over the Mediterranean world and, when the news of it reached western Europe, it created a great wave of sympathy for the Greek cause. Elsewhere, especially in Thessaly, Macedonia, and Asia Minor, the Turks pillaged the Greek churches, massacred the men, and sold hundreds of women into slavery. The attention of the great powers was now focused on Greece, and Tsar Alexander proposed at once to intervene. Metternich, however, vigorously opposed interference and insisted that the insurgents were simply rebels against the established order, like the revolutionaries of Spain and Naples. He rightly suspected that Russia might use the affair as an excuse to continue her advance into the Balkans which she had been making since the time of Catherine the Great. Thus, while Greeks and Turks were fighting in the Near East, there began a long series of diplomatic negotiations which involved all the powers of the Quintuple Alliance, but which produced no joint action until 1826.

On the Greek side there was little organization and much jealousy and double dealing, but the Turkish army was so occupied with fighting Ali Pasha, who was captured and beheaded only in 1822, that the Greeks enjoyed striking successes in the early stages of the struggle and were able to fend off their oppressors for several years. Food and army supplies were sent by the Philhellenes, while a few ardent European and American adventurers went out to Greece to help the insurgents.[45] Even the governments of the powers, although

---

[45] The importance of the contribution of the Philhellenes in the whole struggle is brought out by Finlay. "The empty coffers of the Greek government continued to be replenished with European gold, and the Greek armies reinforced by European volunteers,

they were still officially neutral, found it year by year harder to resist the pressure of these Philhellenes. Diplomats who at first referred slightingly to Philhellenism as "the clamor of a faction," were speaking by 1823 of "the sympathy of all Europe" for the Greek cause.

During the years 1821 and 1822 the Greeks captured and held the fortresses of Navarino, Tripolitsa—where they butchered thousands of Turks in cold blood—Missolonghi, Athens, Nauplia, and Corinth. On the sea they were equally successful. They sank the best of the Turkish warships and drove the others into the Dardanelles, though before this the Turks had massacred or sold into slavery thirty thousand of the Greek inhabitants of Chios, the most horrible incident of the war.[46] On sea and on land the Greeks seemed destined to win a speedy and complete victory. In January, 1822, a national assembly which met at Epidauros proclaimed the independence of Greece and promulgated a constitution which shows American influence. The Greek forces were, however, very disorganized; officials refused to follow the regulations of the central government; military officers would not obey their superiors; bitter jealousies divided group from group. In 1824 a veritable civil war raged on the mainland between the forces of the government and a group of peasants in the Morea who blamed the provisional régime for favoring the wishes of the islanders at the expense of the mainlanders. In spite of this, the Turks were so weak that they were unable to crush the rebellion. Early in 1823 the British government, chiefly to stop the Greeks from preying on British shipping in the Mediterranean, recognized the Greeks as belligerents and opened diplomatic negotiations with them. This move aroused Metternich, who did not want any power to give favors to the rebels and who did not like the idea of England's meddling in Near Eastern affairs. He therefore proposed to the tsar that Austria and Russia move

till Reshid Pasha could exclaim, with bitterness and with truth, 'We are no longer fighting the Greeks, but all Europe!' . . . The greater part of the Greeks who bore arms against the Turks were fed by provisions supplied by the Greek committees in England, Switzerland, France, and Germany . . . while the Greek committees in the United States directed their attention to the relief of the civilian population. The amount of provisions and clothing sent from America was very great. Cargo after cargo arrived." G. Finlay, *History of Greece* (new ed., Oxford, 1877), VI, 437.

[46] Cf. P. P. Argenti, *The Massacres of Chios* (London, 1932).

jointly against Turkey, but, as they could not agree on a course of procedure, no action was taken.

The war entered a new phase when, in February, 1825, Ibrahim Pasha, the son of Muhammad Ali, brought a large military force from Egypt. Mahmud II, the Ottoman sultan, had hoped to crush the Greeks without the help of the Egyptian usurper, and had delayed asking for aid until the insurgents had driven him to the wall. When the Turkish situation became desperate, Mahmud was forced to make a trip to Cairo to appeal for help. Muhammad Ali agreed to send aid, though only on condition that he be allowed to govern Crete and that his son, Ibrahim, be made governor of the Morea. As the sultan was in no position to refuse, an agreement was drawn up on Muhammad Ali's terms and a military expedition left Egypt for Crete. Using Crete as a base, Ibrahim reduced the Greek islands of the Ægean and then took over to the mainland a well-equipped and well-disciplined army. The internal quarrels among the Greeks made it possible for him to seize Navarino and establish a military and naval base on the mainland. From there he began the systematic reduction of the country. The Greeks for a time stopped fighting among themselves, and turned valiantly on the invaders, but their guerrilla bands were no match for the disciplined troops of Ibrahim. In vain did the Greeks appeal to the powers. They tried to place themselves under British protection and pleaded with the English government to send them a king. In 1825, when this appeal was made, Canning was more friendly toward the Greek cause than any other European statesman, but he refused to abandon England's neutrality. So the Greeks were forced to continue the fight alone.

Fortress after fortress in the Morea fell into Moslem hands and in central Greece the Egyptian fleet, coöperating with a Turkish army, besieged Missolonghi, one of the last fortresses held by the insurgents. On April 22, 1826, after it had become clear that the Moslems would finally starve them out, the entire population gathered at the gates, prepared to make a desperate sally. Part of the Greek forces cut their way through, but the besiegers closed in upon the rest and put most of them to the sword. Part of the remnant, seeing all chance of escape cut off, set fire to the powder magazines and perished in the explosion. Some three thousand women and children, the last survivors, were sold into slavery. When the victorious troops took possession of the smoking and blood-stained ruins of the heroic town, they must have believed the final collapse of the Greek cause near.

At Constantinople, Mahmud II, disgusted with the poor showing made by the Turkish troops, turned on the Janissaries. They would neither fight themselves nor allow the sultan to organize an effective army without them. With the help of the conservative Mohammedan religious and social forces they stubbornly interfered with the sultan's reforming efforts. Mahmud now ordered the disbandment of the corps, whereupon, as was expected, the Janissaries revolted. But preparations had long been made to quell them. One June morning in 1826, the inhabitants of Pera, looking across the Golden Horn, saw two great columns of smoke rising above the minarets of Stambul. The smoke announced that the great barracks of the Janissaries had been fired. Inside the old capital of the Byzantine emperors a bloody massacre was taking place. The government troops mowed down the rebels with a fierce artillery fire. Nearly the whole Janissary corps in Constantinople perished. At the same time the sultan ordered the expulsion and confiscation of the property of the Bektashi dervish order, an heretical group closely associated with the Janissaries and with the forces of religious conservatism. The Ottoman government was at last freed of an old burden. This high-handed reform and the fall of Athens, the last important stronghold held by the Greeks, seemed to seal the doom of the revolutionary cause. But the Greeks clung to the hope of defeating the Turks and, while the siege of Athens (1827) was still going on, the National Assembly elected Capodistrias, the most eminent living Greek, president of Greece for seven years.

The course of the war, which had by this time aroused the interest of the whole western world, now took an important turn. Nicholas I, the new ruler of Russia, unlike Alexander, had taken no part in the formation of the Quadruple Alliance, and had no intention of taking orders from Metternich in a question of such vital interest to Russia. In March, 1826, Nicholas made a series of demands on the Sublime Porte in regard to its failure to remove its troops from Wallachia and Moldavia, as promised in 1812 by the Treaty of Bucharest. At the same time, Canning had come to believe that it was to England's commercial and political interest to bring the Greek question to a settlement. He was convinced, too, that the Greeks would some day gain their local autonomy and he did not want them to owe this liberty entirely to Russia. On the other hand, he was fearful of involving England in another war. His was, indeed, a difficult program, for, while it was directed toward curbing Russian influence in the Near East, and toward preserving the Ottoman Empire, it was aimed also at keeping England out of war. Early in 1826 Canning sent the Duke of Wellington to St. Petersburg. Nicholas and Wellington began to go over the situation. They were faced with the fact that Ibrahim Pasha was evidently trying to exterminate the Greek people and intending to settle the Morea with Mohammedan colonists from Africa. This was more than either Russia or England would stand, and the conference soon eventuated in the Protocol of St. Petersburg (April 4, 1826). By this agreement the Russian and British governments were to demand that Greece, though continuing to pay tribute to Turkey, be given self-government. The Sublime Porte made no reply and did not even come to terms with Nicholas on the subject of the removal of the Turkish troops from the Danubian Principalities, and on the question of Serbia, until October. The Convention of Akkerman, signed by Russia and Turkey on October 6, 1826, showed the effects of Nicholas' threats. The Turks yielded completely in Serbian and Rumanian affairs and accepted the Russian demands. Nothing, however, was said about the Greek question.

In the meantime, Canning had grown more impatient. He proposed to the tsar common action to force mediation on the sultan. Efforts were made to get the other powers to join England and Russia. Metternich, who had used all his wiles trying to prevent any action in favor of the Greeks, now attempted to prevent Canning's proposal from being accepted by France. It was useless, for all parties in France, even Charles X, had by this time come to be sympathetic toward the Greek cause. So, in July, 1827, England, France, and Russia signed the Treaty of London. This not only confirmed and extended the agreement made by Nicholas I and

Wellington, but provided in addition that both sides be warned that if they refused to stop fighting the contracting powers would prevent all collision between the contending parties, "without, however, taking any part in the hostilities between them." Ambiguity as to just how the agreement was to be enforced was to make future procedure difficult. In August, 1827, the mediation of the three powers was accepted by the Greeks but refused by the sultan.

The solution of the whole complicated affair—in which England, Russia, and France were proposing to intervene, but also agreeing not to fight—now passed from the hands of the suspicious and hesitating diplomats to those of the naval commanders of the three powers. Codrington, the British admiral in charge of the allied fleets, had received orders to intercept all Egyptian and Turkish ships coming to Greece, but to prevent his action "from degenerating into hostilities." When he asked Stratford Canning, the British ambassador at Constantinople, just how this was to be managed, Canning replied, "The prevention of supplies is ultimately to be enforced . . . when all other means are exhausted, by cannon shot."[47] Ibrahim's fleet was in Navarino Bay and the Egyptian commander was informed that none of his ships would be allowed to leave. But as the Moslem troops continued to burn villages and to massacre or to starve the inhabitants, and as the unreasonable behavior of the Greeks at Patras seemed to make further negotiations impossible, the allied commanders decided to sail into Navarino Bay in order to remonstrate again with Ibrahim and to force the Turks to declare an armistice. On their way in, one of the British ships was fired upon. The fire was at once returned and the engagement soon became general (October 20, 1827). Before the day was over, the Turco-Egyptian fleet was a wreck. Turkey had suffered her greatest naval disaster since Lepanto.[48]

But Greece was not yet freed. The Allies had not intended to go to war with Turkey, but only to force an armistice and compel recognition of the autonomy of Greece. The allied powers did nothing to follow up the victory at Navarino, which Metternich bemoaned as a "dreadful catastrophe." Canning was dead and the

[47] C. W. Crawley, *The Question of Greek Independence* (Cambridge, 1930), 84.
[48] Cf. G. Douin, *Navarin* (Cairo, 1927), and E. Driault, *L'expédition de Crète et de Morée, 1823-1828* (Cairo, 1930).

Duke of Wellington who succeeded him induced George IV to apologize to the Porte and offer regrets "that this conflict should have occurred with the naval forces of an ancient ally."

The attitude of the conservative governments encouraged the Turks to continue the war. Moslem religious fanaticism had by this time flamed high, and the government had great popular support when it denounced Russia and demanded satisfaction. The tsar, too, was not in a mood to yield. Declaring that he was not interested in the Greek rebels but in the maintenance of the rights of Russia, he brushed aside all efforts to restrain him and decided on war with Turkey (April 26, 1828). The situation was really favorable for Russia, for the tsar could claim with some show of justice that he was acting under the terms of the Treaty of London and that the war was only the last method to force mediation upon the Turk. The French government accepted this interpretation without question as did also the Prussians. Metternich was hostile, but unlikely to make an issue of the matter. The English, too, refused to admit the legitimacy of the Russian action, and claimed that the Treaty of London was designed only to effect a peaceful settlement. But the English government was distracted by serious domestic issues and showed no disposition to intervene against Russia.

The Russians ought to have won an easy victory. The Turks were worn out by years of conflict and the Turkish army had not yet been completely reorganized after the destruction of the Janissaries. But Nicholas was overconfident. He departed for the front with an immense retinue and made all preparations for a triumphal entry into Constantinople. The campaign went well until the Russians had crossed the Danube (June, 1828), but then they began to meet with unexpected resistance. The Turkish garrisons at Shumla, Varna, and Silistria fought with desperate valor and religious furor. It was only in October that Varna was taken, and it was then too late in the season to continue operations.

During the winter the Russians made elaborate preparations for a second campaign. General Diebitsch won an important victory at Kulevcha in June, 1829, and thereby opened the road over the Balkans. The Russian forces advanced rapidly, crossing the Balkan Mountains for the first time in history. Adrianople fell in August, the Turkish resistance collapsed and in a short time some of the cavalry squadrons of Diebitsch had advanced to the very outskirts of Constantinople. The Ottoman Empire seemed to be on the point of collapse. But appearances were deceptive. Diebitsch had only about fifteen thousand men with him and many of these were sick with fever. Not only was he unable to take the coveted city; he could not maintain himself in his advanced position for long. The Russians were therefore obliged to give up their aspirations for the time being, and were only too glad to accept the mediation of the Prussian officer, Major von Müffling, who brought the two combatants together.

On September 14, 1829, the Treaty of Adrianople was signed by the Russian and Turkish plenipotentiaries. The territorial changes of the settlement were not great. The Turks lost some coastal territory in Asia Minor, and in Europe abandoned control of the mouths of the Danube, the frontier being moved from the northern to the southern branch. In addition they agreed to pay an indemnity of 15,000,000 ducats in ten years. Pending the payment of this sum the Russians were to occupy the Danubian Principalities, from which all Moslem inhabitants were to be evacuated. The Turkish fortresses north of the Danube were to be razed, so that Ottoman control in what is now Rumania became a purely nominal one. The Treaty of Adrianople gained for Russia tremendous prestige in the Near East and gave her a practical protectorate over the Principalities. Despite the apparent moderation of the terms, the tsar had made a decided advance towards the ultimate goal.

The future of Greece was left to the three allied powers by the terms of the Treaty of Adrianople, and the detailed arrangements were relegated to a conference in London. By the London Protocol, February 3, 1830, Greece was declared an independent kingdom under the guarantee of England, Russia, and France. Prolonged negotiations were necessary before the Greek boundaries were established and before a prince could be found to rule over the new state. The crown was offered to Prince John of Saxony, and, when he refused it, to Prince Leopold of Saxe-Coburg, who accepted and then withdrew because of the inadequate boundaries given the Greek state and because of the dark picture of the Greek situation sent him by Capodistrias, who hoped to remain president of Greece for life. The whole question hung fire until the assassination of Capodistrias by his political opponents in October, 1831. Negotiations between the powers were resumed and finally the son of King Ludwig of Bavaria, an enthusiastic Philhellene, accepted the headship of the Greek state, whose boundaries were now somewhat enlarged. In February, 1833, he ascended the throne as Otto I.[49]

The liberation of the Greek people had made a tremendous impression all over Europe, for it was the first great victory for the principle of nationality since 1815. The classical tradition in education and in art and the religious issue had played into the hands of the liberals of Europe. A greater breach in the bulwarks of reaction had now been made than those effected by England's withdrawal from the European Alliance or by the minor concessions won by the liberals within the various states in the years 1815 to 1830. It was this breakdown of the international forces of conservatism that made possible the liberal victories of 1830.

[49] The new Greek state included only the area south of a line connecting the gulfs of Arta and Volo. Epirus, Thessaly, Crete, and a number of the islands were excluded; thus the majority of the Greek people was left under Ottoman rule and the Greek kingdom began with a great irredentist problem. This unwise decision was due to the British fear that the Greek state would inevitably become a Russian satellite; hence it should be kept weak.

Chapter Nine

THE REVOLUTIONARY MOVEMENTS OF 1830

THE decade from 1820 to 1830 had seen the steady disintegration of reaction. In England the control of the old parties was passing into the hands of younger and more liberal leaders. In spite of the resistance of the king, of the Anglican clergy, and of most of the higher aristocracy, important political and social reforms were being made. It was evident that still more fundamental changes were certain to come either by legal means or through violence. On the continent Austria's power was being undermined by liberal and nationalist movements. Charles X of France was slowly driving his people into a mood of bitter resentment that could eventuate only in revolution. In the Netherlands the tension between the Belgian people and the Dutch authorities was steadily growing. Internationally, the system of reaction, already seriously weakened by England's hostility, broke down completely when England, Russia, and France intervened in the affairs of the Ottoman Empire and freed the Greeks. By 1830 the whole political order was so unstable that a serious disturbance in any of the capitals of western Europe would almost certainly lead to outbreaks in a number of other states.

I. THE JULY REVOLUTION IN FRANCE

The French people had received the news of the appointment of the Polignac ministry, as Pasquier said, "with an emotion impossible to describe"; the *Globe* declared that the news had divided France in two, "on one side is the court, on the other the nation!" Everyone assumed that it was only a matter of months before the king would try a *coup d'état*. In fact, Charles made no secret of his intentions. "The French," he told Portalis, "wanted a charter; they were given one, . . . but in the end this charter cannot keep me

263

from doing my will."[1] In like fashion the Ultra press took for granted that in any conflict between the king and the Chambers it would be the Chambers that would yield. The *Drapeau Blanc*, for example, announced that "the governing power belongs to the king, who has not the right either to alienate it or to destroy it." Later it declared, "if the ministers command a majority, they will save the throne with this majority; if not, they will save it without a majority. The majority is the king!"[2] Already the Ultras were declaring that Article 14 of the Charter, which allowed the king to issue "ordinances necessary for the execution of the laws and for the surety of the state" meant the right to defy parliament.

The liberals of all factions were conducting a lively campaign in the press. The *Constitutionnel* and the *Journal des Débats*, aided after February, 1830, by the *National*, Thiers' new journal, and the *Globe*, criticized the new ministry with increasing bitterness. Their line of attack was to defend the Charter against the king; as Thiers said, "Let us shut the Bourbons up in the Charter, and close the doors tightly; they will inevitably jump out of the window!" Thiers took the lead in preparing the nation for a "French 1688." It was to be a quiet affair, "a change of persons but not of things; . . . everything would take place calmly; one family would replace another"; there would be nothing bloody about such a change; "everything would be legal."[3] This was clever propaganda. Thiers, and his backers, Talleyrand and Laffitte, all of whom were far from being revolutionaries themselves, knew that the middle class would resent any violation of the Charter. It was quite possible, however, that bourgeois fear of revolution would prove stronger than bourgeois devotion to the constitution. The middle class must be convinced not only that the Bourbons were a menace to existing institutions, but that their expulsion need not entail a social or economic upset. The society *Aide-toi, le ciel t'aidera* became more active, revived its local committees, and helped to spread the idea that if the king refused to coöperate with parliament, the liberals would refuse to pay taxes. Among groups of republicans,

[1] S. Charléty, *La Restauration* (Paris, 1921), 346.
[2] Charléty, *op. cit.*, 347.
[3] Charléty, *op. cit.*, 352.

which included workingmen and students, the idea of armed resistance was being discussed.

For several months after their appointment in August, 1829, the ministers went along with no definite program beyond a vague desire to curb the press and to modify the electoral laws—forms of reaction that were in no wise novel. They had six months to plan before the Chambers met, but they devoted this time almost exclusively to foreign affairs. Polignac hoped to distract attention from domestic difficulties by achieving victories abroad. The successful coöperation of Russia and France in the War of Greek Independence emboldened him to form a chimerical plan for the partition of the Ottoman Empire, which he intended to submit to Nicholas I. The King of Holland, so ran this scheme, would replace the sultan at Constantinople, and the Netherlands would be divided; Belgium would go to France, Holland to Prussia, the Dutch colonies to England. Serbia and Bosnia would be assigned to Austria, Wallachia and Moldavia to Russia. The main object of the plan was to reshape the map of Europe so that, without fighting for it, France would acquire the coveted Rhine frontier. Before the project was sent to St. Petersburg, the Treaty of Adrianople was signed, and the proposals actually made to Nicholas were less ambitious. They included, however, the demand that Prussia cede to France territory along the Rhine. When Prussia rejected the idea, the whole plan was dropped.[4] Polignac then turned to an enterprise more nearly within the range of possibility; he would punish the Dey of Algeria for his treatment of French citizens and of the French consul. An expedition against the Dey was prepared. Russia gave her cordial assent, and Austria and Prussia remained neutral, though England protested. The ministers placed their highest hopes on the success of this Algerian expedition.

In March, 1830, the Chambers met, and the conflict between Charles X and the nation soon reached a crisis. The king made veiled threats in his address from the throne, and the liberals, led by Royer-Collard, Guizot, Laffitte, and Casimir Périer, prepared an answer stating that the monarch should coöperate with the majority in parliament and indirectly demanding the dismissal of the

4 Cf. A. Pingaud, "Le projet Polignac," *Revue d'histoire diplomatique,* 1900.

ministry.[5] This defiant address to the king was voted in the Chamber of Deputies by 221 against 181; the ministry replied by dissolving the Chamber and calling for new elections.

The whole country was in a state of feverish excitement. The liberals called for the reëlection of all the now famous "221"; the Ultras and the upper clergy demanded their defeat. The king took the extraordinary step of issuing a royal proclamation appealing for votes favorable to the ministry and so put himself in a position where the rejection of the ministry would also involve his own rejection. On July 9 the news of the fall of Algiers reached Paris. It was hoped that this would bring votes favorable to the king and the ministry. Polignac assured Charles X that the government would secure a majority, but when the ballots were counted it was discovered that the opposition had grown from 221 to 274. The ministers now decided on a *coup d'état*. Nicholas I warned the king against it, but Charles knew that Metternich was favorable and he was being urged on by Polignac, by the Archbishop of Paris, and by members of his own family. After long deliberations the ministers signed a set of five Ordinances on July 25. The first forbade any publication without government authorization, the second dissolved the newly elected Chamber of Deputies which had never met, the third reduced the electorate from 100,000 to 25,000 and changed the method of election, the fourth called for new elections and the meeting of the Chambers in September, and the last contained a list of Ultras appointed to hold high office. Charles X and Polignac could find some legal justification for these measures in Article 14 of the Charter. Three of the Ordinances were concerned with matters that had been regulated by royal decree before, and in none of them was there any mention of abolishing the Chambers or the Charter. But the nation understood these new regulations in a totally different sense, for the mass of Frenchmen believed that the king and the ministry had abrogated the Charter.

The Ordinances were published in the *Moniteur* and the ministers

---

[5] In this address to the king, the attitude of the opposition was summed up as follows, "The Charter provides for the intervention of the country in all deliberations on public questions. This intervention ought to be positive in its results . . . The Charter has also made necessary the agreement of the political views of your government with the wishes of your people. Sire, we are obliged to say that this agreement does not exist." L. Cahen et A. Mathiez, *Les lois françaises de 1815 à 1914* (3rd edition, Paris, 1927), 57.

seem to have imagined that nothing would happen. No military preparations were made; most of the regular army was away from the capital, and Marmont, who had been designated to command in Paris in case of trouble, was not even informed of the Ordinances. Polignac told the king that the nation, being prosperous, was not interested in parliaments and election laws and that there would be no trouble. He also reassured Charles by telling him of repeated apparitions of the Virgin Mary who always promised him success. "Whenever I visit the ministry of foreign affairs," wrote the British ambassador, "I feel as though I were entering the fools' paradise of Milton!"

Paris was soon in revolt. Although the opposition forces had no central direction, a number of groups began to act separately. First the journalists met and delegated Thiers to draw up a protest. In it he announced, "The legal régime has ended, that of force has begun. Obedience ceases to be a duty. We shall try to publish our journals without asking for the authorization which is imposed on us. It is for France to judge how far resistance should go."[6] The intention of the forty-three journalists who signed this statement was not to start a revolution but to force the king to dismiss the ministry. On July 26 the manifesto appeared in the *Temps* and in Thiers' *National*; it was read aloud in cafés and on the street corners. During the evening of the same day crowds gathered in some of the squares and shouted, "Long live the Charter!" and "Down with the ministers!" While this was going on, a group of liberal deputies held an informal meeting in the home of one of their number, but they decided to take no action and to await developments.

The first effective move was made on the 27th by a group of ardent young Republicans led by Auguste Fabre, Cavaignac, Trélat, and Raspail. They coöperated with some of the students in the various higher schools of Paris and with groups of workingmen who had been thrown out of work when the danger of disturbances led to the closing of many factories and shops. In some instances the workmen had been supplied with arms by their employers. Led by students from the École Polytechnique, they threw up

6 Charléty, *op. cit.*, 373.

barricades in the streets. On the 28th the insurgents took the Hôtel de Ville and hoisted the tricolor. The populace sympathized with the resistance; men of the middle classes and workers; "the frock coat cheek by jowl with the blouse," paraded the boulevards. Everywhere shouts of "Down with the Bourbons!" now took the place of shouts of "Down with the ministers!"[7]

The government troops found it impossible to move through many of the streets, especially through the narrower ones. Barricades of paving stones, trees, barrels, boxes, all piled together, met them at every turn, and missiles of all sorts were hurled at their heads from upper windows and housetops. The king was hunting at Saint-Cloud, Polignac was still hoping for divine aid, but Marmont and the royal troops were rapidly losing control of Paris. By the evening of the 29th the city was in the hands of the insurgents. The Parisians in the *Trois Glorieuses* behaved with remarkable sobriety; little damage was done; in fact, the only buildings sacked were the establishment of the Missionnaires on Mont Valérien, and the Jesuit house at Montrouge, which seems to show that the religious, even more than the political, policies of the Bourbons had aroused the French people, at least in the capital. Charles X, looking through a spy-glass from the terrace at Saint Cloud, saw the tricolor floating from the towers of Notre Dame. He sent word that he would withdraw the Ordinances and dismiss the ministers. When he found that these concessions had no effect, he abdicated in favor of his grandson, the Duc de Bordeaux, and when he learned that none of the groups in Paris would treat with him, he fled to England on a vessel belonging to the Bonapartes.

In Paris the struggle now shifted to a quarrel between the young republicans who held the Hôtel de Ville and who wished to make Lafayette president, and a group of deputies and journalists, representing the upper bourgeoisie, who were determined to make the Duc d'Orléans king. This group—which included Talleyrand, Thiers, and Laffitte, who had managed the business affairs of the House of Orléans for twelve years—had been very active since the 28th. On the 30th the Parisians awoke to find the city placarded

[7] Cf. *1830 Études sur les mouvements libéraux et nationaux de 1830* (Paris, 1932), and P. Mantoux, "Patrons et ouvriers en juillet, 1830," *Revue d'histoire moderne et contemporaine,* 1901-02.

with bills praising the activities of the Duc d'Orléans during the French Revolution, proclaiming his present liberalism, and proposing his candidacy for the French throne.[8] The statement had been drawn up by Thiers. In the meantime Talleyrand, still the prince of negotiators, had not been idle. Through his efforts, the diplomatic corps at Paris refused to side with Charles X, even after it was known that he had withdrawn the Ordinances. Talleyrand was also in communication with the Duc d'Orléans. The group of liberal deputies, who had been meeting each day, now sent Thiers to offer the headship of the government to the duke. The stealthy and cautious duke refused to see him, and the matter had to be arranged between Thiers and the duke's sister, the masterful Mlle. Adélaïde. As a result of these negotiations, Orléans came into Paris and on the 31st, wearing the tricolor, he made a progress from his city residence, the Palais Royal, through long lines of silent and sullen men, to the Hôtel de Ville.[9]

Everything now depended on Lafayette. After some discussion within the Hôtel de Ville, the two appeared at a window, wrapped in the tricolor. They embraced, and the populace below shouted, "Long live Lafayette!" and "Long live the Duc d'Orléans!" The next day Lafayette, on his own initiative, went to talk over the situation with Orléans, who, in general terms, declared himself a republican and praised the Constitution of the United States, though he in no way committed himself. Lafayette went away satisfied. The faith of the masses in this "Hero of Two Worlds" is difficult to explain, though his betrayal of the republican cause was undoubtedly due more to his general confusion than to any duplicity. Within

[8] "Charles X can never return to Paris; he has shed the blood of the people.

"The Republic would expose us to dangerous divisions; it would involve us in hostilities with Europe.

"The Duc d'Orléans is a prince devoted to the cause of the revolution.

"The Duc d'Orléans has never fought against us.

"The Duc d'Orléans was at Jemmapes.

"The Duc d'Orléans is a citizen-king.

"The Duc d'Orléans has carried the tricolor under the enemies' fire; the Duc d'Orléans alone can carry it again. We will have no other flag.

"The Duc d'Orléans does not commit himself. He awaits the expression of our wishes. Let us proclaim those wishes, and he will accept the Charter as we have always understood it, and as we have always desired it. It is from the French people that he will hold his crown." J. M. S. Allison, *Monsieur Thiers* (New York, 1932), 68.

[9] Cf. H. Malo, "Thiers et les journées de juillet 1830," *Revue des deux mondes*, 1930.

a few days, 252 members of the old Chamber of Deputies met and revised the Charter, promised other reforms, and formally offered the crown to the Duc d'Orléans, who took the title of Louis Philippe, King of the French People. The new monarch accepted the revised Charter and the tricolor. The preamble to the Charter, in which Louis XVIII had declared it his gift to the French people, with the implication that the king, having given it, could also take it away, was struck out. Some of the terms of the document itself were modified, Article 14 was shorn of its absolutist possibilities, and the article which proclaimed Catholicism "the religion of the state" was changed to read that Catholicism was "the religion of the majority of Frenchmen." The new king promised that "the Charter should henceforth be a reality" and all parties seemed for the time to be contented to have "a throne surrounded by republican institutions." The fighting had been done by the workers, but the upper middle class appropriated the fruits of the victory. The republicans were bitterly disappointed, though, as Cavaignac said, "We only gave way because we were not strong enough. Later on it will be different!"

II. THE BELGIAN REVOLUTION

The news of the success of the July Revolution flew across Europe; it was the most exciting news men had heard since Waterloo. As one German liberal wrote later, "For fifteen years it seemed as if the eternal generative power of the world's history were paralyzed. For fifteen years they had been building and cementing, holding congresses, forming alliances, spreading the net of police supervision over the whole of Europe, forging fetters, peopling prisons, erecting gallows. And then three days sufficed to overturn one throne, and make all the others tremble."[10] In the Low Countries the news of the Paris upheaval soon precipitated a revolt of the Belgians against the Dutch king.

At the end of the Napoleonic wars, the Belgian people had wanted to return to the rule of Austria, but by the Final Act of Vienna the two parts of the Low Countries were united under the House of Orange to form a bulwark against France. The Dutch

[10] G. Brandes, op. cit., VI, 29.

king, William I, had granted a Constitution less liberal than the French Charter—an instrument of government that definitely subordinated the States-General to the will of the monarch. William was an energetic and hard-working ruler, but through too close an attention to details he often lost sight of the main issues. He sincerely wished his people to be happy, but he expected them to follow him unquestioningly. "I can reign without ministers," he announced, "it is I alone who govern and I alone am responsible." The new Constitution was submitted to two assemblies, one in Holland and one in Belgium. The Belgian assembly refused to accept the document, whereupon William decided that he would count as favorable to the Constitution all those who had abstained from voting and all those who had voted "No" because of religious reasons. This was called by some of the outraged Belgians, "Dutch arithmetic."

In the lower chamber of the States-General the Dutch and Belgians had equal numbers of representatives, though Belgium had a population of nearly three and a half million as against the two millions of Holland. Most of the high positions in the administration were given to Dutchmen, no legislation was considered binding unless written in Dutch, and, after laws passed in 1819 and 1822, all pleading in the courts had to be in Dutch. Estranged by such discrimination, the Belgians objected also to the fact that they had to assume a large proportion of the Dutch national debt. The mass of the population in each division of the kingdom cherished a hearty dislike of the other. The Dutch, proud of their two centuries of independence and of their Protestantism, regarded the Belgians, who had never freed themselves, as a race of inferiors ruled by priests and foreigners; the Belgians reciprocated with a growing hatred toward the Dutch.

William I tried to stimulate the economic development of his kingdom. Like the enlightened despots of the eighteenth century, he devoted much attention to building roads and canals, to improving the harbors of Amsterdam, Ostend, and Antwerp (the Scheldt was now opened to navigation), to subsidizing and encouraging industries, and to extending the system of public schools. Belgian manufactures, the only ones in Europe which kept pace with those of England, and Dutch shipping and banking expanded rapidly. Holland and the Dutch colonies furnished excellent markets for Belgian manufactured products, while Dutch shipping provided cheap and rapid means of procuring raw materials for Belgian factories and for distributing Belgian machines, cloth, and glassware. There was some disagreement on questions of tariff legislation. The Dutch, whose chief economic activities were agricultural and commercial, demanded low tariffs; the Belgians, a people with extensive manufactures, wanted high tariffs. But on the whole the union was successful economically, at least for the great capitalists. Among the small landowners and renters, and among the lower middle class and the rising industrial proletariat in the towns, the economic conditions were less satisfactory, and the tendency of the lower classes was to blame their poverty and distress on the Dutch régime. While the governing classes started the revolution, it was the dissatisfied proletarian masses who carried it through.[11]

The growing estrangement between the Dutch government and the upper classes in Belgium arose from the political arrangements made in 1815 and from a bitter quarrel between the Belgian church and the Dutch government. These two currents of opposition had in the beginning little in common. The Catholic opposition to the king, begun by Maurice de Broglie, the Bishop of Ghent, attacked the equality of religious sects provided for in the Constitution.[12] The political liberals, especially those who came of age in the 1820's, wished to free the press and to gain more rights for the Belgians in the States-General. For a time the ardent clericalism of the Catholic clergy, the strongest and bitterest enemies of the Dutch régime, drove the liberals to support William in his quarrel with the Belgian hierarchy. But in 1825 the king prepared the way for a rapprochement of the liberals and the Catholics by trying to force all candidates for the Catholic priesthood to take part of their training in the Philosophical Faculty established by him at the University of Louvain. He then tried to appease the anger of the Catholics by signing a concordat with the pope (1827), and by agreeing to withdraw the regulations for the training of priests.

[11] C. Terlinden, "La politique économique de Guillaume I," *Revue historique,* 1922.
[12] Cf. J. Lenfant, "Broglie, Evêque de Gand," *Revue d'histoire de l'église de France,* XVII.

These concessions proved to be of no avail. In 1827 the liberals, under the leadership of an astute and resourceful journalist, Louis de Potter, approached the clerical leaders, who were turning toward the doctrines of Lamennais. They drew up a common program in which the Catholics agreed to the liberal demand for a free press and the liberals subscribed to the Catholic demand for the liberty of teaching. Both insisted on the principle of ministerial responsibility, on the right of the Chambers to propose legislation, on an annual parliamentary vote on the budget, trial by jury in all cases, and the remission of certain taxes on foodstuffs that fell more heavily on the Belgians than on the Dutch. Nobody seems to have thought of claiming independence; there was not even a demand for self-government. But between 1827 and 1830 dislike of the political régime grew rapidly in nearly all strata of the Belgian population. The Dutch king with the advice of his chief minister, van Maanen, obstinately refused to make any real concessions. The news of the July Revolution in France was received with great interest in Belgium, but was followed at the time by no revolutionary demonstrations. When William visited the Belgian provinces in August, 1830, he found the people more prosperous than they had ever been and he concluded that the political unrest and agitation constituted no danger to the monarchy. On August 15, however, a committee of radicals, meeting in secret, decided that the time for a revolt was near, and sent some of their members to London and Paris to sound out the diplomats.

The Dutch king had visited Brussels to attend an industrial exhibition. It was planned to close the festivities, some days after his departure, with a great pyrotechnic display and a general illumination in honor of William's fifty-ninth birthday (August 24). The unrest beneath the surface was, however, clearly shown in leaflets, broadcast at the time, which contained the extraordinary announcement, "The 23rd August, fireworks; the 24th August, celebration of the king's birthday; the 25th August, revolution!" Because of the bad weather, neither of the first two events came off as scheduled, but the revolution did come as announced. For on the 25th, at a performance of Scribe and Auber's opera, *La Muette de Portici,* which portrayed a Neapolitan rising against Spanish rule, part of the audience, led by some students, started an uproar and later went out into the streets singing and howling, "Down with the Dutch! Down with the ministry!"

The rioters sacked and burned the residence of van Maanen and the offices of a newspaper subsidized by the Dutch government. Attacks were made on the houses of the director of police and of the provincial governor. The military authorities, being unprepared, took no effective steps to stop the rioting. The next day the old revolutionary Brabançon flag was raised, and the royal arms torn from many buildings. To put a stop to the damage being done to property, the nobility, merchants, and municipal authorities, most of whom wanted only concessions from the king, established a provisional guard. On the 28th an assembly of notables from the same groups was held and a deputation of five, including Gendebien and the Comte de Mérode, was sent to present a respectful address to the king, asking him to consider the grievances of the Belgians and to convoke at once the States-General. William answered this request by sending his son, the Prince of Orange, to Brussels. The prince was popular in Belgium and was at least civilly received, but after three days of conferences (September 1-3) no agreement was reached. The prince returned to Holland to confer with his father, but before leaving he ordered the royal troops to evacuate Brussels and confided the rule of the city to its citizens. The king now dismissed the hated van Maanen and called a meeting of the States-General for September 13. On September 29-30 the two Chambers, assembled in special session at The Hague, declared that Holland and Belgium should have separate administrations. This was the last time that Dutch and Belgian deputies were to sit together in the same parliament.

But it was too late for compromise. A group of four hundred patriots from Liège, led by Charles Rogier, as well as other bands of provincials had reached Brussels and were demanding a complete separation from Holland. A struggle ensued between those who wished to negotiate with the Dutch authorities and those who would accept nothing less than independence. The latter group got the upper hand, and when the king's younger son arrived in Brussels with a body of Dutch troops, on September 23, a bloody fight ensued. For four days the Dutch soldiers tried to subdue the city, but, unable to get past the barricades in the lower town, where the working classes fought stubbornly, the Dutch withdrew on the 26th.[13] These days decided the fate of Belgium. Conciliation was no longer possible. The Dutch made matters worse by bombarding Antwerp on October 27. By November 10 Belgian territory was practically freed from Dutch control, and a National Congress had been elected. The Congress voted to establish an independent monarchy, and began to elaborate a Constitution which was not completed until 1831. The most liberal in Europe, it proclaimed the doctrine of the sovereignty of the people, and provided the political machinery for its enforcement. The franchise was given to all those who paid a tax of forty-two francs, a much lower qualification than was provided for in the French Charter after 1830 or by the English Reform Bill of 1832. It wisely gave extensive rights of self-government to the various Belgian provinces and towns. Freedom of the press, of public meeting, of education, of religion were guaranteed. The Belgian Constitution, from the liberal standpoint, was regarded as an even greater victory than the setting up of Louis Philippe's government.

The next step was to get the agreement of the European powers. England and France were both favorable to the new state, though neither showed any desire to intervene in case of a war. The three eastern powers were all hostile. But Austria was occupied with disturbances in Italy, and Russia, although anxious to help the King of Holland subdue his rebel subjects, was entirely wrapped up in the Polish Revolution. A conference of the five powers—England, France, Austria, Russia, and Prussia—met in London, where negotiations fell largely into the hands of Palmerston, the British foreign secretary, and of Talleyrand, the French ambassador. Palmerston wished to keep the new state from becoming a satellite of France, and Talleyrand, anxious above all to maintain peace and to conciliate the English, finally consented to coöperate. By a protocol drawn up December 20, 1830, the powers agreed to recognize Belgian independence; in a further agreement made in January, 1831, they declared the new state "perpetually neutral." The powers decided further to divide Luxemburg; part was assigned to Belgium

[13] Cf. M. Bologne, *L'insurrection prolétarienne de 1830 en Belgique* (Brussels, 1929).

and the rest remained under the government of the House of Orange.[14]

It proved to be much more difficult to choose a king. The Belgian National Congress wanted the Duc de Nemours, the second son of Louis Philippe, or, if that were impossible, the son of Eugène de Beauharnais. England would not agree to the first; the House of Orléans rejected the second. Palmerston proposed the Prince of Orange, and then Leopold of Saxe-Coburg. Louis Philippe withdrew the candidacy of his son, and the Congress finally elected Leopold, the widower of George IV's only daughter, and the prince to whom the crown of Greece had been offered.[15] He refused the Belgian kingship until the frontiers were fixed by the National Congress. This was soon arranged, and on July 21, 1831, Leopold made a solemn entry into Brussels and took an oath to support and defend the Constitution.[16] The King of Holland refused to recognize these arrangements and in August, 1831, he sent an army into Belgium. Leopold appealed to France for help, whereupon French troops drove out the Dutch. William still refused his consent to the terms of the agreements made by the powers. Prussia, Austria, and Russia declined to use further pressure on him, but England and France decided to take joint action. The English fleet blockaded the Dutch ports while a French army was sent to take the citadel of Antwerp, which the Dutch had never relinquished. Not until 1839, however, after eight years of negotiation and diplomatic bickering, did the Dutch king come to terms with the powers and recognize the independence and neutrality of the Belgian state.

III. REVOLUTIONARY DISTURBANCES IN MIDDLE AND SOUTHERN EUROPE

The revolutions in France and in Belgium were paralleled by outbreaks in Germany, in some of the Italian states, in Switzerland, in

[14] Cf. on the diplomatic aspects of the Belgian Revolution, W. E. Lingelbach, "Belgian Neutrality," *American Historical Review*, 1933, and F. de Lannoy, *Histoire diplomatique de l'indépendance belge* (Brussels, 1930).

[15] This arrangement was well received by England, but was accepted only as a compromise by France. Later, to conciliate French opinion, Leopold married the daughter of Louis Philippe.

[16] Leopold proved to be a ruler of great capacity, though he was often much tried by the inexperience of the Belgian leaders and by their naïve enthusiasm for the catchwords and symbols of liberalism. There is a story to the effect that he sent out a servant night after night to pour acid at the roots of a liberty-tree that had been planted in front of the royal palace; the tree died.

Poland, in Spain, and in Portugal. Only in Switzerland, in a few of the smaller German principalities, and in the Iberian states, however, were the movements successful.

In the Confederation the *Burschenschaften* had again become active after 1825, especially in the universities of Erlangen, Jena, and Giessen. The liberals in the parliaments of the South German states spoke out with greater freedom, while the writings of men like Welcker and Rotteck also helped to spread liberal ideas at the end of the 1820's. But as yet there was no general movement which affected the political outlook of all German states. When the news of the revolution in Paris reached Germany, great excitement seized the younger generation. "I was reading Warnefried's *History of the Lombards*," wrote Heine, "when the thick packet of newspapers with the warm, glowing-hot news arrived. Each item was a sunbeam, wrapped in printed paper, and together they kindled my soul into a wild glow. . . . Lafayette, the tricolor, the Marseillaise, —it intoxicates me. Bold, ardent hopes spring up, like trees with golden fruit and branches that shoot up wildly till their leaves touch the clouds."[17] Isolated disturbances broke out. The debauched Duke of Brunswick was driven from his throne and his successor obliged to grant a constitution; the rulers of Hesse-Cassel, Hanover, and Saxony were constrained to make similar concessions. (The Hanover Constitution was largely the work of the famous Göttingen historian, Dahlmann.) New elections in Bavaria, Württemberg, and Baden brought additional liberals into the Chambers; in all three states the press spoke out with courage. The result of these changes was that the radical journalists of several states organized a great liberal and national festival which met at Hambach in Rhenish Bavaria, May 17, 1832. Twenty-five thousand people from all over Germany, together with a number of refugees from the Polish Revolution, attended the celebration and acclaimed the impassioned speakers who denounced the principles of the Holy Alliance.[18]

The course of events from 1830 to 1832 thoroughly frightened the German rulers. Bavaria inflicted severe penalties on the orators of Hambach, and Austria and Prussia took the lead in influencing

[17] Heine, *Sämmtliche Werke* (Hamburg, 1867), XII, 83, 87.
[18] Cf. V. Valentin, *Das Hambacher Nationalfest* (Berlin, 1932).

the Diet at Frankfort to pass the Six Acts of June, 1832. This repressive legislation assured to the rulers of such states as had parliaments the right to override their assemblies and denied the right of any assembly to refuse to the prince the income requisite for carrying on the government or to pass legislation prejudicial to the objects of the Confederation as interpreted by the statesmen of Austria and Prussia. The Diet annulled the press laws of Baden and forced the government at Karlsruhe to dismiss Rotteck and Welcker from their teaching positions. This repressive legislation so exasperated a group of students from Heidelberg and Göttingen that, with the aid of some Polish refugees, they tried a *putsch* in April, 1833. Planning to overawe the Diet, they seized the guard-house at Frankfort and attempted in vain to hold it. Not long afterward the Diet reëstablished the Mainz Commission to ferret out all liberal agitators; in 1835 it condemned the doctrines of the Young German movement for "attacking the Christian religion and the social order."[19] The spirit of revolution had again been conquered in Germany. But, being prosperous and contented, the mass of the German people looked on with indifference while the governments drove a handful of journalists and intellectuals into prison or exile.

The Hapsburg government and the reactionary rulers were even more completely successful in quelling the revolutionary flurries in Italy. In spite of the severe repression that followed the failure of the Revolutions of 1820, the Italian secret societies continued their activities. They had, in fact, entered into relations with the liberal organizations in France and Belgium. A group of Italians in Paris, known as *L'emancipazione italiana*, was in close touch with Lafayette and numbered Buonarroti among its members. It served as a clearing house for the various Italian revolutionary societies. Aided by this group, General Pepe went to Marseilles where, with a thousand volunteers, he made ready to embark for Sicily. Some of the leaders who remained in Italy were negotiating with Francis IV of Modena, who, with large ambitions for the crown of Italy, seems to have so laid his plans that he would stand well if

[19] Cf. G. Ras, *Börne und Heine als politische Schriftsteller* (Groningen, 1926), and the excellent discussion in chap. ii of H. Lichtenberger, *Henri Heine, penseur* (Paris, 1905).

either the conspirators or the Austrians got the upper hand. But when a revolt broke out in his capital in December, 1830, Francis, having decided that Louis Philippe would do nothing to help the Italian revolutionaries, turned on the rebels and arrested their leader, Menotti. The rebels, however, drove the duke to take refuge in Mantua. Within a few weeks Marie Louise of Parma was forced to flee, and in the Papal States east of the Apennines the revolutionaries set up a provisional government. In the Italian Revolutions of 1830-31 the various groups of insurgents coöperated as they had not done in 1820-21, and these revolutions might have succeeded had Austria not intervened.

All the revolts had been undertaken with the hope that the new government in France would be sympathetic and would even send aid. The French ministry had already, in the case of Belgium, proposed as the basis of its foreign policy the Doctrine of Non-Intervention, a formula earlier elaborated by Castlereagh and Canning. Laffitte, the head of the French cabinet, and men prominent in the new régime, like Lafayette and Sébastiani, even encouraged the Italians, as they were encouraging the Poles, to expect French aid. Metternich, however, was not inactive. With the backing of Russia and Prussia he reaffirmed the principles of the Holy Alliance and began to use pressure on the government of Louis Philippe. He attempted to evoke the specter of Bonapartism by recalling the fact that Austria might at any time release the Duke of Reichstadt, that the son of Eugène de Beauharnais was being proposed for the Belgian crown, that Achille Murat was expected to make an attempt to seize the throne of Naples, and that two of the sons of Louis Napoleon and Hortense were taking part in the revolution in the Papal States. At the same time the French Chamber of Deputies made it clear that France would not undertake a war.

The French government now began to beat a diplomatic retreat. Casimir Périer, who had succeeded Laffitte as head of the ministry, announced that the Principle of Non-Intervention could not be carried too far, and that "the blood of Frenchmen belongs only to France." Austria thereupon proceeded to send her troops into Italy and to restore the legitimate rulers in Parma, Modena, the Romagna, Umbria, and the Marches. To save the face of the

French government Casimir Périer, in a memorandum to the newly elected pope, Gregory XVI, demanded reforms in the administration of the Papal States. No real reforms were instituted, the Romagna again broke out in revolt, and Austrian troops entered the Papal States for a second time. Thereupon the French ministry sent an "army of observation" to Ancona, where it remained until 1838. The restored rulers in Parma, Modena, and Rome turned on their defeated subjects; again the prisons were filled with revolutionaries and the executioners were busy. In the Papal States, Cardinal Bernetti instituted veritable massacres.[20]

As part of the papal reaction Gregory XVI promulgated an encyclical condemning the doctrines of the French Liberal Catholics as set forth in their journal, L'Avenir. Lamennais and his followers had welcomed the Revolution of 1830 as the beginning of the liberation of the church from its domination by the state. They hailed the revolutions in Belgium, in Poland, and in Italy, and called on the pope to place the Catholic Church in alliance with the rising forces of democracy. But the hostility of the French hierarchy and of the Roman curia forced the suspension of L'Avenir, and in 1832 Lamennais, Lacordaire, and Montalembert went to Rome to lay their case before Gregory XVI. The pope received them with kindness, but after weeks of waiting, during which they could get no reply to their demands, they started back home. Lamennais was in Munich when he received the crushing rebuke of the encyclical, Mirari Vos. This famous pronouncement condemned and denounced liberty of conscience and of religious worship, and the ideas of the freedom of the press and of the separation of church and state, and all the "other harmful errors of those who, possessed by an undue love for liberty, do their utmost to undermine authority." Far from submitting to the papal condemnation of his doctrines, Lamennais replied in 1834 with his Paroles d'un croyant, an exultant but vague glorification of the ideals of democracy and freedom.

When the liberals in Italy seemed utterly crushed, a new leader suddenly appeared, the greatest the movement had thus far pro-

[20] Cf. C. Vidal, Louis Philippe, Metternich, et la crise italienne de 1831-1832 (Paris, 1931).

duced. Mazzini, son of a professor in the University of Genoa, had dedicated himself early to the cause of Italian unity and freedom. In 1830 he was imprisoned for his activities as a Carbonaro; when he was released, he took up his residence in Marseilles, where in 1831 he founded a new society, Young Italy. Its purpose was to arouse the whole Italian people to a united desire to regenerate and free their country. Mazzini's great power lay in the boldness of his conception, and in his extraordinary ability to convince men of the grandeur of his ideal and to fire them with his own burning faith. Nationalism all over Europe was assuming the form of a new religion; Mazzini soon became its most exalted prophet. His gospel held that the whole populace must be aroused by a great proselytizing movement. This would finally enable the Italians to drive out the Austrians and to set up a united republic with Rome as its capital.[21]

Beyond this goal, Mazzini envisaged Italy as the chosen country of Europe. As the French Revolution had freed the individual, so a great Italian revolution would inaugurate a new era of free nations. By the end of 1834 he had carried his plans far enough to organize, with sixteen other unknown Italians, Germans, and Poles, a movement known as Young Europe, which was to organize national committees to head a Young Germany, a Young Poland, and a Young Switzerland, all in addition to his own favorite project, Young Italy.[22] Mazzini in these years was just at the beginning of his extraordinary career; but by 1833 Young Italy had enlisted 60,000 members. The general movement was directed by Mazzini and a group of Italians in Marseilles, while the central committee for Italy was located at Genoa. Provincial committees were set up in all the important cities of the peninsula, and in a few years there were agents active even in the smaller towns. The members of Young Italy were all under forty years of age, men without wealth or social position, but each one a missionary consecrated to the cause. A fire had been lighted that was not to die out of the heart of this generation until their country was free.

In Switzerland the revolutionary disturbances were local and had no immediate effect on the federal government. Under the

[21] Cf. A. Codignola, *La giovinezza di Mazzini* (Florence, 1926).
[22] Cf. D. Melegari, *La jeune Italie et la jeune Europe* (Paris, 1908).

Federal Pact of 1815 the central government, which rotated in two-year cycles among the cantonal governments of Zurich, Bern, and Lucerne, had little real power. There was a Diet made up of delegates from all the cantons, each of which, regardless of population, had one vote. The cantons, as sovereign bodies, could levy customs duties on one another, were allowed to make alliances with each other, and could conduct diplomatic relations with foreign powers so long as their action was not detrimental to the whole Confederation. Inside the twenty-two cantons the governments were in the hands of the local aristocracies, which guarded their privileges jealously. From 1815 to 1825 these cantonal administrations were, for the most part, reactionary, though they met with little resistance from either the peasants or the bourgeoisie.

After 1825, however, the Philhellenic movement, the activity of groups of students and journalists, and the development of industry started liberal movements which threatened the existing order and in a number of cantons forced the granting of new constitutions. In the July Revolution in Paris, many Swiss soldiers were killed fighting for the French king; shortly afterward Louis Philippe dismissed the six Swiss regiments in the French army and the men returned to Switzerland. These events of 1830 created a profound impression among the Swiss people and emboldened the liberal groups to agitate for further reforms. In many of the cantons public meetings were held, petitions were drawn up, and where the local governments would not yield, riots took place. Between 1830 and 1833 most of the remaining cantons secured new constitutions recognizing the sovereignty of the people, equality before the law, and liberty of the press. The federal government refused to take any part in these cantonal quarrels, and not until 1848 were any fundamental changes made in the Swiss national régime. The liberals, however, regarded the local democratic reforms of 1830 to 1833 as the first steps toward a national regeneration.

The most bloody struggle caused by the upheaval of 1830 was a revolution which broke out in Poland at the end of the year.[23] The growing tension between the Poles and Nicholas I after 1825 had

[23] Cf. A. Lewak, "The Polish Rising of 1830," *Slavonic Review,* 1930, a good introduction.

led to the formation in 1828 of a new secret society, most of whose members were in the officers' school at Warsaw. In 1829, at the time of his coronation as King of Poland, Nicholas was very coldly received, and in the Diet of 1830 his wishes were flouted and his policies severely criticized. When several members of the Polish secret society, detected because of their relations with Russian conspirators, were given light sentences by the Diet acting as a court, Nicholas was furious and remarked, "They have saved the criminals, but they have lost the country!"

The secret society was plotting a rebellion when the rumor was spread about that the tsar was going to lead a Russian and Polish army to France and to Belgium to crush the revolutions there. So on November 29, 1830, the leaders of the secret society started a revolt with the help of some university students. This handful of rebels, without an able leader and without any definite plans, could easily have been put down. But Constantine, the tsar's brother and the head of the Polish army, after some futile negotiations, left the country. A provisional government was set up, and the revolt soon spread over the whole Congress Kingdom. The leaders of the provisional government were landed aristocrats, chief of whom were Prince Czartoryski and General Chlopicki, who had served under Napoleon, and who was allowed to declare himself dictator. Men of this stamp, afraid of a revolt of the masses, tried to negotiate for reform with the Russian tsar, but Nicholas would accept no terms save those of absolute submission. Meanwhile this policy of attempted conciliation led to a split among the Polish forces, for opposed to the Whites, who had the upper hand at the beginning of the revolution, was an ardent group of Reds, led by political radicals, among whom was the historian Lelewel.

The divisions among the Poles themselves paralyzed their efforts. They failed to use their well-organized military forces in a rapid drive against the Russian army, which was exhausted and disorganized after the war with Turkey. The Polish Diet voted the deposition of Nicholas I as King of Poland and in February, 1831, a Russian army entered the kingdom. The Polish forces won a few victories, but were badly defeated at Ostrolenka. The Russians then pushed into the heart of the country. The enemy's advance precipitated disturbances in Warsaw, in which the Reds finally got the upper hand over the Whites. The military and civil leaders were now changed even more frequently than they had been before. The forces of both sides were decimated by cholera, which now made its first appearance in Europe; among its victims were Constantine and the Russian general, Diebitsch. The mass of the peasants remained apathetic. The Diet, composed largely of nobles, passed a few reforms which, in some degree, lightened the burdens of the agricultural classes, but undertook nothing which aroused their interest or enthusiasm in the cause of Polish freedom.

The leaders of the revolution counted rather heavily on the intervention of the western powers to save them. But their hope for help from England and from France—they firmly believed until almost the end that the government of Louis Philippe would save their cause—failed. Austria and Prussia closed their frontiers and stopped the Poles under their rule from sending aid to the revolutionaries. Even the pope denounced the Poles as rebels and ordered them as good Catholics to submit to the tsar, the legitimate King of Poland. On September 8, 1831, Warsaw fell. Within a few weeks the revolution was over. The tsar took a terrible revenge. He renounced all the arrangements made in 1815, and in 1832 promulgated an Organic Statute for the government of the former Congress Kingdom. This affirmed the inviolability of persons and of private property, allowed the official use of Polish, and guaranteed a separate administration. But the document was designed, as it appeared later, to deceive foreign opinion. In actual practice the Poles under Russian rule—especially after a futile rising in 1833—were governed by the most ruthless military methods. An ordinance of 1833 declared the country in a "state of war," a regulation that technically remained in effect until the World War. A tenth of the Polish lands were seized and given to Russians, the Universities of Warsaw and Vilna were closed, and thousands were put to death, imprisoned, or banished.[24] Warsaw, the greater center of Polish cultural life, was transformed into a stronghold of military oppression and police con-

[24] In one of his works Krasinski, the Polish poet, describes Poland after 1831 as "the land of graves and crosses. Thou mayest know it by the silence of its men and the melancholy of its children." E. H. Lewinsky-Corwin, *History of Poland* (New York, 1917), 446.

trol. The Poles who lived in Lithuania and in White Russia were treated even worse than were the inhabitants of the former Congress Kingdom. Practically the whole intellectual élite emigrated; indeed, the Polish emigration was the most extensive in modern history. Poles went to all the countries of Europe and to America, but the largest number settled in Paris, where they exerted a strong influence on the intellectual life of modern France.

The difficulties in Portugal and Spain were the outgrowth of the Revolutions of 1820, though the settlements finally arrived at were the result of the revolutionary movements of 1830. Canning had intervened in 1826 to protect the constitutional régime in Portugal when it was threatened by an intervention from Spain. The regent and the young Portuguese queen, Maria, continued to meet with opposition from the queen's uncle, Dom Miguel, and the Portuguese Ultras. In 1827 Dom Miguel was allowed to reënter the country; in 1828 he seized the throne. Most of the European states broke off diplomatic relations with Portugal, but the Duke of Wellington and the British Ministry refused to intervene. Dom Miguel instituted a white terror and drove all liberal resistance underground. Ultimately the maltreatment of some English and French subjects in Portugal and the insulting language addressed by Dom Miguel to Louis Philippe led the English and French governments to send a French squadron to Portugal in 1831. Dom Miguel apologized, and neither the English nor the French ministry tried to push the matter further.

Pedro, the Emperor of Brazil, who had just been forced to renounce his crown there, now appeared on the scene to defend the rights of his daughter Maria, the legitimate ruler. A civil war ensued which involved Portugese affairs with those of Spain. Ferdinand VII, the Spanish king, was trying to arrange matters to have his infant daughter Isabella succeed him. He therefore set aside a Spanish law of 1713 according to which his brother Carlos, leader of the Spanish reactionaries, the *apostólicos*, would come to the throne. When Ferdinand died in 1833, his daughter was proclaimed Queen of Spain. The queen regent recalled Martínez de la Rosa, who drew up a new constitution modeled on the French Charter. Thereupon the two pretenders, Dom Miguel of Portugal and Don Carlos of Spain, joined forces against their rulers, King Pedro and Queen Isabella. France and England then intervened once more and Dom Miguel and Don Carlos went into exile, though the civil war in Spain dragged on until 1840. Spain and Portugal were, however, lined up with England, France, and Belgium as constitutional monarchies.

IV. THE PASSING OF THE REFORM BILL IN ENGLAND

England passed through the crisis of 1830 without a revolution, although the governing classes were driven to make substantial changes in the parliamentary régime. The Whigs had tried to carry through a reform of the electoral system in the later eighteenth century, but after the rejection of such a project proposed by Pitt in 1785, the matter ceased to be considered seriously. During the long wars with France, to speak ill of the abuses of the electoral system was to "utter seditious words against the matchless constitution," and no reform was possible. After 1815 a series of electoral scandals revealed the corruption of the whole system, which had been left unchanged since the latter part of the seventeenth century and which enabled a comparatively few noblemen to control Parliament. The rapid growth of new urban centers also revealed the absurdity of an electoral régime which allowed small towns or even agricultural villages—the rotten and pocket boroughs—to send representatives to Parliament while great industrial centers like Manchester, Leeds, Sheffield, and Birmingham were unrepresented.[25] The Whigs, after obtaining tariff changes and Catholic Emancipation, now turned to a program of electoral reform. Their principal demand was for a redistricting of the seats in the House of Commons, while the radicals were calling for a wider extension of the suffrage. Now, at the end of the 1820's, the two groups joined forces to make a common front against the Tories.

The death of George IV in June, 1830, and the accession of his brother as William IV necessitated the calling of a parliamentary

---

[25] The abuses of the British electoral system are too well known to require treatment here; a good, brief account is that in E. Halévy, *A History of the English People in 1815* (New York, 1924), 102-130. Recent studies have modified the older views, cf. L. B. Namier, *The Structure of Politics at the Accession of George III* (2 vols., London, 1929), and D. Barnes, "The Myth of an Eighteenth Century Whig Oligarchy," in *Proceedings,* Pacific Coast Branch, American Historical Association (1929).

election.[26] A lively campaign ensued in which the Whigs spoke out vigorously for parliamentary reform. The Tories won the election, but their majority was greatly reduced. Shortly afterward the news of the overthrow of Charles X and the establishment of a new government in France greatly encouraged the liberal forces in England to continue the fight. At the same time the July Revolution strengthened the liberal cause by disproving the old Tory contention that all attempts to meet popular demands would produce anarchy. The leaders of political societies, and popular journalists like Cobbett, aroused the country to a high pitch of excitement. In October, 1830, Earl Grey introduced a Reform Bill into Parliament.

Wellington, the head of the ministry, denounced the idea of reform and went so far as to say he was fully convinced that the country possessed at the present moment a legislature which "answers all the good purposes of legislation, and this to a greater degree than any legislature ever has answered any country whatever."[27] At the very time when the defenders of the old system could say nothing for it but that it worked better in practice than in appearance, Wellington suddenly lavished on it praises which even Blackstone never surpassed. The effect of the speech was exactly the reverse of what was intended; many who were wavering joined the opposition, and a few weeks later Wellington was forced to resign. Lord Grey then formed a new ministry of Whigs and Canningite Tories. When they presented the bill to the House of Commons, it passed the second reading by a majority of only one. The details of the bill were then amended in committee, whereupon Grey decided to dissolve Parliament and to call new elections. These were held in an atmosphere of intense excitement. When the ballots were counted, it was found that the Whigs had a majority in the lower house for the first time in fifty years. The Commons promptly passed the revised bill, but the Lords rejected it by a majority of forty-one. The ministry then advised the king to dissolve parliament once more.

Meetings and processions were held, riots broke out all over the country, the political societies recommended that all Englishmen

[26] Cf. G. E. Thompson, *The Patriot King, William IV* (New York, 1933).
[27] D. C. Somervell, *English Thought in the Nineteenth Century* (London, 1929), 7.

interested in reform refuse to pay taxes, and some of the radical leaders, with the slogan, "Go for gold," threatened a run on the Bank of England. Of the thirty archbishops and bishops who sat with the Lords, only two voted in favor of the bill, seven abstained from balloting, and twenty-one voted against it. Feeling was, therefore, especially bitter against the upper clergy. Some were burned in effigy, others were stoned, and in Bristol the mob set fire to the bishop's palace. The ministry itself was in deep distress, for it was fighting simultaneously on two fronts; it was blocked by the Tory Lords and was at the same time bitterly attacked by some of the radicals. Many thought England on the verge of a civil war.

The House of Lords finally agreed to pass the bill, but with an amendment that would greatly weaken it. The Grey ministry would not consent to such a compromise and proposed that the king create enough new Lords to carry the bill. William refused, the cabinet resigned, and the king next called on Wellington to form a new government. Wellington failed. William was then obliged to recall the Grey ministry and grant it permission to create new peers. Thereupon the House of Lords, to avoid this disaster, passed the bill in June, 1832. As finally adopted, the Reform Bill redistributed a hundred forty-three of the seats in the House of Commons, granting representation to the large urban centers of the north and west of England. No attempt was made to create equal electoral districts, but only to remove flagrant abuses; constituencies still varied greatly in population. The right to vote was given, in the towns, to all owners of property of a rental value of ten pounds a year, and in the country to all owners of property yielding an income of ten pounds; higher qualifications were demanded in both town and country for renters.

The electorate was now increased by half. One out of thirty inhabitants could vote; in France, according to the Electoral Law of 1831, only one out of two hundred inhabitants had the ballot. Although the Reform Bill did nothing for the workers it was a great victory for the middle class in Britain, and was the most decisive blow that the old order had received. It was not only that the Whigs had introduced a change, but that they had introduced the whole principle of change and had applied it to a part of the British Constitution long held sacred. "Whatever some of the Whigs might say about the 'finality' of their Bill," says Trevelyan, "the principle it involved, when once admitted, could brook no limitation until complete democracy had been realized. On the other hand the belief of the Old Tories that the Reform Bill would lead at once to the overthrow of Crown and Lords, Church and property was the exact reverse of the truth. It was due to the Bill that England escaped the vicious circle of continental revolution and reaction."[28]

v. conclusion

The Revolutions of 1830 split Europe into two camps. The reactionary eastern powers—Russia, Austria, and Prussia—drew closer together. In western Europe England and France, both of which now had middle-class governments, joined forces to save the revolutionary cause in Belgium, Spain, and Portugal. Eastern despotism was arrayed against western parliamentarianism.

By a series of diplomatic moves in 1831 and 1832 the eastern powers succeeded in keeping the revolution from spreading beyond France and Belgium. Their threats against Louis Philippe, whom they mockingly named "the King of the Barricades," prevented French interference from saving the liberal cause in Italy and Poland. But Nicholas I was not satisfied merely with crushing the Polish Revolution; neither was Metternich willing to stop after he had pacified Germany and Italy. In 1833 the three eastern powers drew up definite arrangements regarding the future treatment of the Poles, the status of Luxemburg, and the measures of repression to be used in the German Confederation. Beyond this, a formal treaty of alliance, the Convention of Münchengrätz, was signed.

This agreement recognized the right of any sovereign, threatened by revolt, to call to his aid the governments of Russia, Austria, and Prussia. "So long as the union of the three monarchs lasts," wrote Metternich triumphantly, "there will be a chance of safety in the world!" When the Convention was presented to Palmerston, he pushed it aside with a contemptuous remark, and the Duc de

[28] G. M. Trevelyan, *British History in the Nineteenth Century* (London, 1922), 225.

Broglie, the French foreign minister, declared that France would countenance no interference in Belgium, Switzerland, or Piedmont. The next year, when France and England made a pact to intervene in Spanish and Portuguese affairs, Palmerston officially answered the presumptions of the eastern powers, "The treaty establishes among the constitutional states of the West a Quadruple Alliance which will serve as a counterpoise against the Holy Alliance of the East." Time was to prove, however, that the western powers had much less interest in helping liberal revolutions than the eastern powers had in suppressing them.

In England, France, and Belgium—the European states most advanced economically and socially—the middle class had, since 1815, made substantial gains and had succeeded in establishing the political machinery to ensure them. The revolution in France meant not only the curtailment of the arbitrary power of the monarch and the establishment of what Wordsworth called "the miserable and deistical principle of the equality of all religions," but it also assured the advent of a new civil administration. During the Restoration the governmental personnel, both in the offices of the central administration and in those of the departments, was made up largely of men of the Ancien Régime who did all in their power to subvert the purposes of the Charter. This antagonism of the bureaucracy toward the introduction of a genuine parliamentary order in France was the essential political fact of the Restoration. The revolutionary changes of 1830, by bringing in a new body of administrators, marked the beginnings of a régime more genuinely constitutional.

The Belgian Constitution of 1831 was likewise a triumph for the middle class, for it clearly stated the principle of the complete dependence of the ministry on parliament. Moreover, Article 78 stated that "The king has no powers except those formally given him by the Constitution." This meant that in any conflict between liberty and authority the Constitution was to be interpreted on the side of liberty. The revised French Charter and the Belgian Constitution, in the next decades, made the rounds of Europe. They were imitated and pastiched in 1837 in Spain, the next year in Portugal, in 1844 in Greece, in 1848 in Holland, Naples, and Rome, and in 1866 in

Rumania. In England the Reform Bill gave the middle class a much larger influence in Parliament than it had ever had before; indeed, although it involved little violence, the bill effected as true a revolution as did the overthrow of Charles X in France. Despite its far-reaching results, however, the British régime was far from being democratized; the diplomatic service and the higher positions in the church and in the state administration remained in the hands of the aristocracy.[29]

Those who had directed the changes in France and England were immensely pleased and satisfied with their victory. For a generation the middle class had held that the French Revolution of 1789 had erred—that in its policies and acts it had far overshot the mark. Now liberty was advancing with less passionate excitement but with an increased sense of reality. At last the old and the new seemed reconciled, and the leaders of the bourgeoisie believed that "monarchy by the grace of God and the will of the people" would endure forever.

The victors of 1830 were, however, far less aware of the real significance of their achievement than were their opponents in both the reactionary and the radical camps. Metternich's remark that "the mob is now rising against the bourgeoisie," though it simply restates the conventional conservative fear of all change, shows that he recognized that the French Charter of 1830 and the other changes of the time were not the final achievements which their framers imagined them to be. At the same time, the working classes and the radicals in England and in France, who had themselves agitated for reform along with the leaders of the middle class, were not slow in realizing that they had been duped. Thus republican and socialist critics were soon attacking the reign of the upper bourgeoisie as the latter had attacked the rule of the throne and the altar. In all countries of western Europe journalists and literary men began to take up the newer creeds. Romanticism was already divorced from reaction, and poets, dramatists, and novelists of Young Europe filled their works with the ideals of nationalism, political

[29] Cf. B. Mirkine-Guetzevitch, "1830 dans l'évolution constitutionelle de l'Europe," in *1830 Études sur les mouvements libéraux et nationaux de 1830* (Paris, 1932), an admirable study, and M. Deslandres, *Histoire constitutionelle de la France 1789-1870* (2 vols., Paris, 1933), esp. II, 8e partie.

democracy, and economic justice.[30] "We alone have really understood what happened in 1830," declared the *Globe*, now edited by
the leaders of the Saint-Simonian School. "The so-called revolution
has resulted only in the shifting of power from one class that used
the people for its own selfish ends to another."

[30] Cf. F. Baldensperger, "Le grand schisme de 1830; romantisme et jeune Europe,"
Revue de littérature comparée, 1930, and H. Tronchon, "Une crise d'âmes, 1830,"
Revue des cours et conférences, 1926.

Bibliographical Notes

GENERAL WORKS

Among the general books, the best is that of G. Weill, *L'éveil des nationalités et le mouvement libéral 1815-48* (Paris, 1930), in the Halphen et Sagnac series, *Peuples et civilisations*. The bibliographies cover every aspect of the history of civilization in the period. Also of great value is A. Stern, *Geschichte Europas seit den Verträgen von 1815 bis zum Frankfurter Frieden von 1871*, new ed., 10 vols. (Stuttgart, 1913-1928); W. Goetz, Ed., *Die französische Revolution, Napoleon, und die Restauration 1789-1848* (Berlin, 1929), in the series, *Propyläen-Weltgeschichte*, with remarkable illustrations, and the relevant articles in the *Encyclopaedia of Social Sciences* (New York, 1930 ff.). Cf. also F. B. Artz, "European Civilization 1815-50, Some Unfinished Business," *Journal of Modern History*, 1937.

The most useful general histories of the principal countries and peoples—those published since 1920 have extensive bibliographies—are: S. Walpole, *History of England from the Conclusion of the Great War in 1815*, rev. ed., 6 vols. (London, 1902-1905), chiefly political, an excellent narrative; E. Halévy, *History of the English People 1815-41*, 3 vols. (New York, 1924-1928), a more recent account; G. M. Young, Editor, *Early Victorian England*, 2 vols. (Oxford, 1934), very valuable; E. L. Woodward, *The Age of Reform, 1815-1870* (Oxford, 1938), the emphasis is on the relation of economic and political development; P. L. Duvergier de Hauranne, *Histoire du gouvernement parlementaire en France*, 10 vols. (Paris, 1857-1871), the work of a *Doctrinaire*, not a scholarly treatment but ably written and in part based on contemporary material that has disappeared; S. Charléty, *La Restauration* (Paris, 1921), in the Lavisse series, *Histoire de la France contemporaine*, mainly political; and F. B. Artz, *France under the Bourbon Restoration* (Cambridge, 1931), with emphasis chiefly on social and intellectual development. H. von Treitschke, *Deutsche Geschichte im neunzehnten Jahrhundert*, new ed., 5 vols. (Leipzig, 1919-1923), English translation, 7 vols. (New York, 1915-1919), a brilliant work but marred by unfairness to Austria and to Metternich; F. Schnabel, *Deutsche Geschichte im neunzehnten Jahrhundert*, 4 vols. (Freiburg, 1929-1937), excellent work on the scale of Treitschke; A. W. Ward, *Germany 1815-90*, Vol. I (Cambridge, 1916), the best account in English crammed with facts but poorly proportioned; J. G. Legge, *Rhyme and Revolution in Germany* (London, 1918), a clever popularization; J. Redlich, *Das Österreichische Staats-und Reichsproblem,* 2 vols. (Leipzig, 1920-1926); F. Meinecke, *Weltbürgertum und Nationalstaat,* 7th ed. (Munich, 1928), the last two especially valuable for their interpretative comment, though Redlich is brief for this period. H. Baumgarten, *Geschichte Spaniens,* 3 vols. (Leipzig, 1865-1871), covers the political history of Spain from 1788 to 1839, an old-fashioned political history but still useful; H. B. Clarke, *Modern Spain 1815-98* (Cambridge, 1906), the best English account; A. Ballesteros, *Historia de España,* Vol. VII (Barcelona, 1934), the first thorough and scholarly work on the history of Spain after 1814. The two well-known works in English on Italian history after 1815: W. R. Thayer, *Dawn of Italian Independence,* 2 vols. (Boston, 1892), and Bolton King, *History of Italian Unity,* 2nd ed., 2 vols. (London, 1912), are out of date but still of value; good introductions, though very condensed, are A. Solmi, *The Making of Modern Italy* (London, 1925), and G. Bourgin, *La formation de l'unité italienne* (Paris, 1929), but the outstanding general work on Italy is M. Rosi, *Italia odierna,* 2 vols. (Turin-Rome, 1922-1927). For Russia, V. O. Kluchevsky, *History of Russia,* Vol. V (London, 1931), the concluding volume of the best extended history of Russia in English; T. Schiemann, *Geschichte Russlands unter Kaiser Nikolaus I,* 4 vols. (Berlin, 1904-1919), an important, work; K. Stählin, *Geschichte Russlands,* Vol. III (Stuttgart, 1935); and E. Krakowski, *Histoire de la Pologne,* Paris, 1934, the most useful one-volume history of Poland in the languages of western Europe. On the secret societies cf. E. Lennhoff, *Histoire des sociétés secrètes au XIX at au XX siècles* (Paris, 1934) and J. H. Lepper, *Les sociétés secrètes* (Paris, 1933), and on the press, G. Weill, *Le journal* (Paris, 1934).

Chapters I and II

EUROPEAN SOCIETY AFTER THE NAPOLEONIC WARS

There are no general accounts of the European aristocracies of the early nineteenth century, though the memoirs of the time and the more recent biographies and general histories are particularly rich for this period in nearly every country. On the churches and the clergy, the general histories of the church, while brief for this period, should not be neglected; the following are the most useful: K. Heussi, *Kompendium der Kirchengeschichte,* new ed. (Tübingen, 1933); D. H. Stephan and H. Leube, *Handbuch der Kirchengeschichte,* Part IV, 2nd ed. (Tübingen, 1931), both Protestant; and F. Mourret, *Histoire générale de l'église*, Vols. VII and VIII (Paris, 1913), Catholic. On the Jews, there is S. Dubnow, *Histoire moderne du peuple juif*, 2 vols. (Paris, 1933). The most detailed histories of the churches are those for individual countries—for England: S. C. Carpenter, *Church and People 1789-1899* (London, 1933), a good popularization, F. W. Cornish, *The English Church in the 19th Century*, 2 vols. (London, 1910), the standard compend, F. C. Gill, *Romantic Movement and Methodism* (London, 1937); R. F. Wearmouth, *Methodism and the Working-Class Movements* (London, 1937); for France: A. Debidour, *Histoire des rapports de l'église et de l'état en France 1789-1870*, 2nd ed. (Paris, 1911), a scholarly study, though strongly anticlerical; for Germany: Bachem, *Vorgeschichte, Geschichte und Politik der deutschen Zentrumpartei*, Vol. I (Cologne, 1927), J. B. Kissling, *Der deutsche Protestantismus, 1817-1917*, 2 vols. (Münster, 1917-18), A. Hauck, *Kirchengeschichte Deutschlands*, 4th ed., 5 vols. (Leipzig, 1904-1929), the standard work, and G. Goyau, *L'Allemagne religieuse, le Catholicisme 1800-1848*, 6th ed., 2 vols. (Paris, 1923), and by the same author, *le Protestantisme*, 9th ed., (Paris, 1924); for Russia Brian-Chaninov, *The Russian Church* (New York, 1931); for the papacy, J. Schmidlin, *Histoire des papes 1800-* (Paris, 1938 ff.)

Of a dozen or more recent compends on the general economic situation in the early nineteenth century, the most useful is that of A. P. Usher, etc., *Economic History of Europe Since 1750* (New York, 1937). Other good introductions covering more than one country are: J. H. Clapham, *The Economic Development of France and Germany 1815-1914*, 4th ed. (Cambridge, 1936), full of important material; L. Knowles, *Economic Development in the Nineteenth Century* (London, 1932), made up largely of lecture notes, collected after the author's death; J. Kulischer, *Allgemeine Wirtschaftgeschichte*, Vol. II (Munich, 1929), the standard German manual; Laffitte, *Mémoires* (Paris, 1932); E. Corti, *Rise of the House of Rothschild* (New York, 1928), an interesting popularization in a field where there are few works of any type; F. Feldhaus, *Kulturgeschichte der Technik*, 2 vol. (Berlin, 1928-1930); A. P. Usher, *History of Mechanical Inventions* (New York, 1929); these last two works contain much new material on inventions and on the whole story of the mechanization of industry.

For England: there is the admirable work of J. H. Clapham, *Economic History of Modern Britain*, Vol. I, 2nd ed. (Cambridge, 1931), M. and C. Quennell, *A History of Everyday Things in England 1733-1851* 2nd ed. (London, 1939), excellent illustrations; for France, the classic work of E. Levasseur, *Histoire des classes ouvrières et de l'industrie en France 1789-1870,* 2nd ed., 2 vols. (Paris, 1903-4), is still without a rival, though H. Sée, *La vie économique de la France sous la monarchie censitaire 1815-48* (Paris, 1927), with a good bibliography, brings the subject up to date; for Germany, Sartorius von Walterhausen, *Deutsche Wirtschaftsgeschichte 1815-1914,* 2nd ed. (Jena, 1923), P. Benaerts, *Les origines de la grande industrie allemande* (Paris, 1933), E. Kohn-Bramstedt, *Aristocracy and the Middle Classes in Germany 1830-1900* (London, 1937), and L. W. Kahn, *Social Ideals in German Literature 1770-1830* (New York, 1938); and for Italy: C. Barbagallo, *Le origini della grande industria contemporanea,* Vol. II (Venice, 1930), and K. R. Greenfield, *Economics and Liberalism in the Risorgimento 1814-48* (Baltimore, 1934).

On the agricultural classes the best introduction is H. Sée, *Esquisse d'une histoire du régime agraire en Europe aux XVIIIe et XIXe siècles* (Paris, 1921); L. P. Adams, *Agricultural Depression and Farm Relief in England 1813-52* (London, 1932), W. F. Adams, *Ireland and Irish Emigration to the New World from 1815 to the Famine* (New Haven, 1932), and G. S. Ford, *Stein and the Era of Reform in Prussia* (Princeton, 1922).

On the working classes the literature is very extensive; cf. especially G. D. H. Cole, *A Short History of the British Working-Class Movement,* Vol. I, *1789-1848* (London, 1925), M. C. Buer, *Health, Wealth, and Population in the Early Days of the Industrial Revolution* (London, 1926), and P. Louis, *Histoire de la classe ouvrière en France de la Révolution à nos jours* (Paris, 1927).

Chapter III

THE SEARCH FOR A PRINCIPLE OF AUTHORITY

There exists no general work on European conservatism for this period; the best guide to this literature, as also to that on liberalism, is in the bibliographies appended to the biographical articles in the *Encyclopaedia of Social Sciences.* The author found the following works useful: G. Brandes, *Main Currents in Nineteenth Century Literature,* 6 vols. (New York, 1901-1905), a brilliant example of the possibilities of relating literature and history, strongly liberal in outlook; H. Michel, *L'idée de l'état* (Paris, 1896), also of value for the liberal and radical theorists in France; E. L. Woodward, *Three Studies in European Conservatism* (London, 1929); A. Collan, *Edmund Burke and the Revolt against the Eighteenth Century* (London, 1929); C. Brinton, *The Political Ideas of the English Romanticists* (Oxford, 1926); C. Schmitt, *Politische Romantik,* 2nd ed. (Munich, 1925); C. E. Vaughan, *Studies in the History of Political Philosophy,* 2 vols. (Manchester, 1925); P. Rohden, *Joseph de Maistre* (Munich, 1929); C. T. Muret, *French Royalist Doctrines since the Revolution* (New York, 1933); V. Basch, *Les doctrines politiques des philosophes classiques de l'Allemagne* (Paris, 1927); R. Aris, *Political Thought in Germany 1789-1815* (London, 1936), J. Spenlé, *La pensée allemande* (Paris, 1934), H. Meyer-Lindenberg, *Das Problem der europäischen Organisation und des Geisteslebens der Restaurationepoche* (Liège, 1935), J. Hashager, "Der Rhythmus im Wandel von Reaktion und Revolution 1815-52" in *Hist. Vierteljahr,* (1935), E. N. Anderson, "Nineteenth Century Europe, Liberal or Conservative?" in *Social Education* (1938), G. H. Mead, *Movements of Thought in the Nineteenth Century* (Chicago, 1936), also references, Ch. IV.

Chapter IV

THE CREEDS OF LIBERALISM

An excellent introduction to the doctrines of liberalism is G. de Ruggiero, *The History of European Liberalism* (Oxford, 1927), with good bibliography. Particularly valuable are the following works: R. Soltau, *French Political Thought in the Nineteenth Century* (London, 1931), and G. Boas, *French Philosophies of the Romantic Period* (Baltimore, 1925), both also of use for the French conservative theorists; E. Halévy, *Growth of Philosophic Radicalism* (New York, 1928), one of the best studies of any single phase of modern political and social thought; C. Gide et Rist, *Histoire des doctrines économiques,* 5th ed. (Paris, 1926), the standard compend; K. Pinson, *Bibliographical Introduction to Nationalism* (New York, 1935); C. J. H. Hayes, *The Historical Evolution of Modern Nationalism* (New York, 1931); J. W. Adamson, *English Education 1789-1902* (Cambridge, 1930), a comprehensive introduction; E. H. Reisner, *Nationalism and Education since 1789* (New York, 1922), and the work of Meinecke on Germany, referred to among "General Works"; also references, Ch. III.

Chapter V

THE FIRST YEARS OF PEACE 1815-1820

The Congress of Vienna has been entirely restudied in two magistral works: C. W. Webster, *The Foreign Policy of Castlereagh 1812-1815,*

(London, 1931), which maintains the thesis that Castlereagh was the founder of the system of congresses, and H. von Srbik, *Metternich, der Staatsman und der Mensch,* 2 vols. (Munich, 1925), an exhaustive work covering every aspect of Metternich's activity; cf. also C. Dupuis, *Le ministère de Talleyrand en 1814,* 2 vols. (Paris, 1919-20); E. J. Knapton, *Julie de Krüdener* (New York, 1939); Villa-Urrutia, *España en el Congreso de Viena* (2nd ed., Madrid, 1928). Some of the memoirs of the leading statesmen are of great value, both for the history of the Congress of Vienna and for the general history of the period: Charles Vane, Ed., *Memoirs and Correspondence of Castlereagh,* 12 vols. (London, 1848-1853); R. Metternich, Ed., *Aus Metternich's nachgelassenen Papieren,* 8 vols. (Vienna, 1880-1884), also an inferior English version, 5 vols. (New York, 1880-82); Talleyrand, *Mémoires,* 5 vols. (Paris, 1891-92), English translation, 5 vols. (London, 1891-92); Wellington, Ed., *Despatches, Correspondence, and Memoranda of Arthur, Duke of Wellington,* 8 vols. (London, 1867-80), *Supplementary Dispatches,* 15 vols. (London, 1858-1872), F. von Gentz, *Dépêches inédites,* 3 vols. (Paris, 1876-77). For the history of the various states, 1815-1820, besides the general works noted above, cf. Aspinall, *Brougham and the Whig Party* (Manchester, 1927), an admirable study; F. J. C. Hearnshaw, *Conservatism in England, An Analytical, Historical and Political Survey* (London, 1931), brief but suggestive; E. Pasquier, *Mémoires,* 6 vols. (Paris, 1893-1895); Pierre de La Gorce, *La Restauration, Louis XVIII* (Paris, 1926); C. Pouthas, *Guizot pendant la Restauration* (Paris, 1923), a Paris doctor's thesis, dense with new material; E. de Perceval, *Lainé et la vie parlementaire au temps de la Restauration,* 2 vols. (Paris, 1926); H. von Srbik, *Metternich,* 2 vols. (Munich, 1925); E. Kittel, "Metternich's politische Grundanschauungen" in *Historische Vierteljahrschrift* (1928), Vol. XXIV, one of the best recent studies of Metternich's ideas and policies; V. Bibl, *Metternich in neuer Beleuchtung* (Vienna, 1928), attacks Srbik; K. A. von Müller, *Karl Ludwig Sand* (Munich, 1925); G. Spindler, *Follen* (Chicago, 1917); with accounts of the whole *Burschenschaften* movement, and W. O. Henderson, *Zollverein* (Cambridge, 1938); I. Raulich, *Storia del risorgimento politico d'Italia,* 5 vols. (Bologna, 1920-1927), the most valuable of the longer histories of the Risorgimento; A. Luzio, *La massoneria e il risorgimento italiano,* 2 vols. (Bologna, 1925), G. Mollat, *La question romaine de Pie VI à Pie XI* (Paris, 1932), a good manual, and A. Ferrari, *La preparazione intellettuale del Risorgimento* (Milan, 1923).

Chapter VI

THE CRISIS OF 1820

The revolutionary disturbances of 1820-1825 are all discussed in the histories of the period, though a number of special studies of recent date contain new material. For England: W. D. Bowman, *The Divorce Case of Queen Caroline* (London, 1930), a popular account. For France: de Roux, *La Restauration* (Paris, 1930), a royalist apology; H. Dumolard, *Didier et la conspiration de Grenoble* (Grenoble, 1928); G. Weill, *Histoire du parti républicain en France 1814-1870*, 2nd ed. (Paris, 1928). For the Quadruple Alliance and the Congresses: the whole subject has been entirely revised by three important works, C. K. Webster, *The Foreign Policy of Castlereagh 1815-22* (London, 1934); H. Temperley, *The Foreign Policy of Canning* (London, 1925); and D. Perkins, *The Monroe Doctrine 1823-6* (Cambridge, 1927). For the Spanish Revolution and the French intervention in Spain: J. Sarrailh, *Martinez de la Rosa 1787-1862* (Bordeaux, 1930), and by the same author, *La contre-révolution sous la Régence de Madrid* (Bordeaux, 1930); Villa-Urrutia, *Fernando VII, Rey constitucional* (Madrid, 1922); all three contain interesting new material; Geoffrey de Grandmaison, *L'expédition française d'Espagne en 1823* (Paris, 1928); E. Beau de Loménie, *La carrière politique de Chateaubriand 1814-1830*, 2 vols. (Paris, 1929). For the Italian Revolutions: A. Segre, *Vittorio Emanuele I* (Turin, 1928); F. Lemmi, *Carlo Felice* (Turin, 1931); N. Rodolico, *Carlo Alberto* (Florence, 1931), a valuable re-estimate; T. Rossi e C. P. Demagistri, *La rivoluzione del 1821* (Turin, 1927); C. Vidal, *Charles Albert et le Risorgimento* (Paris, 1927); A. Falcionelli, *Les sociétés secrètes en Italie* (Paris, 1936), and J. H. Brady, *Rome and the Neapolitan Revolution* (New York, 1937). For Russia: P. Miloukov, Ed., *Histoire de Russie*, Vol. II (Paris, 1935); T. G. Masaryk, *The Spirit of Russia*, 2 vols. (London, 1919), brief on this period; A. Kornilov, *Modern Russian History*, rev. ed. (New York, 1924), a good compend; J. Mavor, *An Economic History of Russia*, 2nd ed., 2 vols. (London, 1925); A. Koyré, *La philosophie et le problème national en Russie au début du XIXe siècle* (Paris, 1929); G. Vernadsky, *La charte constitutionnelle de l'Empire russe de l'an 1820* (Paris, 1933). For Poland, besides Krakowski and the general works on the Restoration: cf. M. Handelsman, *Les idées françaises et la mentalité politique en Pologne* (Paris, 1927), a series of lectures, thin but containing some material not available elsewhere; B. Winiarski, *Les institutions politiques en*

Pologne au XIXe siècle (Paris, 1928); E. Krakowski, *Mickiewicz* (Paris, 1935). For the Decembrist Outbreak in Russia, the best recent material in the languages of western Europe is in four special numbers of the *Monde slave* (December, 1925, and January, June, and December, 1926); and in articles: by D. Mirsky, "The Decembrists" in *Slavonic Review* (December, 1925), a brilliant analysis; E. Hurwicz, "Zur Charakteristik von Pestel" in *Archiv für die Geschichte des Sozialismus*, Vol. 13, 1928; and A. G. Mazour, *The First Russian Revolution* (Berkeley, 1937).

Chapter VII

THE RISE OF A NEW GENERATION

The best recent manual of the history of science is J. D. Dampier-Whetham, *History of Science,* 2nd ed. (New York, 1932). Valuable studies of the development of individual sciences are: F. Klein, *Vorlesungen über die Entwicklung der Mathematik im 19 Jahrhundert,* 2 vols. (Berlin, 1926-27); E. Rádl, *History of Biological Theories* (Oxford, 1930); E. Hoppe, *Histoire de la physique* (Paris, 1928); M. Oswald, *L'évolution de la chimie au XIXe siècle* (Paris, 1921); and L. Meunier, *Histoire de la médecine,* new ed. (Paris, 1924); nearly all these books contain detailed accounts of the developments of the sciences in the early nineteenth century.

There is no good general history of modern archæological discovery. The history of comparative philology is sketched in the appendix of A. Meillet, *Introduction à l'étude comparative des langues indo-européennes,* 6th ed. (Paris, 1924); a fuller account is in H. Pedersen, *Linguistic Science in the Nineteenth Century* (Cambridge, 1931). The history of history is ably surveyed in E. Fueter, *Histoire de l'historiographie moderne* (Paris, 1914), and more fully in G. P. Gooch, *History and Historians of the 19th Cenutry,* 2nd ed. (London, 1913).

A useful introduction to the romantic movement in literature is P. Van Tieghem, *Le mouvement romantique,* 2nd ed. (Paris, 1923), a collection of texts with brief commentary; for England: O. Elton, *A Survey of English Literature 1780-1880,* 4 vols. (London, 1920), is excellent; for Germany: L. A. Willoughby, *The Romantic Movement in Germany* (Oxford, 1930), a brief account; O. Walzel, *German Romanticism* (New York, 1932), philosophic; W. Kosch, *Die deutsche Literatur im Spiegel der Nationalen Entwicklung,* Vol. I (Munich, 1925), and R. Haym, *Die Romantische Schule,* 5th ed. (Berlin, 1928), the standard work; for France: R. Bray, *Chronologie du romantisme*

(Paris, 1932), and P. Moreau, *Le Romantisme* (Paris, 1932), excellent introductions; and M. Souriau, *Histoire du romantisme en France,* 3 vols. (Paris, 1927-28), the best general work in the field; for Italy: H. Hauvette, *La littérature italienne,* 6th ed. (Paris, 1924), brief but masterful treatment; for Spain: E. Mérimée and S. Morley, *History of Spanish Literature* (New York, 1930), and E. Piñeyro, *The Romantics of Spain* (Liverpool, 1934); for Russia: D. S. Mirsky, *A History of Russian Literature* (New York, 1927), and A. Luther, *Geschichte der russischen Literatur* (Leipzig, 1924); for Poland: A. Brückner, *Geschichte der polnischen Literatur,* 2nd ed. (Leipzig, 1909), contains material on political and social conditions, and J. Krzyzanowski, *Polish Romantic Literature* (New York, 1931); for Hungary: G. Farkas, *Die ungarische Romantik* (Berlin, 1931); for the Czechs: H. Jelínek, *Histoire de la littérature tchèque des origines à 1850* (Paris, 1930). There are two special numbers of the *Revue de littérature comparée* (January-March, 1927, and January-March, 1930) devoted to romanticism.

The history of the fine arts is best followed in A. Michel, *Histoire de l'art,* Vol. VII (Paris, 1925), with full bibliographies; cf. also H. Focillon, *La peinture au XIXe siècle,* 2 vols. (Paris, 1927-28), and three interesting studies in the history of taste: F. P. Chambers, *The History of Taste* (New York, 1932), C. Hussey, *The Picturesque* (London, 1927), and K. Clark, *The Gothic Revival* (London, 1928). For music, a standard work is J. Combarieu, *Histoire de la musique,* Vols. II and III (Paris, 1913-1919), with bibliography. There is some interesting material on the conditions of musical education and of musical performance in E. Newman, *Life of Wagner,* Vol. I (New York, 1933).

On the liberal and socialistic currents, 1820-1830, cf. K. R. Greenfield, "Economic Ideas and Facts of the Early Period of the Risorgimento 1815-48" in *American Historical Review* (October, 1930), and his more extended study referred to above; on Liberal Catholicism: G. Weill, *Histoire du catholicisme libéral en France 1828-1908* (Paris, 1909), a scholarly study, and V. Giraud, *La vie tragique de Lamennais* (Paris, 1933), a good popularization; on Bonapartism: the most recent work, and the best, is that of J. Deschamps, *Sur la légende de Napoléon* (Paris, 1931); also of value are H. A. L. Fisher, *Bonapartism* (Oxford, 1908), P. Gonnard, *Les origines de la légende napoléonienne* (Paris, 1906), and A. L. Guérard, *Reflections on the Napoleonic Legend* (New York, 1924); on Philhellenism (there is no general work on the subject): W. Büngel, *Der Philhellenismus in Deutschland 1821-29* (Marburg, 1917); M. Cline, *American Attitude toward the Greek War of Independence* (Atlanta, 1930), and V. Penn, "Philhellenism in England," "Philhellenism in Europe," *Slavonic Review,* 1936, 1938. On socialism: W. Sombart, *Der proletarische Sozialismus,* 2 vols. (Jena, 1924), and M. Beer, *Allgemeine Geschichte des Sozialismus,* 2 vols. (Berlin, 1922-23), both superior to any works in English or French; C. Bouglé, *Socialismes français* (Paris, 1932); M. Beer, *History of British Socialism,* new ed., 2 vols. (London, 1929); and G. D. H. Cole, *Life of Robert Owen,* 2nd ed. (London, 1930).

Chapter VIII

THE DISINTEGRATION OF THE RESTORATION

England: The change in British foreign policy after 1822 is traced in H. Temperley, *The Foreign Policy of Canning 1822-7* (London, 1925); in domestic policy, in A. Brady, *Huskisson and Liberal Reform* (Oxford, 1928); cf. also A. Aspinall, *Lord Brougham and the Whig Party* (Manchester, 1927); M. W. Patterson, *Sir Francis Burdett and His Times,* 2 vols. (London, 1931), contains some new material but is poorly constructed; D. G. Barnes, *History of the English Corn Laws 1660-1846* (London, 1930); C. R. Fay, *The Corn Laws and Social England* (Cambridge, 1932); G. D. H. Cole, *Life of William Cobbett* (New York, 1924); G. Wallas, *Life of Francis Place,* 4th ed. (London, 1925), the last two are particularly useful; W. H. Wickwar, *The Struggle for the Freedom of the Press 1819-32* (London, 1928), *The History of the Times,* Vol. I (London, 1935); for the Irish Question: D. Gwynn, *O'Connell, the Irish Liberator* (London, 1929), J. E. Pomfret, *The Struggle for Land in Ireland 1800-1923* (Princeton, 1930), and a collection of essays, *Catholic Emancipation 1829-1929* (London, 1929).

France: There is an excellent analysis of the political situation under Charles X in Pierre de La Gorce, *La restauration, Charles X* (Paris, 1928); the government's manipulation of elections is shown in Pilenco, *Les mœurs électorales en France, Régime censitaire* (Paris, 1928), its educational policy in A. Garnier, *Frayssinous, Son rôle dans l'Université sous la restauration* (Paris, 1925), and its attempt to strengthen the nobility in A. Gain, *La restauration et les biens des émigrés,* 2 vols. (Nancy, 1928); the last three works are all based on extensive study of archival material.

Austria: On Austrian policies in Germany and Italy, cf. the general works referred to and also those cited in the bibliographical note to Chapter V. In addition, the following works are of use: V. Bibl, *Der Zerfall Österreichs,* Vol. I (Vienna, 1922); for the cultural nationalist movements among the Austrian Slavs: A Fischel, *Der Panslawismus bis zum Weltkrieg* (Berlin, 1919), and E. Lemberg, *Grundlagen des nationalen Erwachens in Böhmen* (Reichenberg, 1932); for Hungary: D. Angyal, "Széchenyi" in *Revue des études hongroises et finno-ougriennes* (1926), and F. Eckhart, *Introduction à l'histoire hongroise* (Paris, 1928), English translation (London, 1931), and O. Zarek, *Kossuth* (London, 1937); for the Southern Slavs: two works by H. Wendel, *Aus dem südslawischen Risorgimento* (Gotha, 1921), and *Der Kampf der Südslawen um Freiheit und Einheit* (Frankfort, 1925).

The decay of the Ottoman Empire and the Serbian and Greek Revolutions: E. Engelhardt, *La Turquie et le Tanzinat*, 2 vols. (Paris, 1882-83); G. Rosen, *Geschichte der Türkei*, 2 vols. (Leipzig, 1866-67); K. von Sax, *Geschichte des Machtverfall der Turkei*, new ed. (Vienna, 1913); and the extraordinary Ubicini, *Letters on Turkey*, 2 vols. (London, 1856); these are written with more understanding of Ottoman political and economic problems than many of the more recent works. W. W. Wright, *The Process of Change in the Ottoman Empire* (Chicago, 1937), and W. Miller, *The Ottoman Empire and its Successors 1801-1934* (Cambridge, 1934), are two good introductory manuals. Cf. also H. Temperley, *England and the Near East*, Vol. I, Ch. 1, (London, 1936). For the Christian peoples under Ottoman rule: A. Xénopol, *Histoire des Roumains*, 2 vols. (Paris, 1896); Seton-Watson, *History of the Roumanians* (Cambridge, 1934); T. W. Riker, *The Making of Roumania* (Oxford, 1931); M. Emerit, *Les Paysans roumains 1829-64* (Paris, 1937); E. Haumant, *La formation de la Yougo-Slavie* (Paris, 1930), the best work on the history of the Serbs; and A. Hajek, *Bulgarien unter der Türkenherrschaft* (Stuttgart, 1925), a scholarly study. The most detailed account of the Serbian Revolt is G. Yakschitch, *L'Europe et la résurrection de la Serbie 1804-34*, 2nd ed. (Paris, 1917); on the Greek Revolt three older works, K. Mendelssohn-Bartholdy, *Geschichte Griechenlands*, Vol. II (Leipzig, 1874), G. F. Hertzberg, *Geschichte Griechenlands*, Vols. III and IV, (Gotha, 1879), and G. Finlay, *History of Greece*, Vols. VI and VII, new ed. (Oxford, 1877), are still of value; cf. also J. Baggally, *Ali Pasha and Great Britain* (Oxford, 1938), H. Dodwell, *The Founder of Modern Egypt, Muhammad Ali* (Cambridge, 1931), E. Driault, *L'expédition de Crète et de Morée 1823-28* (Cairo, 1930), and G. Douin, *Navarin* (Cairo, 1927), the first scholarly treatments based on study of the Egyptian archives. The diplomacy of the Greek Revolt has been recently restudied in E. Driault et M. Lhéritier, *Histoire diplomatique de la Grèce*, Vol. I

(Paris, 1925), and C. W. Crawley, *The Question of Greek Independence* (Cambridge, 1930); the latter lays emphasis on the English side. Cf. also, A. Dascalakis, *Rhigas* (Paris, 1937), and A. Svolos, "L'influence des idées de la Révolution française sur les constitutions helléniques," *Révolution française,* Vol. I n.s.

Chapter IX

THE REVOLUTIONARY MOVEMENTS OF 1830

The July Revolution in France: Besides the works of Charléty, Pouthas, and de La Gorce, already cited, cf. J. M. S. Allison, *Thiers and the French Monarchy* (Boston, 1926), the author had access to Thiers' papers; G. Gautherot, *Un gentilhomme de grand chemin, le Maréchal de Bourmont* (Paris, 1926); two articles by P. Mantoux, "Talleyrand en 1830" in *Revue historique* (1902) and "Patrons et ouvriers en juillet 1830" in *Revue d'histoire moderne et contemporaine* (1901-2), which have modified the older views on the July Revolution; E. Marc, *Mes journées de juillet 1830* (Paris, 1930), and several important articles in *1830, Études sur les mouvements libéraux et nationaux de 1830* (Paris, 1932), especially B. Mirkine-Guetzevitch, "1830 dans l'évolution constitutionnelle de l'Europe," and G. Huber, *Kriegsgefahr über Europa 1830-2* (Berlin, 1936).

Holland and Belgium: The best introduction to the history of the Belgian question after 1815 is H. Pirenne, *Histoire de la Belgique,* Vols. VI and VII (Brussels, 1926-1932), and to the history of Holland, H. T. Colenbrander, *Vestiging van het Koninkrijk 1813-15* (Amsterdam, 1927); also of value are C. Terlinden, *Guillaume I et l'église catholique,* 2 vols. (Brussels, 1906), R. Demoulin, *Guillaume I et la transformation économique des provinces belges 1815-30* (Paris, 1938); A. Calmes, *Le grand-duché de Luxembourg dans le royaume des Pays-Bas 1815-30* (Brussels, 1932); P. Harsin, *Essai sur l'opinion publique en Belgique de 1815 à 1830* (Charleroi, 1930); M. Bologne, *L'insurrection prolétarienne de 1830 en Belgique* (Brussels, 1929), important, R. Demoulin, *Les journées de Septembre 1830 à Bruxelles et en province* (Paris, 1934); for studies of individual leaders: Louis de Potter, *Souvenirs,* 2 vols. (Brussels, 1839); J. Garsou, *Alexandre Gendebien* (Brussels, 1930); P. de Gerlache, *Gerlache et la fondation de la Belgique indépendante* (Brussels, 1931); F. de Lannoy, *Histoire diplomatique de l'indépendance belge* (Brussels, 1930); W. E. Lingelbach, "Belgian Neutrality" in *American Historical Review* (1933); L. de Lichtervelde, *Le congrès national de 1830* (Brussels, 1922), and by the same author, *Leopold I* (New York, 1930); E. Corti, *Leopold I* (New York, 1923).

Germany: Besides the general works, V. Valentin, *Das Hambacher Nationalfest* (Berlin, 1932); J. Dresch, *Gutzkow et la Jeune-Allemagne* (Paris, 1904); E. M. Butler, *The Saint-Simonian Religion in Germany, A Study of the Young Germany Movement* (Cambridge, 1926); and K. Sternberg, *Heines geistige Gestalt und Welt* (Berlin, 1929); also V. Valentin, *Geschichte der deutschen Revolution von 1848-9*, Vol. I (Berlin, 1930).

Italy: In addition to the studies on Italy already cited, cf. G. Salvemini, *Mazzini* (Rome, 1920); G. O. Griffith, *Mazzini* (New York, 1932), a good popularization; C. Vidal, *Louis Philippe, Metternich, et la crise italienne de 1831-32* (Paris, 1931); G. Ruffini, *Le cospirazioni del 1831* (Bologna, 1931); and M. C. Wicks, *The Italian Exiles in London, 1816-48* (Manchester, 1937).

Switzerland: The two standard histories are J. Dierauer, *Geschichte der schweizerischen Eidengenossenschaft bis 1848*, Vol. V (Gotha, 1917), and E. Gagliardi, *Histoire de la Suisse*, Vol. V (Lausanne, 1925); cf. also E. His, *Geschichte des neueren schweizerischen Staatsrecht*, Vol. II (Basel, 1929); A. Piaget, *Histoire de la révolution neuchâteloise*, Vols. III and IV (Neuchâtel, 1919, 1925); and G. Guggenbühl, *Bürgermeister Usteri* (Aarau, 1924).

Poland: M. Handelsman, "L'état actuel des études rélatives à l'histoire de 1830-1 en Pologne" in *1830, Études sur les mouvements libéraux et nationaux de 1830* (Paris, 1932), and another bibliographical article by Z. Krzemicka in *Jahrbücher für Kultur und Geschichte der Slaven*, new series, Vol. VII. Various new aspects of the Polish Revolt are treated in A. Lewak, "The Polish Rising of 1830" in *Slavonic Review* (1930); J. Rappaport, "L'insurrection polonaise 1830," in *Monde slave*, 1933-8; Müller, *Die Polen in der öffentlichen Meinung Deutschlands 1830-2* (Marburg, 1923); and Grzebieniowski, "The Polish Cause in England a Century Ago" in *Slavonic Review* (1932).

Spain and Portugal: J. Becker, *Historia de las relacioñes exteriores de España durante el siglo XIX*, 3 vols. (Madrid, 1924-26), an important work; Nuñez de Arenas, *La expedición de Vera de 1830* (Madrid, 1927); and Hadenque, "Une équipée française au Portugal (1833)" in *Revue des questions historiques* (1925).

England: All the general works give much attention to the Reform Bill of 1832. Cf. also: G. M. Trevelyan, *Lord Grey of the Reform Bill*, 2nd ed. (London, 1929); Richard Hill, *Toryism and the People 1832-46* (London, 1929); G. K. Clarke, *Sir Robert Peel and the Conservative*

Party 1832-41 (London, 1929); H. W. C. Davis, *The Age of Grey and Peel* (Oxford, 1929); J. R. M. Butler, *The Passing of the Great Reform Bill* (London, 1914); G. Milner, *The Threshold of the Victorian Age* (London, 1934); and the essay by Halévy in A. Coville and H. Temperley, *Studies in Anglo-French History* (Cambridge, 1935); on the consequences of the Reform Bill, cf. O. F. Christie, *The Transition from Aristocracy* (London, 1928), M. Hovell, *The Chartist Movement,* 2nd ed. (Manchester, 1925), a remarkable study, S. F. Wooley, "The personnel of the Parliament of 1833," *English Historical Review,* 1938, and S. Maccoby, *English Radicalism 1832-52* (London, 1935).

Index

THE RISE OF MODERN EUROPE

The above list of titles indicates the scope of this history. The publishers will be glad to answer inquiries as to the publication date of any given volume.